'A fascinating and richly erudite intertwining of theology, history of ideas, scriptural scholarship, and philosophical reflection, this powerfully argued book deserves to rank as Tom Wright's crowning achievement'.

—JOHN COTTINGHAM, *Professor Emeritus of Philosophy, University of Reading, Professor of Philosophy of Religion, University of Roehampton, and Honorary Fellow, St John's College, Oxford University*

'This is Tom Wright at his best—an exegete, theologian, churchman, and public intellectual rolled into one. A creative and arresting contribution to "natural theology", this book argues for the plausibility of the Christian vision of the relation between God and the world by taking seriously the history of Jesus Christ, especially the promise contained in his resurrection of the new creation: the creation become God's and humans' home'.

—MIROSLAV VOLF, *Henry B. Wright Professor of Systematic Theology and Founding Director of the Yale Center for Faith and Culture, Yale University*

'This book offers a wonderful interplay of the history of modernity, natural theology, philosophy, biblical studies, and theology. Written by the most influential biblical scholar of his generation, its constructive conclusions and the promise make this book a necessary read for anyone interested in the light that Jesus can shed on natural theology'.

—TOM GREGGS, FRSE, *Marischal Chair of Divinity and Founding Co-Director of the Aberdeen Centre for Protestant Theology, University of Aberdeen*

'Building on his field-changing New Testament work, N. T. Wright outlines a new theology of history. Against Bultmann's monumental critique of scriptural narrative, he sets a historical drama that unfolds from within the biblical texts themselves. The cosmos as Wright re-imagines it is charged with promise, significance, and bracing responsibility'.

—JUDITH WOLFE, *Professor of Philosophical Theology and Deputy Head of the School of Divinity, University of St Andrews*

'Bible scholars, whether those that specialize in the Old or New Testament, theologians, church historians, or pastors, knowingly or not, trade in the relationship of God to history. The Christian claim is that God has acted in creation in real events and persons both to reveal who God is and to redeem humans. Scholarship, especially since the Enlightenment, has distorted that relationship of God to history by reductionism, historicism, and a series of blinkering false dichotomies. In *History and Eschatology* N. T. Wright turns to the great theme of the Gifford Lectures to respond to the game of history by proposing nothing less than an epistemology of love'.

—SCOT MCKNIGHT, *Julius R. Mantey Chair of New Testament, Northern Seminary*

'In this extraordinary reappraisal of the traditions of "Natural Theology", Tom Wright deploys his intellectual energy with surprising punch to address from an unexpected angle the fundamental problems posed for theology by modernity. Critics may be provoked, but fans will be delighted'.

—FRANCES YOUNG, *OBE, FBA, Emerita Edward Cadbury Professor of Theology, University of Birmingham*

'A tour de force, placing history—and Jesus himself—back at the heart of "natural theology", where the broken signposts of this world lead to the broken God on the cross and creation renewed'.
—JOHN BEHR, *Director of the Master of Theology Program and Father Georges Florovsky Distinguished Professor of Patristics, St Vladimir's Orthodox Theological Seminary*

'N. T. Wright's extensive scholarly work on the New Testament is near legendary. Readers have long wanted to hear him explain the critical foundations for this work, and he now finally provides them, with the same pungency, panache, and provocation for which he is famous. Laying out what he calls an "epistemology of love" that is made possible in the resurrection of Jesus, Wright refashions the debate over natural theology in a way that is able to include, not only the bare phenomena of creation, but the full range of human activity—from politics to art—in the cross-shaped form of divine history. This is a sweeping, passionate, and hopeful plea for seeing, and living in, a world that is God's in origin, suffering form, and final end'.
—EPHRAIM RADNER, *Professor of Historical Theology, Wycliffe College, University of Toronto*

'In this published version of his Aberdeen Gifford Lectures, Tom Wright develops an integrated theology of history and nature, thus overcoming modern strategies that have resulted in their disjunction. This is an impressive and timely publication from a leading New Testament scholar willing to engage with the big questions in his field. Bold, lively, and accessible, it will generate widespread discussion'.
—DAVID FERGUSSON, *Professor of Divinity, University of Edinburgh*

'Accessibly written without any loss of academic rigour, Wright's book opens up new and productive conversations between biblical interpretation and philosophical theology. By eschewing unhelpful either/or oppositions Wright shows the vitality of both biblical and natural theologies—and how they might not be quite so far apart after all. Lord Adam Gifford would be proud'.
—RUSSELL RE MANNING, *Reader in Religions, Philosophies, and Ethics, Bath Spa University*

'With a stunning breadth of research Wright takes his Gifford Lectures as an occasion to deepen the paradigmatic shift in biblical studies that he has shaped over the last thirty years. Wright offers a model of historical exegesis that just might release us from our Platonic bondage. This book combines breathtakingly creative brilliance with a lovely eloquence. Since an "epistemology of love" is at the heart of Wright's natural theology, we wouldn't have expected anything less. Read this book, then read it again. It takes its place in the esteemed tradition of Gifford Lectures becoming classics'.
—BRIAN J. WALSH, *co-author of* Romans Disarmed: Resisting Empire, Demanding Justice

History and Eschatology

Jesus and the Promise of Natural Theology

N. T. Wright

BAYLOR UNIVERSITY PRESS

Cover Design by Daniel Benneworth-Gray
Book Design by Savanah N. Landerholm

The Library of Congress has cataloged this book under ISBN
978-1-4813-0962-2.

In loving memory of Rosemary Wright

2 June 1923–1 June 2018

Contents

Preface and
Acknowledgments

My mother, in her 94th year, asked me what the Gifford Lectures were supposed to be about. I explained that some people used to think you could start from the natural world and think your way up to God; that other people thought that wasn't such a good idea; but that fresh thoughts about history might lead to fresh ideas about Jesus and by that route eventually to the God of creation; and that on the way we might learn something about the nature of knowledge itself. My mother thought for a few moments and then said, firmly, 'I'm glad I don't have to listen to those lectures'.

Anyone who agrees with my mother should feel under no obligation to read on. But let me explain a little more. What might 'natural theology' be, and how might a biblical scholar come to grips with it?

The phrase 'natural theology', like all shorthand theological terms, is best understood as a drastically abbreviated version of a full sentence. (Thus the word 'atonement', in regular Christian discourse, is a shorthand for 'the Messiah died for our sins in accordance with the scriptures', or one of several other accounts. It is only when we deal with the longer versions, the full sentences, that we can be sure we are not talking at cross purposes.¹) But what is the implied longer sentence of which 'natural theology' is the dense abbreviation? There are several possibilities, and past Gifford Lectures are full of them. Karl

Barth, famously, defined the term in a decidedly polemical fashion: 'natural theology', for him, meant any attempt to pronounce upon a theological point of discussion by appealing to a source other than God's self-disclosure in Jesus Christ, as witnessed to by scripture.[2] The political pay-off from this in the 1930s is well known: he was opposing those who claimed that one could discern God's will in 'history', meaning by 'history' here the observed rise of German National Socialism. Barth's strictures have not, to put it mildly, prevented a lively ongoing discussion.[3]

Two recent surveys show something of the range of current possibilities.[4] Christopher Brewer lists five options: (1) natural *religion*; (2) a proof or argument for God's existence; (3) signs of God's existence within creation; (4) 'Christian natural theology', that is, starting from already Christian premises and using arguments from the natural world to expand upon or confirm the knowledge of God already given in Jesus Christ; (5) a theology of nature.[5] (Each of these, of course, is itself a shorthand in need of further unravelling.) Alister McGrath, for his part, offers six options: (1) 'the branch of philosophy which investigates what human reason unaided by revelation can tell us concerning God'; (2) 'a demonstration or affirmation of the existence of God on the basis of the regularity and complexity of the natural world'; (3) 'the intellectual outcome of the natural tendency of the human mind to desire or be inclined toward God'; (4) 'the exploration of an analogy or intellectual resonance between the human experience of nature on the one hand, and of the Christian gospel on the other'; (5) 'an attempt to demonstrate that "naturalist" accounts of the world and the achievements of the natural sciences are intrinsically deficient, and that a theological approach is required to give a comprehensive and coherent interpretation of the natural order'; (6) 'a "theology of nature"—that is, a specifically Christian understanding of the natural world, reflecting the core assumptions of the Christian faith, which is to be contrasted with secular or naturalist accounts of nature'.[6]

Even to display and discuss these views one by one, and engage in the debates which surround them, would take a course of lectures in itself. I have taken it for granted that underneath all these various ways of understanding 'natural theology' there lies the great theological and philosophical challenge of talking about God and the world and the relation between them. And I have assumed, on the basis of being invited as a biblical scholar to address the 'Gifford' topics, that my task was to see whether there might be new ways of bringing biblical insights to bear on the traditional questions and topics—or, to put it more positively, to see whether a biblical theology might offer some fresh parameters within which the old questions would appear in a different light. I have concluded that it might. This book represents the thought experiment that results.

Biblical scholars have not usually been involved in the discussion of 'natural theology'. (Thus, the last exegete to give the Giffords was James Barr, in 1991, while the last New Testament specialist was Rudolf Bultmann in 1955.[7] If we exegetes are thus to be rationed to one shot in every generation, perhaps my successor in 2050 or thereabouts will pick up the conversation from here.) They have left it to the philosophers and systematic theologians, with biblical scholars only chipping in when asked whether 'the Bible' is 'for' or 'against' the whole project. In the present book I intend to go beyond this strictly limited task by trying to understand something of the origins and shaping of the relevant modern debates and suggesting what seem to me to be potential ways forward. The fact that, as a biblical scholar, I was asked to do these lectures indicates that some people at least would like to see whether for once we can step outside our academic siloes and engage in some cross-fertilising discourse. While on the subject, I should add that biblical quotations in what follows will be from the New Revised Standard Version for the Old Testament, and from my own translation, *The New Testament for Everyone*, or in its American version, *The Kingdom New Testament*.[8]

One of the obvious reasons for biblical scholars not being involved in the discussion is that, in the modern period at least, 'natural theology' has been defined negatively in terms of *not* including 'special' or 'supernatural' revelation, for which the Bible, along with Jesus himself, has been seen as the primary source. But whatever meaning we give to 'natural theology' itself, and however we evaluate it, there is something strange in excluding the Bible from 'nature'. The Bible was, after all, written and edited within the world of space and time, by a large number of individuals situated in 'natural' communities and environments. This insight had a mixed reception amongst writers in the eighteenth and nineteenth centuries, producing an odd kind of double-think. On the one hand, the Bible was long presupposed to be 'special revelation' from God, and it was thus ruled out of consideration for natural theology; on the other hand, the development of critical historical studies recaptured the reality that the Bible is on par with other ancient books—at which point, one might have thought, it should have been allowed back into the conversation. But these confusions—whose wider contexts we shall study in the first two chapters—seem not to have been properly noted.

The Bible, after all, purports to offer not just 'spiritual' or 'theological' teaching but to describe events within the 'natural' world, not least the public career of Jesus of Nazareth, a first-century Jew who lived and died within the 'natural' course of world history. If we appeal to history—as did Hume, Gibbon and Reimarus in the eighteenth century—then to history we should go. And that means investigating the actual historical world of Jesus of Nazareth, a turbulent and much-studied world about which real knowledge is available, and which, when studied carefully, includes core beliefs about the overlap of God's world and the human world ('heaven' and 'earth') and the regular interplay of the Age to Come with the Present Age. These contextualise Jesus and his kingdom-proclamation in ways remarkably unfamiliar in 'historical Jesus' studies through the nineteenth and twentieth centuries.

But integrating 'history', in any sense, especially the actual history of Jesus and his first followers, with the current discussion of 'natural theology' is not easy. We are entering stormy seas, and the winds and waves appear to have pulled the question out of shape.

There are, actually, several storms that have converged, into the now familiar image of the 'perfect storm'. First, there have been large abstract issues in philosophy and theology: how to relate God and the world, heaven and earth, and how to address the big problems which such relation throws up, not least the 'problem of evil'. These perennial questions have joined up, second, with certain topics of debate which have become prominent in the modern world, loosely referred to by labels like 'science and religion' and indeed 'church and state'. Third, there have been various movements of would-be Christian 'apologetics', drawing in some cases on much older theological styles to construct an argument for the existence of a 'God', perhaps even a 'perfect being', and working out from there. One of the rules of the game, for most practitioners in the modern period, has been to keep Jesus and the Bible out of the question, to avoid the suggestion of Christian 'cheating' that would trump the supposedly 'neutral' enquiry into the 'natural' world by an appeal to a supposed 'supernatural' authority. At the same time, however, the reductionist approach to Jesus and the Bible which has been rampant in European and American culture forces the question back into the open: if Jesus was a real human being within the 'natural' world, and if the Bible is a genuinely human book, then one cannot rule them out of the enquiry at the outset. And, when we allow them back in, things may change. Jesus was known, after all, for calming storms.

I am not, then, simply proposing a new and hopefully 'biblical' approach to 'natural theology' as conceived and discussed in the modern period. I am suggesting that the conception and discussion in question was distorted in specific ways by the cultural and philosophical trends of the eighteenth and nineteenth centuries, resulting in many flaws; and that the historical study of Jesus in his first-century context will allow us to approach the underlying questions (looking at the world, thinking about God) in different ways. 'Natural theology', in other words, has become a loose label for a string of questions, all of which have to do with the relationship of the world and God. Some of those questions have been isolated, highlighted, and posed within what with hindsight we can see to be distorting frameworks. I am proposing that we relocate them within the larger sets of questions to which, historically, they themselves belong, and that we do so with a fresh historical look at Jesus himself (indeed, with 'history' itself clarified and rescued from its own similar distortions).

It is of course open to anyone to say, 'You just changed the rules of the game'. My response would be that the game as currently played has been artificially shrunk; rather as though a cricket match were to be played on a baseball diamond, thus ruling out two-thirds of the cricketer's field of play and allowing both sides to contest any 'results'. Once we switch the game to the full-sized field and provide the proper equipment, things may work out differently.

History, in other words, matters; and thus Jesus and the New Testament ought by rights to be included as possible sources for the task of 'natural theology'. In saying this I am certainly not attempting to revive the kind of rationalist apologetic that would seek to 'prove' the Christian faith by a supposed 'appeal to history'. 'History' is far more complex than that, as I shall show in chapter 3. Neither in method nor in results will I be following normal apologetic pathways. To make the case for including Jesus in the topic at all, I shall dismantle some of the now standard misunderstandings of his public career and teaching and go on to argue for a fresh placing of him within the Jewish symbolic as well as historical world of his day. I shall then suggest that, with Easter, the raising of Jesus from the dead, we are faced with a renewal of creation which, by redemptive transformation, constitutes the *revalorization of the original creation itself*. The new world, brought to birth at Easter, is neither a mere adjustment within the present world nor the totally new replacement of the present world with something quite different (as was widely assumed when it was held that Jesus and his first followers believed that the present world would end in order to make way for 'the kingdom of heaven'). There is *continuity* as well as *discontinuity* between the old and the new, and between the modes of knowing necessary for understanding the one and the other. Easter says the divine 'yes' to the original creation, affirming in a new way, through the new kind of knowledge required for this new kind of world, those inferences that were already drawn from the world in the biblical and cognate traditions. (In other words, Easter does *not* affirm the 'natural theology' of, say, Epicureanism, Perfect Being theology, or the musings of the German Christians in the 1930s.) This, expounded in chapter 6 on the basis of the previous argument, and developed and applied in chapters 7 (via a consideration of Jesus' crucifixion) and 8, lies at the heart of my proposal in this book. With Jesus' resurrection comes the possibility, and perhaps even the promise, of a renewed 'natural theology'.

The lectures as conceived and delivered, and the book as presented here, consist, like a symphony, of four 'movements' of two chapters each. Within an overall continuity of argument, each 'movement' has its own integrity and appropriate style of presentation. The first pair set the historical context for the topic; they need, and here receive, quite detailed historical annotation. The second two analyse three key concepts ('history', 'eschatology' and 'apocalyptic') and begin to apply them to the subject matter. The third pair, lectures 5 and 6, plunge us into the first-century Jewish world to explore ways in which God and the world were seen together and to locate the question of Jesus' resurrection within that world. The final two, in a reflective mode now which requires less detailed annotation, reflect on broad themes of human experience and relate them first to the story of Jesus' crucifixion and then to the larger world of eschatology and mission, in order to round off the case for a new approach to the questions surrounding 'natural theology'. The final pair aim at the sense you might have if, having climbed up a long flight of stairs, you opened a trapdoor and could suddenly see a large vista in all directions. The mood is then one of describing what we can see, rather than arguing, step by cautious step, for a particular reconstruction. The title for the Gifford Lectures as delivered, reflecting this train of thought, was 'Discerning the Dawn', and I have allowed some echoes of that new-creation phrase to remain even though the book now bears a different title.

In my earlier 'academic' books I drew together subjects and themes which I had studied and taught for many years. With this book, however, I am entering what is for me comparatively new territory.[9] New possibilities have opened up, shedding light in various directions including, excitingly, on the history of my own main discipline. But such a moment, at my age, is also daunting. With every step, I am treading on the turf, and perhaps on the toes, of those who have worked for decades in fields which I have just been discovering. The dangers of oversimplification and strange omission are always present. I trust that colleagues in these other fields will at least appreciate that I am trying to bring our disciplines into conversation, even if I make a few blunders along the way.

Let me briefly describe the sequence of thought which carries the argument through the four movements. I shall begin by putting the earlier quest for 'natural theology'—including Lord Gifford's bequest—into its determinative eighteenth- and nineteenth-century cultural context. There, following in particular the blow dealt to older possibilities by the Lisbon Earthquake of 1755, the philosophies of the Enlightenment were quick to reshape the discourse around new forms of Epicureanism.[10] This, I shall suggest, has distorted subsequent discussions to this day, introducing false alternatives and truncating assumptions about knowledge itself, including historical knowledge.

In the second lecture I will show how the same distorted perspectives have worked their way through modern biblical studies. This includes Bultmann's interpretation, in his 1955 Giffords, of 'history and eschatology', to which my own title alludes. The historical study of the Bible, which often to this day pretends at least on the surface to an 'objective' or detached stance, has itself been radically shaped by the variegated revivals of Epicureanism, which encouraged people to study the world without reference to God, and to study God without reference to the world—in particular, to study theology without reference to history. What is sometimes called 'methodological naturalism' exemplifies the first (the world without God), and the god of 'perfect being' theology the second (theology without history). This climate of opinion has made it more and more likely that devout Christians and theologians would first construct a picture of 'God' from other sources and then try to fit 'Jesus' into the picture: much systematic theology in the eighteenth and nineteenth centuries was concerned with the First Article of the Creed, i.e. God the Father/Creator, rather than the Second or Third Articles, on the Son and the Spirit. But such a procedure can easily result in a Docetic or 'supernatural' Jesus, untouchable by historical criticism but also unknowable by any form of genuine history—which fits with what many unreflective modern Christians believe, but which also generates an equal and opposite sceptical reaction.

One might almost think that Docetism had won the day in the eighteenth century, and perhaps that is part of the problem. The easily assumed 'divine' Jesus of the then Christian orthodoxy, and the equally easily assumed 'divine inspiration' of scripture, meant that appeals to either were seen by the devout and the sceptic alike as settling the question in advance. No real historical work was required, and indeed to propose such a thing might be taken (as it still sometimes is) as a sign of infidelity to the gospel, a collusion with an implicit denial of God. The 'natural' and the 'supernatural' worlds were split apart, with those words themselves changing their meanings so as to support just such a complete disjunction. This resulted on the one hand in a 'Jesus' who appeared to float free of the 'natural' world, giving up without a struggle that full humanity for which some early Christian teachers (starting in the

New Testament itself) fought so hard;[11] and, on the other, in a 'Jesus' who was located in a badly researched hypothetical Jewish world, with any ascription of 'divinity' being seen as a later ecclesial corruption.

That in turn would produce, and did produce, a natural reaction, as sceptics and critics, including some in the churches who could see the damaging effects of Docetism, came to think instead of Jesus as 'merely human'. All this makes it much harder to do what ought to be done, and what this book will attempt to do, namely, *to relocate Jesus and the New Testament within the real first-century world without sacrificing their 'theological' relevance.* In the split-level world of the modern Epicurean revival, with the gods and the world divided by a great gulf (related to Lessing's 'broad, ugly ditch' between the eternal truths of Reason and the contingent truths of history), it was bound to appear that Jesus must belong on one side or the other, but not both. The first two chapters of this book will therefore address the larger cultural context and show how the study of Jesus has been significantly flawed by factors other than the strictly historical.

This, however, raises the question as to what 'history' really is, and what it can and should achieve. This is the subject of chapter 3, where I will argue that the notion of 'history' itself has been pulled and squeezed out of shape by the same cultural pressures. 'History', too, and its relevance for theology, has been affected by the assumed split between 'God' and the 'natural world', with the sceptics claiming that 'history' favours a reductionist picture and the anti-sceptics referring grandly to 'history' to mean 'everything that ever happens', with no reference to the actual historical task of understanding Jesus of Nazareth and his kingdom-proclamation within his own day.

Once all this is clearer, however, we will have to turn our attention (in chapter 4) to two other widely used terms, 'eschatology' and 'apocalyptic', whose slippery meanings have frequently made historical work on Jesus difficult if not impossible. This is not, however, simply a matter of using words clearly. These two terms have become slogans in the service of the theory that Jesus and his first followers expected the imminent end of the space-time world—a theory which merely parodies the historical imperative to locate Jesus within his first-century Jewish context. This in turn is related directly to the question of 'natural theology'. If the present world must come to an end so that a new one may begin, how could anyone argue from the present world up to the God who was about to abolish it? Here is a paradox indeed: Jesus has been kept away from 'natural theology' on the one hand (by many Christians) because he counted as 'divine revelation' and on the other hand because, in predicting the end of the world, he was wrong (and thus was not the embodiment of Israel's God). Neither theology nor exegesis ought to collude with such muddles.

Chapters 3 and 4 thus clear the way for the main positive proposals of the book, which begin in chapter 5 with the first-century Jewish world and its symbols. The Temple spoke of the overlap of heaven and earth, directly contradicting the split-world view of Epicureanism ancient and modern. The Sabbath spoke of the Age to Come being *truly anticipated* within the present time, challenging any suggestion that, if the kingdom of heaven was to arrive, then 'earth' would first have to be abolished. And if humans are made in the image of the creator God, then the idea that one might (somehow) discern something of God from thinking about humans and their vocational imperatives is not after all so strange. This then contextualises the argument of chapter 6, that with Jesus' resurrection (a strange event, to be sure, within the present world but the foundational and paradigmatic event within the new creation) a new ontology and appropriate epistemology are unveiled, a new and transformative dimension of the 'epistemology of love'. This does not, however, create a private 'spiritual' world, sealed off from 'ordinary reality' and hence from the possibility of looking at the world and drawing inferences about its creator. On the contrary, the resurrection opens up instead a new public world in which the questions raised by humans within the present creation can be seen as provisional signposts to God.

They are, however, 'broken signposts', since the highest and best aspects of the human vocation, from 'justice' to 'love', all create paradoxes and sharp disjunctions. None will lead us to Utopia, let alone to God. The argument of chapter 7 is that precisely at this moment of dark paradox the story of the cross—always the most powerful 'apologetic', and in this chapter we begin to understand why—comes into play. At the point where human vocational instincts might be thought to point 'up' to God, but fail to do so, the story of Jesus comes 'down' to where justice is denied, love betrayed, and so on. At this point the particular kind of 'natural theology' which comes into view, unlike most kinds in the last three centuries, takes a specifically Trinitarian form. Reflection on the 'broken signposts' and the paradoxical way they point to God challenges the older implicitly Deistic models which either leave Jesus out of consideration or try to fit him in at a late stage into a picture of 'God' generated on other grounds. This approach is then complemented by the missiology expounded in chapter 8. The present spirit-driven mission of the church is to anticipate, by freshly embodying the previously 'broken' signposts, the promised time when God will be 'all in all'. If the 'natural' world of time and space will be rescued from its corruption and decay and transformed by the glorious divine presence, this eschatological vision will not only sustain the church in its vocation but will enable the retrospective approach to 'natural theology' for which I have argued in chapter 7.

Knowledge itself forms a vital sub-theme throughout the book. I will explore 'love' as the missing link in those various modernist epistemologies which have either grasped at 'objectivity' as a form of power or retreated into a 'subjectivity' which is in fact a self-serving projection.[12] Modernism has screened out the dimension of 'love', a drastic move acknowledged in our culture in the Faust myth and elsewhere. But one cannot, I suggest, understand ordinary knowledge of the ordinary world without 'love' in this sense; which means that we must challenge *both* the reductionist visions which have done without 'God' altogether *and* the would-be 'apologetic' strategies which have tried to answer them. Equally, 'love' itself shifts into a new mode when we are confronted with the possibility of a 'new creation' which is, perhaps surprisingly, neither simply a modification of the old nor yet its straightforward replacement. Rather, it is to be seen as its *redemptive transformation*. Love itself thus moves into a new mode, a new dimension, producing a new kind of knowing. Yet this new 'knowing' is not a private knowledge of the new world only: returning to the world of 'ordinary creation', it not only knows it for the first time but rightly hears it telling the truth about its maker.

That, expounded in the sixth lecture and explored further thereafter, is at the heart of my proposal.

I owe to the University of Aberdeen a great debt of gratitude for the unexpected and flattering invitation to give the Gifford Lectures in the first place. I am equally grateful for the warm welcome and hospitality which I enjoyed over the four weeks in which the lectures were given, and the cheerful encouragement with which, undaunted by the largest snowstorm eastern Scotland has seen in living memory, my hearers turned up, listened attentively, and engaged energetically with my proposals. Professor Philip Ziegler hosted and organised the whole event; one would not have known, from the generous and friendly spirit in which he entertained and introduced me, the extent of our ongoing theological disagreements.[13] Many of the distinguished Aberdeen faculty, not least Professors Tom Greggs and Grant Macaskill, made sure I was well looked after. Amber Shadle took care of hundreds of practical arrangements large and small with friendly efficiency. My own then research assistant, Simon Dürr, helped with the detail of the text, and produced and ran a splendid sequence of

PowerPoint presentations. It was an extraordinary experience of high-octane academic and personal interaction.

I must also thank those who offered me the chance to try out aspects of the argument in earlier settings. I first tried out the sequence of thought on the Right Reverend Robert Forsyth, who gave me his usual shrewd assessments of what might and might not be wisely attempted. Thanks to the kind invitation of the Revd Dr Angus Morrison, I gave a lecture at the Scottish Church's 'Grasping the Nettle' event in Glasgow on September 1, 2016, on 'Wouldn't You Love to Know', outlining the 'epistemology of love' which runs as a thread through the whole train of thought. I presented a single-lecture summary of the overall argument of the lectures at the Lanier Library in Houston, Texas, in March 2017, and I am deeply grateful to Mark Lanier for his hosting of that lecture and to his colleague Charles Mickey for his work behind the scenes. I gave an early version of the third chapter as the 'Analytic Theology Lecture' during the annual meeting of the American Academy of Religion in Boston, Massachusetts, in November 2017, and I am very grateful to Professor Michael Rea and his colleagues for the invitation and their hospitality. (That original lecture, duly expanded, is now published in the *Journal of Analytic Theology* and may be seen as a somewhat more technical version of the analysis of 'history' now to be found in the third chapter of the present book.[14]) Drafts of several of the lectures were inflicted on members of the Logos Institute in St Andrews during 2016 and 2017, and I received a great deal of helpful comment and discussion. My old friends Oliver O'Donovan, Simon Kingston, Bob Stewart and Kimberly Yates all read early drafts with care and insight and gave me much wise comment. None of these, of course, is responsible for any of the mistakes or muddles that may remain.

I must then thank those colleagues and students who came together on June 25, 2018, for an extraordinary colloquium, discussing the lectures one by one in front of an audience in St Andrews, under the auspices of the Logos Institute for Analytic and Exegetical Theology, hosted by Prof. Alan Torrance. My interlocutors on that occasion were Tom Greggs, David Fergusson, Andrew Torrance, Carey Newman, Judith Wolfe, Elizabeth Shively, Amy Peeler, Scott Hafemann, Mahdavi Nevader, Christa McKirland, Jonathan Rutledge, Philip Ziegler, Angus Morrison, Jeremy Begbie, Mitch Mallary and Trevor Hart. Brendan Wolfe subsequently also contributed substantial and very helpful notes on all the lectures. It was a truly extraordinary day in which I was both flattered by the attention and humbled to be reminded how much I still had to learn. It made me realise, as I had already started to think, that there was no point trying to pretend that the present volume, in which the lectures have been edited with a certain amount of expansion and further explanation, could be other than an interim report on an intellectual (and I hope spiritual) exercise very much still in progress. I much regret that it has not been possible to incorporate all the points that were well made at that remarkable meeting, and all the reflections that I might have had on them. I hope I shall be spared to reflect on them all in the days to come. I have not, in other words, tried to do with these lectures what Charles Taylor did with his Giffords, allowing them to grow into *A Secular Age*, his extraordinary *magnum opus*. In terms of scale, the present book is much more like what Rudolf Bultmann did with his Giffords, clarifying and annotating but not altering the original shape and argument. I hope it will redirect some of the current theological and exegetical debates into fresh and fruitful channels.

Among these debates, the ongoing question of Jesus' resurrection continues to puzzle many. I hope that this book, and chapter 6 in particular, will go some way to explaining things in my earlier work that have seemed opaque to some recent writers, and to addressing further issues they have raised. I have in mind particularly P. Carnley, *Resurrection in Retrospect: A Critical Examination of the Theology of N. T. Wright* (Eugene, Ore.: Cascade Books, 2019), which arrived when the present volume was at proof stage.

In the process of clarifying and editing for publication, the expert continuing help of Simon Dürr and Mitch Mallary has been beyond praise. They have rescued me from numerous blunders, pointed out places where I was failing to give my own argument the clarity they could see it needed, and steered me towards numerous sources of help. I have been richly blessed by several research assistants over the years, and these two young colleagues are the equal of any.

I am particularly grateful to Dr Carey Newman of Baylor University Press, and his staff, for his enthusiasm for this project and his encouragement and wise direction at various stages. I continue to be grateful to my London publishers, SPCK, and especially to Philip Law, for their happy partnership which now extends nearly thirty years. And I am, as ever, deeply indebted to my wife and family for their love and support—especially for one memorable morning when my son Julian was kindly reading a draft of chapter 3 while Carey Newman was reading a draft of chapter 6, at the same table, and both were giving me their candid running comments. Such moments enrich both family life and scholarly community.

My mother, having given me the backhanded encouragement I mentioned earlier, died on June 1, 2018, one day short of her 95th birthday. This book is dedicated, with love and gratitude, to her memory.

Tom Wright
St Mary's College, St Andrews
Eastertide 2019

List of Abbreviations

11QMelch	Melchizedek Scroll
1QS	Community Rule
2 Bar.	*2 Baruch*
2 En.	*2 Enoch*
AB	Anchor Bible
Ant.	Josephus, *Antiquities of the Jews*
Apoc. Mos.	*Apocalypse of Moses*
ARN	'Abot de Rabbi Nathan
Barn.	*Epistle of Barnabas*
bRos Has.	Babylonian Talmud tractate Rosh Hashanah
CD	Damascus Document
Civ.	Augustine, *City of God*
Dial.	Justin Martyr, *Dialogue with Trypho*
Ecl.	Virgil, *Eclogues*
H&E	Bultmann, *History and Eschatology*
Hist. eccl.	Theodoret, *Historia Ecclesia*
JBL	*Journal of Biblical Literature*
JSJ	*Journal for the Study of Judaism*
JTI	*Journal of Theological Interpretation*
Jub.	*Jubilees*
JVG	Wright, *Jesus and the Victory of God*
LAE	*Life of Adam and Eve*
Mek. Exod	Mekhilta on the book of Exodus
mTamid	Mishnah tractate Tamid
Nat. d.	Cicero, *De natura deum* (On the Nature of the Gods)
NTPG	Wright, *The New Testament and the People of God*
OHNT	Re Manning, ed., *Oxford Handbook of Natural Theology*
PFG	Wright, *Paul and the Faithfulness of God*
PRE	Pirqe Rabbi Eliezer
PRI	Wright, *Paul and His Recent Interpreters*
Rep.	Cicero, *Republic*
Rer. nat.	Lucretius, *De rerum natorum* (On the Nature of Things)
Revolution	Wright, *The Day the Revolution Began*
RSG	Wright, *The Resurrection of the Son of God*
ShirShabb	Songs of the Sabbath Sacrifice
Test. Dan	*Testament of Dan*
TynBul	*Tyndale Bulletin*

I

Natural Theology in Its Historical Context

1

The Fallen Shrine

Lisbon 1755 and the Triumph of Epicureanism

INTRODUCTION: THE PUZZLES WE INHERIT

When I was Bishop of Durham, my study in Auckland Castle held a wonderful collection of books left by previous incumbents. We had Bishop Lightfoot's copy, a first edition, of Tennyson's *In Memoriam*. We had Bishop Handley Moule's copy of his own commentary on Romans. And much beside. But one of my favourite memorabilia, which fell out of a book when I was looking for something else, was a postcard dated 1717. It was an invitation to an afternoon of tennis in Oriel College, Oxford, addressed to a young man who had recently decided to abandon his earlier Presbyterianism and to seek Anglican ordination. The young man was Joseph Butler, destined to become one of the great names of eighteenth-century theology and philosophy. He became Bishop of Bristol in 1738 at the age of forty-six and was translated to Durham in 1750. There he made quite an impression, even though he lasted less than two years before dying at the age of 60.

Bishop Butler represents an old order which was about to disappear. That disappearance, and the way in which very different movements of thought replaced Butler's approach, has given particular shape and emphasis to the subsequent discussions of what has long been called 'natural theology'. This fresh shaping of that question coincided, for closely related reasons, with new questions and challenges about Jesus. These two sets of questions, and their mutual relationship, form the theme of the present book.

The questions of 'natural theology' and of 'who was Jesus?' have been held apart in most subsequent theology. One way of defining 'natural theology' might almost be 'sorting out God while bracketing out Jesus'.[1] But if Jesus himself was a fully human being and thus a genuine part of first-century historical reality, as the church has always taught, and as modern critics have indeed sharply insisted, it makes no sense to exclude him from the 'natural' world.

The problem here is that 'history' itself has been anything but a stable category. The larger movements of culture and thought that swept across Europe in the eighteenth century had a profound effect not only on 'natural theology' and on the study of Jesus but on the notion of 'history' itself. Since I am intending here to get inside these questions, to see why they have been understood the way they have, and to suggest new ways of bringing them all fruitfully together, it is important to sketch the story of how it happened. This touches on many complex and interlocking questions, some of which—but by no means all—I shall discuss later in this book. But the inevitable dangers of oversimplification are far outweighed by the dangers of trying to address the questions of God, creation, Jesus and history as though each existed in a vacuum, sealed off from the others and from the wider world in which the questioners lived.

Bishop Butler's best-known work is a classic of the early eighteenth century: the *Analogy of Religion*. Written in 1736 while he was Rector of Stanhope, a few miles up the River Wear from Auckland Castle, he argued that there was a series of what he called 'analogies' between the world of nature and the truths of the Christian faith which lent strong support to the latter. He made the point, against the then prevailing Deists, that the problems they had perceived in scripture—the mysteries and cruelties of 'sacred history', not least in the books of Joshua and Judges—were matched by the mysteries and cruelties inherent in the world of nature as we know it. It looked as if the world of creation and the world of scripture belonged closely together.

That summary does scant justice to a work of subtlety and learning.[2] But Butler is important not just for what he said but for what he represented: a mood of optimism, of *Christian* optimism no less, which expressed itself in many forms in British society. The missionary movements of the time were mostly postmillennial in inspiration. That is, they believed that the kingdom of God was growing and extending, and that Jesus would soon be hailed as lord around the world.[3] Handel put this into immortal music in the *Messiah*, composed in 1741. The music, well known though not always theologically understood, reaches its climax, not with a heavenly 'life after death', but with the mission of the church through which 'the kingdom of this world is become the kingdom of our God'. That is the theme of the 'Hallelujah Chorus' which ends Part II, prior to the general resurrection in Part III.

The same mood of optimism, of a theology which makes sense of creation in parallel with a gospel which transforms the world, is visible in Joseph Addison, one of the most famous essayists and politicians of the early eighteenth century. In the year 1712 he published a hymn, 'The Spacious Firmament on High', which expressed a similar point of view to Butler's: the sky, the sun, the moon and the stars all declare the praise of the creator.[4] At one level this is simply an English version of Psalm 19. At another level, it bears the stamp of the same Christian faith which Butler put into his anti-Deist arguments:

> What though, in solemn silence, all/ move round the dark terrestrial ball?
> What though no real voice or sound/ Amid their radiant Orbs be found?
> In Reason's Ear they all rejoice,/ and utter forth a glorious Voice,
> For ever singing, as they shine,/ The Hand that made us is Divine.

This, one might suppose, is Christian engagement with the natural world at its best: a scripturally sourced acknowledgement (resonating closely, as well, with Plato's *Timaeus* and Cicero's discussion of the dream of Scipio) that the natural world speaks, indeed sings, of its creator.[5] And, importantly, that human Reason can hear the song. If one were to regard the implicit scriptural reference as an optional extra, making the engagement with the natural world one thing and the Bible something quite different, one might even call this 'natural theology'.[6]

At another level, but still indicative of the mood of the early eighteenth century, we might note the great Northumbrian artist Thomas Bewick (1753–1828). Bewick took commissions, from farmers who wanted to show off their stock, to engrave prize bulls, sheep and horses. But when they asked him to make the animals look even larger and fatter than they actually were, he refused. For the devout Bewick, 'Nature was God made visible'.[7]

A noble vision; and then came the crash. Literally, a crash: the earthquake that struck Lisbon on All Saints Day 1755 destroyed 85 percent of the buildings in the city, killing around a fifth of the city's population (thirty or forty thousand citizens out of roughly two hundred thousand). Many of the dead had been devoutly assembled in church for the festival. Many others, rushing down to the sea to escape falling buildings, were overwhelmed by the subsequent tsunami. The same event killed a further ten thousand or so in Spain, and even Morocco, partly through the tsunamis and fires.[8]

These shattering geophysical events, and their catastrophic human effects, brought into sharp focus a moment of philosophical and ideological devastation.[9] The fallen shrine of Lisbon symbolized the fallen shrine of an optimistic variety of 'natural theology' which had tried to read off divine benevolence from the course of historical events. (That is not the only, or even the normal, meaning of 'natural theology', as we shall see.) How could one believe that the world was getting better and better, under the benevolent guidance of a wise providence, if things like this were allowed to happen? There were, of course, many other reasons for the reaction which followed. Lisbon did not generate Voltaire's scepticism *ex nihilo*, just as the First World War did not generate Karl Barth's *Romans* commentary out of nothing—and just as the events of September 11, 2001, did not generate from scratch the anti-religious rhetoric of the so-called 'new atheists'.[10] The cultural and philosophical mood I shall shortly be describing had been well under way some time before the disaster, but Lisbon gave it a new focus and energy.

Some Christians, to be sure (including John Wesley) interpreted the earthquake as a sign of divine judgment. (This too, of course, might be seen as a form of 'natural theology', deducing divine acts from occurrences in the 'natural' world.) This position was in line with the kind of 'interpretation' in which James Begg, a distinguished Free Church minister, saw the 1879 Tay Bridge disaster as a judgment of God, both upon the train—which was running on a Sunday—and upon various supposedly wicked persons on board.[11] Similar interpretations of disasters have continued to this day. But my point is simply that arguments like Bishop Butler's, which had seemed convincing to many in the 1730s and 1740s, appeared a lot less so after Lisbon.

Earthquakes, famines and the like were not, of course, new. Devout Jews and Christians had always known about them. Such occurrences had not normally been seen as a *problem*, as such, for Christian theology. Paul's readers were troubled by many things, but not those. Neither the early Fathers nor the great mediaeval thinkers, nor the sixteenth-century reformers, supposed that (what we have come to call) 'natural disasters' might threaten the very foundations of faith. Augustine addresses the question as to why both the righteous and the wicked remain vulnerable to this-worldly catastrophes, and he replies that this has no effect on the eternal salvation of God's people, who were in any case going to die one day.[12] Perhaps such events only posed an apparent threat to faith when the form which Christianity took was either Deism or the Butler-like response to it. To that extent, Lisbon may have been more of a symptom than a cause of a scepticism which had been growing quietly in the background of European thought. It may be that the optimistic proponents of a postmillennial Utopia had been inclined to downplay such events. Did they suppose that the spread of the gospel would eradicate volcanoes and earthquakes as well as human sinfulness?

Scepticism itself was not, after all, a new option.[13] It was over a century since Descartes's *Cogito* had unleashed (despite, it seems, the great Frenchman's intentions) a wave of critical thinking which some were riding in the sceptical direction.[14] Memories of the Thirty Years' War, and other intra-religious conflicts, functioned like winds to whip up that wave and turn it into an intellectual tsunami to rival the actual one that struck Lisbon. In other words, people already had what we might call socio-political reasons for wanting Christianity to be untrue, or at least for doubting its absolutist claims. Now they had epistemological tools for advancing that case.

One marker in this narrative is the Frenchman Pierre Bayle (1647–1706), a Huguenot refugee living in Holland. He argued that atheism was more rational—and more likely to produce social harmony—than Deism.[15] The Lisbon earthquake was then seized upon by those who wanted (for various reasons, not least the corruption of the French church) to reject mainstream European Christianity, whether Catholic or Protestant. Voltaire's sarcastic comments about God and Lisbon—will you now say, he asks the devout, that this terrible event will merely illustrate 'the iron laws that chain the will of God'?—expressed what many others were thinking.[16]

The result, when the dust had settled, was that the Deism which Butler had opposed was steadily being overtaken by a similar but sharper worldview, namely a revival of the ancient philosophy of Epicurus. At least things were now more explicit. People had often confused Deism with Christianity (as they still do). That was far less likely with Epicureanism. Deism would continue—some have suggested that it remains a default mode for many Western people who think themselves Christian—but the public mood and widely held assumption has shifted.[17]

Epicureanism had in fact been increasingly popular in Europe, as an alternative to the official religion, since the 1417 rediscovery of Lucretius, Epicurus's greatest expositor.[18] It was enthusiastically promoted by Pierre Gassendi (1592–1655), who saw it as a substitute for Aristotelian analyses of the world, and who attempted to create a synthesis with Christian ideas—something his successors increasingly saw as impossible.[19] Epicureanism had been influential, though inevitably controversial, in the complex and politically charged debates of the seventeenth century, including the rise of new scientific endeavours. Edmund Halley (1656–1742) used Lucretius as a model for the Ode he wrote to celebrate the mathematically coherent system of Sir Isaac Newton (1642–1727).[20] Canon Robert South of Oxford, eager to say the worst thing he could about the members of the Royal Society, described them in 1678 as 'sons of Epicurus, both for Voluptuousness and Irreligion'.[21] Diderot, in his famous

Encyclopedia, suggested that France was full of Epicureans of all sorts.[22] Writing to a friend in 1715, Leibniz commented on the rise in England of 'materialism' and 'mortalism', movements that had sprung up (in Catherine Wilson's words) 'in the anti-authoritarian upheavals and sectarian fragmentation of the English Civil War'.[23] Thomas Hobbes was routinely denounced as an atheist and an Epicurean.[24] The explosive combination of scientific enquiry, political radicalism and theological scepticism had been in the air for some time. A case can be made for discerning the roots of some at least of all this in the Nominalism of thinkers like William of Occam, several centuries earlier.[25]

Epicureanism, then, had been on the increase for quite a while. But now, after 1755, it had become both mainstream and (up to the present day) permanent. Forget those stars and planets singing the praises of God; if there is a god, he or it is a long way away and takes no notice either of us or of the whirling stars. Religion is a human invention designed to keep the masses docile.[26] The world does what it does under its own steam. It develops and changes in random ways without outside interference as atoms move randomly and, sometimes, swerve in such a way as to bump into one another and produce new effects. That's all there is to life. And when we die, we die; so there is, in both senses, *nothing to be afraid of.* That is Epicureanism in a nutshell, from the great man himself in the third century BC, through Lucretius's poem in the first century BC, all the way to Machiavelli, Bentham, and a great multitude since, including as we shall see Thomas Jefferson.[27]

These names—people who intended to make, and did make, quite a difference in the world—highlight two main differences between the ancient and the modern forms of the philosophy. Ancient Epicureans thought there was nothing much one could do about the course of the world. The atoms swirled about and did their own thing; all one could do was to make oneself as comfortable as possible. The modern Epicureans, however, have seen in this cosmology an opportunity to pursue new goals.[28] Ancient Epicureans were a minority, a self-styled small elite. Modern Epicureans have attained a majority, making the Western world—their natural habitat—the new self-styled global elite ('the developed world', with all the heavy irony which that phrase now possesses). Friedrich von Schlegel (1772–1829), a German Romantic philosopher, lamented that Epicureanism had become the dominant philosophy in the second half of the eighteenth century.[29] Karl Köppen, one of the closest friends of the young Karl Marx, pointed out the close relation between the eighteenth-century *Aufklärer* and Epicureanism, claiming that Epicurus was the great 'Enlightener' of antiquity. Marx himself echoed this view in his doctoral dissertation.[30] This robust 'materialism', as Catherine Wilson argues in her compelling book, has become so much the stock in trade of the modern Western world that we don't even realise its ancient roots.[31] When we read summaries of Lucretius, the ideas seem 'deeply familiar', says Wilson, because 'many of the work's core arguments are among the foundations on which modern life has been constructed'.[32]

Lucretius has, in fact, helped the modern world to articulate its standard polemic against religion.[33] The growing influence of Epicureanism (whether explicit or not) on modernity created an intellectual as well as social environment in which it was now felt fitting and appropriate to study and organise life in this world without reference to God or the gods—and to study and reflect upon God or the gods without reference to the contingent truths of this-worldly, 'historical', life. This is the point at which our brief sketch of the philosophical climate provides the vital context for understanding why the whole project of 'natural theology', as conceived before, has become a whole lot harder. For the great mediaevals, with their largely Aristotelian universe, various kinds of commerce between the present world and divine truth were to be expected. Within an Epicurean framework, the theologian is apparently being challenged to make natural-theology bricks without straw. A great gulf has opened up, with 'the real world', including 'history', on one side, and any divine beings on the other. Arguing from the one to the other—particularly to the *Christian* God—might seem akin to humans trying to fly.

Might there, however, be other gods towards whom the argument might more naturally point? This distinction is worth pondering. From Democritus through Epicurus to Lucretius and on to our own day, there *is* a kind of 'natural theology' going on. But, unlike what might appear the 'normal' kinds within Christianity, it would go like this: we look at the whirling atoms doing their own thing, and we conclude that the gods were never involved in this world and they still aren't. A more cynical account might suggest that the real logic was running the other way: we don't want any gods getting involved in our lives, so when we study the natural world we close up the 'gaps' where divine influence had previously been detected. This account—turning scepticism against itself, as it were—would be just as plausible for the eighteenth-century revolutionaries as for the modern 'new atheists'. And this question of the direction of travel (are we arguing from the observed world to the absent gods, or from the hoped-for divine absence to the observed world?) would then present an eerie parallel to the same question within a would-be 'Christian' natural theology. Are Christians really reasoning from the observed world to the Christian creator, or are they assuming the creator and seeing the world as his handiwork? In which case, which 'creator' precisely would they be assuming?

Once the new situation became established, philosophers started to talk about 'the problem of evil' in a new way.[34] They separated out the question of human sin, and the proffered divine solution, from the question of why apparently 'bad' things happen in the 'natural world'. The first question (sin and salvation) was passed on to systematic theologians writing about 'atonement', usually as quite a separate question from 'theodicy' (the problem of God's justice), often without noticing that the most famous first-century writing to address such things arguably held them together (Paul's letter to the Romans, discussing 'the righteousness of God'). The question of theodicy then had to face, not the problem of God's dealing with human sin, but rather the problem within various versions of Deism, namely that if the present world is the handiwork of a good God, then, as a famous contemporary satirist said, he seems to be a bit of an underachiever.

The result of all this, as we shall see throughout the present book, was not only that a would-be Christian 'natural theology' would then be required to make bricks without straw. It would have to build on land already liable to subsidence. It is, no doubt, for reasons like this that (as we shall see later on) Jewish thought regularly regarded the teachings of Epicurus as the last word in false and wicked worldviews. A properly Christian theological engagement with the natural world clearly requires a robust alternative to Epicureanism.

So far, I have offered a quick, rough sketch of the climate of thought in which contemporary debates about 'natural theology' took shape. It may now be helpful to pause and clarify a few points.

History of Ideas

First, on the history of ideas. I shall be talking about various leading opinion-formers, but I do not assume that they were all fully consistent. All of us, no doubt, have inconsistencies, more obvious from a distance than in the rough-and-tumble of everyday life. Nor do I suppose that societies in general adopt new worldviews because someone later seen as a great thinker made a particular point. Histories of philosophy, as of theology, sometimes appear to imply that, once (say) Descartes or Hume had said something, everyone quickly read it and believed it, until the next philosophers developed it further. Real life is more complex than that.[35]

We need, in particular, to distinguish pioneers from popularisers. The ideas of some innovative thinkers take time to percolate into the popular mind. Legend has it that the young William Temple (1881–1944), subsequently himself Archbishop, asked his archiepiscopal father Frederick (1821–1902) why the philosophers didn't rule the world, and received the reply, 'Of course they do—a hundred years after they're dead!'[36] On the other hand, some thinkers catch a public mood and express it strikingly, clarifying, as in great poetry, something 'that oft was thought, but ne'er so well expressed'.[37] The pioneers hack their way through the jungle; the popularisers put up vivid signposts beside an increasingly well-trodden path. Some, no doubt, belong in between; some pioneers are seen in hindsight as popularisers, even though—like Voltaire and Hume in the 1750s, and Marx in the 1850s—they were, in their own day, voices in the wilderness. Sometimes it works the other way around. Nietzsche in the 1880s caught, and articulated sharply, one of the moods of the times, but people today look back and see him as a wild-eyed prophet.[38]

If we choose to call this new world 'modernity', or 'enlightenment', or any of the other available options, we are using such labels heuristically. The key figures seldom thought of themselves like that. We think of Schubert as standing on the bridge between classical and romantic music; but Schubert himself was thinking of love, death and the next tune. Only with hindsight do we fit people into a larger category, which itself will always be a sketch, often inevitably a caricature. My aim, in any case, is not to attempt a precise genealogy of the developing ideas. I want, rather, to draw attention to different currents of thought which have shaped the intellectual milieu within which people have addressed the questions of the world, history and God, and to propose that, after the shrine of a Butler-like 'natural theology' had fallen, it was replaced, in the popular mind, with something quite different which created new and lasting challenges. For our own purposes, the upshot is clear: neither the modern quest for 'natural theology' nor the modern historical search for Jesus comes to us as a 'neutral' project, unconditioned by its own times.

We must not, of course, regard a many-coloured phenomenon through monochrome spectacles. As in the ancient world, where the Stoic Seneca could cheerfully borrow Epicurean ideas on the grounds that if something was true it was true no matter who said it,[39] so the great European thinkers of the seventeenth, eighteenth and nineteenth centuries were capable of all kinds of eclecticism.[40] Epicureanism in the period 'was anything but a unified doctrine . . . it was built out of a variety of components, often applied independently of one another, in different contexts and with multiple strategies'.[41] Some analysts have seen the major philosophical conflicts of the time as being between a latent Augustinianism and a revived Stoicism, with Epicureanism playing a lesser role. In my view, the evidence suggests that Epicureanism became increasingly dominant until (as Wilson points out) it becomes the native air of the modern West.[42] The specifics of Lucretius's scientific theories have been left far behind, but in many other ways he bestrides our world like a Colossus. 'The brooding Epicurean [i.e. Lucretius] inspired the youthful Voltaire and the mature Holbach, and his memory sustained the dying David Hume'.[43]

Deism and Epicureanism

So to my second question: how did this newer Epicureanism differ from the Deism which was already widespread in the seventeenth and eighteenth centuries?[44] Deism, I have suggested, formed an easy transition point into full-on Epicureanism. So what is the difference?

Deists and Epicureans share the view, which has now become widespread in Western culture, that there is a great gulf between God (or the gods) and the world we live in. Here we need to be careful. For the Epicureans at least, the gods are made of atoms just like everything else, so that they are the same *sort* of creatures as we are, only completely separated from us.[45] This contrasts with the mainstream view of Jews and Christians, and I think of Deists as well, for whom the referent of the word 'God' is different in *kind* from us, as well as in *location*, since God is believed to inhabit a different kind of space from ours, though one which overlaps and interlocks with ours. (For Christians, the incarnation of the second person of the Trinity obviously bridges the gap both of ontology and of place, resulting in complexities and possibilities we shall explore later.) For the Deist, there is one God who made the world, the supreme watchmaker who set the machine running and keeps it well-oiled. For some Deists like Newton, inconsistently, the watchmaker has to come back from time to time to wind the watch up or perhaps adjust the time (which is why some Deists, like some of the American Founding Fathers, were happy to pray, and to encourage others to do so, for particular outcomes).[46] For the Epicurean, however, the gods had nothing to do with making the world, and they have nothing to do with its maintenance.[47] Nor is the world a well-oiled rational machine, since its ongoing life is a matter of irrational trial and error, with atoms bumping into one another at random—and thus offering no hope of 'progress', an idea whose origins I will deal with presently. There is no 'problem of evil' in Epicureanism; the world is what it is. We may not like it, but to assess the 'morality' of what happens in a random universe is to ask a meaningless question.[48] For some Deists at least, God cares how we behave, and may eventually call us to account. For Epicureans—and this has always been its attraction, in ancient, late mediaeval and modern times—the gods don't care, and they won't judge, so how we behave is up to us, and death dissolves us into nothingness.[49] Lax Epicureans have taken this as an invitation to licentiousness; serious ones, as a counsel of moderation.⁵⁰ Many people today, hearing the word 'Epicurean', think of morality, or more likely immorality. When I use the term in this book, my focus is particularly on the cosmology in which the domain of the gods is totally removed from our own, and utterly incompatible with it—however much it serves as a model for the Epicurean philosopher who wants to separate himself, similarly, from the common herd.⁵¹ Any divine beings are out of our reach; you can acknowledge them if you like, offering a distant, cool appraisal of their superiority, but you shouldn't imagine that prayer, devotion or holiness will have any effect on them (however much some kinds of devotion might have beneficial effects on ourselves). When modern surveys suggest that far more people say they 'believe in God' than go to church, here is an obvious explanation: why would you get out of bed on a Sunday morning for the distant Deist god, still less for the absent Epicurean one?⁵²

Enlightenment

Third, then, to the meaning of 'Enlightenment'. Answering this question will lead us straight in to my main exposition.

The English word 'Enlightenment' is a nineteenth-century coinage, picking up the German *Aufklärung*, used by Immanuel Kant in 1784. Kant was resonating with the French thinkers who produced the famous 'Encyclopedia' in 1751, which referred to *lumières*, the 'lights' that were now appearing. Theirs was a common noun, putting a label on what seemed to be happening; his was active, naming an agenda to be followed. Kant's own definition, in his famous essay *Was ist Aufklärung?*, had to do with the freedom to make public use of one's reason with the goal of liberating humankind from its self-imposed immaturity.⁵³ The polemical edge in almost every word here tells us that *Aufklärung* was already being seen as a campaign slogan.

The English word was still being used with contempt in the late nineteenth century, justifying one of the definitions in the *Oxford English Dictionary* which refers to 'the spirit and aims of the French philosophers of the eighteenth century, or of others whom it is intended to associate with them in the implied charge of shallow and pretentious intellectualism, unreasonable contempt for tradition or authority, etc.'.⁵⁴ The standard English scorn for strange continental theories, however, cannot mask the fact that the genesis of the Enlightenment belongs not least in seventeenth-century England. Kant himself looked back to John Locke's sense-based epistemology. Other British thinkers like Francis Bacon, Thomas Hobbes and David Hume were leading lights in the same movement, even if they didn't give it the name we now all use.[55] By the early nineteenth century William Blake (1757–1827) could shake his fist not only at the movement's French leaders but also at their underlying Epicurean philosophy.[56]

The project of 'Enlightenment', then, was always many-sided. Historians differ as to which thinkers and movements they choose for particular focus, and note the national differences between the German, French, English and Scottish Enlightenments, not to mention the American variety. But they all look back to something like Kant's definition, and to the sense of a *shared project* which it invokes and a new worldview which it assumes. New *knowledge* had opened up a new era of *freedom*, a human coming-of-age. Freedom from traditional theology or religion, along with new forms of political freedom, were seen as bound up with, and in a sense consequent upon, new scientific discoveries and theories. Again, the direction of travel of this implied argument raises questions about the way an implicit 'natural theology' actually works. Did scientific Epicureanism come first, leading (in politics) to revolution and (in theology and religion) to an absentee God and a 'merely human' Jesus? Or was it the other way around? Or was it a more complex mixture of all these and more?

Such a complex movement, containing philosophical, theological, social, cultural and political elements, does not appear in a flash, with Albert Schweitzer or A. J. Ayer springing fully armed from the head of Kant like Athene from the head of Zeus. And, of course, throughout the eighteenth and nineteenth centuries there were leading thinkers, and Christian movements, who showed little signs of 'Enlightenment' tendencies. John and Charles Wesley were among the great names of the eighteenth century, as was the devout Samuel Johnson. The equally though differently devout John Henry Newman was one of the most influential writers in nineteenth-century England. But there was a tide running in the other direction, so strongly that when we open a book entitled *God's Funeral* we find that it is not about the 1960s Death-of-God movement, or the Dawkins-and-Hitchens 'new atheists', but about the Victorian era.[57] Atheism is the end of the Epicurean road. There isn't much difference between having distant divinities, unknowable and uninvolved, and there being no god at all. By the end of the nineteenth century, many—particularly those in a position to profit from it all—had embraced that new vision. And they supposed it to be based on 'science'.

The word *Enlightenment*, in fact, says it all, at least in retrospect. Everything that had gone before was darkness and superstition: now came sudden illumination. Alexander Pope's famous couplet catches the mood:

Nature, and nature's laws, lay hid in night:
God said 'Let Newton be!' and all was light.[58]

This sense of new light replacing previous darkness had always been the appeal of the great Epicurean poet Lucretius: a new world, free from ignorance, free in particular from fear of divine interference or final condemnation. This 'new world' was in fact the retrieval of one of the great ancient philosophies and was hailed as such by many at the time. This undermines the widespread assumption today that 'the modern world' as a whole has been 'discovered' by scientific research, leaving ancient worldviews far behind.[59] In this implicit assumption, the scientists have discovered how the world works and as a result we can and will do things our own way. We have come of age, we are grown-up, able not only to understand our own destiny but to take it forward. Humans must therefore stand on their own feet and accept the dark fatefulness of the random world. All this (apart from specific modern scientific discoveries) was in fact a well-established worldview of the first century BC. At that time, as we said before, it was the view of a small minority, but it has now become the implicit understanding of a majority at least in the Western world.[60] That is one of the central points of this present chapter.

For a good nineteenth-century example of all this, we may consider the poet William Ernest Henley (1849–1903), who was as influential in the mid-nineteenth century as Samuel Johnson had been in the eighteenth. His 'Invictus', written in 1875, is well known for its last lines, 'I am the master of my fate;/ I am the captain of my soul'. The poem accepts the new philosophy and announces a human self-confidence from within it. 'My head is bloody, but unbowed', he declares. Death itself, approaching as 'the menace of the years', 'finds, and shall find, me unafraid'.[61] This shout of defiance should be put in context. Having suffered from tuberculosis as a boy, Henley had had his lower left leg amputated when he was twenty. (He was the model for Robert Louis Stevenson's energetic one-legged pirate, 'Long John Silver'.) The poem expresses something of a Stoic resolution, but it is set in the context, not of a pantheism, in which the speaker is somehow part of the divine (or vice versa), but of a detached independence, characteristic of a robust Epicureanism. Whatever the gods may be up to, I will live my independent life, and death will be 'nothing to be afraid of'. Twenty years later, the University of St Andrews awarded Henley a Doctorate of Letters.[62]

The result of all this, we shall now see, was a climate of opinion which steadily pulled things apart. 'Natural theology' would become 'theology without history' (particularly without Jesus in his first-century context); 'biblical studies' would become 'history without God'. The former would lead to types of 'classical theism', looking for a 'perfect being' God with whom it might then prove difficult to associate the real Jesus. The latter would lead to the scepticism of Jesus-scholars, from Hermann Samuel Reimarus in the late eighteenth century to Robert Funk in the late twentieth. These movements of thought are themselves contingent, not necessary. Understanding their contexts, and the forces which drove them, will help us to see how to put back together things that should never have been separated.

Straws in a Strong Wind

In order to frame our exploration, we have to look wider than theology and exegesis. Our disciplines have been prone to tell their own stories as though they were detached from the wider world. In my own field, the story of New Testament scholarship is often told with minimal reference to the larger cultural scene.[63] But this is myopic. (There is a parallel here with the history of philosophy itself. As Jonathan Israel points out in his introduction to Isaiah Berlin's studies of *Three Critics of the Enlightenment*, philosophers tend to tell the story of how particular ideas developed as though in a vacuum, whereas Berlin was concerned to put that story in its wider cultural framework.[64]) This task is necessarily generalized and broad-brush. But at this stage in my exposition there are strong, clear indications of the wider mood.

I note in particular five features of late eighteenth-century culture. These might initially appear to be unconnected and to have little to do with natural theology or (except for the last one) biblical exegesis. But together they form a pattern.

First, there were the Revolutions, in America (1775–1783) and France (1789–1799). Taking them in the reverse order, France had witnessed a long-developed attack (originating in Jansenist pietism) on the high religion of the Roman Catholic court. Increasingly politicized in the later eighteenth century, this attack combined with a new intellectual analysis of, and reaction to, the colluding corruptions of crown and church.[65] We should not suppose that ordinary French people were, at the start, eager to destroy the church. But the Revolution gave political force to the idea that society was now to be reordered from top to bottom. This led to the 'dechristianization' campaign of 1793, which unleashed a particular vein of latent anti-god philosophy, setting up the goddess of Reason in Notre Dame Cathedral, with an inaugural Festival on November 10 that year. Getting rid of princes and getting rid of God and his earthly representatives were, to the most radical French revolutionaries, two ways of saying the same thing.

Robespierre, however, tried to mediate with a form of Deism. In his last speech to the Convention, he claimed cryptically that death was not an eternal sleep, but the beginning of immortality. He gave his support in June 1794 to a proposed 'Cult of the Supreme Being'. But his opponents on the hard left were implacable. When they guillotined him seven weeks later (July 26, 1794) they were insisting, in language everyone could understand, that something like Epicureanism, rather than Deism, was now the new orthodoxy.[66]

America, meanwhile, had been eager to get rid not only of the British monarchy but also of the intertwined theological and ecclesial structures which appeared to support it. Thomas Jefferson, after all, later declared, 'I too am an Epicurean', though to be fair he was a great many other things as well.[67] Most of the Founding Fathers were in fact Deists, though theological consistency was not their strongest suit: some were quite devout in worship and in calling people to pray for God's help and guidance. The tension between that cautiously integrative approach and the more powerful Deism persists to this day in America, emerging in debates about prayer in schools, about the slogan 'One Nation Under God', and other similar points of tension. I suspect that at least some American attempts at 'natural theology' may have been aimed at finding, not the Christian God, but the Supreme Being who still presides over much American religion.[68] A dangerous compromise, one might suppose: it had cost Robespierre his head. The leaders of the new American project persisted. They didn't want to reject bishops; they just didn't want the public servants George III had been sending them. Having seen the dangers of politically sponsored church leadership, they wanted bishops of their own who would live in a parallel universe, enforcing a strict separation of church and state. That reflected exactly their underlying Deistic separation of God and the world. Both France and America were determined to bundle God off the public stage.

I suspect that some of the continuing differences between America and France today reflect that difference between Epicureanism and Deism. Their respective approaches to multiculturalism might be a case in point. Their respective revolutions, though, have generated puzzles of democracy and revolution which are with us yet. But in both, the net result was to get God out of the way and let the political process (like the swerving atoms of Epicurus) do its own thing.[69] Everything would be better that way. This was, for them, the political application of Epicureanism—or at least, an Epicureanism newly linked, as we shall see, with the idea of 'progress'. A sterner retrieval of Epicurus and Lucretius might have pointed out that swerving atoms were not guaranteed to produce anything which humans might find 'good' or even enjoyable. A cynical observation of two centuries of quasi-Epicurean political life might agree.

The irony of the American project echoes the underlying irony of the Enlightenment itself: is this really a new world, or is it the glad retrieval of an ancient one, or is it somehow both? The rhetoric works either way, framing the shift in meaning whereby the word 'new' has gone from meaning 'dangerous, shallow and disruptive' to meaning 'fresh, recently discovered, and life-giving'. Anyway, those who framed the American Declaration of Independence chose for the Great Seal, and for the one-dollar bill to this day, an adapted quotation from Virgil: *Novus Ordo Seclorum*, 'a new order of the ages'.[70] Did the Founding Fathers suppose that history went in great cycles, with a 'new order' emerging every two millennia or so? Or did they see the Age of Augustus, celebrated by Virgil, as a false dawn, with their own day as the ultimate long-range fulfilment? Did they mind if people spotted that they were re-employing a slogan heavy with past imperial overtones? Mediaeval Christians, following Lactantius and the Emperor Constantine himself, had seen Virgil's poem as a prophecy of the coming of Christ (an idea still visible in the Christmas hymn, 'It came upon the midnight clear', with its startling suggestion that the 'ever-circling years' will result in a new 'age of gold'[71]). Reapplying Virgil to the American constitution meant making explicit what was always implicit in the Enlightenment: Jesus was now, at best, a forerunner of the new age of independence.[72]

Alongside the political revolutions, there was, second, the rise of pre-Darwinian evolutionism.[73] Note the 'ism': this wasn't just a theory about biology; it was a worldview in which an evolution without divine guidance played a necessary role. Some have called this 'naturalism', but that is inadequate and misleading. With hindsight we can see, as some at the time saw, that it was an explicitly *Epicurean* programme. It was developed by people like Charles Darwin's grandfather Erasmus (1731–1802), who like Addison lived in Lichfield but who took a very different view of the world. Erasmus Darwin and his colleagues ('the Lunar Men') were eagerly inspecting the creation for signs of change and development driven internally from within rather than being imposed from on high, while equally eagerly exploring new technologies to enable humans to take matters into their own hands.[74] Living as he did at the west end of the Cathedral Close, Darwin literally had Canons to the right and the left of him, and one of them, Canon Thomas Seward, seeing only too clearly the implications of Darwin's choice of shells as symbols of a new theory of origins, wrote a poem in 1770 angrily accusing him of Epicureanism.[75] Darwin published his findings in *Zoonomia* (1794–1796), explaining the laws of organic life on the evolutionary principle. Whether or not he and his colleagues wanted to draw the fully blown Epicurean conclusion about the absence of God, their theories and their practice were all tending in that direction. Like Democritus's atoms, which were the scientific heart of Epicureanism, the organisms they were studying (and interestingly also the machines they were inventing) would do their own thing without outside interference.[76] Put the question of God to one side, they were implying, and science would flourish.

Third, there was the radical economic theory of Adam Smith, who in 1776 published *The Wealth of Nations*. Here we have to be careful, because a recent study of Smith argues strongly that the great Scotsman was not advocating the full-on laissez-faire view of economics with which he has subsequently been associated.[77] A wide-ranging polymath, Smith wrote about many topics other than economics, and the famous metaphor of the 'invisible hand' appears only three times in his entire work, and only once in *The Wealth of Nations*. Nevertheless, his ideas have ever since been taken up in the direction of a self-driven self-interest that would automatically guide the flow of money to bring about social improvement—or at least wealth and harmony, which many will have thought would amount to the same thing. (Even though Thomas Hobbes did not, as people sometimes suppose, describe the human community as a world full of wolves, his undoubted pessimism forms a stark contrast here to Smith's optimism.) Analysing Smith's complex proposals is way beyond our present task. Like others at the time, he was eclectic, and held together elements of Stoic, Epicurean and Platonic thought.[78] But the mood of the times seems to have swept him along with it. The way he was read, in the eighteenth century and ever since, amounted to a proposal that, like Newton's mechanistic universe translated into money, the clock would work by itself. This has become highly influential in subsequent economics, being used to justify unfettered industrial expansion within the spreading imperial worlds and ending up with the greed-is-good philosophy of Ronald Reagan and Margaret Thatcher. No allowance needed then to be made for such radical ideas as organising care for the poor, let alone the remission of large debts (the 'Jubilee' principle). Smith himself, strongly on the side of the poor, would have been horrified. But he has been read in accordance with the larger cultural movement.

In the same year, fourth, there appeared the opening volume of Edward Gibbon's *Decline and Fall of the Roman Empire* (1776–1789). Gibbon argued, *inter alia*, that Christianity helped to sow the seeds of imperial decline by its otherworldly teachings, its internecine squabbles, and its un-Roman pacifist leanings. Gibbon is one of the main back markers (along with David Hume) for what we today think of as 'historical criticism'. He used comprehensive documentary research and a caustic style to dethrone an easy-going view of

Christianity as the start of a straightforward force for good in the world, the launching pad for the optimistic expansionism of the early 1700s. If there was to be optimism, it would have to find grounds other than standard Christian ones. Gibbon wanted to return to the ideals of the ancient classical world, conceiving of his task as being to construct 'a bridge thrown across the swamp of the Christian millennium'.[79] The shrines were falling to left and right.

Fifth, and right in the middle of all this, there was the beginning of what came to be called 'The Quest for the Historical Jesus'. Hermann Samuel Reimarus (1694–1768) was a Deist with a difference. He believed in a good and wise deity discoverable by reason without divine help ('natural theology' of a sort)—which was just as well, because for him not only were the Old and New Testaments not divine revelation but the Old was full of misleading nonsense and the New was a self-serving fiction invented by the early Christians. Jesus himself, said Reimarus, was a deluded would-be revolutionary Messiah who died a failure and whose followers, hiding his body, invented the new movement. If you're going to have a Deist view of God, it helps to get rid of the Gospel portrait of Jesus. Gottfried Ephraim Lessing brought Reimarus's work to posthumous public attention by publishing it in fragments (1774–1778) after the author's death; previously it had circulated anonymously among friends.[80] Albert Schweitzer saw Reimarus's work as the start of the 'Quest' which Schweitzer himself summarized and moved into a new mode.

Something like Reimarus's proposal was always going to be necessary for the overall Enlightenment agenda. If the new socio-cultural mood was to thrive, it would need to be calibrated with a fresh reading of the Gospels, making their central figure fit the theory. Conversely, if the Gospels made good historical sense within the world they were ostensibly describing (whether or not every detail might be true), the entire project of modernist revisionism would be called into question.

Lessing himself is known for his 'broad ugly ditch' between the eternal truths of reason and the contingent truths of history. This gives a particular focus to the Epicurean split between the gods and the world. Granted that 'the eternal truths of reason' are not the same as 'theology', and that 'history' is but one aspect of 'the world', it seems clear enough, not least from the succeeding centuries, that the disciplines of theology and history were being pulled far apart. Reimarus's account of the 'contingent truths' about Jesus made the point: first, how could you possibly base any 'eternal' conclusions on such a story? Theology would therefore have to proceed without a well grounded historical base, as it has regularly done to this day. Second, even if the historical investigation were attempted, Jesus would turn out to be neither like the New

Testament had portrayed him nor like the later church had imagined him. Heaven and earth would thus remain mutually opaque. Though Lessing later announced his conversion to Spinoza's pantheism, at this point his conclusions, building on the theories of Reimarus, fit neatly within the undercurrent of Epicureanism guiding the flow of modern scholarship.

All these things go together: politics without God, science without God, economics without God, history without God,[81] and finally Jesus without God. All of them take for granted a kind of über-Reformation: against the corruption, not only of the mediaeval church, but of 'the church' in general, and traditional Christianity as a whole. All these movements studied the world, and acted in the world, on the assumption that the world makes itself as it goes along, without divine interference. Their immediate and influential predecessor—their godfather, if that isn't exactly the wrong word—was David Hume, whose *Enquiry concerning Human Understanding* of 1748 still forms the classic argument against believing in 'miracles'.[82] Hume converted Descartes's epistemological caution (how can we be sure this *is* so?) into ontological scepticism (we can be sure that it *isn't* so).[83] The mood of the times was with him. Ever since, anyone in the Western world who believes in 'miracles' has been swimming upstream.

The five features I have mentioned—and a sixth to which we must shortly devote a slightly longer section—are in some ways significantly different from one another. But they are united in their philosophical thrust. They are not just straws in the wind. They are flags flying strongly to announce a new world, a new day. Thus the word 'Enlightenment', used with various angles of hindsight, covers several movements in the seventeenth and eighteenth centuries. These movements drew eclectically on many different philosophies and aimed at various different targets (though usually including Christianity and the perceived oppressive social structures of their time, often linking the two). But by 1800 the shrine of the earlier assumed theology (that of Joseph Butler and many like him, including their versions of 'natural theology') had fallen. A brave new independent world had been born.

My proposal so far, then, is that the developed thought of the Enlightenment was shaped (in different ways, of course) by a revived Epicureanism. To be sure, there are many differences between the ancient and modern versions. For a start, the ancient Epicureans believed that the gods were made of the same stuff as ourselves. But the key point at issue is the great gulf separating them from us, together with the apparent randomness of the world and the non-intervention of outside divine forces.[84] Much of the claim to be new, 'modern', and indeed 'scientific', at the time and ever since, has thus been simply the attempted justification of a much older worldview by appeal to new scientific discoveries and technological achievements. We glimpse all this, to repeat, after the event, seeing how things in fact turned out and the way in which this idea of a 'modern age' has subsequently taken hold on the Western imagination. I do not envisage a conspiracy in which people were saying, 'Now, how can we re-launch Epicureanism without saying that's what we're doing?' My case is more about long-term effects than explicit intentions, though the intentions, not least in their social, political and ethical dimensions, were often at least implicit. What matters is the way in which the newness of certain scientific discoveries was used rhetorically to press the claim to the newness of the worldview. At the time, many leaders of the movement knew perfectly well that they were rekindling ancient fires. Those who today invoke 'the modern world' either ignore this or choose to forget it.

My point in underlining the Epicurean framing of the Enlightenment is therefore, first, to unmask the claim that the cosmology was 'modern' rather than 'ancient';[85] second, to suggest (as I shall do presently) that today's common distinction between 'natural' and 'supernatural' has now become a function of that philosophy, and that continuing to use the distinction hands a free pass to Lessing; third, that understanding the Enlightenment in this way gives fresh insight into why both 'natural theology', and the study of Christian origins, and the meaning and practice of 'history' itself, took the turns, and ran into the problems, they then did. Before we can develop these points, however, we need to note the remarkable development, not itself originally Epicurean, though coming to birth alongside its modern form, of the idea of 'progress'. The old shrine had fallen, but that became an apparent reason, not for despair, but for a new secular optimism. The older 'Puritan' hope, that the Christian God would continue to implement the victory of the gospel, was replaced by the newer secular hope, that better times were somehow coming along all by themselves.

Epicureanism and 'Progress'

Many of the central features around which modern life has been oriented are thus not new ideas, despite the regular assumption to that effect. They have an Epicurean undercurrent which goes back to antiquity, older than Christianity itself. But at one point in Enlightenment thought we find genuine novelty: the idea of 'progress'. Up to now we have seen (as I said) politics, science, economics, history and even Jesus without God. Now—a breath-taking claim—we also find eschatology without God. Or, at least, without the Christian God. The gospel-driven optimism of the early eighteenth century retained the optimism but dropped the gospel. It translated itself into a sense that the world was steadily improving, but under its own internal steam, not by divine energy from without.[86]

How could this happen? Ancient philosophers didn't think they were heralding a new age. They left that to Augustus's tame writers, Virgil, Livy and others. The philosophers were simply trying to provide wisdom, and a calm personal serenity, for anyone who adopted their ideas. Lucretius said nothing about 'progress' in our sense. There was, as we saw, no guarantee that randomly swerving atoms would produce outcomes anyone might like. But the philosophers and social activists of the Enlightenment made this philosophy into a major social principle, announcing that a new day had dawned for the world, and that it would go on getting brighter and brighter. The French philosopher Condorcet (1743–1794) said what many were thinking: the human race, set free at last from its shackles, was now 'advancing with a firm and true step along the path of truth, virtue and happiness'.[87] Adam Smith can be seen as a 'cosmic optimist' who believed that the unintended consequences of human economic actions would work out for the best.[88] When John Stuart Mill wrote his great book *On Liberty*, it was not, as has been well said, a book about Liberty. It was a book about Progress.[89]

This resulted in a parody of Jewish and Christian eschatology: a new form of *inaugurated eschatology*. The French Revolutionaries were the most explicit about this, in that (like bar-Kochba in AD 132) they restarted the calendar with Year One. Though that experiment did not survive, French political thought has been haunted ever since by the sense that the new day has yet to reach the promised high noon of its full promise—or perhaps we should say, as they did, the 'grand soir' of the 'bourgeoisie'.[90] Though there were many other voices in that debate, some on the Left were ready to invest later moments (such as the 1848 revolutions, the 1871 Paris Commune and above all the Bolshevik Revolution of 1917) with the possibility that they might be 'the events' which, like a long-awaited ship, would finally deliver the eschatological cargo.[91] But the modernist belief that a new day had dawned and that it was now to be implemented (indeed, as you might expect within Epicureanism, that it was implementing itself from within) constituted a new phenomenon. Without having ever been part of classical Epicureanism, it nevertheless repristinated many features of its distant ancestor while co-opting the Jewish and Christian sense of divine purpose. That is the origin of the modern doctrine of progress. We often associate this with Hegel; but Hegel was only a boy when Adam Smith and Edward Gibbon were writing. Like Beethoven and Wordsworth, he was born in 1770. He did not invent the idea of progress. He gave decisive shape, and a particular philosophical underpinning, to something already widely believed.

This idea of progress was, then, in part a secularisation of the Christian optimism (itself fuelled by Jewish eschatology) evident in the early eighteenth century, and, with that, an older doctrine of Providence.[92] It drew also, however, on ancient mythology, as we can see (for instance) in Keats's *Hyperion*.[93] Its central claim, which took root in European thought, was that the old order was being swept away and that new and better days were not just happening but that they were, in some sense, happening *automatically*. All one had to do was get on board (and push aside any who didn't see the point).[94] Hegel represents a high point in this teaching. He believed that rational progress was demonstrable not only in science but also in philosophy, the arts, and even history and religion.

Hegel's work provides, I think, the clue as to how the cuckoo of 'progress' came to be born in the apparently unlikely nest of a revived version of Epicureanism. It wasn't just that the new hard-nosed materialism was looking for a happier outcome. Once it was decided that the old Deist divinity was neither involved in the world's creation nor interested in its ongoing maintenance,[95] there arose the intriguing possibility of discovering a divine-like quality within the process itself.[96] Theology, like nature itself, abhors a vacuum. That is why atheism can sometimes beget new forms of pantheism (which is perhaps what was going on when Lessing adopted the views of Spinoza). Thus with Hegel you can even get God too, after a fashion: Democritus's world of swirling atoms, the 'scientific' basis for Epicureanism, turns out to be the vehicle of Hegel's immanent *Geist*, moving forwards inexorably (though dialectically) to a new goal, a new kind of *telos*. Marx suggested, in his doctoral dissertation, that Epicurus anticipated Hegel's principle of self-consciousness.[97] This would become a key element in Marx's own developed proposals.

For the right-wing Hegelians, however, 'progress' was to be a smooth evolution. From this there emerged the social and cultural implication that within 'progress' lay hidden the steady advance of the kingdom of God itself. It may seem a big step from Jefferson, Adam Smith, Edward Gibbon and the rest to Albrecht Ritschl. But with Hegel as the bridge, and with only a little oversimplification, the goal was in sight. Kierkegaard, who nearly made up in prophetic insight what he lacked in charm and tact, had already protested against exactly this kind of thing.[98] The same philosophical energy that had fuelled revolutions at the end of the eighteenth century was now marshalled in service of a comfortable, and comfortably 'religious', bourgeois life ('now that we have arrived at the sunlit uplands, let us develop them smoothly'). All this could then be incorporated into ongoing religious life, in a way very different from the early eighteenth-century view that the preaching of the gospel and the conversion of the heathen would bring the nations to bow down before Jesus. By the end of the nineteenth century it was widely assumed, in Britain and Germany at least, that the spectacular achievements and advances of Western civilisation were part of what Jesus must have meant when he said that 'the kingdom of God' was at hand. This was 'natural theology' made easy: look at our wonderful civilisation and see the handiwork of God! The nineteenth century had many faults, but low self-esteem was not one of them.

There is a sense, but only a sense, in which the Enlightenment's developed doctrine of 'progress' was bound up with evolutionary theory. The new wrinkle, quite a big step away from the random 'swerve' of atoms, came with the Darwinian idea of 'survival of the fittest': suddenly the 'swerve' was brought under teleological control, giving the theorists (from their point of view) the best of both worlds: functional atheism on the one hand but a sense of providence-from-within on the other. In the same way, every new mechanical invention was 'better' than the one before it, with 'better' here meaning more efficient, hence more cost-effective, hence more profitable for the entrepreneur—not necessarily 'better' for the environment or for those losing jobs through mechanisation. These worlds of biology and engineering lent to quite other discourses the sense that the world was in fact improving: in politics and society, European reformers had now 'discovered' that things were steadily getting 'better', through democratic reforms, extension of the franchise, and so forth. This, however, has little if anything to do with actual biological evolution, though the popular 'evolutionism' (in which 'history' is moving inexorably in a 'progressive' direction) regularly supposes itself, as we saw, to be rooted in scientific observation. (It is often pointed out that Darwin's theories were eagerly embraced by those in Britain and elsewhere who saw in them a kind of validation of the new upward mobility, the social evolution if you like, of the middle classes.)

But even if you embrace the theory of the survival of the fittest—actually, especially if you embrace that!—it remains the case that the majority of evolutionary developments have not meant changes for the 'better', even supposing we knew what 'better' might mean in that context ('survival-value', for instance? But that would be tautologous: 'you survived because you had survival-value'). Most of nature's experiments end in blind alleys. What else could you expect from swerving atoms? Likewise, the idea (particularly invoking developments in medicine) that science and technology are making the world a better place is more than a little ambiguous. Industrial pollution, atom bombs and gas chambers tell a different story. At the popular level, however, the ideology of progress simply ignores these counter-examples. Like the eager British socialists who visited the early Soviet Union and returned to say, 'We have seen the future, and it works', the ideology of 'progressive' thought and 'forward-thinking' movements sweeps all before it on every television or radio chat show. This is what is implied every time someone says, 'in this day and age' or 'now that we live in the twenty-first century . . .'.[99] Social Darwinism, based on the survival of the fittest, was in fact a harsh reality in British society long before Charles Darwin figured out its biological equivalent. In a judgment anticipating on other grounds the view I shall shortly expound, A. N. Wilson argues that, as we look at the early nineteenth-century industrialists, 'the struggle, the eternal warfare between the weak and the strong, the inexorable survival of the fittest, seems . . . to be a law of Nature, cruelly replacing the older belief that it was love which ruled the sun and the other stars'.[100] The modern Epicurean overthrow of Christianity provided 'freedom'—for those with the power and opportunity to take advantage of it and of their fellow human beings.

By the end of the nineteenth century, then, the following intriguing combination of philosophical and cultural beliefs had become widespread. First, there was the ongoing Epicurean framework: God or the gods were effectively out of the picture, though you could worship them at a distance if you wanted. But the world was making itself, evolving and developing under its own steam; steam engines, indeed, were part of the excitement of the time. Second, the scientific investigations which were supporting Epicureanism by showing how organisms evolved without divine interference were also giving credence to a belief that the whole world was steadily, and automatically, becoming 'better'—though whether that would happen through step-by-step advance or sudden revolutions remained unclear, as we shall see. This coincided, third, with actual political movements of social reformation and/or revolution. It was a toxic combination whose long-term results are with us still.

Protests have of course been loud. Rousseau thought that 'advances' in arts and sciences had damaged the human race rather than making it better. Charles Dickens graphically portrayed the seamy side of the Industrial Revolution. Nietzsche foresaw nothing but a great crash. Karl Barth's *Romans* commentary was a massive theological counter-blast, a divine Word of rebuke to the nineteenth-century Tower of Babel: look where your 'progress' has landed us now! So too with Walter Benjamin at the end of the 1930s, and with Theodor Adorno in the late 1940s: unlike Barth, they could not draw on the idea of a fresh word from above (hence their unrelieved gloom at the turn of events), but their critique of false expectations of 'progress' amounted to the same thing.

The movements hailed as 'postmodernity' in the later years of the twentieth century were, among other things, direct challenges to the narrative of progress. Wisdom, many have insisted, does not advance chronologically. But even with the horrors of the twentieth century to brandish as counter-examples, the postmodern protest hasn't made much headway. The idea of progress has embodied its own principle: it has just gone ahead, pushing everything else out of the way. Sustained in its optimism by the exciting fruits of science (not least in medicine) and technology, it has been assumed more and more widely.[101] It has applied, to the future as a whole, the principle that had already been applied to politics, science, economics, history and even Jesus: rethink them all without an external divine figure directing the traffic. We can do it all ourselves. Providence without God.

Like its theological antecedents, the modernist doctrine of 'progress' has faced choices. Will 'progress' happen automatically, or do human thought and action play a vital part? Do we sit back and watch, or must we campaign to make sure that 'history' actually moves in what we know to be the 'right' direction? Will new developments occur gradually (Hegel), or will there be convulsions (Marx)? Where will suffering and death fit in? The line from the eighteenth-century thinkers, through Hegel, to both Schopenhauer and Feuerbach and thence to Marx and Nietzsche, with Richard Wagner an intriguing middle term to whom we shall return, can already be glimpsed. But despite the *Götterdämmerung* which took place on the stage at Bayreuth and then on the battlefields of the Somme, the myth of progress has retained its hold on Western consciousness, so that every imaginable kind of 'enlightenment' or 'liberation' is now routinely advocated and justified not so much on its own merits but because we all somehow 'know' that this is the way 'history' is going. From this there flow a thousand follies, not least of which is the slipperiness of the word 'history' itself, to which I shall return in the third chapter. There is also, indeed, the myth of scholarship, that scholars build firmly on the solid foundation of their predecessors, so that the subject automatically 'advances'. Folly indeed. But the point is that 'progress', as a kind of providence-without-god, or even (through Hegelian pantheism) a quasi-divine force in itself, is a new construct. It combines the memory of Jewish and Christian eschatology with eighteenth-century Epicureanism. Emboldened by its one-sided reading of the evolutionary principle of 'survival of the fittest' (the myriad random 'experiments' that turn out to be 'unfit' are simply ignored), those who advocate the 'progress' ideology today seem to assume that every passing decade will see moral, social and cultural 'advance' to match the technological 'advances' of smart phones, driverless cars and, not least, high-tech weaponry.

This has produced one very important corollary—important, that is, for contextualising our topic, that of natural theology and Christian origins. This is a strong sense of innate superiority. Part of the point of classical Epicureanism—and the reason it remained the preserve of a small minority—was that its devotees would want to withdraw from the mess and muddle of ordinary life, imitating the gods whose happiness depended on keeping their distance, on their non-involvement with the space-time world. Few people in the ancient world could afford this. The well-functioning Epicurean needed money, a nice vineyard, and compliant slaves. But with the new skills developed in Europe it seemed possible at last that a whole society might attain the goal. The doctrine of progress has thus enabled the societies shaped by modern Epicureanism—Western Europe, America and their satellites—to assume the social prestige envisaged by their philosophical ancestors, rising above the common herd to be 'the enlightened ones', the 'developed' or 'advanced' countries, operating on different principles and, tellingly, living by different standards.[102] We today in the Western world live in an Epicurean paradise. It comes at a cost. The cost is borne by others, some of whom are washing up on our shores as we ponder the problems from a safe distance.

Modern Western housing, heating, communications and particularly healthcare, and many other things besides, are indeed innately desirable. That is why so many from outside the Epicurean bubble want to share them. But to infer from this—as happens all the time at a popular level—that the latest Western cultural or moral fads are likewise 'superior' to beliefs and practices in less 'developed' societies is a laughably false inference. It is no wonder that we can't easily cope with the combination of multiculturalism and postmodern identity politics. We have no narrative to generate or sustain wise reflection. Our philosophical basis gives us neither a clear analysis of what's happened nor the tools to cope with the results.

The protests of postcolonialism have often been shrill, simplistic and merely pragmatic. But all this shows the direction in which the eighteenth-century ambitions were leading. The social and *political* implications of Epicureanism remain powerful to this day in many Western assumptions and policies. Our 'secular' debates now often mirror the earlier theological ones, with the question of geopolitical 'intervention' producing an eerie reflection of the theologians' question about divine 'intervention'. Newtonian Deists in America want to 'intervene' in global problems; Epicureans in France want to hold back. (The British, as usual, pretend not to understand the question, and they settle for short-term pragmatic decisions and gestures.) Debates about natural theology, and about biblical exegesis and Christian origins, have regularly reflected this in turn; not least, sadly, in the severe limitation whereby such discussions, including the present work, remain at the level of in-house Western discussion.

If the secular world of the Enlightenment was able to discover a form of progressive pantheism within its Epicurean framework, those who wanted to hold on to Christian belief often invoked a different model. Many found themselves going back to Plato for help. To see how this happened, we must return to the theological world within the complex context we have now sketched.

THE TASK RE-IMAGINED

Where does the powerful rise of Epicureanism leave the questions which are raised by the phrase 'natural theology'? The main question—whether we can arrive at truths about God by observation of, and inference from, features of the world around us—is flanked by two other essentially modern questions, which sit in uneasy tension with one another. First, does God 'intervene' in the world by doing 'miracles'? The appeal to the miraculous was, and has remained, a central plank particularly in the Anglo-Saxon resistance to Epicureanism, or, to put it more positively, in the case for inferring Christian truth from the supposedly historical events concerning Jesus. But it is in tension with the second question: what about so-called 'natural evil'? If God could 'intervene' to raise Jesus from the dead, why didn't he stop the Lisbon earthquake, or for that matter the Holocaust, or the horrors of September 11, 2001?

I take it that Lord Gifford's intention, in setting up his Lectures, was to see if one could address the main question (inferring truths about God) while assuming that one could not appeal to 'miracles', all the while hoping that the 'problem of evil' might not be so much of a problem after all. That, indeed, is a larger topic again. As I have argued elsewhere, one of the strange results of the Epicurean turn is that theology proper was left with a question about 'atonement' (how can my sins be forgiven?), while the so-called 'problem of evil' (why do earthquakes happen? and so on) was handed over to something now called 'philosophy of religion', without the two questions being joined up.[103] But the missing element in the discussion is *history*—more particularly, the history of Jesus. History has to do with things that actually happen in the 'natural' world. Why should the human life, thoughts and intentions of Jesus then be excluded from 'natural theology'?

The answer is that it ought not to be. Indeed, many sceptics from at least Reimarus onwards have made a reductive 'historical' account of Jesus and the Gospels part of their polemical arsenal.[104] In other words, history is indeed allowed into the conversation, but it is assumed that history will disprove the truth-claims of the 'religion', specifically here of Christianity.

Leaving aside the slipperiness of the word 'religion' for the moment, we here encounter a paradox within the 'natural theology' discussion. Our historical evidence for Jesus consists almost entirely of the New Testament. For many in the eighteenth and nineteenth centuries, the New Testament was the key document of 'special revelation' and hence precisely the sort of thing to which 'natural theology' could not appeal. But this is muddled, and it seems that the muddle, originating from the defensive posturing of Christians, has leeched over to involve the sceptics as well. It seems to assume that the New Testament offers a kind of detached abstract teaching descended from heaven with no human involvement. Much popular Christian tradition, particularly after the Reformation when the Bible was summoned to bear the weight of authority previously shared with the church's tradition, has tended to see it like that. But great swathes of the Bible, and obviously especially the Gospels, purport to be about history, about things that actually happened in the 'natural' world, and actually point away from themselves to those actual events. That, indeed, is why the Gospels have not always been easy for 'theologians' to use, except as a ragbag of illustrations for abstract ideas whose basis may be found elsewhere. But the result has been that the sceptics have adopted the 'special revelation' view of the Bible and so have often set it aside with minimal actual study, relying on well-known demythologising treatments to back up their dismissal.[105]

Sauce for the goose, then, and also for the gander. If Hume, Reimarus and others can appeal to 'history' to show that Jesus was just a man of his times, perhaps others can appeal to history as well to test the claim. In fact, the more one goes down the route of Hume and Reimarus (Gibbon, even when discussing the primitive church, has virtually nothing to say about Jesus himself), the more we are indeed told that Jesus is to be seen as part of the regular flow of history, part of the natural order. That is then made the basis for the Deist version of 'natural theology': we have looked at the evidence for Jesus, and it seems he was not particularly special after all! And, though the Gospels are indeed the major sources for Jesus, many thinkers in the eighteenth century read Josephus in Whiston's translation of 1737, and many also read Tacitus, likewise translated in the sixteenth and seventeenth centuries. Both mention Jesus. One could not claim that he was only to be found in the writings which supposedly constituted 'special revelation'. He required investigation, and true historians should not assume in advance that certain persons or events ought to be studied differently than others just because the church and theologians tell them they should.

One cannot, then, have it both ways. Hume, Gibbon and Reimarus, quite accidentally I think, offered a challenge: history is part of the 'natural world', so what are you going to do with it? It was a good question, which both church and theology had long avoided, or at least failed to deal with. Hume and the others, by calling into question the superhuman Jesus of much popular Christology, inadvertently paved the way for a rediscovery of the actual first-century Jew from Nazareth. As Ben Meyer delightfully puts it, with Reimarus the instinct for historical imagination is present, 'diseased but alive'.[106] Precisely by saying that the real Jesus was truly to be found within actual history, Reimarus invited further study of the Gospels themselves, which the intervening centuries have been eager to provide. But the problem here has been that *the same cultural presuppositions which have shaped Enlightenment thought as a whole have also shaped the practice of history itself, and with it the historical study of Jesus.* As a result, would-be orthodox theology has by and large ignored, or even sneered at, the would-be 'historical' portraits of Jesus and has continued with a Christological construct projected backwards onto the first century from the subsequent formulations of the Fathers, the Mediaevals and the Reformers. Subsequent theology has, in fact, often seemed to agree *de facto* with Lessing: we want the eternal truths, so let's not worry too much about the history. Since the gospel must be contextualised in different settings, why worry about the original one? But Lessing's challenge can just as easily work the other way.[107] Supposing we did the history for ourselves, to see if Reimarus was right? You cannot then logically keep the question of Jesus himself, Jesus as a real first-century human being, out of the possible sources for 'natural theology'. At least, you can't do it without begging a central and vital question. The problem is then how to stop both questions (history and theology) being fatally distorted by the pressures of the surrounding culture.

Here we meet a vital point to which I shall return. When I say that Enlightenment presuppositions have shaped the study of Jesus, I do *not* mean that if people have studied Jesus from the point of view of something called 'naturalism' then we should respond with something called 'supernaturalism'. I shall return to this presently. My point is that both 'sides' in that debate have bought into a false either/or, an over-bright apparent contrast, which is itself the either/or of what I have characterized as Epicureanism, with heaven and the gods radically separated from the world in which we live. That simply repeats Lessing's point in a different register. The either/or, as we shall see in the second chapter, has produced influential misreadings of Jesus and his first followers which have then conditioned several theological discussions, not least that of 'natural theology' in its various guises. The problem is how to stop both questions (Jesus within history, and 'natural theology') being distorted by aspects of the surrounding culture. And one feature in particular of that culture, invoked to help Christians face the rising tide of secularism, has hindered rather than helping. I refer to the Christian retrieval of Plato.

What happens, you might ask, if you want to be a thoughtful Christian within a world where Epicureanism has triumphed, where it is assumed that God and the world are utterly detached from one another? One might have hoped that the obvious answer would be, Read the Bible and discover how the ancient Jews and early Christians thought of God and the world and their interaction. Discover that the assumed splits between God and the world, between 'natural' and 'supernatural', and between God's promised future and the present, are category mistakes; are, after all, quite foreign to the way that Jews and early Christians actually saw the world. That is what I shall be proposing in due course. But this answer seems not to have been given.

Why has this happened? Three reasons suggest themselves.

First, there is a long Christian tradition, dating back at least to Clement of Alexandria in the late second and early third centuries, of philosophical interpretations of scripture and doctrine. Such interpretations have attempted to achieve, by philosophical analysis, what in Jewish and early Christian thought was achieved within the Hebrew or Jewish cosmology we shall study in later chapters.[108] The interpretations, however, have become better known than the original cosmology. Indeed, the interpretations, shorn of the original cosmology, have often been seen as normative. This has often left the Bible, in its Jewish context, as a generalized and uncomfortably 'historical' signpost pointing vaguely towards the supposedly clear truth which the later interpreters then discerned—as though the Bible lacked a metaphysical framework and needed one to be supplied from elsewhere.

Second, the Reformers, particularly the Lutherans, were wary of anything too 'Jewish'. This is partly due to earlier European anti-Judaism, but equally to the sixteenth-century polemic in which the picture of a corrupt mediaeval Catholicism, legalistic and priest-focused, was projected back on to the Jewish teaching of works-righteousness supposedly opposed by Paul. The multiple confusions in this picture have been widely exposed in recent decades, but their influence is still apparent.[109]

Third, and darker still, that same residual anti-Judaism, transformed into anti-Semitism through the nineteenth-century 'racial' theories which floated like marine detritus on the foetid sea of popular social Darwinism, meant ruling out anything which might invoke such Jewish symbols as Temple or Sabbath as the clues to cosmology or eschatology, or indeed as clues to anything from Christology to spirituality and even (as I shall later propose) to natural theology. It was exactly in this period that Graf and Wellhausen were proposing that the 'priestly' material in the Hebrew scriptures was a late, degenerate form of Israelite religion: *Spätjudentum*, in fact, a term now mentioned, if at all, with a shudder.[110] Not for nothing had Hegel seen Judaism as the archetypal 'wrong sort of religion', based as it was—oh, the irony!—on blood and soil.[111] The Jewish world was off limits. Genuine Christianity (so it was thought) must have had different roots (hence the futile quest for a 'pre-Christian Gnosticism': anything would do as long as it wasn't Jewish!) and must be shaped differently. Paul's polemic against 'works-righteousness', misunderstood and generalized, had been co-opted into an ideological programme of ethnic cleansing.

Thus if the devout Christian, faced with the sceptical attacks of the eighteenth century, was not to invoke the Jewish world and its modes of thought (within which, as I shall later explain, the earliest Christian ideas meant what they meant), what was the alternative? One natural possibility was to invoke Plato—or at least, though Plato himself remained important, the Middle Platonic thought of Plutarch and others, and particularly the Neoplatonism of Plotinus and his successors. Since this had been the context, and the shaping assumption, for many of the most influential teachers of the third, fourth and fifth centuries, one could travel some distance down this road without noticing that the scriptures, like recalcitrant children taken for a walk against their will, were dragging their feet and pointing in a different direction. The Fathers, rightly resisting any form of Marcionism, found ways to make the scriptures come into line. They have their modern successors.

There are, once again, a thousand implications here, of which I can only mention two as particularly important for our question.

First, it is remarkable how easily modern Western Christianity abandoned the biblical hope of new creation and bodily resurrection. The way had been prepared by the later mediaeval thought in which heaven, hell and purgatory dominated the eschatological horizon; but (as I pointed out ten years ago)[112] there was a decisive shift in the popular view in Britain at least, visible on tombstones and other memorials, somewhere between 1700 and 1900. The older hope was still for resurrection. *Resurgam*, 'I shall arise', spoke of a present rest and a future re-embodiment.[113] But the classic nineteenth-century language, not least among devout Evangelicals, spoke of 'going home', of being 'with God at last', and so on. Western Protestantism, having given up Purgatory, came to think in terms of a single-stage post mortem reality: 'going to heaven', with no thought of new heavens *and new earth* or indeed of 'new creation' at all. The hymns of Charles Wesley, brilliant and rightly beloved in other respects, embodied and powerfully reinforced this mistake.[114] This trend has been so widespread that respected Christian theologians can speak without embarrassment of our 'souls' being at present 'in exile' in this material world and body, and of our longing to return to our proper home, namely heaven. This, however, is the explicit teaching, not of Jesus or the New Testament, but of Plutarch.[115] The problem here is one of popular perception. The old going-to-heaven teaching is now so engrained in our culture that any mention of new creation, or of bodily resurrection, is either 'translated' into a fuzzy metaphor for 'heavenly life' or met with shock and incomprehension.

The theme of new creation will occupy us later in this book. My reason for highlighting it here is twofold. First, its frequent absence in the eighteenth and nineteenth centuries shows the extent to which devout Christians were actually colluding with the Enlightenment's agenda, accepting the split-level world of Epicureanism (in other words, leaving politics, economics, science and history and the world itself to the secular authorities, and trying to snatch a docetic Jesus back from the reductionists) and none the less finding an alternative way to express a kind of faith. Some may even have welcomed and encouraged the split world of the Enlightenment, enabling the church to focus on 'spiritual' matters rather than 'worldly' concerns (though of course many devout Christians, with William Wilberforce as an obvious example, solidly resisted such a split). Second, it highlights the way the 'natural theology' problem was intensified, and with it the attendant problems of so-called 'natural evil' on the one hand and 'divine action in the world' on the other. If it is true that 'this world is not my home' and that our true home is radically, ontologically different from this present world, then any attempt to look at this present world and figure out truths about God becomes not only far harder than it was for, say, the Psalms, Isaiah or even Jesus; it becomes suspect. Why look at the corruptible world in order to learn about the holy God? Even the dry possibility we noted before, of a kind of 'natural theology' within Epicureanism itself ('the world makes and runs itself; *ergo*, God is out of the picture'), was thus ruled out within a Platonic dualism.[116]

By the same token, the need to explain 'natural evil' is reduced. This world is a mere vale of tears; we should never have expected it to be pleasant; the sooner we escape it the better. ('Heaven's morning breaks,' says the Victorian hymn, 'and earth's vain shadows flee'.)[117] Meanwhile, for several devout Christians the idea of God 'intervening' in the world, in 'miracles' and in the incarnation itself is unproblematic. This is, in fact, what many assume Christian belief entails. This dogged devotion has continued, like Daniel's prayers, even from within the Epicurean Babylon. The paradox of a basically Epicurean or at least Deistic framework (God 'outside' the process of the world) with occasional 'interventions' (something a self-respecting Epicurean god would never do, but a Newtonian Deist god might just manage) is exactly how many Western Christians to this day envisage the world, as we shall see presently when discussing the idea of 'miracle'. God 'intervenes' in the world in order to provide temporary help in the present. (This has produced in recent years some worrying examples, such as tales of people being 'miraculously' prevented from reaching their offices in the Twin Towers on September 11, 2001 . . . ignoring the fate of those who went to work as usual.) The extreme version of this envisages a final intervention, the 'rapture', which will snatch Christians away altogether.[118]

It might seem an awkward balancing act to imagine someone holding a Neoplatonic spirituality within an Epicurean metaphysic. Epicureanism was, after all, the one thing the original Neoplatonists ruled out, since the commerce they envisaged between earthly and heavenly was precisely what Epicurus had rejected. But that, I think, is part of the ongoing dilemma of Western Christianity: trying to re-express, in different contexts, ideas which might not naturally combine in that new environment and ending up with an eclectic and not altogether consistent mix. Thus for us to address, as I propose to do, the questions of natural theology and historical Christian origins in relation to one another simply highlights the problem. If we are to address it coherently, we need to understand how it has been shaped by its larger context.

The second implication of trying to hold a Platonic spirituality, particularly a mystical openness to 'the divine' in the present and the immortality of the soul here and hereafter, all within an implicit Epicurean metaphysic, is that it offers an open invitation to various forms of Gnosticism. This, not surprisingly, has been seen by some critics as the default mode for American religion in particular.[119] The élitism of Epicureanism, interiorized and individualized, combines with the Platonic sense of a secret interior reality—a 'soul', perhaps—to generate, not the sense of a sinful soul that needs redeeming and transforming, as in classic Christian theology, but the sense of a 'true self' which needs 'saving'—from the distortions that the outside world, and even one's own body, might try to impose upon it. Onlookers cannot guess the secret 'identity' which is known only to the possessor. The Gnostic believes, not in 'redemption', but in 'revelation', the unveiling of the true self rather than its death and resurrection. Like 'progress' itself, this kind of low-grade Gnosticism has recently become almost the only orthodoxy in some quarters, where 'finding out who I really am' is the ultimate imperative, and any challenge to this project is seen as the ultimate denial of one's human rights. Such a view easily takes on apparently Christian colouring, appropriating the biblical distinction of the outward appearance and the state of the heart.[120] Thus the socio-political élitism which allows 'enlightened' Westerners to look at the rest of the planet and bestow upon it blessings (or, as it may be, bombs) goes well with an inward élitism of the 'enlightened' ones who know themselves to be the spiritual high-fliers, the real moral heroes.

Thus an ancient minority option has become the new majority—at least in the West. Epicurus never gained much traction outside a small circle in ancient Greece and Rome but has finally come into his own, producing what Charles Taylor in his *magnum opus* designated as 'a Secular Age'. The situation is of course far more complex than can be sketched here. But we have said enough to indicate that the resurgence of Epicureanism in the modern West has been the major contextualising factor, culturally as well as philosophically, within which the great questions have been posed and answers given. That is the new thing. Even those who have wanted to modify it, whether by postulating a pantheistic 'progress' within it or finding a Platonic escape route out of it, have lived within that world. Never before has there been a time in world history where, in a culture as a whole, people could and did organise personal and social life on the basis that our world and the world of the gods, if any, were radically separate. Never before, then, was there a time in which it would be harder (particularly for a Christian seeking to be faithful to the God revealed in Jesus of Nazareth) to obey Lord Gifford's instructions and talk about 'natural theology'; or, indeed, to attempt what I see as the necessary step towards that, which is to talk about Christian origins. And if someone were to respond that 'natural theology', to be true to itself, must function irrespective of cosmological presuppositions, the answer would have to be that there is no neutral territory.

Charles Taylor's thesis alerts us, however, to four crucial points which we must put on the table, in concluding this chapter, in order to set up our later discussions.

CONCLUSION

First, 'the modern world'. The idea that modern science has discovered a new view of the cosmos, rendering all earlier worldviews obsolete, is unwarranted.[121] The current Western worldview is a variation on a well-known ancient one, advocated in the early modern period on social, cultural and political grounds long before Charles Darwin or even his grandfather hunted for possible scientific evidence. Whether the worldview is true or not is another matter; what it is not is new. The appeal to 'progress' is itself ambiguous, fusing together a dehistoricized Jewish and Christian Providence-theology with either the (more or less) atheistic world of Epicurus or the pantheistic world of Hegel.

In that context, second, the word 'religion' is all but useless. The modern split between 'religion' and the rest of life was unknown, perhaps even unthinkable, in the ancient world.[122] Contemporary usage regards the early Christian movement as a 'religion' in the modern, Enlightenment-driven sense, which was designed precisely to marginalise its social, political, philosophical and cultural identity. This confusion has divided the relevant disciplines: 'philosophy of religion' (usually excluding biblical exegesis) has taken charge of key areas including 'natural theology', while 'history of religion' has, until recently, dominated the study of early Christianity, implying that early Christianity was at bottom a 'religion' in the modern sense, to be placed historically in relation to other ancient Near Eastern cults (usually, as we saw earlier, excluding the Jewish world).[123] The actual historical study of early Christianity yields a very different result, a different meaning of 'religion', a different set of analytic tools, and the prospect of very different results.

This brings us, third, to the question of 'naturalism'—or rather, the supposed split between nature and 'supernature'. An older usage (no doubt with many variations across many centuries) envisaged the creator always at work within the 'natural' world, and sometimes doing 'supernatural' things, displaying, not the *abolition* of nature by grace, nor the *invasion* of nature from the outside, but the *superabundance* of grace over nature. (The word 'nature' itself, in any case, may also be hinting at some kind of independence from the creator.) Now, however, 'nature' and 'naturalism' are regularly used in relation to one half of the Enlightenment's false antithesis, the implication being that 'methodological naturalism' rules out 'supernaturalism' and vice versa.[124] The word 'miracle' is similarly distorted, denoting an 'invasion from outside' which 'naturalists' (from Hume onwards) will deny and which 'supernaturalists' will affirm. These fresh usages, however, merely collude with Lessing.[125] They agree that his 'ugly ditch' exists, and simply assert that we either can (with God's help) or can't leap over it, thereby ultimately reinforcing a false and indeed unbiblical antithesis of heaven and earth.[126] It wasn't just the Neoplatonists, after all, who rejected Epicureanism. It was also the Rabbis, and earlier Jewish writings such as the Wisdom of Solomon.[127]

These questions all come back, finally, to epistemology: how do we know? In what follows, I shall argue that the *ontology* of the mainstream Enlightenment views, owing much to its latent Epicureanism, was in a symbiotic relationship with its implicit *epistemology*, a theory of knowledge from which one crucial element had been screened out. The missing element is 'love', a word rendered almost meaningless by over-use, but employed here heuristically. 'Love', as I shall explain, overcomes the false polarization between 'objective' and 'subjective', and between the Idealist and the Empiricist. Love jumps the gap—or rather, love insists that there was never really that kind of a gap in the first place.

Classic Epicureanism was always wary of love. Lucretius, like Oscar Wilde, advised that falling in love would get in the way of properly appraised erotic pleasure.[128] This forswearing of love has become an epistemological principle. Detached rational enquiry is the epistemological correlate of atomistic materialism.

This is encoded, almost prophetically, in the legend of Faust. Mephistopheles promises Faust everything he could possibly want, on one condition: he must never actually *love* what he is enjoying. Faust makes his promise: he will never say, to the blissful moment, 'Verweile doch! du bist so schön'.[129] Thomas Mann makes this explicit, with his satanic messenger instructing the hero: '*Thou maist not love*'.[130] It is a parable for our time.[131] The rationalist Enlightenment, screening out the god-dimension of reality, screened out love at the same time *and for the same reason*: It claimed instead the 'objective' knowledge of the physical world, obtained and exploited through science and technology, and wrote off the 'subjective' elements as mere opinion or, worse, mere projection. The result, one way or another, was Frankenstein's monster.[132]

Of course, our culture has also reacted sharply. The Romantic movement, and with it much fervent Christian discipleship in the pietist and Methodist traditions, went the other way, focusing on what warms the heart, what we 'know' deep within. But unfortunately one can be strangely moved by things which turn out to be false. Romanticism is not enough. Both Goethe and Wagner, I think—two of Albert Schweitzer's greatest heroes—tried to address exactly this problem, to transcend the false polarities they saw developing.[133] We need, to put it simplistically, both the subjective and the objective pole, the romantic and the rational, just as we need the ongoing dialogue between the Ideal and the Empirical (which, like the chicken and the egg, may turn out to have no obvious starting point). What account can we give of such a both-and knowledge?

As we will see more fully in due course, 'love' simultaneously *affirms and celebrates the otherness* of the beloved (be it a person, a tree, a star) and wants it to be itself, not to be a mere projection of one's own hopes or desires, and also *takes appropriate delight* in this knowing, leaping beyond mere cool appraisal to a sense of homecoming, of belonging-with.[134] Love, in this sense, includes the other modes of knowing within it, reframing many debates, including that with which the Gifford Lectures are concerned.[135]

In Christian theology, of course, love became human in Jesus of Nazareth. But this claim can be advanced in such a way as to close down further thought, or it can be scorned as uncritical fantasy without historical basis. In this book, however, I propose to resist both those tendencies. Having proposed in the present chapter a particular interpretation of the social, cultural and political contexts in which the question of 'natural theology' has been addressed, we move in the next chapter to the ways in which the same contexts shaped, and often distorted, readings of the New Testament and historical constructions of its central figure.

2

The Questioned Book

Critical Scholarship and the Gospels

INTRODUCTION: CONFUSED DEBATES

In the first chapter I sketched the contexts in which, over the last few centuries, the debates about what has come to be called 'natural theology' have taken place. (To be sure, discussions of 'natural theology' go back to ancient times, but it is the particular modern approach that has concerned us.) The debates were neither neutral nor disinterested. Nobody asks questions about God and the world from a detached standpoint. A pretended objectivity is merely naïve. The larger movements of culture and politics, of philosophy and revolution, have all been interlinked within a multi-dimensional historical reality which we must acknowledge even though we can never describe it adequately (or, indeed, 'objectively'). Better an admission of impossible complexity than a false assumption of simplicity. And within this same swirling mixture of elements we find the question of Jesus and the Gospels.

The English Deist Matthew Tindal (1657–1733) and the Irish rationalist John Toland (1670–1722) had already raised critical questions about the Gospels.[1] Whether questioning the Gospels led them to Deism or vice versa, or whether both arose through wider seventeenth-century concerns, in the way I suggested in the previous chapter, we cannot investigate here.[2] But they undermined the standard orthodox answer to sceptics. The sceptic would question divine involvement in the world; the orthodox would respond that God had revealed himself in and as Jesus of Nazareth, not least his 'miracles': Q.E.D. Thus, if one wanted to maintain any sort of Deism, the Gospel record would have to be challenged; or, to put it the other way, if people were challenging the

41

Gospels, perhaps Deism might be the only possible place of retreat. In any case, Hume and other sceptics chipped away at the miraculous, as we saw; and it was left to Reimarus, and to Lessing, who published his *Fragments* after his death, to set out the revisionist case about Jesus and the Gospels more systematically.[3]

Albert Schweitzer was right about many things, not least to place Reimarus at the head of his famous chronicle of German writings about Jesus.[4] Since what Reimarus, and thence Lessing, was saying about Jesus was intended as a crucial element in the overall Deist agenda, which as I have argued above was by this stage heavily influenced by the Epicureanism of the surrounding culture, it is an indication of their success that comparatively few people who have written about natural theology have engaged with these questions at all.[5] In fact, 'natural theology' has normally been lined up as though questions about Jesus are excluded automatically. Some who have reacted against 'natural theology' have reinforced this impression by insisting on placing 'Christology' ahead of it.[6] These problems appear to go back a lot further than simply the last century. Some Catholic theologians already in the sixteenth century were advancing arguments for the existence of God on purely philosophical grounds, being careful not to seem to beg the question by referring to Jesus, or for that matter to the spirit.[7] Once we call all these assumptions into question, however, we may find that Jesus himself, a flesh-and-blood human being, really was part of the 'natural' world of space, time and matter, and ought thus not to be exempted from the questions which surround 'natural theology', however fashionable that bracketing out may have been.

Such a claim is difficult to advance not least because the problem is double-edged. On the one hand there are the sceptics who have wished to exclude Jesus from the question lest that should mean smuggling in 'God' by a back door. But, on the other hand, there are would-be orthodox teachers who have thought of Jesus in what has been effectively a Docetic way, so that any mention of him—particularly when he is referred to simply as 'Christ' as though that were a 'divine' title!—gives the impression of wearing a halo. He is then, by implied definition, removed from the rough-and-tumble of real life, however much all four Gospels place him exactly there. This seems to be the case, for instance, for those who like the Barth of the 1930s believe that 'Christology' is the means by which we can *avoid* 'natural theology', as though the 'Christ' of Christian faith is only tangentially related to the space-time-matter Jesus, which flies in the face of John's claim that the Word became 'flesh', and of that of the writer to the Hebrews who insists that Jesus was 'like us in every way'. Thus Jesus has been excluded from the question both by the sceptic (lest the argument should be tilted towards a Christian result) and by the orthodox (lest it be dragged down into historical uncertainties). And since I am advancing in this book the unfashionable proposal not only that we must include the question of Jesus and the Gospels within the discussion of 'natural theology' but also that by fresh historical investigation of these questions we may be able to find new ways into the heart of the matter—going into the dragon's den, in other words, to recover the stolen treasure!—we clearly need to examine the factors which, over the last two centuries and more of scholarship, have apparently pulled the study of Jesus and the Gospels away from any apparent theological usefulness.

Before we go any further into the question of what critical scholarship was doing with the Gospels and with Jesus himself, contributing thereby to various ongoing theological questions including that of natural theology, we must put one particular observation on the table. In popular British culture today the only real theological debate that most people are aware of is the one which took place between the two main parties in the mid-eighteenth century, namely, those who think the distant (perhaps Deist) God sometimes 'intervenes' in the world and those who think he doesn't. This has then been flattened out into the now standard assumption that Christians are supposed to believe in a God who does strange things (like virgin births and resurrections), while those who 'know' that God doesn't do things like that are *de facto* atheists, though many may still profess to believe in some kind of non-interventionist deity. This emerges when journalists interview church leaders such as, for instance, newly appointed Archbishops: do they really believe in the virgin birth and the bodily resurrection? This functions as the equivalent of the trick questions people asked Jesus himself: The Archbishop will be shown up as either a naïve fundamentalist or a dangerous liberal.[8]

This now standard cultural assumption (that the two available options are an interventionist divinity and a non-interventionist one) is reflected in an exchange made famous by the sociologist Grace Davie. An interviewee, when asked, 'Do you believe in a God who can change the course of events on earth?', responded, 'No, just the ordinary one'.[9] The poet Donald Davie (Grace Davie's father-in-law) comments on this exchange that

> The ordinary kind
> Of undeceived believer
> Expects no prompt reward
> From an ultimately faithful
> But meanwhile preoccupied landlord.

The metaphor is telling: God as a landlord who, if not actually an absentee, is 'preoccupied'. Within this 'moralistic therapeutic Deism',[10] God cares how we behave; believing in him may be good for us, at least in the long run; but he doesn't get involved. He is normally 'preoccupied'. If you ask someone in the street whether they believe in God, this is the God they assume you are talking about. There is, you might suppose, good biblical precedent, with Jesus asleep in the boat; but the point of the story is that he then wakes up and stills the storm. The popular either/or of 'natural' versus 'supernatural' does not, in fact, fit the evidence.

Stilling storms, after all, is not what you'd expect 'the ordinary god' to do; hence the protest from Reimarus and a host of others. The Gospels, they said, were written up partly to hide the original politically revolutionary message (Reimarus lived, of course, at a time of revolution as well as of Epicurean-ism) and partly to launch a new religion in which a being called 'God' became embodied in a man called 'Jesus' and proved it by doing supernatural tricks. Hence the questions about the Virgin Birth and the empty tomb. It is assumed, in the modern conversations that reflect these eighteenth-century moves, that we all know what 'real Christianity' is about, namely believing in this kind of a God, who does indeed 'intervene' in certain ways; a God of whom Jesus was the 'son' in some 'supernatural' sense (as opposed to any of the senses available for that phrase in the first-century Jewish world). And it is often assumed that when people investigate 'natural theology' on the one hand, or the Gospels on the other, this is what they are trying to test out. Does such a 'God' really exist?

I do not know in how many other countries this low-grade British theo-logical stand-off is replicated. (It was of course in the British context that Lord Gifford established his Lectures.) But it bears little relation to the debates that were taking place in Germany at least between 1800 and 2000, debates which have had a massive influence in shaping the ways the questions have been asked. (It also has very little to do with the first-century Jewish world, but that important point must be left on one side until chapter 5.) German debates about God and the world, and about Jesus and the Gospels, were always part of much larger and more complex discussions, framed by the massive schemes of Kant and Hegel and pulled and pushed this way and that by the various proposals of Schelling, Schopenhauer, Feuerbach and others, as well as the tur-bulent political movements that swept across Europe throughout the period. The British usually didn't get it. They were too busy running an empire and ruling the waves to concern themselves with such things. When Schweitzer wrote his *Von Reimarus zu Wrede*, he was studying Jesus-writing in its wider context. The English translation retitled the book, assuming it was about *The Quest of the Historical Jesus*, just 'trying to get at the facts'.[11] But life was more complicated than that. Schweitzer was not trying to 'find' a Jesus who (the

English title seemed to imply) was 'lost' somewhere. That was a subtly different question. The writers Schweitzer surveyed, and indeed Schweitzer himself, along with later writers like Bultmann and Käsemann, were not engaging in a quasi-positivist attempt to 'find' or 'prove' Jesus, to 'get at the facts'. Their Jesus-investigations were part of a larger cultural whole to do with the German church and its conflicted relations with social, cultural and political issues. And my point is just this: that this larger whole was routinely ignored in the Anglo-Saxon world, where it was assumed that, since the Germans were such thorough historical critics, they must really be trying to 'get at the facts' in some neutral or, again, positivist sense.[12] The North Sea was thus functioning as Lessing's 'broad, ugly ditch'. The British were looking for contingent truths of history; the Germans, for eternal truths of reason.

An oversimplification, of course, but it makes the point. Proposals advanced within German cultural settings were 'heard' in Anglo-Saxon circles as 'assured results'—particularly by those to whom such conclusions would be congenial. These 'results' could then be set in stone and defended, not by arguments, but by that peculiar kind of scorn which English theologians and critics borrow from their world of social snobbery. To question the 'assured results' of the great Germans would be like turning up to a smart dinner in jeans and T-shirt. If you want to sit at the top table, you'd better learn your manners. The challenges of Reimarus (that Jesus was a failed Jewish revolutionary) and of Schweitzer (that Jesus was a failed end-of-the-world visionary), though interestingly incompatible, were enough to generate the negative 'assured result' that the Gospels had got it wrong. Jesus was not after all what he had been made out to be. Any non-biblical Jesus, 'reconstructed' or at least reimagined, would do for this purpose. (Gibbon, and before him Tyndall and Toland, had mentioned the end-of-the-world point, but it had not really stuck before now.[13] Certainly Reimarus, who followed them in their Deism, saw Jesus not as a failed apocalyptic prophet but as a failed messianic revolutionary.) You then need alternative explanations; hence the ongoing popularity of William Wrede's ingenious (some would say bizarre) but long-running theory about the 'messianic secret', according to which, since Jesus had not thought of himself as Messiah, Mark must have made up *both* that claim *and* the command to keep it secret. Hence, too, Rudolf Bultmann's proposals about form criticism: Bultmann presupposed a Wrede-like picture of Jesus and developed his theories about the story-telling habits of the early church to fit.[14]

It was thus assumed, on both sides of the North Sea, that 'the scholars', with their rigorous historical study, were siding with the eighteenth-century Deists. Science had proved evolution; scientific economics insisted on laissez-faire policies; scientific historiography had proved that God doesn't intervene; scientific study of the four Gospels had shown them to be largely fictitious. Meanwhile the supposedly 'simple believers', who took incarnation, miracles, resurrection and all the rest at face value, were still living, it seemed, in the early eighteenth century or even, in the silly polemical usage one now meets all the time, in the 'mediaeval' period. These false antitheses are played out to this day, especially in America, in terms of the 'culture wars' in which all kinds of other issues, including creation and evolution, get bundled up together in false and damaging polarizations.

All this is at stake as we plunge into the multi-faceted 'Quest', alert for the ways in which what was said about Jesus and the Gospels both reflected and conditioned the larger questions about God and the world.

The so-called Quest for Jesus was part of the complex world of modern biblical criticism. This combined at least two quite different strands.

(1)   First, the Reformers and their successors appealed to the 'original mean-ings' of scripture, as prime evidence for the 'real' early Christian faith as opposed to the accretions of later speculation and 'tradition'. From Luther to Wesley and beyond, the search was on for a purer, more authentic form of the faith than was to be found in the Middle Ages or in the sleepy and corrupt churches, as many saw them, of the sixteenth, seventeenth and eighteenth centuries. Thus the Bible was, at least in theory, made to bear more and more weight within the life of the church. 'Original meanings' were investigated to give substance and direction to Christian faith.

(2)   But, disturbingly intertwined with that, there was a quite different move-ment. This was the rationalist or sceptical appeal to 'original meanings' as the key evidence that might *undermine* early Christian faith and any attempt to retrieve it in modern Europe. Thus the Protestant impulse for early meanings by which the church might be *rejuvenated* could be harnessed to support a sceptical search for early meanings by which the church might be *undermined*. History would (so many supposed) expose the falsity of dogmatic Christianity, not just to combat corruption and oppression in the church, not just to replace wars of religion with 'toler-ance', but to replace 'superstition', including Christianity itself, with sci-entific rationality.

Since both reformers and rationalists were opposed to mediaeval Christianity and its continuing legacy, their quite different tasks accidentally but effectively combined. This brought a Protestant energy and style to the sceptical task, leaving Protestants who wanted to hold on to Christian faith with a largely ahistorical Platonic Idealism. If that sounds confusing, it was and is. But these confusions, rampant in Continental scholarship, have largely been flattened out in British (and American) retrievals into the effectively positivist question: did it happen? Are the Gospels 'true'?

The story of what followed is thus quite different from what we find in some histories of biblical scholarship, with their supposed *wissenschaftlich* progression from one 'assured result' to another.[15] It is much more the confused noise which follows from the pursuit of social and cultural agendas by other means, as well as the shrinking of perspective sketched by Iain McGilchrist as the left brain usurps the role of the right in Western culture.[16] Thus we find the rationalists denying key elements of the faith, such as the resurrection of Jesus, and the romantics trying to put them back by other means (think of Ernst Renan as a reply, of sorts, to David Friedrich Strauss).[17] We find the debates between the right and left wings of Hegelian philosophy being played out in the implicit stand-off between (a) theories of 'progress' such as those of the liberals like Ritschl and the conservative nineteenth-century advocates of *Heilsgeschichte*[18] and (b) the revolutionary apocalyptic proposals of Schweitzer and then of that well-known Swiss Marxist Karl Barth.[19] All this, taught to bemused Anglo-Saxon students as the solid and assured results of modern historical-critical study, has made it increasingly difficult for actual study of Jesus and his first followers to play any serious role in theological reconstruction, not only in 'natural theology' (the attempt to find out about God) but even, with considerable irony, in Christology itself (the attempt to speak truly about Jesus Christ). To talk about 'the Christ'—which is often shorthand for a metaphysical entity floating free from history—without talking about Jesus himself can only be a high road to fantasy.[20] Since I am arguing here that studying Jesus himself is a vital element in the larger task of articulating Christian theology, and particularly in the more focused task of 'natural theology' itself, reasoning from the created world to the creator, we cannot avoid plunging in and seeing what was going on, and why, before we come up with alternatives.

I want in the present chapter to argue in particular that the idea of the literal and imminent 'end of the world' as a central belief of first-century Jews, including Jesus and his early followers, is a modern myth. The 'end-of-the-world Jesus' has become a vital part of the argument for keeping Jesus himself off stage in theological construction, just as it was a vital part of the position advanced by Rudolf Bultmann in his Gifford Lectures and elsewhere and emphasised by his followers to this day.[21] But it is a myth.

By 'myth'—itself of course a highly contentious term—I mean not only the popular sense of 'an untrue tale' but the more technical sense of a story told by a community to sustain a particular view of its common life and purpose.[22]

Such myths are accompanied, as often as not, by a ritual—in this case the regular murmuring of the words 'well, of course, Jesus expected the end of the world at any time', followed by a selection of congregational responses such as 'so we have to rethink traditional theology' or 'so we can relativize Paul's ethics', accompanied by a solemn but smug shake of the head at the weird things people used to believe in the pre-Enlightenment days. This entire programme is, in effect, a fatted sacred cow in need of slaughter. Any prodigals wishing for a feast should come home right away.[23]

The mainstream view in twentieth-century Western scholarship has been that in the late nineteenth century two pioneering young German scholars, Johannes Weiss and Albert Schweitzer, stumbled upon a hidden truth: that Jewish 'apocalyptic' writings were predicting the end of the world; that Jesus shared this view; and that after his disappointed death his followers went on with the same message. This time it was pegged to Jesus' *second* coming or *parousia*, but this was still expected imminently.[24] That hope, too, was disappointed.

The question we ought to ask about this supposed 'discovery' of Weiss and Schweitzer is: why did it catch on so quickly? And why did it become, within a couple of decades, the received orthodoxy across at least German and much Anglo-American scholarship? The answer is certainly not that Weiss and Schweitzer had discovered texts which actually predicted the end of the world. There is no evidence that either of them had made extensive or careful historical study of the relevant Jewish texts in their social, cultural and linguistic contexts. Had they done so, they would have realised that their end-of-the-world reading was a naïve literalistic mistake, cognate with supposing that when Isaiah described the fall of Babylon by speaking of the sun and the moon being darkened, and the stars falling from heaven, he was really talking about astral events that could be seen in the sky. In fact, as Klaus Koch points out in his still very important monograph, Western (particularly German) theology and exegesis was studiously ignorant about Jewish apocalyptic writing at the time.[25] So why the sudden rush into modern myth?

To answer this, and to unpick the myth of 'hope deferred' itself, we must glance quickly at the roots of the confusion, as they appear in certain key writers. Our underlying point is this: the intellectual and cultural debates we studied in the first chapter have had a significant, and arguably damaging, effect on the way in which Jesus himself has been perceived. The 'delayed *parousia*' myth is a prime example of this. So long as this myth persists, any hope of bringing Jesus back into the question of 'natural theology', or indeed ordinary systematic theology, will be lost. But to understand how this myth arose, we need to look quickly at the key moments in the ongoing scholarly discussions.

FROM STRAUSS TO KÄSEMANN: HISTORY, ESCHATOLOGY AND MYTH

D. F. Strauss

We have already introduced Hermann Samuel Reimarus as part of our eighteenth-century contextualisation, but we now start with a very different character. David Friedrich Strauss (1808–1874) is strangely described in Wikipedia as having portrayed a 'historical Jesus' 'whose divine nature he denied'. This is a classic example of the point I just made, of Anglophone misunderstanding of German contexts and meanings. Strauss, in fact, argued a sophisticated case, framed in Idealist philosophy and rooted in the extensive German fascination with ancient mythology. His point was that the Gospels were to be thought of as the 'mythologising' of larger truths, in the way that the Nordic or Germanic myths were telling great, sprawling truths about the world and the human condition when they spoke of the ancient gods and their ways. In particular, Strauss was applying Hegel's dialectic to the sources, arguing that there were conflicting forces at work in the early Christian movement from which, as in a Hegelian synthesis, a higher religious truth would emerge. By the second century, he argued, the Gospels were being written as the legendary embodiment of the hopes and beliefs to which, at that stage of development, the community had arrived. Since, for him, religions in general and Christianity in particular were fundamentally constituted by ideas, not events, this ought (he supposed) to be unproblematic. The important ideas were still present and intact. They could stand on their own, with no need to be grounded in actual events. Strauss went on to expound them, in dogmatic style, in a work of 1840.[26]

The reason I refer to the summary in Wikipedia is that it illustrates the slippage in understanding I have already mentioned between German and Anglophone thinking. Its comment about Strauss as denying Jesus' divine nature is making the same mistake that John Hick and his colleagues were inviting British readers to make in 1977 when they published *The Myth of God Incarnate*. To the average person, the word 'myth' in the title simply meant 'people used to believe Jesus was God incarnate but we now know it isn't true'. This oversimplification was continued by the American Westar Institute, the parent body for the now defunct Jesus Seminar, which instituted an 'Order of David Friedrich Strauss', honouring scholars who, they say, had 'rigorously applied the historical critical method to the study of the Gospels and creeds that Strauss pioneered'. There was, in fact, no such thing in Strauss's day (just as there is no one single thing in our own day) that can be called 'the historical critical method'. Strauss was doing neither of the mainstream activities (actual historical investigation; essaying historical narrative) which now go under that title, as we shall see in the next chapter.

Of course, if we come to Strauss with the question 'Did the events in the Gospels happen?', he will give the same answer (more or less) as the Jesus Seminar. But that was not his primary purpose. Strauss, I think, saw his proposal as far more positive; he was opposed to the rationalists (and the 'Jesus Seminar' was precisely rationalist in inspiration and method) just as much as to the 'supernaturalists'. He was trying to get away from what he saw as the trivializations of the faith, particularly the naïve piety that supposed the Gospels were a mere transcript of things that had happened, but his aim was not simply to say (with the rationalists) 'therefore nothing of great significance is found here'. He was inviting his readers to contemplate the vast reaches of supra-historical truth as reflected in mythological dress. 'Myth' was very popular in mid-nineteenth-century Germany, enabling one to explore, like the Greek tragedians, the *inside* of events and human motivations in a universally relevant way.[27] Strauss was making a post-Lessing move: forget those historical contingencies and go straight for the eternal truths.

It is of course true that Rudolf Bultmann muddled up different senses of 'myth' a hundred years later.[28] I do not think that Strauss did that in the same way. He was pleading for an Idealist version of Christian faith for which actual events in first-century Palestine would be more or less irrelevant. (Just to be clear: by 'Idealist' here I do not mean 'fanciful or impractical', but *philosophically* 'Idealist': seeing historical events as merely illustrative of timeless or absolute principles, or seeing the ideas themselves, such as 'freedom' or 'justice', as the main causal or driving forces in the unfolding process of historical events. Though this does not necessarily mean a fully blown Platonic scheme, the effect of giving up on a faith grounded in first-century events and finding a 'ground' somewhere else has close analogies to the Platonic division between the eternal, timeless 'ideas' and the changeable, transient material world.) That is the point at which he does look forward to Bultmann, who was nothing if not a neo-Kantian Idealist. Neither Strauss nor Bultmann was, at heart, a rationalist or 'naturalist', as the Westar Institute imagined, and as 'supernaturalist' apologists too have supposed. They were philosophical Idealists.[29] They represent one aspect of the Platonic turn within the larger Epicurean framework. For them, God and the world were still completely distinct. But Plato, or something like him, would enable them to bridge the gap. If that meant that they would have to set aside, or turn into 'myth', the supposedly this-worldly events which were now rendered suspect by 'historical criticism', so be it.

Albert Schweitzer

We jump from Strauss in the 1830s to Albert Schweitzer in the 1890s and early 1900s, pausing only to note the stress laid by both Richard Wagner and Friedrich Nietzsche on 'myth'.[30] Schweitzer, deeply influenced by both, is famous for a great many things, from his extraordinary book on Bach to his lifetime of medical missionary work in Africa. But for us what matters is his belief that Jesus and his first followers expected the imminent end of the world.[31]

Here too, as with Strauss and indeed Reimarus, among the interesting points are the contrast between the cultural and philosophical context of the original proposal and the flat-footed positivistic reception of the notion within the Anglo-Saxon world.[32] But the central point is that the end-of-the-world proposal was conceived within, and then eagerly propagated as part of, the complex cultural and philosophical world we have all too briefly sketched. It was emphatically not an 'assured result' of the historical study of first-century texts.

Two factors in particular must be put on the table to make this point. First, as we have seen, the ongoing attempts at kinds of 'natural theology' in the nineteenth century had avoided engaging with the task of history, particularly the history of Jesus. They had assumed something like Lessing's ugly ditch (itself, as we saw, a close cousin of the Epicurean heaven/earth split), and something like Reimarus's critical questioning of the Gospels, and thus focused on the first article of the creed (God the Father) rather than on the Son (let alone the spirit, which might have raised the spectre of 'enthusiasm'). They had followed the standard arguments (ontological, cosmological, teleological and moral), often working towards some variant on what is loosely known as 'classical theism'.[33] Fitting the Jesus of the Gospels in to the resultant picture was difficult, especially when we consider the agony in Gethsemane and the 'cry of dereliction' from the cross.[34] The tendency was then to read the four Gospels docetically, presenting Jesus as an exception to the normal rules of 'nature'. This applied equally to the devout, who therefore believed that Jesus had indeed 'claimed to be God' in an uncomplicated way, and to the sceptics, who therefore argued that the Gospels were obviously written up later, falsifying the 'merely human' original Jesus. 'Natural theology' then proceeded to construct a 'perfect being' with scant reference to Jesus or the Bible. This opened the way for quite different construals of Jesus, whose theological results could not easily be foreseen.

At the same time, second, the secular optimism of nineteenth-century Europe had developed to the point where many genuinely believed that the apparent social 'progress' really was the arrival of the kingdom of heaven on earth. Fuelled philosophically by Hegel's developmental pantheism, this reached something of a peak in the optimistic theology of Albrecht Ritschl. One could still suppose that God was somehow in charge of this process, but for practical purposes the eighteenth-century Epicurean assumption of a split-level world still held true. The 'progress' was arriving under its own steam. But this generated serious protests. Kierkegaard is the obvious example from earlier in the nineteenth century; Nietzsche, from later. In between the two came Marx, whose doctoral dissertation had been on Epicurus.[35] As with the eighteenth-century signs of Epicureanism (science without God, history without God, and so forth), Hegel's 'progress' was basically providence without God (except for the pantheistic divine force immanent within the process); Marx's revolutionary ideology was basically apocalyptic without God. A new world order was needed, and for that the old would have to be abolished entirely.

Schweitzer laid great emphasis on the sheer strangeness of his proposed 'Jesus' in the modern world. That was necessary for his project, to translate the 'moral will' and 'personality' of Jesus into the fresh challenge he saw as required for the new day (and to which, with conscious heroism, he devoted his own life).[36] Jesus, he said, 'passes by our time and returns to his own'.[37] This means that 'it is a good thing that the true historical Jesus should overthrow the modern Jesus, should rise up against the modern spirit and send upon earth, not peace, but a sword'.[38] Here and elsewhere we detect echoes of Nietzsche, and perhaps also of Marx. For Schweitzer, Jesus and his first followers had announced a 'supernatural' version of the protests of the former and the prophecies of the latter. As one would expect within an Epicureanism which assumed the radical incompatibility of heaven and earth, for heaven's kingdom to arrive the earth would have to disappear. Schweitzer's understanding of the 'eschatological' Jesus owed much to the genuine historical insight that Jesus was announcing not just a new or strengthened morality but a new world order. But his interpretation of Jesus' new vision owed far more to the underlying Epicurean cosmology of his culture (in which 'heaven' and 'earth' were radically incompatible) and the revolutionary ideology of his two great heroes, Nietzsche and Wagner: the moralist and the musician.

Thus a different analysis of Schweitzer's proposal is called for. Schweitzer and his contemporary Johannes Weiss are sometimes credited, in surveys of New Testament studies, with going off like intrepid Victorian explorers into the wild jungle of ancient Jewish apocalyptic thought and coming back with the alarming news that some Jews of the period believed in the imminent end of the world, and that Jesus himself shared this belief, and that he was of course disappointed. But at this point the rhetoric of radically different cultures (Jesus' apocalyptic culture over against a modern culture of steady progress) was smokescreen. Schweitzer himself relished, lived in, *wallowed* in a musical sub-culture whose controlling myth reached its climax in the coming end of the world. He was a Wagner fan.

This fact has, remarkably enough, been missed in most studies of Schweitzer. Theologians interested in his end-of-the-world theories have not enquired after his musical tastes; musicians interested in his attempted bridge between the 'pure music' of Bach and the expressive emotionalism of Wagner have not enquired after his theories about early Christianity. Biographers have noted his love of the music, his trance-like state after hearing *Tannhäuser* at the age of sixteen, his ongoing friendship with Cosima Wagner and then with Wagner's son Siegfried. Schweitzer's own massive work on Bach returns again and again to comparisons with Wagner, arguing indeed that Wagner's music had prepared Germany for a fresh appreciation of Bach himself.[39] But they pay little attention to the cultural and philosophical outlook to which Wagner was giving expression, and hence they underestimate, or fail to consider at all, the 'end of the world' motif in Wagner's work as a significant factor in the youthful Schweitzer's development of his basic thesis about Jesus and early Christianity.[40] A recent book on Schweitzer and music concentrates, naturally enough, on Bach.[41] One very recent article probes into the key area, but there remains much to explore.[42]

Consider this, for a start. One of the most important ideas in the whole of the *Ring* is the sense of the world coming to an end. A recent book of reflections on the tetralogy is entitled *Finding an Ending*.[43] When the musicologist Deryck Cooke died young in 1976 he had not brought his massive work on the *Ring* cycle as far as *Götterdämmerung* itself, but the published title even of the early part of the projected work was *I Saw the World End*.[44] This theme clearly had its impact on Schweitzer as a young man, overwhelmed by Wagner in general and the *Ring* cycle in particular. He went to the *Ring* cycle, in Bayreuth—all twenty hours of it—when it was revived in 1896, and he shared with his keyboard teacher Eugène Munch the excitement of the final pages of *Götterdämmerung* 'when all the themes of the trilogy are massed together and engulfed, when the world falls into ruins!'[45]

Munch died not long after that shared experience, but Schweitzer went to Bayreuth again no fewer than three times in the very same years that he was writing his three-part work on Jesus (the books on the Last Supper and on the secret of the Passion and then *Von Reimarus zu Wrede*) and then his history of Pauline scholarship. (Throughout this time, he was also, of course, giving organ recitals around Europe and writing articles on organ-building.) Here is the (almost unbelievable) schedule:

1892, J. Weiss's *Jesus' Proclamation of the Kingdom of God*
1894–1895, Schweitzer's military service (reading the Gospels in Greek in his spare time)
1896, Schweitzer's first visit to Bayreuth
1898–1899, in Paris and Berlin, studying Organ with Widor and Theology with von Harnack
1899, Philosophy PhD on Kant
1900, Licentiate in Theology (*The Problem of the Last Supper*)
1901, second visit to Bayreuth
1901, Habilitation (*The Secret of the Messiah and the Passion*) (published the same day as Wrede's book on the messianic secret)
1903–1906, Principal of St Thomas's College, Strasbourg
1904–1905, writing the two-volume study of Bach
1905, starts studying medicine
1906, third visit to Bayreuth
1906, *Von Reimarus zu Wrede*
1909, fourth visit to Bayreuth
1911, *Geschichte der paulinischen Forschung* (ET 1912); qualifies in medicine
1912, doctorate in medicine (*The Psychiatric Study of Jesus*).

The parallels between Wagner's epic and Schweitzer's reconstructions of Jesus are far too close to be coincidental. It would be going too far to suggest that Schweitzer's portrait of Jesus owed anything to Wagner's Siegfried, though I think if we were to investigate a combination of Siegfried and Brünnhilde (the children of Wotan who both do and don't do his will), we might find some fascinating insights, at least in Wagner if not in Schweitzer too. But my point here is that the myth of Valhalla, of the old gods, of their struggle with love and power in the face of dark and dwarvish forces that have renounced love for the sake of power, is all heading for the great climax in the ultimate and necessary destruction of Valhalla itself. Valhalla, of course, is not in itself the whole world; it is the home of the gods. Strictly speaking it is the gods who are condemned in the final *Götterdämmerung*, not the whole world. But, as we have seen, Schweitzer's excitement was already kindled by his (perhaps over-exuberant) interpretation of Wagner in terms of the world falling into ruins. After all, already in the *Das Rheingold*, the first opera in the sequence, we find Erda informing Wotan of 'the truth that everything ends'.[46] At the end of the entire cycle, Brünnhilde, faced with the utter corruption of the world of gods and mortals, recognises 'that in some sense all is as it had to be' and performs 'an act that burns all this corruption away'. In this 'twilight of the gods', 'her will coincides again with Wotan's, and what he suffers passively she, in a magnificent gesture, wills on them all'.[47] Some have credited this ending, different from Wagner's original conception, to his switch in philosophical allegiance from Feuerbach to Schopenhauer. But it has recently been convincingly argued that the traffic might have been going in the other direction: that, in other words, Wagner was led to the conclusion of a 'resigned acceptance', of *Götterdämmerung* itself, by his own artistic intuition for how the myth, and equally importantly the music, had to work out, and that it was this that generated his admiration for Schopenhauer rather than the other way around.[48]

My point is simple. There are obvious differences between Wagner's implied eschatology, in which the twilight of the gods leaves a purely secular world to fend for itself, and Schweitzer's view of Jesus' proclamation, in which the divine kingdom abolishes the world in order to replace it. But the two converge, not least in Schweitzer's hermeneutical proposal for what one might now do, granted that the early Christian end-of-the-world prediction came to nothing. The supernatural world is now out of the picture. Humans must act heroically to bring about a new way forward.

All this bears the unmistakable stamp of the broadly Epicurean cosmology, the incompatibility between the heavenly and earthly worlds, which characterised the times. Wagner's great epic, coupled of course with Nietzsche's philosophy, gave Schweitzer the clue he needed: the idea of a culture and its horizon heading for disaster. This enabled him to portray Jesus as a new kind of moral hero, announcing the imminent tragedy and going straight to meet it, to take its full force upon himself. At a certain but powerful level of generality, the notion of the world's end (in some sense!) as the necessary outcome of all things, simultaneously tragic and heroic, the result of a new sort of power, the power of self-sacrificial love—all this was there in the opera before it was there in the books which Schweitzer wrote in between his trips to Bayreuth. The imminent end of the world was not, in other words, a first-century Jewish idea which Schweitzer (and Weiss) had discovered and expounded as something alien to their times. It was a glorious piece of late nineteenth-century German mythology.

Of course, it appeared novel and strange—rather as Kierkegaard had done—in a world full of Hegelian optimism. Johannes Weiss, often seen as Schweitzer's partner in advocating the end-of-the-world Jesus, reverted in his own theology to the Hegelian and Ritschlian view of the gradually emerging kingdom.[49] Some suggested that if Schweitzer's proposals about Jesus were true then Jesus must have been suffering from psychological delusions. Schweitzer took this challenge sufficiently seriously to write a refutation of it as his medical doctorate.[50]

Schweitzer himself did not draw the conclusion that some might have done, that Jesus was simply wrong and that we should have nothing more to do with him. Nor did he, like Weiss, turn back in his own teaching to a steadily arriving kingdom. At the risk of oversimplification, one might say that, faced with the end-of-the-world Jesus, Weiss reverted to right-wing Hegelianism and Schweitzer to the left-wing variety. For him, one could not wait for the kingdom to arrive gradually. One must act heroically. And he did. His scheme was therefore much closer to his hero Nietzsche (whom he imitated down to the detail of the famous moustache). Of course, by then Nietzsche had become disenchanted with Wagner, and said so. But the differences between the philosopher and the composer do not affect the conclusion that when Albert Schweitzer proposed the end-of-the-world Jesus he was reflecting—as he himself said in a candid moment—ideas that were in fact 'in the air' at the time. This public mood has been extensively demonstrated recently by the German historian Lucian Hölscher.[51]

The end-of-the-world ideas were in the air in other contexts, too. It is quite a leap to go from Wagner's epic to the novels and short stories of the day. But these may be straws in the same wind. H. G. Wells's *The Time Machine* (1895), challenging the idea of endless progress, supposes that the world might after all come to an end. And, in a different register again, Oscar Wilde, in *The Picture of Dorian Gray* (1890), offers a revealing flicker of dialogue. One character, commenting on the degenerate lifestyles all around in the 1890s, murmurs '*Fin de siècle*'. His companion answers sorrowfully, '*Fin du globe*'. Not just the century; the world.

Metaphorical? Perhaps. Wagner, Wells and Wilde were not, most likely, saying exactly the same things. But the point is precisely the general mood. One of the reasons why Schweitzer's ideas found a ready market not least in Britain was the sense in the Edwardian decade that the Babel-like tower of Victorian optimism was tottering and could not long remain upright.[52] People easily demythologised Schweitzer's portrait of Jesus, applying it to the perceived end of a particular way of life: a very Edwardian sentiment. Hensley Henson, Dean of Durham in this period and then Bishop, used often to preach on the psalm text, 'I see that all things come to an end; but thy commandment is exceedingly broad' (Psalm 119.96).

In all this—and this is my underlying point—from Gospel scholarship to Edwardian cultural anxieties we find a massive implication for 'natural theology'. If the world is coming to an end, to be replaced by the wholly other 'kingdom of God', the chance of being able to infer anything about the latter from the former is effectively nil. One might still, of course, look at the old world and work back to the creator. But then as now the question of 'nature and grace' was closely correlated with the question of 'the present age and the age to come'. Thus, if the 'age to come' was the complete unknown, the arrival of the 'other' to replace the present world, the implication was that a similar epistemological barrier existed between earth and heaven. Thus the so-called 'apocalyptic' mood of the times, embodied exactly by Schweitzer, told heavily by implication against any kind of 'natural theology'. There is a straight line, in other words, from Schweitzer's end-of-the-world ideas—and their cultural context!—to Barth's post-war *Romans* commentary and then his angry rejection of Brunner. He was reacting, like Schweitzer and arguably with much more recent political reason, against the progressive liberalism embodied in their teacher Adolf von Harnack.

The puzzle, however, remains. Weiss and Schweitzer were claiming to tell the world what 'kingdom of God' meant for Jesus, on the basis of the supposed discovery of Jewish apocalyptic texts. *1 Enoch* is regularly cited, along with *4 Ezra* and *2 Baruch*; I do not know whether Schweitzer and Weiss looked much further.[53] But the question must be posed: what in those texts made them think anyone was talking about the actual end of the world? A glance at Josephus, and even a nodding acquaintance with the revolutionary movements of the Herodian period and then of the 60s and the 130s, would not suggest that people were expecting the world to end. Josephus discusses the different parties and movements—Sadducees, Pharisees, Essenes, and the revolutionary 'fourth philosophy'—but he never mentions end-of-the-world speculators. He has no category resembling the modern fiction 'apocalyptists'. All our recent work on texts from Ezekiel and Daniel on to 4 Ezra and 2 Baruch indicates that what they were talking about was actually the *transformation* of the present world by the *end of the present state of affairs*—the state of affairs, that is, in which the Jewish people perceived themselves to be in a state of ongoing slavery and in a sense 'exile', and looked back to Daniel and other texts which assured them that through the strange and powerful outworking of divine promises this state would not last for ever. And, common to most Jewish schools of thought, including the much later Rabbis, we find the notion of 'the present age' and 'the age to come'. This is not, as used often to be suggested, peculiar to 'apocalyptic' literature, or indeed theology.[54] It is a biblically rooted way of looking at the ultimate purposes of the God of creation and covenant.[55] This two-age scheme of history is frequently invoked by the Rabbis, who almost by definition rejected the 'apocalyptic' dreams that had led to disastrous revolutions. The expectation, then, was for a great transformation, not for the end of the world of space, time and matter.

So why would anyone think otherwise? Here we look not only to Wagner, Nietzsche and the other anti-Hegelian thinkers of the late nineteenth century but once more to how the Epicurean framework shaped reflection on many topics. To expand what we said above: if we are talking about 'the kingdom of heaven' or 'the kingdom of God' arriving 'on earth as in heaven', then, if we have accepted as axiomatic that heaven and earth are radically unalike, and that in particular 'heaven', the abode of the gods, is sharply removed from the present world and wants nothing to do with it, then the only way 'the kingdom of heaven' can become a reality is if 'earth', the present world, is abolished. Epicureanism itself, of course, had no such eschatology. Humans would cease to exist at death, and one day the whole world would go the same way, with nothing to take its place. But when the heaven/earth split frames a would-be Christian eschatology, it produces a zero-sum game. You can't have heaven and earth together. Transposed into the famous rationalist slogan of Lessing from over a century earlier, if there is a broad ugly ditch between the eternal truths of reason and the contingent truths of history, then the only way for the eternal truths to become real will be through the abolition of history itself—in the sense of the world of space, time and matter coming to a stop.

So, darkly, if 'history' (the ongoing flow of this-worldly events) is to be abolished, why bother doing real 'history' (the study of the past) yourself?[56] A quick 'historical' glance through some more Jewish texts—Josephus, say, or the admittedly more sketchy evidence for the bar-Kochba revolt—would have shown that the 'end of the world' picture bore no relation to what actual first-century Jews believed.[57] Some Jews did indeed expect the kingdom to come through miraculous acts of divine providence, but the new 'kingdom' would still consist of *a new state of affairs on earth*, not the abolition of earth and its replacement with something completely different.[58] Jews debated how to help this project forwards. The Sadducees collaborated with Rome; the Pharisees urged Israel to obey Torah more strictly; the Essenes said their prayers and waited; the revolutionaries sharpened their swords. 'Apocalyptic' is in fact a *political* genre. It is about a major upheaval *within* the space-time world. We have no evidence of people thinking the world itself would end.[59]

But this Jewish view was neither understood nor wanted in the late nineteenth and early twentieth century. The true historical reading fell between two stools. On the one side there was the Western view of 'salvation', 'going to heaven', mocked by Nietzsche as 'Platonism for the masses'. On the other side there was 'Jewish theology' as imagined by, and reviled by, liberal Protestants: blood, soil, priestcraft, works-righteousness. The actual Jewish expectations, and the actual early Christian reworkings of them, were not in sight. History as a *task* had been left to one side.

So what could 'the kingdom of heaven' actually mean? Here, as so often in the period, what Epicureanism lacked (any definite view of heaven) Platonism could supply. The usual Victorian images of 'heaven', with disembodied souls sitting on clouds playing harps, were radically discontinuous with the present world. The normally imagined 'heaven' wouldn't fit either into Queen Victoria's drawing room or into Albert Schweitzer's study in the *Stift* in Strasbourg. Neither Epicureanism nor Platonism could get heaven into earth or vice versa. So if the kingdom of heaven was coming, earth would have to be abolished.

Schweitzer, then, claimed to put Jesus into his first-century context and to discover that he believed in the end of the world. I am returning the compliment. By putting Schweitzer into his late nineteenth-century context, I conclude that he believed what he did about Jesus because, in the complex swirl of philosophies and worldviews available to him, this was what he was almost bound to suppose 'the kingdom of God' must have meant, and the idea of the world 'coming to an end' was in any case, as we have seen, readily available in a part of his cultural context by which he had been thrilled to the core. Then, when Europe was set ablaze by the follies of Queen Victoria's muddled grandchildren—the Kaiser, the Tsar, the King and all the rest, trundling off to what everyone hoped would be a good brisk war in 1914—there was a sense in which it all came true. The European Valhalla fell, and with it the easy-going *Kulturprotestantismus* of the great theologians of the day, von Harnack and Hermann among them: the teachers, in fact, of Barth, Bultmann and Schweitzer himself. When, right after the war, Barth wrote his *Romans* commentary, insisting that one could not build up from below but that one needed a fresh word 'vertically from above', he was, to be sure, reading St Paul as well as Karl Marx. But he was, in this sense, looking out on the world described by Albert Schweitzer: the world which had had to come to an end so that something new could be born.

It was, of course, Barth who later said 'NEIN' to Emil Brunner. That is where my narrative about Schweitzer joins up most obviously with the ongoing question of 'natural theology'. Schweitzer had, in a sense, prepared the way, though Barth's turn to eschatology does not seem to have been directly influenced by him, but rather by the Blumhardts and Franz Overbeck. What Schweitzer saw as the necessary 'end' for the present world is parallel, in some respects, to what Barth saw as the natural incapacity of human reason. Either way, if the world is coming to an end, there is a very broad, very ugly ditch between that world and any truth about God. What Anglo-Saxon thinkers then and subsequently have thought of as 'results', in a fairly straightforward positivist sense, about the historical Jesus—that he was an 'apocalyptic prophet' expecting 'the end of the world'—is thus umbilically related to the larger theological issues. It is only by exploring how both sides of this equation actually work that we can attempt any kind of biblically based, Jesus-based reconstruction.

Rudolf Bultmann

With that we move rapidly forward into the 1920s and 1930s, and greet with due caution my predecessor as Gifford *Neutestamentler*, Rudolf Bultmann.[60] For him, famously, the end-of-the-world language in the Gospels and Paul had of course been falsified in the literal sense but was now to be retrieved through *demythologisation*. That confused slogan combined three senses of 'myth': (1) the flat sense of 'myth' as 'old stories we can't believe today'; (2) the more interesting sense of 'myth' as 'the stories cultures tell themselves to explain the human predicament', as with ancient Greek tragedies, and including particularly (3) the cosmic myths in apocalyptic writings which encode a different kind of truth. Bultmann used this third sense to focus on what for him was central. The main thrust of his Giffords was to label as 'eschatology' the existentialist experience which for him was the vital thing, to 'translate' into those terms the 'apocalyptic' language of Jesus, and to use the resultant construction to oppose the deterministic historicism which he saw as the major threat of his times.[61]

Bultmann was thus simultaneously retrieving the Idealism of David Friedrich Strauss, picking up the post-Hume modernist rhetoric about what we moderns can and can't believe, and combining both in his own retrieval of Schweitzer. (We should include Ernst Troeltsch in this picture, too, and I shall return to him briefly in the next chapter.) This combination has, I think, obscured the fact that there was an important grain of truth in the demythologising programme. Many were anxious about Bultmann's apparent capitulation to the modernist agenda, and they failed to focus on the fact that he was quite correct to say that the ancient Jewish language of myth was not to be taken literally. The question, of course, is what the intended referent actually was. No wise reader of *1 Enoch* in the first century, or indeed the twenty-first, imagines the writer to be predicting an actual white bull leading a herd of other farm animals. If 'demythologising' means decoding the picture-language used by such writers, we should simply say that this is learning to read. But what is the language a picture *of*? As we shall see in a moment, all the evidence suggests that it was (what we would call) *political*. For Bultmann, however, it was 'internal', 'existential' or (in that sense) 'spiritual', with no obvious relevance to the world of space, time and matter. Several different questions and agendas are thus muddled up with one another. When we affirm the point about ancient myth as picture-language, but confuse that with community-forming narratives on the one hand and 'things we can't believe today' on the other, we are back to *tohu wa'bohu*. Confusion and chaos.

Part of the problem here, relating directly to the God-and-world question underneath both exegesis and 'natural theology', is that though Bultmann was (from my point of view) within an ace of touching the truth he could never make the final move. His theopolitical stance (see below), like a thick and prickly hedge between two adjacent pathways, would not let him switch tracks. As virtually all students of *1 Enoch* or *4 Ezra* and indeed Daniel would now say, the vivid apocalyptic language is indeed coded script—but for (what we would call) *political realities*.[62] Nobody in the first century thought that Daniel's dream of the statue with its four metals, and the stone cut out of the mountain which smashes it and replaces it with a new mountain, was a prediction of an actual compound statue and an actual miraculous stone. Daniel 7 is not 'about' sea-monsters and primitive human space travel. Daniel 2, Daniel 7 and the later works that echo and develop them were about the actual kingdoms of the world (and, to be sure, the dark powers that stood behind them and operated through them) and the actual kingdom-establishing victory of God that would challenge, overthrow and replace them.

This caused Bultmann what with hindsight we can see as a double problem, to which the twists and turns of demythologising (not to mention the still more tortuous theories of Form Criticism) were his inadequate and inappropriate response. First, he didn't want to find a this-worldly political message; second, he didn't want to countenance the possibility of dark non-human powers that might stand behind political realities. The irony of this double problem, in the 1920s and 1930s, should not be overlooked. Let me briefly unpack both of these.

First, Bultmann was never going to accept a 'political' reading. This was partly because of his Lutheran 'two kingdoms' theology, which, when read without the nuance it may once have had, resulted in a straightforward split: God and politics don't belong together. It was partly because of his neo-Kantian Idealism: ultimate truth was to be found in quasi-Platonic abstraction, not in concrete particulars. It was partly because of the elements of liberal modernism still evident in his work: he simply assumed that the resurrection of Jesus had not occurred (and that Paul's appeal to eyewitnesses in 1 Corinthians 15 was a worrying error on the apostle's part), so that neither at Easter nor at any other time was there any sign of real new creation coming to birth within the old world, nothing to challenge the *status quo* on the ground. It was partly because of his existentialism, in which strange apocalyptic language became code, not for political realities but for the personal decision of faith, and so had to be stripped of its association with an unacceptable ancient cosmology.

Bultmann's reading of the first century was conditioned not least by the rise of the Nazi party. The only political statement that Bultmann could, and did, extract from his reading of first-century Christian apocalyptic was an appeal for quietism. Throughout the 1930s, his favourite preaching text was 1 Corinthians 7, where Paul says that because of the present distress (he probably has a large-scale famine in mind, but since Schweitzer it has been fashionable to say that it's because the end of the world was about to occur) one should live in the present world 'as if not': the married, 'as if not' married; the traders, 'as if not' buying and selling, and so on.[63] For Bultmann, this was to be read as a down-to-earth way of saying what he said in his Giffords: that the response to historicist political claims ('this is the way history is going') was to grasp the eschatological moment.

One can easily sympathise. If you were preaching in Marburg in those years, particularly if you were a friend and philosophical disciple of Heidegger, a member of the Nazi party (though apparently tolerant of other views in the university setting, and also increasingly uneasy), perhaps that was all you could say. Bultmann returns to the point quite explicitly in his 1955 Giffords: the theologian and preacher has nothing to say to the present political situation except that we are living on a different plane and therefore touch the world only at a tangent, 'as if not'. The analogy with Barth's early position on natural theology is fascinating, though Barth was of course able to launch a much fiercer protest, partly because he was back in Switzerland, and so could speak 'vertically from above' into the situation, and partly because he was a Calvinist not a Lutheran. (To be fair: Barth had of course opposed Hitler openly while still teaching in Bonn; and many Lutherans such as Bonhoeffer and Niemöller were, and still are, famous for active opposition to the regime.)

If Bultmann's first problem was his unwillingness to recognise that the texts were addressing (what we would call) political realities, and prophesying real socio-cultural change, the second can be stated more briefly. Bultmann had no desire to acknowledge the reality of dark supra-human powers. This, I think, was partly because of his post-Hume modernism but also because of his existentialism. When Paul spoke of 'sin' as a *power* that acts on humans, not simply as a human act, Bultmann was committed to understanding this in terms of the mythologisation of the internal human struggle to which the answer was that one should grasp, or awaken, the latent eschatological possibility.[64]

One can, as I say, sympathise with Bultmann personally and politically. But his position is exegetically inexcusable from someone world-renowned as *a historical critic*, the foremost heir in his day of the so-called 'historical-critical movement'. To understand Jesus and early Christianity historically, one would have to understand the Jewish world of the first century. But one of Bultmann's foundational principles, in his theological DNA from Luther and Kant, and indeed from Hegel and F. C. Baur, was the rejection of all things Jewish. Judaism meant works-righteousness, whether in its supposedly Pelagian moralistic form ('doing good deeds to earn God's favour') or the existentialist's version of that ('grasping my own identity'). Had Bultmann simply said, 'My construction is not intended to be historical; it is a theological and/or existential proposal', that would have been one thing. But he did not. He was continually engaged in an attempt to find a *religionsgeschichtlich* genealogy of early Christian ideas in the non-Jewish world. This led him from his early interest in mystery-religions to his later heavy (and completely unhistorical) investment in Gnosticism. Neither worked—as real history. When it came to the actual first-century Jewish world, he took little real interest in it, remaining content (as Sanders pointed out a generation ago) with the caricatures of Schürer and Billerbeck. He never visited the Holy Land to see for himself, quite literally, how the land lay. He ignored the historical movements of revolution (Reimarus was long forgotten), and he screened out the way in which key texts such as Daniel were being read as part of that national aspiration. After all, one did not want to base one's faith on history: that, for the Lutheran neo-Kantian, would risk turning faith into a 'work' as well as muddling up the 'two kingdoms'.[65]

The end-of-the-world myth thus suited Bultmann's philosophy, his theology, his politics and his exegesis. His followers to this day continue to suggest that anyone who questions this foundation must be engaging in special pleading. I think the boot is on the other foot.[66] And since Bultmann's work has shaped a good deal of continuing Gospel scholarship, one will look there in vain for anything that might help us in trying to gain a fresh vantage point on the question of God and the world, whether the *action* of God *in* the world or the *inference* of God *from* the world.

'Delay' Reworked: Conzelmann, Käsemann, Werner

The third movement to seize upon the end-of-the-world myth as a hermeneutical tool consisted of pupils of Bultmann, such as Hans Conzelmann and Ernst Käsemann, and the systematician Martin Werner, the latter a lifelong friend of Albert Schweitzer. This too needs contextualising.[67] In the middle and late 1930s many in Germany had pinned their hopes on something new and wonderful emerging from the dangerous turbulence of European events. Perhaps it would after all be a Hegelian 'progress', a steady movement towards the light; or perhaps, more likely, it would be a Marxist-style revolution, also emerging from within the world though more like a volcanic explosion. One way or another, a new day would arise in which ancient wrongs would at last be put right. Among the hopeful was the cultural critic Walter Benjamin, a close friend of Gershom Scholem. When it didn't happen—for Benjamin, when Molotov and Ribbentrop signed the pact between Stalin and Hitler—hope crashed to the ground. Benjamin's final work, shortly before his suicide, denounced 'history' as without meaning or hope. Paul Klee's famous picture, 'The Angel of History', was invoked: history, after all, was just a pile of trash. So much for 'progress', and particularly for Hegel.[68]

The mood of disaster, of hopes dashed to the ground, continued in the post-war period. Barth returned from Switzerland and, lecturing in Bonn, spoke of the young men in his audience who had forgotten how to smile.[69] Käsemann would later speak of his generation being 'burnt children' who were unwilling ever again to put their hands into the fire of 'salvation history'.[70] Conzelmann argued that Luke, seen as the pre-eminent voice for *Heilsgeschichte* in the New Testament, represented the radical failure of nerve on the part of the post-70 church. Instead of living by a 'vertical' faith in God's imminent victory, the Third Evangelist had offered a 'horizontal' account of Israel, Jesus and the church, an apparently immanent history into which one would immerse oneself rather than expecting God to do something radically new.[71] To write a 'gospel' at all, then, was already to lose the plot, to imply that the 'good news' was a *story* about *things that happened sequentially in the space-time universe.* Käsemann and Conzelmann, and with them an entire generation, thus kept Schweitzer's end-of-the-world belief for Jesus and his first followers and *projected back onto the early Christians the radical disappointment that all their generation in Germany felt at the dashing of their hopes.* This then brought into articulation a new form of the standard Protestant rhetoric: the first generation got it right (in their 'vertical' trust in God), and the second generation went to the dogs, looking instead to 'ongoing history'. No wonder Bultmann and many of his followers then looked to Gnosticism, exactly as many disappointed Jews began to do in the middle of the second century after the failure of the bar-Kochba revolt. Indeed, as I have argued elsewhere, the parallel between the disappointment of AD 135 and the disappointment of 1940, and their respective aftermaths, is telling.[72]

That whole school of criticism thus articulated a two-stage problem. First, Jesus expected the end very soon, and it didn't happen. He went to his death in disappointment. (Actually, that summary itself elides two stages for Schweitzer: first, Jesus expected 'the son of man' to arrive soon, and he didn't, so he went to his death to force God's hand, and that failed as well.) Then, second, his first followers transferred this hope to their own generation: the end would come while they were still alive. This didn't happen either. That second disappointment forced the church to reshape itself—to turn, in fact, into 'early Catholicism'. Like Barth rejecting Brunner's version of 'natural theology' with heavy-duty weapons borrowed from standard protestant rhetoric, calling something 'catholic' was meant to sound damning.

There are of course two (but only two) pieces of early evidence that anybody in the early church thought in the way Bultmann's successors were suggesting. There is a well-known passage in Second Peter which seems to reflect an anxiety that the apostolic generation is dying out; and there is John 21.[73] The Petrine passage has sometimes been read as a version of a Stoic eschatology, expecting a cosmic conflagration. But in Stoicism the fire which eventually consumes the world is the inner divine life, finally and gladly drawing the entire world into its flame, whereas for 2 Peter it seems that the fire executes judgment. In any case, the passage is unique among early Christian writings and cannot be used as an index of what Jesus and his first followers believed. The passage also contains some of the oddest textual puzzles anywhere in the New Testament, presumably a sign that early scribes found it as perplexing as we do.

These passages have regularly been drawn upon to support an entire exegetical project, apparently measuring where different early Christian movements and writings stood in relation to the shock of AD 70—despite the fact that in the Apostolic Fathers, and on into the second century, there is no sign of any such problem. Käsemann and others then used this analysis as a means to produce a heavy critique of the way in which German bourgeois piety had settled down after the war and made itself comfortable once more: a kind of quasi-theological parallel to the heavy-handed secular critique embodied in J. B. Priestley's play *An Inspector Calls*.[74] Käsemann in particular could see only too clearly how dark and dangerous the world still was. So he and others redeployed F. C. Baur's category of *Frühkatholizismus* to describe the supposed world of the deutero-Paulines, the Pastorals, and especially that wretched would-be historian Luke. 'Apocalyptic', in Käsemann's sense, was the mother of genuine Christian theology; but the second generation had given it up and gone in for a less stressful existence.

All this made a lot of sense in the second half of the twentieth century. But it bore little resemblance to how people thought in the first century. A moment's reflection on what little we know of Jesus' followers between AD 70 and AD 150 will show just how much this was a projection of post-war Germany rather than a historical assessment of second-generation Christianity.[75] The end-of-the-world notion had worked well for Schweitzer and his immediate followers; demythologised, it worked well for Bultmann in the 1930s; the *disappointed* end-of-the-world notion now worked well for the post-Bultmann generation in the 1940s and 1950s. And, as I am emphasizing in our present context, this multiple and essentially unhistorical reconstruction helped to sustain a theological climate in which Jesus himself, and the writings of his first followers, would simply not be available for use by theologians puzzling over the interface between God and the world. Worse: the received view of Jesus and his first followers—that they thought the world would end and it didn't—*reinforced* the tendency to think of God and the world as being at arm's length, thus rendering 'natural theology' on the one hand, and divine action within the world on the other, increasingly incredible.

Meanwhile, in England and America, something rather different was happening with the same data. In England at least (Scotland, the home of the Gifford Lectures, might be different) few people had read Hegel. Few people believed in his inexorable if dialectical progress—though the British Empire had had its own version, too: 'wider still and wider', indeed! Many people were worried about Marx. Schweitzer and Barth were greeted with respect but also alarm; Bultmann, with anxious incomprehension. The British tend to be suspicious of theory, preferring muddled pragmatism. (And, after all, Britain and America had won the wars. We had other problems, but we didn't expect our theologians, let alone our biblical scholars, to help us solve them.)

Here we see a phenomenon of cultural non-transference which turns up in other areas as well. Take Ludwig Wittgenstein. Born and brought up in the highly cultured world of late nineteenth century Vienna, he carried into his philosophy all that multi-layered culture, addressing to the end questions he had puzzled over in his earlier life. But in Britain, once he had been teamed up with Bertrand Russell, Russell himself and more or less everyone else assumed that Wittgenstein was basically a linguistic philosopher whose work could function within some kind of positivism.[76] The English have an effortlessly Procrustean tendency with high-flown Continental ideas: let's just chop off the incomprehensible philosophy and use what's left to answer the questions we were interested in anyway. The same thing happened with the great historian von Ranke. He was himself a historicist (in a sense I will discuss in the next chapter). But his famous statement of intent, that he was trying to find out 'what had actually happened', has often been misunderstood. Von Ranke was trying to say, with considerable care, that he was *not* trying to provide vast ranges of historical 'meaning' but only trying to ascertain the raw material from which one might move to such larger theories. But his cautious statement has been taken by generations of English readers to mean that he was a positivist who thought history could yield unvarnished facts.[77]

Something similar has then happened with Bultmann. English-speaking readers left to one side his seemingly tortured and contested philosophical explorations. All they saw was a massively learned German reading the Gospels, and all they wanted to know was: does this turbo-charged scholar think Jesus did and said what the Gospels say he did and said, or not? Does he support an interventionist Deism or a non-interventionist Deism? Bultmann, however, wasn't addressing that question. He was, and still is, revered by many in Germany for his preaching and spirituality, with his quiet stance under Hitler being excused or overlooked, but in English-speaking circles he has simply been regarded as a 'liberal'—a word which, like so many others, has a very different meaning when you cross the North Sea, let alone the Atlantic. Those who have championed Bultmann in the Anglo-Saxon world, such as Norman Perrin in America, or John Robinson or Dennis Nineham in England, have hailed him as a master exegete, finding in his work a useful foundation for the theology and ethic they wished to promote: a theology which trimmed off the bits that modern science had rendered questionable, and an ethic more suited to progressive modernity.[78] For many on both sides of the Atlantic, he was seen simply as the enemy, the denier of the faith.

My aim here is not to enter into that debate but simply to point out that when people in England or America saw Schweitzer's 'end-of-the-world Jesus', and Bultmann's attempts to demythologise the Gospels, they misunderstood both the motivation and the meaning of the whole sequence. Often the pay-off amounted to little more than the open-ended invitation to revisionism. Jesus and the early church (so it was thought) expected the end of the world and structured their theology and ethics accordingly; they were wrong, so we can structure our belief and behaviour differently. That is the real cop-out, the real flag of convenience. And that is no way to build a theology, whether a natural theology or any other kind.

But (the reader might object at this point) are the texts not clear? Did not Mark's Jesus declare that some standing there would not taste death until they had seen the kingdom of God come with power? What are we to do with passages like that, and many others? To this question, fraught as it is with challenges both historical and theological, we shall return. But not quite yet.

CONCLUSION: THE NEED FOR HISTORY

The provisional conclusion we may reach from this survey of the questioned book—the challenges to the Gospel portrait of Jesus and what it might mean in a new day—is that the actual historical task, the study of Jesus within his own complex first-century Middle-Eastern Jewish culture, is still waiting to be addressed, however much this might appear to be what Reimarus and others were, officially at least, meant to be doing. But, as we shall see in the next chapter, the challenge of all genuine historical investigation is to think into the minds of people who think very differently from ourselves. Twentieth-century studies of eschatology, whether they have gone with Schweitzer into end-of-world theories or whether like Bultmann they have demythologised and seen 'eschatology' as an existentialist's inward turn, have signally failed to grapple with the demonstrable historical setting of Second Temple Jewish aspiration, retrieval of key texts, and agendas. As we shall see in the next chapter, the movement which has sailed under the flag of 'historical criticism' has regularly had too much criticism and not enough history. What if we did it differently? Might it after all help us approach the questions surrounding 'natural theology' in new ways? Can we, after all, look at anything in the world, *history included*, and see it as a genuine (if broken) pointer to the new creation, and hence to a reaffirmation of the Creator himself?

I have stressed that the whole varied and complex movement of European thought, from the mid-eighteenth century onwards, was increasingly shaped by the Epicurean mood. Heaven and earth were set radically apart from one another, as the theological analogue of Lessing's ugly ditch between the ultimate truths of reason and the mere contingent truths of history. God's sphere was removed from the earthly realm, with the former uninvolved in the latter and the latter conceived as the random play of chance forces. But, as I shall argue throughout this book, the point we need to grasp is that few if any first-century Jews would have seen it like that. The modern Western philosophies and their variations remain alien to the texts, the thought-forms, and the world-views of Jesus and his contemporaries. At this point, of course, the familiar chronological snobbery sets in: they had embraced an ancient worldview, but we have embraced a new one and the old one is no longer available to us now that we have modern medicine and electricity (Bultmann said this explicitly). Actually, of course—this has been one of my underlying points—this is a fiction. The supposed new worldview is simply a fresh version of an ancient one, Epicureanism, with some radical new twists (the doctrine of 'progress') and claiming to offer some new supporting evidence (modern science). This has normally been ignored. The modernist rhetoric, even while sometimes deliberately evoking the ancient classical (but not Christian or Jewish) world, has not wanted to admit that its underlying proposal is simply a new version of a very old worldview.

It is of course true that we today know things about the physical world which Aquinas and Calvin did not know. How much more with Plato or Aristotle, Plutarch or Seneca, Jesus or Paul! But that isn't the point. The point is not that they were ancient, and we are modern. Epicureanism is also ancient. Modernism used scientific advances as the pretext for a comprehensive worldview which they do not in fact demonstrate. The implicit argument was going in the other direction: the already powerful seventeenth-century Epicureanism offered a socially, culturally and politically attractive worldview for which signs of biological evolution (as well as dramatic medical and technological advances) could be judged to offer support. So the split between heaven and earth, between God and the world, continued to dominate the discussion, whether on the part of those who wanted to emphasize the world and question God (Feuerbach and his followers) or on the part of those who wanted to emphasize God and his revelation and set that over against the world (Barth and Bultmann, in their different ways).

The theological relevance of the history of Jesus was by no means the only casualty in this long-running discussion. History itself—history as a discipline, as a task—was pushed out of theology's way. In particular, a historical account of how first-century Jews themselves understood their world, including their own long story, was lacking. It was assumed that Jewish ways of thinking were by definition antithetical to those of the early Christians and particularly of Jesus himself, thus providing apparent theological justification for ignoring the real historical task of examining the first-century world from every angle and trying to understand what it might mean to see Jesus within it. Not doing this means that 'criticism' has expanded to fill the whole agenda and 'historical' has disappeared altogether. We cannot make any headway without a historical account of how first-century Jews themselves understood their world, including their own long story. That is what we must now try to provide.

As the first step, however, we need to take a good look at what 'history' itself might mean. The meanings of 'history' have themselves been caught up in the very turmoil I have been describing, and they need sorting out. Since the discipline of 'history' claims to be studying events and motivations in the 'natural' world, one cannot study that 'natural' world, or ask the theological questions we want to ask about it, without understanding how the discipline itself has been affected by the cultural climate we have been sketching. That will be the subject of the next chapter.

II

History, Eschatology and Apocalyptic

3

The Shifting Sand

The Meanings of 'History'

INTRODUCTION

In the autumn of 1973, just as I was beginning my doctoral studies, I happened to meet Professor Henry Chadwick, then Dean of Christ Church, by the cross-roads near the Sheldonian Theatre in Oxford. I was, of course, greatly in awe of this man, whose lectures I had attended; the adjective 'magisterial' might have been invented just for him. I had not long before heard him on BBC radio, doing a broadcast review of the recent publication of Geza Vermes's new book—still a landmark—*Jesus the Jew*.[1] He had entitled his talk, with an ironic glance at a famous line from Swinburne, 'A Rather Pale Galilean'.[2] We talked briefly about the book and about Vermes's claim to be writing simply 'as a historian'. 'When people who invoke the word "history"', commented Chadwick, 'show us that they understand what "history" actually is, then we shall take them seriously'.

There may be some kinds of 'theology', even with a strong pedigree within the tradition, which neither need nor want history; but a specifically *Christian* theology has no choice.[3] Christian theology needs history, even though it hasn't always known how to do it or what to do with it. It isn't just that biblical exegesis—the attempt to discover what the original texts meant in their contexts—is a branch of ancient history. It goes to the heart of the central Christian claims. There is a reason why Pontius Pilate turns up in the Creed. The Christian theologian faces questions about incarnation, 'salvation history', and so on. But that is just the start. 'History' is not simply a lump of clay preventing Docetic hot-air balloons taking off vertically into the clouds, never being seen again. Those who pray that God's kingdom will come and his will be done 'on earth as in heaven' are *ipso facto* committed to focusing on real life, real space-time-and-matter existence, *not as an illustration of abstract truth but as the ultimate reality to which the best 'abstract truths' bear humble witness.* According to the New Testament, Jesus himself—the human being, the man from Galilee who died on a cross—is the full, definitive revelation of who the One True God really is and what he is up to. He is not an 'example' or 'illustration', even the ultimate illustration, of an abstract principle or a true doctrine. Principles and doctrines refer to him and must defer to him. This means history. History is inescapable. Doing theology (including natural theology) without engaging in the tasks of history is like playing the violin without a bow. Pizzicato theology, if you like.

Part of my main argument in this book is that the task of history is a necessary, but normally absent, ingredient in 'natural theology'. Jesus lived in the 'natural' world of first-century Galilee. Reimarus and others insisted we look for him there. That might have been, from their point of view, an 'own goal': supposing we did, and there he was? The fact that our main historical sources, the Gospels, are part of Christian scripture ought neither to be invoked as special help ('we Christians have an inside track') nor to be dismissed as special pleading ('that's special revelation, so it doesn't count'). The texts are still there, still claiming to talk about real events—events in the 'natural' world.

Let me fill this out a bit. I want to suggest—though this will be a tentative probe rather than a full-dress exposition—that history, properly understood, might be a missing ingredient to help theology accomplish what appears, to an outside observer, to be among its goals. It sometimes seems to the onlooker that certain movements in today's natural theology are trying to achieve, by logical inferences alone, what Bishop Butler had hoped to achieve roughly three hundred years ago but which had seemed nearly impossible after 1755: a Christian apologetic which might begin in the world of space, time and matter and end by speaking of the one true God. Of course, if we were to begin with Jesus, and the biblical writings about him, this will not be what most have meant by a 'natural theology', since if we start there we shall be using sources normally regarded as part of 'revealed truth' rather than as part of 'nature'. But Jesus himself was a figure of the real world. The Gospels are real documents from the real world. To refuse to treat them as 'natural' evidence because the Christian tradition has seen them as 'revelation', and to dismiss Jesus similarly because the Christian tradition has confessed him to be God incarnate, looks like the sceptic bribing the judges before the trial. Once a post-Humean 'history' demonstrated to its own satisfaction that the docetic Jesus of popular Christian imagination was not to be found in the texts, it was only a small step to conclude (wrongly, but understandably) that he was of no theological significance, natural or otherwise. But this is a mistake. Ruling the Gospels out of consideration is just as unscientific as putting them on a pedestal, safeguarded against rigorous historical investigation.

All of this hints, in fact, at a fallacy in the way 'natural theology' is often set up. Human beings and their writings are part of the 'natural world'. Or was the idea always to exclude from the start those elements of the 'natural world'—the writings of the first Christians—which some Christian traditions had seen as 'divinely inspired'? Some critics demanded that the case for belief in God be made without appeal to such sources; others set about undermining the sources themselves, seeing them as later self-serving propaganda, leaving Jesus himself as simply a Jewish teacher or revolutionary. The latter position is still widely held. Christian theology cannot walk away from these challenges. If the early Christians were wrong to claim that Jesus himself was the 'image of the invisible God', one might still want to salvage some elements of Christian theology or spirituality from the resultant wreck; but the enterprise itself would be a very different kind of thing. For a fully Christian theology we need history, even though—no, precisely because of the fact that—history deals with the uncomfortable and messy 'real world'. And it is in that messy 'real world' that Jesus was crucified—the event above all which his first followers came to see in the light of Easter as the unveiling of the nature and saving purpose of the Triune God.

To take this further, we must begin at the beginning, with some careful reflections on what 'history' is and how we 'do history' in relation to the New Testament. This may turn out to be more than simply a necessary adjunct to the theological task; it may be the central motor. Those whose encounter with supposedly historical study of early Christianity has been confusing and negative may not welcome this conclusion. But that itself, as the argument progresses, may be part of the point.

'History', after all, is not neutral. It is shifting sand. The notion of 'history', and the discipline which bears that name, have themselves been part of the cultural, sociological and political struggles discussed so far. Earlier times understood an easy connection between past and present. But from the Renaissance onwards the idea of a temporal break became more apparent.[4] *This is the equivalent, in the understanding of time, of the Epicurean break between our world and the divine.* The past was now remote and opaque. Revolutions were shaping the present and the future. A new professional historiography was therefore required, with professional historians appointed to official chairs in universities, training people to grasp what before was assumed to be familiar. And, as the rationalists separated past from present, the romantics looked back sadly, trying to glimpse a lost world. 'Schöne Welt, wo bist du?' asks Schiller. Schubert, setting that stanza,[5] moves poignantly between minor and major. Only in the magic land of song, says the poem, does the sweet springtime of nature live on. 'Keine Gottheit zeigt sich meinem Blick': no divinity appears to my gaze. Lessing's ditch separates not just contingent and eternal but also past and present. Only a shadow remains.[6]

So does 'history' now mean rationalistic investigation, romantic imagination, or both, or neither, or a mixture, or what? Other voices soon proposed new ways of linking past and present. Perhaps there were overarching themes, patterns, inner movements, a sense of an onward journey which might be 'scientifically' retrieved. A sense, perhaps, of a goal, a *telos*: 'history' was all along *going somewhere*, and perhaps it was almost there. . . . Perhaps one might grasp it by revisiting the myths from that old Greek world and allowing them to speak to the human condition again. Nineteenth-century Germans loved those myths, seeing in them a genuine reconnection with the past, and hence with deeper meaning. That is where D. F. Strauss came in. Casting the Jesus-story as 'myth' was his way of saying that *this* was how to connect with the past, whereas Anglo-Saxons, deaf to the cultural point, only heard him saying, 'So most of that stuff didn't happen'. These proposals were closely connected with the political movements of the time, in a Europe full of new possibilities and dangers. 'History', it was supposed, might be a new way to find out who we are and where we're going in the strange, rootless new world now opening up.

Thus the modern discipline of history was born out of the same cultural crisis that I have already described. There is no reassuring, neutral area called 'history' to which we can retreat, nurse our wounds, and plan further strategies. 'History' is itself contested territory, part of the battlefield. The discipline which investigates the contingent has itself developed contingently. The sands were shifting then, and they're shifting still.

Part of my purpose in this book is to stress that, from a theological point of view, this is as it should be. A glance at our primary subject matter makes the point. History is, I suggest, the risky public discourse which matches and celebrates the divine risk, the divine humility, of incarnation itself. Shying away from that risk has been endemic among Jesus' followers from the start. Christians in general and theologians in particular are regularly tempted to copy Peter at Caesarea Philippi, assuming, against Jesus' own protest, that we know what his Messiahship (still more, his 'divinity'!) ought to mean and where it ought to lead. They are then tempted to copy Peter in Gethsemane, one minute trying to defend Jesus and the next minute denying him. (The evangelists hint, perhaps, that the attempted defence was itself a form of denial.)[7] These are the standard Petrine temptations, demanding the penitence and recommissioning of John 21.15–17 ('Simon, son of John, do you love me?'). Jesus—the Jesus of our sources, historical and theological—resists attempts to define him or defend him, knowing that both may already involve, or may well end in, denial. He demands that we pay attention to what he is actually doing, saying and being. And that means taking history seriously.

History, I therefore suggest, requires humility, patience, penitence and love. Just because we want to think clearly, that doesn't mean we can escape the methodological demands of Christian virtue. To cash these out: it requires humility, to understand the thoughts of people who thought differently from ourselves; patience, to go on working with the data and resist premature conclusions; penitence, to acknowledge that our traditions may have distorted original meanings and that we have preferred the distortions to the originals; and love, in that genuine history, like all genuine knowledge, involves the delighted affirmation of realities and events outside ourselves, and thoughts different from our own.

In this chapter I shall try to do six things. First, I shall disentangle the quite different meanings which the word 'history' itself regularly bears. Confusion here often derails discussion before it really gets going, and clarity is vital. Second, I shall lay out some initial results of this clarification, looking particularly at historical study of the New Testament and arguing for a particular understanding of the historian's task. Third, I shall attempt to bring some clarity to the vexed term 'historicism', issuing a health warning against its casual use. Fourth, I shall return briefly to the question of Jesus within his historical context. Fifth, I shall argue for a fresh understanding of what history can and should contribute. Sixth and finally, I shall reflect more broadly on the task of the Christian historian.

WHAT IS 'HISTORY'?

So what do we mean by 'history' itself? Many professional historians have written books asking, 'what is history', dealing with the subject at a large scale; but I want to go behind that to some even more basic data.[8] The word itself is slippery and ambiguous, and there are signs that some discussions, particularly of the interplay between history and theology, have slid to and fro across different meanings, producing confusion.

At a popular level the slipperiness is so common that we scarcely notice it. A sports commentator, watching a racing driver crash his car, declares, 'He's history'. The next minute a politician says it's important to be 'on the right side of history'. The first of these means 'past events that are gone for good'; the second is 'the inexorable movement of events towards a desired goal'. An article in the periodical *Foreign Affairs* says that 'history is full of surprises' and then, in the same paragraph, that 'history is driven by the interaction of geopolitics, institutions and ideas'. The first of these means 'the sum total of all past events', and the second 'the way that important events happen'.⁹ In the same issue a reviewer describes a book as 'an exhaustive history' and reports on someone saying to a Prime Minister, 'I hope history will be kind to you'. The first of these is 'history' as an *assemblage* of all that is known about the relevant past; the second is 'history' as *subsequent evaluation* of a particular set of actions.¹⁰ Alan Bennett, playwright and diarist, comments sardonically on Hilary Mantel's *Wolf Hall*: 'History is a playground. The facts are Lego. Make of them what you will'.¹¹ History, in other words, is not just about collecting facts; it's about arranging them into patterns that make sense to us. Bennett, thinking of tutors from his Oxford undergraduate days, separates out historians who focused on 'what actually happened' from those for whom 'history was a skating rink on which they could show off their techniques, turn their paradoxes'.¹² The novelist Malcolm Bradbury, alive to multiple ironies, introduces his quasi-historical novel *To the Hermitage* (whose hero is the eighteenth-century French intellectual Denis Diderot) by explaining that 'history is the lies the present tells in order to make sense of the past', and that Diderot himself knew that 'history was the future's complaint against the present'.¹³ At this level of popular usage, to be sure, there is little confusion. We shift easily enough between these and other shades of meaning. But in theology they cause real problems, and theologians ought not to rest content, here of all places, with serial ambiguity.

Tracing the English word to Latin and Greek originals, 'history' is often defined in terms of an *account* of past events; a continuous written *narrative* of select past events; the *discipline* which deals with such things; and then the *past events* themselves. This ordering, as in the *Oxford English Dictionary*, follows etymology, where the Latin *historia* refers primarily to a written account, from which the larger meanings branch out into the general, arm-waving gesture of 'the aggregate of past events in general'.

Many today, however, would do it the other way around. As one recent writer puts it, 'history' can refer to the past, to the study of the past or to the representation of the past.¹⁴

Two other meanings, not noted in the *OED*, have crept in over the last two centuries. First, there is the opening up of 'events in general' to include the future as well as the past ('the future history of our country' meaning 'whatever course of events will occur here'). This might be justified in terms of the perspective of future historians, looking back on what now seems future to us. But when someone now says, 'at any time in history', meaning either events long past or events in the distant future, that perspective has gone and been replaced with an arm-waving generalisation. Second, linked to this, another meaning of comparatively recent coinage is to treat 'history' in terms of *a particular direction in which events are moving* (hence, 'being on the right side of history').

To get a handle on all this—and to prepare for our biblical and theological reflections—I propose here a reasonably rigorous account of current usages of the word 'history', starting where the *OED* ends ('events') and working back, though with more refinements on the way. The four options are to have 'history' refer to *events*; to *narratives* about events; to the *task* which historians undertake; and to the *meaning* they and others discern in events, especially in the sequence of events. Only so can we then take stock of the ways in which different cultural and theological agendas have tended to favour one or another of these meanings, and, with that, of the methods they require.

Here, then, is the first meaning. **'History' refers to events**, normally in the past, but sometimes even in the future as well: the vast accumulation of events, almost all unknown and unknowable. When we say, 'at some point in history', this is the sense we have in mind. Thus, if we were to say that 'history is the theatre of sovereign divine action', we would mean the entire sweep and flow, not only of past events but of future ones too. To refer to 'history' in this sense requires no research. Claims about it are unfalsifiable, since they emerge *a priori* from a theological commitment. When theologians refer to 'history', this totality is normally what they mean.[15]

An important sub-category uses the word for **the knowable past**, the far smaller accumulation of events for which, frequently by accident, we have evidence. This would include some events for which there is no written record. We know, beyond any doubt, that the dinosaurs were wiped out at a certain point, even though neither they nor anyone else wrote about it at the time. Fossils and other archaeological evidence speak for themselves. One can postulate a series of steps: the whole of the past, the hypothetically knowable past, the demonstrable past.[16]

The question then arises as to what counts as 'knowable', introducing us to the sliding scale of epistemology. The Cartesian sceptic (or the ironic cynic, as in the quotations above from Bennett and Bradbury) will cast doubt in all directions, but in real life we almost always settle for what appear strong probabilities. People sometimes talk as if all historical events are uncertain. But, to anticipate where this discussion will take us, almost nobody doubts that Jesus of Nazareth died by crucifixion or that Jerusalem was destroyed by the Romans in AD 70. And, as we shall see, fixed points like those often provide a solid platform for much else.

This bifurcated first meaning (history as *events*, unknown or known) will include the perceptions, reflections and reactions, if any, of participants or observers at the time. As we shall see, 'history' in the sense of 'what happened' regularly demands that we study the motives and intentions of the characters involved. Investigating what Josephus was thinking as he toured the walls of Jerusalem, looking at thousands of crucified Jews and trying to rescue his friends, is itself part of the overall 'history' of AD 70. Asking whether Jesus of Nazareth believed it was his vocation to be crucified, and if so what meaning he attached to that, is part of 'history' in this sense. History, as we have already said, regularly involves the attempt to think into the minds of people who think differently to ourselves.[17] This task of describing how people thought at the time is then closely related to the task of analysing *why* particular events happened, which points to further meanings below.

With this meaning ('event') we associate the adjective 'historical'. Like the noun, this regularly conveys the assertion that something *actually happened*, as opposed to its being fictitious. Thus 'the death of Mr Rochester's first wife' is not 'historical', but 'the death of the last pterodactyl' is: we know it happened even though we don't know when or where. There is a muddle to be cleared up here. English uses the adjective 'historic' to indicate that an event, or even a place or building, *carried particular significance*. The election of the first African American President was a *historic* event; nobody doubts that it was 'historical', i.e. that it really happened. But 'historical', confusingly, is often used today to mean 'significant', where 'historic' would be technically correct.[18] Saying that something is 'historical' thus normally means that it *really happened* in the past, that it is *not fictitious*, and that it is *in principle knowable*.

The next meaning is **'History' as the *written account* of past events.** An important distinction here is between 'history' itself and mere 'annals' or 'chronicles'; 'history' tells a whole story, making continuous *sense* of events, looking for and displaying connections and consequences. It implies continuity—some sense of causes and consequences, of a sequence with developments, disruptions, recapitulations and results. History includes 'story', logically as well as etymologically; and this implies more than an undifferentiated eagle's-eye view of everything that has ever happened. Sometimes a 'history' might over-confidently make a claim to be exhaustive or definitive (*The* History of the Civil War), but in fact all history-writing proceeds by selection and arrange-ment. The only time you can say everything is when there is almost nothing to be said. Selection and arrangement, of course, involve the interpretative judg-ment of the historian (see below); but so far we are talking about the way the word is used, differentiating 'history' as *events* (e.g. the war that actually took place between Athens and Sparta in the late fifth century BC) and 'history' as *written account of events* (e.g. Thucydides' book *The Peloponnesian War*).[19] This is why we sometimes speak of 'pre-history' or of 'pre-historic' events: things that happened before anything we can write about and/or before anyone back then wrote about them. Ancient historians sometimes speak of the moment, whether with Herodotus or with the Solomonic Succession narrative, when we move from pre-history to 'history'.

These first two meanings present us with an important linguistic prob-lem. In German, 'history as past events' is *Geschichte*, while 'history as written account' is *Historie*. Rudolf Bultmann, however, used these terms differently. For him, *Historie* combined these two, while he used *Geschichte* to denote events and/or narratives that carried theological freight.[20] This, as we shall see, has produced considerable confusion in discussions of 'the historical Jesus'. Many still use that phrase in the first sense: 'Jesus himself as he actually was'. Others insist on using it—and frequently critiquing it—in the second: 'Jesus as historians reconstruct him'. To this, too, we shall return.

The next definition is that of **'History' as the *task*: of researching and writing about things that actually happened,** as opposed to producing fiction or fantasy. This is what actual historians think they are doing: 'doing history'. Theologians who are inclined toward 'classical theism' normally do not refer to this meaning of the word, except perhaps when discussing 'historical criticism' as a problem for theology.

We distinguish 'doing history' in this sense from, as we say, *making* history, i.e. doing things which bring about certain meaning-laden effects. Julius Cae-sar both *made* history and *wrote* history; so did Winston Churchill; but this is rare. Most Romans would only ever know what Caesar had done in Gaul through Caesar's own account, so that he was not only accomplishing 'facts on the ground' but, through his writings, ensuring the victory of his way of looking at the events over any possible rivals. Churchill was doing something similar in writing the history of the Second World War, though in his case of course there were and are millions of other sources against which his account could be checked. Historians normally have to spend too long grubbing around in the sources, and wrestling with copy-editors, to be able to change the world, except insofar as their writings, like the flapping of a butterfly's wings, may sometimes cause a storm somewhere.

The distinction between the two parts of the task—finding out what happened and then arranging it in a meaningful sequence—is subtle but important. When a distraught relative arrives at the scene of a tragedy, he or she might say, 'I just want to know what happened'. There will be a time for evaluation, for blame or excuse, but the first thing is to establish the facts. When the great nineteenth-century German historian Leopold von Ranke declared that his aim was to tell the reader 'wie es eigentlich gewesen' ('as it actually happened'),[21] he was not declaring an ambitious positivism, as some have supposed. He was, rather, modestly declining to offer grand overarching interpretative schemes, such as some of his contemporaries were attempting, in which the past could be 'judged' and lessons learnt for the future.[22] He was not, as people sometimes imagine, claiming that everything could be known or indeed that what could be known could be verified quasi-mathematically. He was merely contrasting his own attempt at simple *description of events* with the then popular ambition of large-scale *evaluation and prediction*. He was setting himself the task of researching and producing a *narrative* telling about *events* that actually happened—including things that, though themselves leaving no trace, were certainly to be inferred from events for which there was evidence. On the way, he was forswearing any big-picture evaluations such as the Hegelians wanted to offer. Of course, he too needed to select and arrange. He was perfectly aware that through that door, necessarily left open because the only alternative is mere unsorted 'chronicle', more subtle kinds of personal evaluations could creep in.

Here the complexity of usage begins to come fully into view, as we see how the various currents of philosophical and theological thought have affected what people have supposed 'history' itself might be. The philosophical Idealists (Hegel and his followers) will treat 'history as past events' as the incidental raw material for big overarching theories. Von Ranke, in sharp distinction, saw 'events', 'what actually happened', as the goal.

Von Ranke was here echoing an aim going way back in history-writing. The fourteenth-century John Barbour knew, and displayed, the difference between (a) the pleasure of a good tale (whether true or not), (b) the importance of remembering the great deeds of those long gone and (c) the pleasure of learning what actually happened ('the thing rycht as it wes').[23] But, since all history that goes beyond mere chronicle or annals involves selection and arrangement, and since all 'selection and arrangement' involves some principle, and since the principles are held by the human beings who do the selecting and arranging, this is bound to move towards a further definition: that of history as *meaning*. It would, however, be a juvenile mistake to suppose that, because selection and arrangement are always involved, we can never attain to true knowledge of the past but must always collapse into subjectivism, into 'knowledge' of the inside of our own imaginations.[24] Just because I have a reason for wanting to tell you something, that doesn't mean I'm making it up.

'History' as *task* can further imply the work of **discerning and displaying some kind of connection, pattern or principle—and hence, some** *meaning*—**within things that actually happened**. Selection and arrangement involve some kind of principle, and the question then is whether the historian allows the evidence to suggest the principle or insists on superimposing an alien principle on the evidence.

So what might 'meaning' itself mean in this context? If, following the philosopher Ludwig Wittgenstein, we see the meaning of a word as its use in the sentence, and the meaning of a sentence as its use in a paragraph or larger unit, then the 'meaning' of an event or a sequence of events will be *its perceived role within some larger narrative or symbol-set*. But: whose narrative? Which symbol-set?

This might vary. Someone in a Sarajevo bar on June 28, 1914, might have said that the assassination of Archduke Ferdinand 'meant' that you could never trust those coach-drivers; the fellow took a wrong turning, and there were the assassins. Gavrilo Princip, the assassin himself, might have deduced a very different 'meaning', namely a stroke of amazing luck: he'd botched the first attempt and then was presented with a second chance. Vienna newspapers the next day might have seen it as 'meaning' that the Serbs now needed to be taught a lesson. The *Chicago Daily Tribune* got it wrong: now Ferdinand has gone, said the paper, there's a better chance of peace.[25] Generals and crowned heads around Europe, fatefully, saw it as the call to arms for which they had been preparing. *They had seen that history was 'going this way' and were eager to help it along*. In hindsight, a century later, *we* give it a different meaning again: the trigger for four years of crazy butchery and fifty years of inhumane wickedness. We see it as tragedy, recognising in long retrospect that Ferdinand was the one man who might have prevented it all.[26] The meaning of an event is its use in a larger narrative.

Those examples work differently. The man in Sarajevo, and the journalists, would simply be adding new twists to old stories. Our long hindsight, as the consequences continue to unfold, generates a head-shaking penitence for nineteenth-century optimism. But for Europe's royalty, and especially the generals, there was already a solid, larger narrative in place. Plans were drawn up.

Troops were prepared. They 'knew' which way history was going. They'd been saying so for some time. People now just had to get on board. Meaning varies according to the story.

To return to von Ranke: however much he disclaimed any grand ambitions, he had to have some organising principles, some overall narrative, or he couldn't have even begun work. He had no intention of saying 'what actually happened' at every moment of every day in every house and street in Germany. He, like everybody else, had to select and arrange. The reason for this, and the criteria by which it is done, has to do with the 'meaning' we are discerning. As we shall see presently, the task of the historian, in this respect quite like the task of the scientist, is to bring the evidence and the hypothetical meaning (and hence the proposed selection and arrangement) into dialogue. To work with no evidence and only a hypothetical 'meaning' is to capitulate to some sort of Idealism; to pretend that there is no guessed-at meaning, that we are simply working inductively from raw data, is naïve. That is the fulcrum across which the see-saw of modern debate has taken place, with those on either side accusing the other of methodological impropriety.[27] That is why, I shall suggest, we need a mature form of critical realism, the careful application of the epistemology of love, in which the hermeneutical spiral of hypothesis and attempted verification is allowed to proceed at its own pace.

'Meaning' regularly involves the study of consequences. When I was first introduced to the work of Martin Luther I was told, in effect, that the mediaeval church had covered up the Bible and the gospel, and that Luther had given them back to the world—resulting, it was assumed, in a new flourishing of Christianity. That is not everybody's perception. Some have now widened this, seeing Luther (for good or ill) as the precursor of the Enlightenment. Some have hailed him as the father of modern Europe and North America, including its ambiguous ideology of 'freedom'. Many current 'historical' retellings of Luther's story are designed to bring that out, whether to exalt the hero who launched the modern world or to shake one's head over the villain who opened the Pandora's box of modernist horrors. All these retellings are concerned with 'meaning'.

The task of investigating the 'meaning' of events includes, though it often goes way beyond, the study of *human intentionality*, as part of the answer to the question 'why' something happened. Comparatively few events (except things like earthquakes) are a matter of random inanimate causation. Even an earthquake might have effects which involve the fact that humans had chosen to build towns in dangerous locations. A large part of the task of investigating meaning within events therefore involves the study of the intentionality of the characters involved, which as we saw is in any case implicit already in the study of the event itself. This means looking for what is sometimes referred to as the 'inside' of events, not just the 'outside' physical facts. And this in turn, as we shall see, involves studying the larger world, and worldview, of their societies and cultures, always alert of course for the possibility of radical innovation or mutation within those worldviews. What this variation within the 'task' means in practice we will discuss presently.

The term 'History' is also used to mean 'History as a meaningful *sequence* of events', either in the sense that the sequence or the events have meaning in themselves or in the sense that they are 'going somewhere', that they have a 'goal' in view. This is the sense of 'history' invoked when people speak of being 'on the right side of history': a popularized version of Hegel, Marx or others, that world events are necessarily or automatically proceeding in a determined way, in a closed continuum, to a foreordained goal, perhaps in a grand return to an earlier golden age. The claim to know 'where history was going' was made explicitly on behalf of the new monarchies in Britain in the late seventeenth century and the new republic in America in the late eighteenth: history (so the message ran) has turned a corner, and we are the future, recapitulating the great classical civilisations of old![28] Actually, this kind of reading of a nation's history goes much further back. Ever since people started telling the story of Britain in terms of Magna Carta, the principle of 'increasing liberty' has been a controlling theme, appealed to both by Cromwell's men in the 1640s and by the Restorationists in the 1660s.

This brings us back to the clash of narratives in the eighteenth century. The question asked by historians was seldom if ever simply 'what happened?' but 'what does it mean?' European culture had lived off various narratives, including versions of the Christian story in which (a) God is ultimately in control, (b) the story reached its climax with Jesus, and (c) we are doing our best, often with pain and trouble, to trust (a) and live up to (b). However, as Deism gave way to full-on Epicureanism, all three elements had to go—or rather, they had to be replaced with 'secular' equivalents. Thus (a) the story was controlling itself from within; (b) it had just reached its climax in the Enlightenment itself; (c) we must 'get on the right side of history' by advancing the cause of 'liberty'. This complex but powerful 'meaning' lay behind the so-called 'rise of historical consciousness' associated with David Hume, William Robertson and Edward Gibbon.

This was emphatically not a delight in the past for its own sake. It did not pretend that no previous history had ever been attempted; Hume and the others knew their Herodotus and Thucydides. But it had to be more explicit about worldview. As in other spheres, if God was out of the picture, events must be taking their own course. We note the 'must': an inner sense of causation has taken the place of providence.[29] Thus the telling of the past, both positive and negative (think of Gibbon's debunking of the early church), was seen as part of a larger Epicurean project, worked out in politics, science and economics as much as in history. The 'historical movement' was a way of claiming control over the past in order to seize control over the present and the future, as with Voltaire and others.[30] For Hegel, *the events themselves* were the 'history' that beckoned people to join 'the right side'.

I will come in a moment to the attempt at meaningful *writing*; the point here is that writers in this period were arguing that *the events themselves carried the meaning of 'progress'*. The high-water mark of this, producing many streams and rivers of subsequent thought and political action, was Hegel himself. In theology, and I think philosophy as well, and certainly in popular culture, this theme is everywhere apparent. Thus when people say that 'history teaches us' this or that, they do not mean that those who write history (narratives displaying events) have inserted a 'moral' into their narrative (though that might be true as well). They mean that the events themselves convey a message, often about the internally driven 'progress' through which culture is moving inexorably towards the fulfilment of the libertarian Enlightenment dream. 'Meaning', in other words, is found in the significance of the events themselves as they are perceived to carry an inbuilt purpose and a definite final goal. *A great deal of philosophical and theological writing about 'history', as opposed to the writing of historians themselves, has something like this in mind.* If, with standard modern Epicureanism, there is no 'god' in this picture, then events, on both the large and small scales, must either be completely random and meaningless or carry some meaning within themselves. Since theology abhors a vacuum, such 'meanings' can easily come to invoke different kinds of divinity (Mammon? Mars? Aphrodite?), though this is usually left implicit.[31]

To display this sense of meaning, of course, writers resort to a further usage: that **'"History" is a meaningful *narration* of events'**. We think once more of Hegel and Marx, and those who have written history to display their theories in practice. But we also think of ancient Hebrew writing. The compilers of the Pentateuch, of Joshua and Judges, of the books of Samuel, Kings and Chronicles, all wrote with a sense that the events of Israel's past were to be seen as part of a larger, if often perplexing, divine purpose, and that they themselves were called to display the events in such a way as to bring out, or at least hint at, that purpose. Sometimes this was done in a heavy-handed way, as when the books of Kings ascribe good and bad behaviour to this or that king and point out almost mechanically what happened as a result. But it could also be done with a light touch. The writer of 2 Samuel does not say that David's adultery resulted in Absalom's rebellion, but we are invited to infer it. The Hebrew text of Esther, having explained that Jews in Susa were holding a three-day fast to pray for deliverance, then says, laconically, 'that night the king could not sleep' (Esther 6.1).[32] Divine action is often to be inferred, not least by means of intertextual allusion. When the early Christians wrote the story of Jesus their clear implication was, 'Let us explain to you that these events were the goal of Israel's long story and, through their world-changing significance, the launching of a new story upon the world'. Within that, their textual allusions were also saying, 'The person whose story we are telling is to be seen as the living embodiment of Israel's God'.[33] The only other people we know of in the ancient world who did anything like this were Virgil, Livy and their antecedents, explaining that Rome's long history had been a preparation for the glories of Augustus and his golden age. A complex narrative with a teleological meaning: this was 'where it had all being going'.[34]

There are doubtless many other sub-meanings which the word 'history' has carried in popular or academic usage. But these four—'history' as *events*, as *narration*, as *task* and as *meaning*—are a start. Of course, when people are actually 'doing history', most of these senses may be in play at once. I am not suggesting that these meanings denote different or mutually exclusive *activities*. My point is that *the way the word is used* slides to and fro between these meanings, and no doubt others as well. That is where confusion easily arises—especially in theology.

INITIAL RESULTS

This analysis invites three initial comments. First, we must consider the question of historical epistemology (including the proposals of Rudolf Bultmann); then, more briefly, historical ontology; then, finally, the combined questions of cosmology and eschatology.

Historical Epistemology

The first usage of 'history', 'history as *event*', sets up a classic dichotomy in modern thought: the lure of positivism can generate its opposite, radical doubt.[35] Hardly any questions of 'what happened', even in modern history, admit of absolute precision, especially when we add, as we noted above, that historical investigation includes the study of human motivation. Can we really 'know'? Lawyers meet this problem all the time. A jury steeped in Descartes, or even in Troeltsch, might be dogged with radical doubt; but, whereas the historian can wait forever, the court must reach a verdict. Juries detect guilt, or infer it, and convict on the balance of probabilities. Actually, we all work with the balance of probabilities. Scientists sometimes pretend to absolute knowledge—until new data shows up, requiring hypotheses to be revisited.

In the field of historical investigation of the Bible and early Christianity there is another factor to be considered. The story we have told over the previous two chapters has influenced the way the word 'history', and the activities and products associated with it, are understood and performed. Much of the early historical investigation of the New Testament was done in Germany between the late eighteenth and the early twentieth century, just when the German Enlightenment, with Kant as its patriarch, Hegel as its Moses, and a line of prophets from Goethe to Feuerbach and beyond, was eager to challenge traditional Christianity and cut it down to size. The aim was precisely not to find 'what actually happened' in some supposedly 'neutral' fashion but to 'discover' *what ought to have happened* if the ideals of the Enlightenment, and with them the great new European culture-project as a whole, were to be valid. Hence *the pressure to epistemological caution, if not downright scepticism, was powerfully reinforced by the social, cultural and theological pressure towards forms of radical Protestantism.*

Here is the ambiguity of the vexed phrase 'the historical-critical method'. For many in Germany, up to and including the exegetes of the 1960s, the 'historical-critical method' was a way of using 'historical' tools—source criticism and the like, but also an innate scepticism, sometimes associated with Ernst Troeltsch (see below)—to produce the 'results' of a slimmed-down Christianity, indeed a slimmed-down Protestantism, to fit the philosophy and culture of the times. However, many in the Anglo-Saxon world, not being tuned in to Hegel, Feuerbach and the rest, have continued to use the phrase 'historical-critical' in a much more apparently 'neutral' sense. Thus C. K. Barrett declared that the great J. B. Lightfoot used only one method in his commentaries, namely 'the historical-critical method', meaning that 'the primary and inescapable task of exegesis is to determine the precise meaning of the words in question in the context in which they were first spoken or written'.[36] With that statement of method on the table, if you said you were *not* following 'the historical-critical method', you would be confessing to arbitrary and home-made pseudo-exegesis, quite possibly determined by some kind of fundamentalism, and producing historical dishonesty. So when English speakers were told that the Germans, using the historical-critical method, had produced assured 'results', they heard this within an assumed Anglo-Saxon philosophy tending towards positivism, rather than a German one borrowing from Idealism. This has produced a backlash where some, seeing the negative results on offer, have rejected not only the sceptical agenda but the Barrett/Lightfoot method as well. Thus the phrase 'historical-critical', now widely used with the more general meaning, is still often heard to carry the stridently negative sense, producing suspicion and confusion. Cautious theologians sometimes cite the negative meaning as a way of absolving themselves from worrying about history at all—as though, hearing a broadcast of unpleasantly raucous music, one were to throw away the radio instead of tuning to a more congenial station. That is the context within which some have preferred to invoke 'history' in the broad sense not only of 'events' but of 'everything that happens' as a kind of outflanking movement. Since we know that God is the lord of 'history' in this sense, there is nothing more to be said, and even trying to say it, trying to do actual historical research, would constitute a form of unfaithfulness.[37]

So how, epistemologically speaking, does history 'work'? Not, to be sure, by following the three principles of the theologian, philosopher and politician Ernst Troeltsch. Troeltsch (1865–1923) taught in succession at Bonn, Heidelberg and ultimately Berlin. He laid down the criteria of (1) scepticism or 'criticism' (the Cartesian assumption that one must doubt everything that cannot be totally proved), (2) analogy (we can only admit events which have analogies in our own experience) and (3) correlation (events must be shown to belong within a cause-and-effect closed continuum).[38] These have had a good run for their money, though each is obviously flawed. Scepticism is necessary to rule out unthinking or naïve positivism, but it must lead on to fresh truth-seeking narratives. Nobody in real life lives by scepticism alone. Analogy fails to take account both of well-attested ancient practices unknown in our modern world (exposure of female infants, for instance) and of the possibilities of radical innovation (the first flight to the moon). Correlation, and the essentially Epicurean reading of history it presupposes, is designed to ward off the kind of 'interventionist Deism' which invokes sudden divine action 'from outside' to explain puzzling phenomena. But that was never a good model in the first place. A great many things in the world happen because of human desire, intention, and decision. The determined determinist may hope for the day when all of that can be logged scientifically, and in principle even predicted, but the proposed 'closed continuum' would be just as much an *a priori* as any possible Jewish or Christian commitment. The Jew or Christian might want here to suggest that the minds and hearts of those made in God's image might be one place (among others, perhaps) where divine action—not 'intervention from outside'—might be expected to play a quiet but sometimes decisive role. 'That night the king could not sleep'.

Rudolf Bultmann: History and Eschatology

One major influence on 'history' in New Testament studies has been Rudolf Bultmann, not least in the published version of his Gifford Lectures, *History and Eschatology*. We studied the overall themes of his work in the previous chapter, and we must now consider Bultmann's proposals about history in particular.

Bultmann worked with a particular notion of 'history', which within its own limits was relatively uncontroversial. He, like von Ranke, was determined to reject the 'historicism' of the type which saw the whole sweep of history itself as a seamless whole, a 'closed continuum' though now with social and political, not merely scientific, significance.[39] Looking back in hindsight from the 1950s, Bultmann like many of his contemporaries (such as Karl Popper in his famous book, *The Poverty of Historicism*) could see that the problem had been not simply with one crazy leader but with an entire ideology. (We shall discuss types of 'historicism' presently.) Bultmann saw with great clarity that this produced only a prison from which humans could never get free. God's future, he argued, could never be the natural result of historical development.[40] To make his point, he followed the Italian Benedetto Croce, the German D. F. Strauss and the Englishman R. G. Collingwood in looking (as von Ranke did not) not only at the 'outside' (the physical event) but at the 'inside' (the human motivation and intentionality) and using that as a way of avoiding the determinist conclusion.[41] 'History' as a monolithic juggernaut might appear to be rumbling on its inevitable way, but human beings have the chance, the responsibility even, to take decisions for themselves, awakening what Bultmann calls 'the eschatological moment', and so to write about the past in such a way as to bring out what Bultmann called its *geschichtlich* meaning, as opposed to its merely *historische* event-character, a distinction which might cautiously be rendered into English as its 'historic' meaning as opposed to its merely 'historical' meaning.[42]

Putting all this together, one's own self-identity becomes the clue to thinking about others. True historical knowledge is thus a form of self-knowledge.[43] 'Faith' is basically the 'decision' to be open to God's future, and it is therefore precisely opposed to 'history' in any sense that would restrict that freedom.[44] Believers thereby receive their own reality, rejoicing that it is after all not determined by 'history'. These intentions, which appeared good to Bultmann—his insistence on the inward turn away from outward constraints, coupled with his leaning towards Heideggerian existentialism and his putative 'historical' derivation of early Christian theology from non-Jewish sources—paved the road to something disturbingly similar to Gnosticism. This, ironically, has proved to be among the least historically sustainable of his proposals.

The 'historicism' which Bultmann was rejecting started with a particular construal of history-as-meaning and applied that backwards to history-as-event, without going through any of the steps required in history-as-task (no actual investigation was required) or attempting to produce, by selection and arrangement, a historical narrative in which human motivation would play a central role. Another irony: Bultmann seems to have done something very similar. Puzzlingly for a would-be historian, he seems not to have been interested at all in the actual *realia* of first-century Palestine; he never visited the Holy Land and showed no concern for the social and political movements that featured so prominently there in the first century. His strong neo-Kantian Idealism needed none of that. Like the historicists he was opposing, he knew in advance 'where history was going', and had no need to take prisoners, still less to convert them. His Lutheran inclinations had long been conditioned to see the Jews and their Law as part of the problem. They were not needed in his picture of early Christianity, except as a dark foil for the timeless, ahistorical gospel.

Bultmann's rejection of the truly historical disciplines, and his attempt to replace what he then called 'history' with what he called 'eschatology', have close analogies with what others have done more recently with what they have called 'apocalyptic'.[45] Invoking this word means, we are told in one recent account, putting a 'theology of history' first, before all else, so that 'the knowledge given to us in Jesus' history, expressed in the confession of who he is, is a knowledge of the end of human history and the beginning of a new kind of history'.[46] This, we are told, 'is an argument about the large sweep of human events and their ultimate meaning'.[47] Thus, to amplify what we said a moment ago, like the Hegelian historicism which Bultmann rightly rejected, this view skips between 'history-as-all-events' and 'history-as-ultimate-meaning' without going through—indeed, while rejecting as 'naturalistic' or 'immanentist'—any sense either of the historical task or of a historical narrative. It knows in advance what to 'find'. One can simply look down from a supposed great height, seeing world history from start to finish and believing that God in Christ is its true 'lord', shaking one's head in frustration over those poor benighted souls who insist on studying historical evidence and trying to produce coherent narratives about it as though for some reason that sort of thing mattered, denouncing them as 'methodological naturalists'. This supposedly 'supernaturalist' position now sometimes also claims the word 'apocalyptic', on the grounds, presumably, that that word gestures towards the sovereign freedom of God without reference to human events, or indeed human *investigation of* events. This approach thus *knows in advance what we ought to find*, and so finds it, astonishingly calling this process 'historiography'.[48] This is the 'end' of history in both senses. (1) It claims that in Jesus the history of the old world has come to a full stop, and (2) it uses that *a priori* position as a reason for refusing to do 'history' in the sense of 'task' or 'narrative', on the grounds that such activity 'must' be 'naturalistic', must be rejecting 'transcendence' and embracing 'immanence'. (Those categories, by the way, are almost as misleading as 'supernatural' and 'natural'.) As we saw earlier, 'history' in this broad sense neither requires nor desires research. It cannot be falsified. It is not only 'history' that comes to a stop here. Scholarly discourse, too, runs into a brick wall.

History, however, like other disciplines, abhors a vacuum. Bultmann advanced several actual proposals, trying among other things to make sense of his unquestioned belief that Jesus' resurrection was not an event involving an empty tomb or an actual living person who had once been dead, and that Jesus and his followers all expected the end of the world within a short time and were of course disappointed. His most famous proposal, which we have already mentioned, was that there must have been some kind of pre-Christian 'gnosis'—not necessarily a full-blown Gnosticism such as we find later—which formed the matrix for the early faith as Bultmann understood it. Second, and cognate with this, he saw the four Gospels as primarily witnesses to the self-expression of the church's faith, not as intending to report on actual events. (This has then become a classic example of cross-channel misunderstanding: Bultmann thought he was highlighting faith, but pragmatic Anglophone positivists thought he was arguing for doubt.) Third, he therefore regarded as a sad second-generation decline those works which seemed, after all, to think that history mattered: here he even included Paul's listing of eyewitness testimony to the risen Jesus in 1 Corinthians 15.3–8, but his obvious targets were the two-volume work of Luke and the supposedly high ecclesiology of Ephesians and Colossians. Rejecting these two has remained the fashionable position in much New Testament studies. Bultmann's other proposals have fallen by the wayside, for the rather obvious reason that they lacked basic evidence and failed to cohere with the increasing emphasis on the Jewish setting.

For Bultmann, then, with the gospel of the crucified Jesus, 'history' has come to a stop. Seeing the horror of the Third Reich, Bultmann decided to live, and indeed to preach, 'as if not'.[49] The believer is taken out of the world, while in another sense still living in the world.[50] At the climax of his book Bultmann takes nearly a whole page to quote enthusiastically from Erich Frank, who insists that the events to do with Jesus constituted 'an event . . . in the realm of eternity, an eschatological moment in which . . . this profane history of the world came to its end'. The believer is thus 'already above time and history', because 'an eternal event' has happened 'in the soul of any Christian'.[51] This is where Bultmann's simultaneous retrieval and demythologisation of the standard end-of-the-world hypothesis reaches its own goal. With the gospel, history has come to an end. Though Bultmann did not himself show any instinct for anything called 'apocalyptic', nor any inclination to retrieve it for himself, his conclusion has been eagerly seized upon by those who want to say that because the gospel is an 'apocalyptic' event this means that normal 'history' cannot, as it were, touch it.[52] If 'history' has come to a stop, something quite new, quite discontinuous, must begin in its place. This produces simply a new version of Lessing: doing ordinary history cannot contribute to the truths of theology.[53] This whole discussion highlights my underlying point in the present chapter. The word 'history' has become far too slippery for its own good. In the hands both of Bultmann and of recent writers like Rae and Adams, 'history' both as task and as necessary narrative is ruled out.

Thus, though there is much about Bultmann's account of history that overlaps with mine (his rejection of deterministic historicism and his stress on the 'inside' of events), here in particular we radically part company. He was, understandably both philosophically and politically, fighting hard against the 'historicism' which put together the broadest meaning of 'history-as-event' (everything that happens) with an *a priori* understanding of 'history-as-meaning'. The 'meaning' in question for him was the Hegelian notion of 'progress', imposed on the world with no possibility that fresh data could or would challenge it, even as, in the 1930s, the actual data all around was doing precisely that. He found his own way out of that dilemma by taking 'eschatology', clearly a major theme for Jesus and his first followers, and simultaneously misunderstanding it (supposing that it meant the end of the space-time universe) and demythologising it (turning it into a form of Platonic existentialism, or even of gnostic self-discovery). He rightly saw that actual historical research required a sympathetic look into the world of the 'other'. But Bultmann's own attempts at real history—his understanding of the ancient Jewish world, for instance, or of putative sources for early Christian faith-expressions in Hellenistic religions or philosophies—make it seem as though the sympathetic look was actually into a mirror.[54] There is truth in the dictum that historical knowledge is a form of self-knowledge. Taken by itself, however, it looks as though self-knowledge is all one is left with. No effort is then needed to think into the minds of people who think differently to ourselves.

What then can we say about Bultmann and history? He has very little to contribute on genuine historical method. For him, 'history' is always in danger of lapsing into either a misunderstood Jewish salvation-history or—which is not that different, for him!—a Hegelian determinist historicism, which he knows to have been politically disastrous. He sees that history has an 'inside' as well as an 'outside', allowing for the possibility of individual decision, motivation and so on, and this can and does disrupt the apparently iron determinism on the surface. But he does not explore how this two-sidedness might apply to actual first-century history (exploring the 'inside', the human motivations, of Jesus, Paul, and the rest). His aim was always to talk about the believer's present self-understanding. When he says that historical research needs a subject/object dialogue, he tends to collapse this each time towards the subject.[55]

History, in fact, always appears threatening to Bultmann, despite his supposed status as a leading 'historical critic'. I do not think this was solely due to his rejection of 1930s political historicism. It was deep in his theological and cultural DNA from much earlier. His early teachers, including J. Weiss and A. von Harnack, stood in a tradition for which 'faith' was, almost by definition, a 'present event' rather than having to do with 'objective events in the past'. (This might claim to look back to Melanchthon's emphasis on the essential *pro me* of the gospel, though that is another story.) His placing of the early Christians within a 'history of religions', especially when their native Jewish frame of reference was screened out, was pushing him this way too. His own historical reconstruction of the first century was entirely determined by his desire to place Paul and John in particular outside the flow and hopes of Jewish life in the period, which means relegating to a second (degenerate) generation anything which might look too Jewish—anything to do with the Law, with Apocalyptic, and so on.[56] He celebrated the demythologization of the 'imminent *parousia*' in terms of 'history coming to an end', but what this really meant for him was that *we are not to be determined by history* in the sense of being imprisoned by the blind forces of historical process. We are, rather, to make the existential decision which results in freedom. That existential moment, he says at the conclusion of the lectures, is always there as the true possibility, and 'you must awaken it'.[57] This has analogies with the theme which Walter Benjamin retrieved from Gershom Scholem: in every moment lies the possibility that the Messiah might arrive.[58] Here, whether he realised it or not, Bultmann was perhaps at his closest to genuine Jewish insight.

It should be clear that I regard Bultmann's methods and conclusions as historically unwarranted and theologically unhelpful. The way he uses the word 'eschatology' (see chapter 4 below) with an existentialist meaning is trying to say something very important—and it was certainly important to him and his congregations at a very difficult time—but it uses very misleading language, carrying all sorts of unwarranted connotations. As a result, his actual historical constructions lacked, at every point, the genuine dimension of New Testament thought which for all sorts of reasons he had already ruled out, namely new creation. That is the theme we shall pursue later in this book.

Critical Realism and the Historical Task

So if the scepticism of Troeltsch and the existentialism of Bultmann must themselves be subjected to damaging critique, how then is the *task* of history to be undertaken? When people try to research and produce written historical *narratives* which genuinely point to true past *events*, what place is there for any sense of *meaning* in history, and how can we be sure that this emerges from the study rather than simply being superimposed upon it?

I have proposed elsewhere, following Ben Meyer and Bernard Lonergan, a form of *critical realism*.[59] That phrase has been contested and controversial; I adopt it in a common-sense heuristic mode. To put it crudely, fake news exists, but that doesn't mean that nothing happened. A problem emerges at once, though: when we examine the critical-realist paradigm for doing history, it soon becomes apparent that the historian's own *sympathetic imagination* must play a vital role. Does that not invite the comment that this leaves the door open for the historian simply to make it all up?

In fact, no. The critical-realist historian operates with strict controls. The accumulated and detailed evidence is basic and must always remain so: evidence, that is, both about the central subject matter and about the wider world, and the wider worldview(s), within which the central events took place and were perceived and recorded. There is also the 'control' of the overall sense of the narrative that is finally offered, and its coherence with larger areas of study. Actually, the potential charge of subjectivism, because of the personal involvement of the historian with the reconstruction, is not so very different from the problem of the observer in scientific experiments. As physicists have long recognised, the 'observer effect' comes into play: you can't measure a system without affecting the thing you're measuring.[60] This personal involvement, so far from calling historical work into question (as being insufficiently 'objective') actually constitutes one key element in the task of critically realist historiography.

How then do historians go about it? The task has three normal phases. First, you investigate source materials (that is the original meaning of *historia* as used by Herodotus). Second, you form hypotheses about how the evidence might 'make sense', and you test these hypotheses against both the data and any rival theories that may have been advanced. Third, you work towards a *narrative* through which readers will know and understand the *events*.[61] This normally involves some gestures towards 'meaning', though there the ways diverge.

Let us expand this just a bit. The various activities involved in these three tasks are interlocking and mutually informative; they can in principle be distinguished even though, when at work, they are often all in play simultaneously. They are not (in other words) sequential, as though you had to complete each in turn before proceeding to the next.

First, *the historical task is always rooted in close attention to the data*. This may seem obvious, but some will find it to be the 'boring' bit and will be tempted to skimp. Trevelyan describes it as 'the day-labour that every historian must well and truly perform if he is to be a serious member of his profession'.[62] In the study of Christian origins there is no escape from total immersion in the world of the first century—Jewish, Greek, Roman and early Christian. Every text, every coin, every inscription counts.

Second, and no doubt commencing while the first task is under way, *history proceeds by hypothesis and verification*, just as science does. The hypothesis itself is formed in the imaginative mind of the person who has been immersed in the data, the raw material: is there a pattern, a common theme, a way of making sense of disparate or puzzling data? Are there connections, vital links, hidden causes and consequences? The hypothesis is tested rigorously against the data, with exactly the same three questions that the scientist asks: does this hypothesis get in the data? Does it do so with appropriate simplicity? Does it shed light on other areas beyond the original object of study? Of course, these are as flexible for the historian as they are in many cases for the scientist: what counts as 'getting in the data'? What sort of simplicity is 'appropriate', and how do we know? What will count as 'shedding light' on other areas? All of these questions invite further reflection. What matters is the interplay of the *carefully studied data* with the *interpretative human imagination*. Your developing 'big picture' and the study of the data are in ongoing dialogue.

There are two main differences between the study of the so-called 'hard sciences' and the study of history. First, science studies the repeatable—that which can be repeated in laboratory conditions (the exceptions to this would include astronomy and geology); history studies the unrepeatable—that which has already happened and will always remain unique (thus calling into question Troeltsch's principle of analogy).[63] The 'repeatable' element in history lies elsewhere: the 'experiment' that is repeated in scientific historical study is that historians all study (in principle) the same evidence.

The second difference takes us to the heart of the historical task. History, unlike (say) chemistry, includes centrally *the study of human motivations*. We want to know 'what happened', of course. But we also want to know, if we can, *why it happened*, not just in terms of physical causation ('the Archduke died because he was shot') but more especially in terms of human intention ('the Archduke died because Gavrilo Princip was a highly motivated revolutionary'). Sometimes human intention will appear on the surface of the data, as when Julius Caesar writes about what he was trying to do in his military campaigns (though the historian will always want to probe, too, for the hidden motives behind what is written). Normally it is an ongoing question at many different levels, and these levels gradually emerge as part of the hypothesis-formation as the evidence is being studied.

As this study proceeds, a central element, as we said before, is the task of thinking into the minds of people who think differently from ourselves. The 'sympathetic imagination' required for the formation of hypotheses must never mean that we imagine people in other cultures and ages to be just like our-selves. This was already central to the anti-Cartesian protest of Giambattista Vico in the seventeenth century. Isaiah Berlin, summarizing Vico's insistence on the study of human motivation, puts it like this:

> In short, we judge human activity in terms of purposes, motives, acts of will, decisions, doubts, hesitations, thoughts, hopes, fears, desires and so forth; these are among the ways in which we distinguish human beings from the rest of nature.[64]

This is part of what I am loosely calling the 'epistemology of love': we are not flies on the wall, 'neutral observers', but nor are we collapsing the evidence into our own ways of thinking. Thus, in Berlin's summary of the German philosopher J. G. Herder (1744–1803),

> It was Herder who set in motion the idea that since each of these civilisations has its own outlook and way of thinking and feeling and acting, creates its own collective ideals in virtue of which it is a civilisation, it can be truly understood and judged only in terms of its own scale of values, its own rules of thought and action, and not of those of some other culture: least of all in terms of some universal, impersonal, absolute scale.[65]

Thus, in the words of Herder's mentor J. G. Hamann,

> Each has its own vocabulary, [which can be grasped only with the passion of] a friend, an intimate, a lover.[66]

A lover! Yes indeed: one who simultaneously enters sympathetically into the life of the beloved while honouring and celebrating the vital differences between the two of them. This is the paradox of the epistemology of love, and we see it as clearly in the work of the historian as anywhere else. And, as we saw in chapter 1, it is precisely love that has been screened out by the epistemological tradition, traceable back to Descartes, that became dominant in many strands of post-Enlightenment thought—and of which Vico, Hamann and Herder were early and profound critics.

We may not get it right. That is part of the ongoing 'scientific' work. The evidence must be given every opportunity to answer back, to suggest alternative nuances. The question of what then counts as appropriate sympathetic imagination (how it arises, and how we stop it collapsing into an Idealism which would simply superimpose its own narrative on the evidence) remains important. Examples of people getting it wrong abound.[67] But it is possible, and necessary for the task of history, to discern, to describe, and imaginatively to inhabit other minds, other worldviews, and to see how people who saw the world like that would plan, make decisions, respond to events, and so on. This is fundamental to what historians do.[68]

To attend to the aims and motives of people different from ourselves, I and others have developed models of worldviews, 'social imaginaries', and the like.[69] As with other tools of thought, I use 'worldview' heuristically, not wishing to import any large abstraction but rather intending to be explicit about the reconstruction of aims and motives other than our own. The worldview model I have developed, composed of stories, symbols, praxis and key questions, enables us to be sure that we are not resting content with generalisations and in particular that we are not simply projecting our own assumptions on to people very different from ourselves, and to ensure that we really are essaying, at every step, hypotheses about the other minds we are investigating, hypotheses which can themselves then be tested against historical data. This is not, as has recently been suggested, a way of squashing events into a pre-formed pattern or importing a 'naturalistic' presupposition which would prevent us ever speaking of God.[70] The natural/supernatural split was in any case the wrong way of addressing these questions, as I argued earlier.[71] Using a tool like 'worldview' in the way I and others have done is simply the due diligence of the historian. It respects the many-sidedness of the actual circumstances and mindsets involved.

We can see the effect of this in some obvious examples. People used to think that Jesus got into trouble over apparent Sabbath-breaking, and over his Temple-demonstration, because the Jews were legalists or ritualists while he believed in free grace. This is simply a mistake. Sabbath and Temple were central *symbols* with known meanings that functioned within strong (if usually implicit) *narratives*, giving rise to particular *praxis* and providing implicit answers to the key worldview *questions* (who are we, where are we, what's wrong, what's the solution, and what time is it?). Jesus' radical kingdom-announcement resonated in his world in a way that has been opaque to ours for many generations (though careful study of known Jewish sources might have revealed things a long time ago, were it not that many theologians were conditioned to regard Jewish thinking as automatically dangerous).[72] The worldview-model is a way of disciplining the sympathetic imagination, alerting us to the danger of merely projecting our own ideas (even our own ideas of radical newness) back onto a fictitious screen.[73] Thinking into the minds of people who think differently from ourselves is thus, to say it again, one aspect of the *epistemology of love*, in which, rather than trying to drag people into our world, we relish the fact that they live in theirs.

This task is vital but fraught. Vico's insistence on studying other minds is different from Voltaire's anthropocentric reductionism, though even Pannenberg can write as if they were doing the same thing.[74] For any historian of the early Christian movement (whatever their own personal beliefs) it is vital to take fully into account the question of what the first followers of Jesus thought they were doing and why, and of course to enquire similarly about the human vocation of, and aims of, Jesus himself. Investigating human motivation remains central to the historical task. It has no connection either with 'naturalism' or with 'reductionism'.

The second phase of historical work is thus concerned with the formation and testing of hypotheses, within which the careful study of human motivation and mindset is likely to be central. This brings us to the question of how hypotheses are formed and tested: how, if at all, 'verification' can happen.

The process of hypothesis and verification is often misunderstood. There is a technical term for this, 'abduction', as expounded by the philosopher C. S. Peirce.[75] Scholars sometimes speak as though history simply meant accumulating data, with no hypotheses involved. Any attempt at a larger narrative, showing how it all fits, is then dismissed: oh, we are told by a critic, you had that story in your head all along, and you're imposing it on the data, in other words, doing 'deduction' rather than 'induction'. Since some people *do* have narratives in their heads ahead of time and *do* impose them, we need to distinguish.[76]

Think of the alternatives. Starting from below, 'induction', is never enough. No scientist merely collects specimens at random. You need to sift and sort, to select and arrange. That requires some framing principle or question. That in turn arises from informed and disciplined imaginative leaps to hypotheses, which are then ruthlessly tested against the evidence.[77] That is abduction.

Likewise, starting from above, 'deduction', is never enough. Big theories need testing and modifying, or abandoning altogether, in the light of the evidence. Without that, it might be right, but it might be fantasy. You only get real knowledge through abduction.

So, to sum up so far: the historical task proceeds by the collection of evidence; it focuses on the construction and the rigorous testing of hypotheses, particularly about the human aims and motives that make sense within their own complex culture and worldview, always working abductively towards the larger narrative that will best explain the evidence. Then, third and finally, *history works towards a narrative display of results*. The historian's narrative is more than chronicle. History proposes, and attempts to display, causes, connections and consequences. Once more, this will be a hypothesis, and the looked-for verification will include the confirmation of others who have studied all the evidence. Once more, too, this involves *selection and arrangement*. Selection: as we saw earlier, you can only say everything when there is almost nothing to say. Arrangement: you can't just list 'what happened'. You must display the narratival ligaments, highlighting events and showcasing motivations.

When these three tasks are all working well and in harmony, the result is that *history produces real knowledge.* It does not simply result in 'opinion' or 'belief' (as a nervous Platonist might see it). It is a real mental, and quite possibly emotional, grasping of something other than ourselves. As with hard science, this is always provisional, but that doesn't mean it isn't knowledge. As the philosopher Karl Popper used to insist, even well-tested scientific hypotheses, though regarded as 'laws', are in fact only hypotheses that are thus far unfalsified. Only mathematics escapes provisionality—at least when viewed from outside the discipline. The historian, like the scientist, uses educated and disciplined guesswork to form hypotheses. But the hypotheses don't stay as guesses. They are put to the proof. There is thus a continuum, rather than a great gulf, between 'science' and 'history'. We have real knowledge about the fall of Jerusalem in AD 70, just as we do about the fall of the Twin Towers in AD 2001. We can, in principle, get inside the minds of the Romans besieging Jerusalem, as we can those of the terrorists who attacked New York. By the same token, we have real knowledge of what the phrase 'kingdom of God' meant in the first century, and of the fact that Jesus of Nazareth redefined that meaning around himself and his forthcoming death.

Again, as with science, there is a range of possible results, from virtual certainty to continuing indeterminacy. We know that the Romans destroyed Jerusalem in AD 70 just as securely as we know that 'water' equals 'hydrogen plus oxygen'. We do not know what Paul got up to in the silent decade he spent in Tarsus before Barnabas came looking for him to help with the church in Antioch, though we can infer all kinds of things from what we securely know about the person he was in the next twenty years.[78] But—and here is the payoff for our present project—*if history is real knowledge about the real world, it must take its place near the heart of any theological investigation which seeks to bring that real world into engagement with the question of God.* It is thus intrinsically wrong to exclude history, in all the senses we have explored, from the question of what can be known about God, and how we might know it.

If that seems a sudden jump, let us fill in the argument somewhat more. The 'real world', of course, includes human beings, at two levels. Human *decisions* and *actions* are central to the subject-matter under investigation. Likewise, as we have seen, the human *aims* and *motives* of the agents under investigation form the joints and tendons of the story itself. This is what some have meant by the 'outside' and 'inside' of events. Both matter vitally. Keeping humans out of the equation, at either level, would produce a truncated epistemology in the service of a particular conclusion (perhaps, that history might be a closed continuum of physical causes). There is a theological substructure here: if you get rid of the image-bearers, you might glimpse some kind of a god, but it won't be the Jewish or Christian one.

All this brings us to a vital point, over against Lessing in particular but also the great many who have followed him. The historical task, investigating historical events in the natural world, is actually a close cousin of the hard sciences which investigate objects and organisms in the same natural world. It works by very similar rules and has very similar results. That is why, to say it again, history in all senses does indeed belong within the overall project of 'natural theology'. Lessing seems to have been operating within a mixture of philosophical influences, in which what he meant by 'history' could never attain any real 'certainty' and therefore could not be used as the basis for any conclusions about Christian doctrine. But, as the proponents of 'abduction' have insisted, this is mistaken in its invocation of something called 'certainty'. There is a continuum. Lessing's head-shaking over the inability of history to produce the 'certainty' he would need to draw theological conclusions may be beside the point. Not only does this put 'history' on a broad and bumpy plain alongside other investigations. It assumes what remains to be proved: that theological truths would in fact be out of reach from there. Lessing had thereby already denied what the New Testament writers were affirming. He had set up the experiment in such a way that it was bound to fail. No wonder he was keen on publishing Reimarus. A more probing account of Jesus within his historical context might just have blown the whistle on his entire project.

At the heart of this question—as Rudolf Bultmann saw clearly—is the role of *humans* at both key levels, that is, in both the subject-matter and the investigation. Humans, their aims, ambitions, motivations, hopes and fears, and the actions which result from all these, are the central subject of historical research. And the humans who are called to do this sympathetic imagination are themselves inevitably involved in the process. They are not neutral flies on the wall. This means that *not only is history a necessary part of the 'nature' involved in 'natural theology'; history, centred upon its human agents and investigated by human researchers, contains vital clues for the 'natural theology' quest.* This after all is what we should expect if—whatever we mean by this!—humans are in any sense made in the divine image. Screening out 'history' from the quest, perhaps because it appears too uncertain to form the basis for further theological investigation, means shutting out what might be the most promising area of all.

History, then, proceeds by *abduction* (hypothesis and verification); it includes the study of *human aims and motivations*, mapped by *worldview-analysis* or the like; it results in a *narrative* displaying causes and consequences; this involves the exercise of the disciplined but sympathetic *imagination*, just as in the formation of hypotheses in the hard sciences; and this produces *real knowledge*. Sometimes when scholars talk about 'scientific historiography' they mean starting with Cartesian scepticism or Humean reductionism, or indeed ending with a 'scientific' projection into the future. Some line it up like that as a way of insisting that 'scientific historiography' will disprove central Christian claims; others, in order to 'prove' Christian claims in a quasi-rationalist fashion; others again, as a way of insisting that since we believe the central Christian claims to begin with there should be no place for this kind of historical work. But once we allow for the difference in subject-matter, history is fully 'scientific' in its method. Historical enquiry, like science, must go around the spiral of questioning everything and then telling fresh stories which approach real knowledge by hypothesis and verification. When it does this it achieves the kind of knowledge appropriate for the subject-matter. The critically realist *task* of history, producing a historical *narrative*, really can put us in touch with *events*, not indeed in a positivistic or 'certaintist' way (a hypothetically detached 'objectivity' seen from a 'neutral' point of view) but through appropriate engagement (the 'epistemology of love', allowing the sources to be themselves), leading not to mere random guesswork but to the kind of 'knowledge' on which real people really do stake their real lives.

As this work is under way, the historian is obliged to engage with the question of *meaning*. This is required already by the challenge of selection and arrangement, as well as by the imperative of thinking into the minds of people who think differently from ourselves. History, like all human knowledge, is self-involving. The question then is: How is the self involved? How can this avoid the risk (which we saw already in Bultmann) of merely making the past in one's own image?

That risk can be illustrated by two well-known examples. First, there is Gibbon's *Decline and Fall of the Roman Empire*. Gibbon's settled aim, in line with other mid-eighteenth-century agendas, was to destabilize the comfortable and self-serving received narrative about the early church. Second, there is Ronald Syme's famous work on the Emperor Augustus, written in the first half of the twentieth century with a clear eye to the implicit parallels between first-century dictators and their modern successors.[79] In both cases there is an implicit appeal to the reading public: does this selection and arrangement of the data make sense, or does it not? It is open to anyone to remind Gibbon (and his successors!) of all the good things the early church did.[80] It is open to anyone to write further on Augustus and to suggest that Syme's intended parallel with Hitler and Mussolini may have skewed the portrait. In particular, it is open to anyone studying the sources to ask *what people at the time were making of it all* and whether that sense of immediate 'meaning' is retrievable by us today.

Part of the answer to all this is once more the epistemology of love. The point of love is that it is neither appraisal nor assimilation: neither detachment nor desire, neither positivist objectivity nor subjective projection. When I love I am delightedly engaged with that which is other than myself. Part of the delight is precisely in allowing it—or him, or her—to be the 'other', to be different. For the last two hundred years, as I suggested in the first chapter, Western epistemology has oscillated between the poles of objective and subjective, rationalism versus romanticism, logic and lust. The dream of scientism is for an objective certainty through which one can rule the world; genuine science explores and looks on in wonder and humility. The historian, recognising that all human knowledge is self-involving, learns to discipline the involved self so that the mind is open to different ways of thinking, to hitherto unsuspected motivations and controlling narratival worldviews. And, whether or not the historian calls it 'love', that exercise of sympathetic imagination is precisely the point at which the quest for *meaning* comes in, enabling us within the *task* of history to give an *account* of the past, which highlights real *events* in the knowable past and does so in such a way as to discern *the meaning or pattern of the events within the worldviews of the people concerned.* And perhaps also—the theologian's task?—within the worldviews of people in our own day.

The question then presses, as it has in biblical scholarship over the last two generations: in what sense can we then make the first-century meaning our own? Do we have to pretend (as people often ask, sometimes with a sneer) that we are first-century apocalyptic Jews like them? That is a whole other question, but the answer is yes and no. We do not have to pretend that we are living in the first century, but it is nevertheless part of being a faithful Christian that we believe that with the events concerning Jesus of Nazareth the creator God brought Israel's history, and with it world history, to its single great climax. That of course is deeply counter-intuitive in a world whose presupposition is that world history reached its climax in the late eighteenth century. Part of the deep resistance to real first-century history on the part of theologians—and even of some 'historical critics'!—comes from the resultant clash of metanarratives, and the resistance is sustained by the implicit ecclesiological critique: if Jesus really launched the new covenant and new creation, how is it that the church, never mind the world, is still such a mess? At this point the narrative of modernity (the world reached its climax in the eighteenth century) joins forces ironically with the narrative of postmodernity (all the big stories are trash). Together they make it very difficult for anyone, even practising Christians, to get inside a worldview in which what happened in and through Jesus really was the climax of history, the one-off, unrepeatable moment which changed the world. But that is what all the early Christians believed.

This is the point at which the *task* of history offers itself as the 'point of contact', the necessary central mode of some kind of chastened Christian apologetic. I say 'chastened' because, despite what some have suggested, I am (to say it again) not proposing that history can 'prove' the truth of the Christian faith in an older unreconstructed positivist fashion. I am not offering a historical version of a foundationalist apologetic. I shall argue presently that historical study is good at defeating the defeaters and dismantling the distortions, and that, when historical study is allowed to direct the discussions, instead of being relegated to the odd footnote, a new coherence emerges which offers, not a positivistic proof, but *the kind of proof appropriate within critical realism*, the appeal of a fully rounded hermeneutic of love—in this case, the (provisional) verification of hypotheses. History as a discipline is after all a *public discourse*. Anyone can play; the materials are in the public domain; and the different meaningful narratives people offer compete in the way any historical constructs, or indeed scientific hypotheses, compete. At this level, the Christian does not have an inside track, and any attempt to pretend that one does will be spotted at once. As C. S. Lewis once said, illustrating his point that 'Christian literature' has at least to be literature, there is no specifically Christian way of boiling an egg.[81] There may be Christian motives for doing it here and now; it may be an act of charity or an act of selfishness depending on the circumstances. In the same way, there is a task called 'history' which, like boiling an egg, is actually the same for everyone; and refusing to engage in it because we ought to be doing something more 'specifically Christian' is to refuse the path to what I believe is the heart of all true apologetic. *These things were not done in a corner*, as Paul said to Agrippa.[82] Or, as Lesslie Newbigin used to insist, the Christian gospel is *public truth* or it's nothing. The public truth of the gospel is found in its historical roots; and the historical roots are open to inspection by anyone and everyone.

Of course, the Christian comes with assumptions about the basic truth of the gospel story. But this doesn't mean that when a Christian does history it is all a matter of projection. Back to the epistemology of love: Christians too, precisely because they are Christians, must humbly allow the sources to tell them things they hadn't expected. History will continually dismantle the distortions, whether it's at the level of the lexical investigation of a single word in the New Testament or at the level of the first-century meaning of an entire train of thought such as those connected with the 'coming of the son of man'. If we don't do history this will never happen. If we reduce 'history' to the free-floating idea that we know ahead of time that the real 'meaning' is found in the Nicene Creed and the Chalcedonian Definition, it will never happen either. And not only will this fence us off from any fresh scriptural insight. It will reduce our discourse to the status of a private game. And that, right there, is to falsify the gospel.

Historical Ontology

From epistemology to ontology. Much theologically contextualised discussion both of science and of history has assumed a split between 'naturalism' and 'supernaturalism' (see chapter 1), without seeming to notice that this is simply handing a free pass to G. E. Lessing, whose 'ugly, broad ditch' separated the contingent truths of history from the necessary truths of reason.[83] This has had the effect—and this may sometimes have been the point!—of ruling out any kind of 'natural theology' based upon the task of history before it can start. If, however, we relabel 'naturalism' as 'Epicureanism'—which is after all what it is—we will see what's going on. The supposed 'natural/supernatural' split has migrated into history-discourse from science-and-religion discussions; it was the wrong tool there, and it is worse here. The word 'supernatural', which in the Middle Ages meant the superabundance of grace over nature (without denying that God was active in nature as well), has been squashed into the dualist Epicurean paradigm, producing an either/or: either one is a 'naturalist' in some sense, or one is a 'supernaturalist' (and to reject the latter would be to incur the displeasure of many devout Christians whose sense of God's presence and love has been interpreted in terms of 'believing in the supernatural'). Both, then, come with strong implicit evaluation in different communities.

But supposing the either/or of the Epicurean worldview was radically mistaken? Supposing we went with some kind of ancient Hebrew or first-century Jewish worldview, in which heaven and earth were supposed to overlap and interlock? Supposing Jesus really was launching God's kingdom on earth as in heaven, so that *we needed to study earth in order to find out what heaven was up to*, rather than assuming that we knew heaven's mind in advance: what then? Leaping from the broad sweep of 'all events' to 'meaning', or indeed the other way, while rejecting both the *task* and the *narrative product* of history because they appear 'naturalistic' is not to do history at all. What's more, it guarantees bad theology.

Cosmology and Eschatology

From epistemology and ontology to cosmology and, with it, eschatology: will history get where it's going by 'progress' or 'irruption'? Here we must recapitulate earlier arguments. Hegel believed in progress, with God as part of that process, so technically he wasn't a 'naturalist'; but there have been many 'naturalistic', or as I have argued Epicurean, versions of this theory. This is basically Jewish Providence-theology with Israel's God left out, just as Marx's dialectical materialism was Jewish apocalyptic theology with God left out. Reacting to Hegel, we have the Danish Søren Kierkegaard (1813–1855) in the nineteenth century and the Swiss Karl Barth (1886–1968), partly channelling Marx, in the twentieth century. Both were challenging 'progress' and the comfortable *Kulturprotestantismus* that saw in modern European culture the gradual arrival of the kingdom of God. The idea of 'history' has itself been caught in the crossfire of these battles, so that, as I indicated earlier, some now hear any appeal to 'history' as a give-away indication that the speaker believes in 'naturalism', perhaps in an 'immanent process'.[84] The assumed guilt here comes from the twentieth-century events which 'prove' that Hegel at least was wrong and that 'history' leads only to disaster—a conclusion that, however warranted by actual events, was already assumed by anti-Hegelians. This brings us back to Barth's insistence on revelation 'vertically from above' and to Benjamin's disappointment with 'history', about which I wrote in the previous chapter. Benjamin, and Paul Klee's painting 'The Angel of History', have recently been invoked by some who for quite other reasons use the misleading label 'apocalyptic' to retrieve an agenda which rejects not only the salvation-historical version of 'meaning in history' but the historical *task* of research, the historical *goal* of a fresh narrative, and the possibility that real knowledge of historical *events* would ever be helpful for theology.[85] These muddles need sorting out.

The debate about progress and irruption (as theories of how history works and what it might mean) has been played out in the misshapen debate between 'apocalyptic' and 'salvation history'. I have written about this elsewhere and will be returning to 'apocalyptic' in the next chapter.[86] Genuinely historical study of the relevant Jewish and early Christian material produces a narrative about beliefs that were actually held and that, through the consequent human motivations, generated actual events, in the light of which we can and should construct a mature, genuinely grounded picture of Jesus and his first followers within their historical and cultural settings. That picture includes the Second Temple Jewish sense that the course of events was indeed guided by God, certainly not through a smooth evolutionary progress but through covenantal and creational judgment and renewal seen as the sudden and startling fulfil-ment of ancient promises.[87] This conclusion points forward to some of our later remarks both in its *form* (real historical exegesis challenging spurious top-down schemes) and in its *content* (Christian retrieval of Second Temple Jewish ideas challenging later Western ideologies).

What then is the significance of the events the historian discovers? The widespread appeal to 'the authority of scripture', as I have shown elsewhere, only attains coherence when seen as shorthand for the authority of God exer-cised in Jesus and by the spirit somehow *through* scripture.[88] But scripture does not offer a closed, private world, however attractive that looks within some theological circles. The Gospel narratives do what Paul did in his travels: they display the Jesus-story as *public truth*, the truth of *events* which were told in coherent historical *narratives* by people who believed themselves called to the *task* of researching, editing and arranging them so as to display (their view of) the *meaning* which these events carried. They gesture at an overall mean-ing for the whole of history, *but they insist that this meaning is to be found in the actual events as researched and displayed*, not in an *a priori* discovered else-where, and not simply in a private world created by their writing. In fact, they insist that God's decisive saving self-revelation has taken place precisely *not primarily in their writing* but *in the events to which they bear witness*. That is why we must hold together 'history' as task, with its various sub-disciplines, and 'history' as *narrative*. These cannot be trumped by a grand *a priori* appeal to an arm-waving sense of 'history' as 'all events, ever' combined with an equally arm-waving sense of 'meaning' in terms of theological generalizations.

Throughout this prolonged discussion, one technical term has been waiting in the wings. It occurs so frequently when these matters are considered that we need now to take some time to investigate what is going on. The term in question is 'Historicism'.

HISTORY IS NOT HISTORICISM–WHATEVER THAT MEANS

The Meaning of 'Historicism'[89]

The question of what 'history' is, what it could or should be, of how it is to be done and what it's useful for and why, has always been bound up with, and bounced around by, the various social and cultural situations in which prominent historians have lived and worked. The most obvious example is the upsurge of interest in history within Germany from the late eighteenth century onwards, as writers who were concerned with and active within various political movements offered versions of German, European and world history as ways of reflecting on and contributing to the questions of their own day.[90] This was where some of the chickens hatched in the movements we looked at earlier came home to roost. To what extent were past events random, to be studied in isolation from one another, and to what extent were they part of the relentless unfolding of some great, if normally invisible, process? This question produced a large-scale, corporate version of the old philosophers' puzzle of determinism and free will: to what extent were events in the past, and presumably the future as well, somehow 'fixed', so that one could even 'see where they were going'? And to what extent were humans able to do new things, to break free from the iron hand of fate?

This is where the word 'historicism' is often found. If it is hard, but necessary, to disentangle the different common senses of the word 'history', it is much harder, but equally necessary, to disentangle the senses of the word 'historicism', which haunts discussions of early Christianity and still more the meta-discussions of relevant methods of study. Unlike the quite different uses of 'history', it is by no means clear what different users mean, especially since the word often appears to carry polemical overtones.[91]

I am aware of, and will try to describe as simply as I can, several senses of 'historicism' in fairly regular use today. The common factor linking them all is *the belief in the interconnectedness of events, ideas and cultures*. Events do not occur in a vacuum. Ideas are neither thought nor expressed in isolation. They belong within a wider network of social, cultural, political, religious life, practice, belief, imagination and so on. We can of course refer to actions and events in isolation: we can say that 'the church agreed the Chalcedonian Definition in AD 451' or that 'a massive earthquake struck Lisbon on November 1, 1755'; but the only point in drawing attention to such things would be to say something about the *meaning*, real or imagined, of these events. And for that we need context.

But how do we describe that context, and what role does it then play in our understanding? One standard answer is to look at the social sciences. Describing human societies and their multi-level functioning has played a major role in various historicist theories, leading some to postulate that if we could give a complete description of all the sociological factors we would be able, like an astronomer predicting the next eclipse, not only to give a complete explanation of events but to predict where the events were leading. One still meets this kind of top-down sociology, not least in some branches of biblical study.[92]

This pathway leads straight to the first and perhaps best-known sense of 'historicism': that which Karl Popper attacked in his famous 1957 book *The Poverty of Historicism*.[93] As with his other famous work *The Open Society and Its Enemies*, Popper saw Idealist historical thinking as the root cause of the totalitarian horrors of the twentieth century, singling out Hegel and Marx for particular blame.[94] Pantheism and materialism had claimed to know hidden laws not just about what *had* happened but also about what *would* happen. *This is the way history is going*, said the theory, *whether you like it or not*. For Hegel, the quasi-divine *Geist* is progressively displaying itself, and we know in advance the direction it is taking.[95] Exceptions don't matter; they'll be sorted out within the dialectic. The same, *mutatis mutandis*, with Marx. His material world has an inner consciousness, collecting itself in the mind of each class. Thus, if 'the divine' is in everything (pantheism), or if 'everything' behaves according to hidden laws (materialism), we can not only study what *has* happened; we can predict what *will* happen—indeed, what *must* happen. That 'must' is the regular tell-tale warning sign, the soft footfall of the historicist burglar in the vulnerable house of human wisdom.[96] Popper's pressing of the panic button at this point is exactly cognate with the reaction of Käsemann and his colleagues to any suggestion of 'salvation history'. The scars were fresh.[97]

Critics disagree over the appropriateness of the term 'historicism' for what Popper was attacking. They also question the accuracy of his critique, especially of Marx.[98] But what matters for us is the sense he gave the word, and the inevitable opprobrium which was thereby built into it. 'Historicism' in this sense meant that by looking at the past and present one could *tell which way 'history'* *was going*, producing an effectively determinist teleology and an inescapable political agenda. Whatever we call this view, it was clearly present and powerful in the nineteenth and twentieth centuries, and its effects linger on in the popular belief in 'progress' we examined in the first chapter. For Popper, if 'historicism' caused Hitler and Stalin, it was obviously a Bad Thing. Today, many who have never heard of Hegel or Marx (or Popper for that matter) but who believe that 'history is going' in a particular direction, or that 'history teaches us' this or that, are 'historicists' in this first sense.

Popper was not the only person to single out this view, to call it 'historicism', and to critique it as such. It wasn't, it seems, just the moderns like Hegel and Marx who had espoused this dangerous idea. In 1950 C. S. Lewis published an essay, the substance of which was repeated in one of his literary monographs, critiquing a similar viewpoint.[99] Lewis regarded as 'historicist' any attempt to 'read off' a metahistorical or transcendental truth from this-worldly events, from the trivial interpretation of a misfortune as a 'judgment' upon someone to the large-scale theories of Hegel and Marx. He put these together with Virgil and his predecessors, whose long narrative told of the divinely ordained rise of Rome, and of Augustine and other early Christian writers giving their view of what God had been up to in history. He brought this forward to modern times, citing Carlyle and Keats.[100] Lewis's target was, I think, broader than Popper's. Popper was after the teleological schemes which claimed to tell you not only what was 'going on' behind events already taking place but where those events were inexorably leading and thus what humans had to do to make it all happen.

Nor was Popper the only one to see Marx as a historicist. F. M. Turner explains that Marx saw his own age both as the culmination of past historical development and as containing the seeds of future historical development, and that he understood from history that change often happened violently; so he extrapolated forwards to the necessity of revolution.[101]

If Popper's is one of the best-known meanings of 'historicism', another is that of E. Troeltsch (1865–1923). Troeltsch shared the widespread optimism and belief in 'progress' of late nineteenth-century Germany and regarded liberal Protestantism as the ultimate form of 'religion'. But when people speak of 'historicism' in connection with him they usually mean something quite different from what Popper was attacking, a determinist prediction of the future. Troeltsch is known for his criteria for historical research, already discussed, which together encapsulate the belief that events in this world are part of a 'closed continuum' of cause and effect. I suspect that this is what many theologians mean when they refer disparagingly to 'historicism', on the grounds that Troeltsch is ruling out from the start any possibility of divine action in the world.[102] There is a sense in which Troeltsch is offering a specific focus for a larger scheme of the sort opposed by Popper, in that for him the 'development' of human society and particularly religion had reached its goal from within, as it were. There was no need for outside, divine 'interference' in his now perfected type of religion.

These two meanings of 'historicism' (the one attacked by Popper and the one proposed by Troeltsch) may be the best-known senses, but the insistence on understanding events and ideas within their wider social and cultural setting can go in quite different directions. The more you see things in their own contexts, the more you see them precisely not as part of a grand universal scheme but as distinct, and hence relative. This is why 'historicism' is often associated with 'relativism': 'they believed X in that time and place because of factors A, B and C; but of course people in other times and places wouldn't believe it'. This is the sense of 'historicism' expounded by Steve Mason in his recent book on historical theory in relation to ancient Roman Judaea.[103] For Mason, it was the *positivists* who embraced the large-scale vision of 'progress', hoping 'to tame the chaos of the past, as scientists brought the chaos of nature to ordered principles'. Meanwhile in his account, the practitioners 'embraced the mess and were suspicious of large-scale explanations', devoting their energy 'to figuring out who did what to whom when, and why, specifically'.[104] It is clear why Mason thinks Popper is completely off-track: for Mason, 'historicists' represented 'the turn toward the specific and particular', staking their claim 'on the scientific virtues of precise observation and accounting for detail, ahead of theorizing'.[105] No wonder we all get confused. For Popper and Lewis, and a great many at a popular level, the 'historicists' are the people with the big theories who impose them not only on the past but also on the present and the future. For Mason and those he follows, the 'historicists' are those who refuse to do that but who concentrate instead on locating words, documents, people and events within their own specific culture and time.

The relativism implicit within Mason's version of 'historicism' can, however, emerge just as well from a Hegelian understanding (see below). 'If all things are a product of a particular time and place and a particular culture *or a particular stage of Absolute Spirit coming to understand itself*, then the Bible as a document must also be similarly time-bound'.[106]

The apparent stand-off between a 'historicism' which imposes a grand scheme on particular events past and future, and a 'historicism' which refuses to do just that, may reflect the nineteenth-century stand-off between arguably the greatest German historian of the day (Leopold von Ranke) and his successors, on the one hand, and the Hegelians, on the other. Von Ranke has often, as we saw, been thought to have expressed a naïve realism in his famous statement that he was only trying to describe the past *wie es eigentlich gewesen*. (In Anglo-Saxon contexts people sometimes describe the naïvely realist view as 'positivism', but this too is far more complicated, as Mason's use of it to mean almost exactly what Popper meant by 'historicism' indicates.) The point at stake—and here I think we see the roots of the confusion—is that von Ranke throughout his life was bitterly opposed to Hegel and to Hegelian schemes which tried to predict or even control the future on the basis of the past, but that von Ranke himself had his own meta-historical view of the meaning of events. This was, in fact, an in-house German debate, tinged with ongoing political questions. The combatants may have grasped some things which are vital for healthy historical work, particularly the insistence on the careful study of the wider contexts of events and motivations. But the battle spread out, as other wars have done, over larger territory than was originally envisaged.

For Hegel—and this was Popper's target, whether he labelled it appropriately or not—the Absolute Spirit was developing and expressing itself in historical events in such a way that one could and should see where it was going and get on board. The proposal was developed, albeit in very different ways, by Nietzsche, Spengler and Toynbee, who proposed 'a form of history which shaped the events of the past into a grand philosophical system'.[107] Their views and others like them remained at the basis of the social determinism which drove both Nazi and Soviet regimes. History was marching forward, and everyone should get in step. This was the future, and there were ways of making it work. (For the Marxists this took a different form: in Bentley's apt phrase, Marx 'escaped the system by hijacking it and running it off in a new direction'.)[108]

For von Ranke all this was anathema. He 'prided himself on his loathing for Hegel'.[109] Like many others of his time and place (to do to him what historicists determinedly did to everyone else) he regarded the events of 1813, with the establishment of the Prussian monarchy, as a high point in the history of human freedom, or at least of the German concept of freedom.[110] Von Ranke was the classic type of the new professional historian, eager to get to the details rather than sweep them all under the carpet of a grand developmental scheme. That was what he meant in his famous anti-Hegelian slogan about 'how things actually happened'. He saw 'states'—a newish concept at the time—as corporate individuals and, as such, as expressions of divine thoughts (an interesting idea for anyone thinking of 'natural theology'). Every age, he believed, and every state, was equally accessible to God, which was the fundamental reason for rejecting Hegel's teleology. He would look *backwards* to see what God *had* been doing, not forwards to predict what *would* happen in either the immediate or the ultimate future.[111]

Von Ranke's disciple Meinecke rammed the point home: history is not 'predictive' or determinist.[112] On the contrary: the essence of history was for him 'the substitution of a process of individualizing observation for a generalizing view of human forces in history'.[113] This he described not as *Historizismus* but as *Historismus*, 'historism', a distinction which Michael Bentley has attempted to maintain but which seems not to have caught on.

The key point was, in fact, lost in translation. As in other matters, in the Anglo-Saxon world the German subtleties got flattened out. There was a sharp debate in the 1930s in which the leading American historian Charles A. Beard (1874–1948) championed a form of relativism (urging that the historian, like the subjects under study, was historically situated amid pressures which would influence research and results) over against a naïve realism represented then by Theodore Clark Smith. Beard's positive case for relativism would be almost universally accepted today, but in presenting it he made three remarkable assumptions. First, he assumed that von Ranke's statement about history *wie es eigentlich gewesen* indicated a programme of naïve realism such as he took Smith and others to be championing; second, he took it for granted that because von Ranke was known to be a 'historicist' this meant that 'historicism' and naïve realism were more or less the same thing; third, he was therefore able to attack them both together, treating 'historicism' as an 'extension' of the 'von Ranke formula'.[114]

In England the battle was joined differently. The Cambridge historian J. B. Bury expounded a form of historicism in his 1902 inaugural lecture as Regius Professor of Modern History (where he followed Lord Acton). What he said then amounts, I think, to a kind of social Darwinism, which was indeed popular at the time. History was now to be put on a 'scientific' basis, requiring that we grasp 'the idea of human development', the great 'transforming conception, which enables history to define her scope'.[115] Now at last, he claims, long after the Greek tragedians had taken a leap forwards, 'human self-consciousness has taken another step', as humans can now grasp 'the notion of their upward development through immense cycles of time'. This idea, he claims, 'has recreated history', bringing it out from its former colleagues, 'moral philosophy and rhetoric', and instead entering into close relations 'with the sciences which deal objectively with the facts of the universe'.[116] People must therefore be taught history so that they will not only understand but also contribute to the new developments: history will itself be 'a factor in evolution'.[117] History, in fact, 'is a science, no less and no more'.[118]

Bury apparently revised his views quite considerably after the First World War, as well he might.[119] But he was trenchantly answered in 1903 by G. M. Trevelyan,[120] speaking for a kind of British pragmatism against the vast reaches of Hegelian theory. 'There is no way of scientifically deducing causal laws about the action of human beings in the mass' from historical data.[121] Only in retrospect do the events of the past seem inevitable. One twist of fate and it would all have gone differently.[122] (Think again of the coachman taking the wrong turn in Sarajevo.) The scientific spirit is required when a historian is collecting and weighing evidence ('just as it is for a detective or a politician').[123] But then there comes the 'imaginative', the formation of the hypotheses, and finally the 'literary' stage, writing it all up. Therefore, 'when a man begins with the pompous formula—"The verdict of history is"—suspect him at once, for his is merely dressing up his own opinions in big words'. No one historian can see more than a small part of the truth, and 'if he sees all sides he will probably not see very deeply into any one of them'.[124]

Trevelyan is here rejecting, via Bury, the possibility of grand schemes like those of Hegel. He does not mention 'historicism' by name, but he is agreeing with Popper, and Lewis, in showing the folly of attempts, on the basis of a supposed 'scientific' reading of history, to predict where 'history is going'. This points us back to an earlier argument than those of Hegel or von Ranke: to the work of Giambattista Vico, whom Isaiah Berlin regarded as the father of a true historicism. Historicism, says Berlin strikingly, is 'a doctrine that in its empirical form has stimulated and enriched, and its dogmatic, metaphysical form, inhibited or distorted, the historical imagination'.[125] Here and elsewhere Berlin seems to understand these two senses of 'historicism' in terms of (1) the need to locate events and ideas in their own contexts, described as richly as possible (what we might now call 'thick description') and (2) the attempt to deduce from social-scientific observation of the past the 'meaning' of the present and the direction of the future. The irony of these two meanings, as we have now seen, is that they quickly become exact opposites: the first (perhaps closest to Ranke) insists on the local, specific and retrospective; the second (that of Hegel) on wide (and wild) generalisations and predictions. The first can easily be used as a form of relativism ('of course, they thought like that back then, but we are different'), though it need not be. As Collingwood saw clearly, the fact that we all see things from our own point of view does not reduce history to something arbitrary or capricious. Historical knowledge remains genuine knowledge.[126]

All this (and I have given a very short summary of highly complex issues) means that we should exercise considerable caution in the use of 'historicism' as a technical term. Its meaning varies wildly. But, taking this risk, and using the labels offered above, there is a vital point to be made. We will return to Troeltsch on another occasion. For the moment I follow Berlin's distinction which, as I have said, seems to gesture towards a Rankian 'historicism' (of which Berlin approves) over against a Hegelian type (of which he disapproves). Hegel's historicism, however, is alive and well, not only in popular political discourse but in theology. One of the main reasons for the present rather long chapter is the need to name it and shame it.

Hegel's historicism has no need to bother with 'history' as either narrative or task. Nor, indeed, does it concern itself with the question of which events in the past can actually be known. It makes grand statements about 'history' meaning 'everything that has happened and will happen'. It leaps across to statements about 'meaning', in terms of the inevitable progress of the divine spirit. This (to say it again) requires no investigation, no study of sources. All this, quite naturally, gets 'history' a bad name among natural theologians, as well as making real historians gnash their teeth at seeing their subject thus distorted beyond recognition. It is all a bit too easy.

The obvious answer to the Hegelian historicist is that we know hardly any of the past, and none whatever of the future.[127] This, to repeat, is why von Ranke, often misrepresented as a positivist, determined to avoid such grand schemes and focus as best he could on 'what actually happened'—for which, confusingly, he is himself sometimes called a 'historicist'.[128] Nineteenth-century Hegelian historicists ignored this and, with Ritschl, sailed the boat right into harbour. Here comes the kingdom of God. Except that what then happened was the twentieth century.

Historicism in Practice: Politics

Politicians have often been predictive historicists. When seventeenth-century radicals called themselves 'fifth monarchy men', they were (however devoutly) Hegelian historicists. The book of Daniel pictured four monstrous regimes being succeeded by a very different ruler who establishes God's kingdom. This gave them the clue: history was going in that direction, and they were on the crest of its wave. When Hillary Clinton declared in 2011 that it was important to back the Arab Spring in order to be 'on the right side of history', she was using a Hegelian trope. She claimed to know where 'history' was going. Of course, history didn't go the way it was supposed to. But people often still think it will, if only we can sort out the logistics and persuade distant peoples whose thought-forms we don't understand to think like us.[129]

The claim to stand at the leading edge of history is hardly new. The earliest examples I know are Augustus's court poets and historians, seeing the inexorable rise of Rome as the meaning of all history.[130] A century later, of course, nobody saw it that way. The cynicism of Tacitus and Suetonius functions like the mould on an overripe historicist cheese.

Historicism in Theology

So much, briefly, for the political application of Hegelian historicism; what about theology? Do Christians have an inside track on the *telos*, the 'goal'? From one point of view, the answer is Yes: in Romans 8 we have a vision of creation rescued at last from its 'slavery to decay'; in 1 Corinthians 15 we are told that when death itself is defeated God will be 'all in all'; in the book of Revelation (and in Second Peter) we are promised what Isaiah promised: new heavens and new earth.[131] Jesus told his first followers to watch out for warning signs that indicated the imminent fall of Jerusalem; but the early Christians regularly referred to the ultimate future as a surprise, like a thief in the night.[132] Neither their hoped-for future nor their remarkable claims about the recent past—the events concerning Jesus—enabled them to read God's action off immediate circumstances. The book of Acts is full of scenes in which would-be faithful followers of Jesus have no idea what is going to happen next. They did not try to deduce it from what had happened so far. They knew the ultimate goal, but they did not suppose it would emerge from within the ongoing processes of the world. That is the great difference.

When some early Christians did propose a larger picture of historical meaning, of what God was doing in the ongoing events they knew, they were to that extent acting out of character. Augustine himself, writing *The City of God*, was answering those pagan writers who, anticipating Gibbon, accused Christianity of undermining Rome by stopping people worshipping the ancestral gods.[133] Writing like that drew neither on Jewish nor on New Testament theology. Jewish salvation-history worked differently, as we shall see. The early Christians believed that with Jesus the new creation had appeared. As far as they were concerned, Jesus himself was the one and only Fifth-Monarchy Man; they looked for no others. This is the grain of truth in Bultmann's claim that history came to a stop. But new creation didn't mean 'no more history' in the sense of 'no more events'—only a radically new focus of interpretation.[134] The early Christians lived within ongoing history and looked for God to act within their world. But, with the important exception of the fall of Jerusalem, they never claimed to read God's action off the surface of events.

I regard modern attempts to sidestep the actual historical task, therefore, as succumbing to what I earlier called the Petrine temptation: to protect Jesus against his own vocation. Real history, including the investigation of Jesus and his first followers, has the character of the Pauline *kenosis*. Jesus did not wear a halo. His redefinition of power, in word and in deed, in action and in passion, was the opposite of what his friends expected, just as those who start their theological investigations with an assumption of an 'all-powerful' deity would do well to look closely at the radical redefinition, in the New Testament, of power itself. The discipline of actual history, history as *task* and history as *narrative*, matches that strange redefinition of power in terms of weakness with the seeming 'weakness' of an investigative method in which we put large-scale conclusions about 'meaning' on hold and allow the evidence to make its impact on the enquiring mind. The shifting sand is where we are called to stand.

So what happens, after all this, to Jesus and historical criticism? And what might that contribute to the possibility, or even the promise, of 'natural theology'?

HISTORY AND JESUS

The question of Jesus and History is still sometimes dismissed with scorn by theologians reacting to the latest sceptical proposals.[135] But if we are talking about the interface between God and the world, we cannot tiptoe around the topic and pretend it doesn't matter. Where can we begin?

The old implicit moratorium on historical-Jesus work is long gone.[136] Controversy still rages at every level, but options are narrowing down. Nobody of course comes to Jesus 'neutral'. Such claims, for instance those made by Geza Vermes or Ed Sanders, are falsified both by their own published autobiographical remarks and by their very different constructs.[137] So: does everything reduce after all to historians bringing their own 'meaning' and adjusting the evidence to fit? Is it all a back-projection from subjective *a prioris*? Certainly not. The *task* of history is a public discipline; the debates continue. Like all genuine knowledge, that task involves *both* the full engagement of the interpreter *and* the full allowance that the evidence may suggest things which don't fit the original assumptions.

That is why the phrase 'historical Jesus' remains ambiguous. Many, particularly in the implicitly positivistic Western world, assume without question that 'historical' is to be taken in the sense of 'Jesus *as he really was*', 'the man from Galilee', and so forth. As we have noted before, however, the bright light of a positivist ambition has a dark side, namely, the scepticism or even cynicism when 'absolute proof' appears lacking. That has fuelled the movement, particularly among those schooled in the tradition that runs from German Idealism to Anglo-Saxon liberalism, to take the phrase 'the historical Jesus' in the sense of 'Jesus *as the historian reconstructs him*', 'our picture of Jesus', and so on (not least because that's what the German phrase *der historische Jesus* means)—often with the clear implication that this 'reconstruction' is a mere projection, the subjective fantasy of this or that ideology or theology. Theologians often use that ambiguity to suggest that, while you may think you're talking about Jesus himself, you're only really dealing with 'your construction of Jesus', and so on. All this has generated a long-running reaction, from Martin Kähler one hundred years ago to C. S. Lewis seventy years ago, from Luke Timothy Johnson in recent American scholarship to a good many post-liberals today: please don't supply us with a 'historical Jesus', because that will only be your attempt to create a fifth gospel, to find a Jesus 'behind the text' rather than relying on the Jesus in the Gospel texts themselves.[138] This is where accusations of 'methodological naturalism' are thrown around, generating more heat than light.[139]

Now of course many historians from Reimarus onwards have indeed said, 'Don't believe the Gospels, believe me instead'. That approach has challenged church tradition in the name of an Epicurean agenda which, as we saw, banished the rumour of God to an inaccessible heaven and tried to make sense of the godless world—Jesus included!—in its own terms. But there is a big difference between saying, 'Now that we know miracles don't happen, don't believe the four Gospels, believe my reconstruction instead', and saying, 'Perhaps the church has forgotten, or not fully understood, what the four Gospels were trying to tell us in their own context and their own terms; so let's dig deeper into the Gospels themselves, in their own first-century context, and see what happens'.

This last suggestion is eminently reasonable. Jesus and his first followers lived in the Second Temple Jewish world which became increasingly opaque to Christians, and actually to Jews too, after the tumultuous events of AD 66–70 and 132–135, and particularly by the fourth and fifth centuries. The turn to 'Jewish' readings after the Second World War was a welcome and long-overdue development in New Testament studies, but the early tendency was to look at the Rabbis—whose work, in the Talmud and related texts, dates from several hundred years later and, crucially, after the leading Jewish thinkers had firmly turned their backs on the dangerous political quest for God's kingdom to come on earth as in heaven.[140] The Pharisees of Jesus' day were not simply early versions of the later Rabbis.[141] The recent massive advances in our knowledge of the Jewish world of the first century itself shed copious light on what the Gospels (in their different ways) were actually saying. *This does not require the back-projection of a theological construct culled from subsequent Christian thought, any more than it requires the back-projection of a Humean scepticism.* It requires *history*: through the task of collecting data and forming hypotheses, thereby producing narratives which, like scientific knowledge *mutatis mutandis*, will more and more approximate to the events and motivations themselves, opening up new possibilities for fresh proposals about 'meaning'—proposals which have not been brought in *a priori* but have emerged through the actual practice, the task, of research and narration. Just as the massive nineteenth-century advances in discovering and collating early Christian manuscripts led to major revisions of the text of the New Testament (resisted in some quarters, partly on the grounds that if God had wanted us to have this new text he would have given it to us a lot sooner), so the major twentieth-century advances in our knowledge of the ancient Jewish world, of which the discovery of the Qumran scrolls is just one example, have opened up new possibilities and insights which systematic theology has barely noticed but cannot afford, in my view, to resist or discount.

Nor should one be put off from this task by the suggestion that it involves 'going behind the text'. That phrase often implies that we are doing something sneaky or underhand, surreptitiously second-guessing what the writers were doing. This is ridiculous—though the accusation picks up some extra if unwarranted energy from the postmodern literary mood of questioning whether there can be any real world 'outside the text'.[142] This cultural mood has coincided with the neo-Kantian existentialism of Bultmann and his successors, imagining the Gospels to be self-referential mythmaking, not historical memory. But when texts have a *prima facie* intention of describing actual events (compare Luke's prologue, for a start, and his accurate dating of John the Baptist),[143] doing one's best to understand what those events meant in their context is not 'going behind' those texts. It is accepting their invitation to explore the world of the real-life past which they intend to open up.[144] When the newspaper reports that the local team won the match, the cheerfully partisan spirit of the article doesn't hide, but rather insists upon, the actual events that took place on the pitch. The goals were not scored in a private intra-textual world. The task of history *is not to substitute a new construct for the texts we possess but to understand better what those texts were saying all along.*

Reading the Gospels historically requires, of course, sensitivity to their genre.[145] The Gospels purport to be history as *narrative*, referring to history as *event*, the result of historical research and selection as *task*, pointing strongly to specific *meanings*. The Gospels also contain, of course, sub-genres, such as parables, which—apart from occasional topical allusions—do not intend to refer to actual events. To ask where the prodigal son lived, or who bought his half of the property, would be to miss the point. But to ask what first-century factors would have generated the hostility to which Jesus' parable is responding is to get the point. The Gospels as a whole, and the stories about Jesus which they contain, are not presented as parables whose 'point' is independent of historical truth.

The question of hostility to Jesus illustrates all this. The Christian tradition has often assumed that Jewish hostility arose from a 'legalism' that was offended by Jesus' offer of love, grace and forgiveness. We now know—and I mean 'know'—that this doesn't work historically. It is a hopeless caricature.[146] Jesus was offering a fresh construal of 'God's kingdom' in a world where there were other construals on offer, and that meant a social and political challenge, not simply a clash of theologies or soteriologies in the usual sense. In particular, as we shall see in chapter 5, Jesus' actions on the Sabbath were controversial not because his contemporaries believed in 'legalism' and he believed in 'freedom' but because the Sabbath was seen as an anticipation of the Age to Come, and Jesus was acting as if the Age to Come were being inaugurated in his own work—with consequences very different from what had been expected. In other words: the *task* of history needs to challenge received interpretations, *not to substitute a new construct for the Gospels we already have but to understand what those Gospels were saying in the first place.* This is not to 'go behind the text' except in the sense to which the texts themselves urge us.

WHAT CAN HISTORY DO?

Defeating the Defeaters

So what can history do for us? Three things, I believe. To begin with, it is particularly good at what some have called 'defeating the defeaters'. Every year or two someone writes a blockbuster claiming that Jesus was an Egyptian Freemason, a Qumran visionary, married to Mary Magdalene, or whatever—always with the implied corollary, 'so therefore traditional Christianity is based on a mistake', and we should go back to atheism or, at best, eighteenth-century Deism. These proposals, and the equally strange though apparently scholarly proposals of groups like the 'Jesus Seminar', come and go, and can be seen off quite easily. One should not judge a discipline by its distortions. But what will see off the sceptics is not a dogmatic reassertion of the tradition, nor the dismissal of the discipline of history with the slur of 'methodological naturalism', but history itself.

Another example: many have suggested that Jesus and his first followers couldn't have thought of him as 'divine', partly because they were Jewish monotheists and partly because that would make him 'insane'. But contemporary studies of monotheism, and of the Temple as God's dwelling and of humans as image-bearers in God's Temple, have shown that this was mere ignorance.[147] Problems remain; but the old dismissal of Christian claims on the assumption of an original 'low' Jewish Christology—and their mirror image in the suggestion that for a proper Christology we have to forget history and look to the Fathers or to Aquinas—has been shown to be out of line, not by an *a priori* culled from later orthodoxy but by historical research into actual historical evidence, challenging unwarranted narratives and suggesting the possibility of different meaningful narrations. I venture to suggest that this kind of complex 'history' could be seen as part of obedience to the kingdom itself, coming on earth as in heaven.

All this moves into a different register with the resurrection. We shall return to this in the sixth chapter, but for the moment we may just say this. Historical study of the sources suggests that the earliest church's testimony to Jesus' resurrection precipitated a radical mutation within Jewish understanding of history and eschatology, which then formed a new interpretative grid: Jesus' rising was interpreted simultaneously as a very strange event within the present world *and* the foundational and paradigmatic event within God's *new* creation.[148] This points to the fundamental argument I am making throughout this book. The idea of new creation operating from within the womb of the old—perhaps we should say, from within the *tomb* of the old—makes sense, albeit new sense, within that Jewish world in which God's space, time and matter and human space, time and matter were designed to overlap and interlock. I shall develop this particular point in the next chapter. For the moment I focus on the limited but vital point: just as the sceptic cannot appeal to a Humean *a priori*, so the Christian cannot simply say, 'I believe in the supernatural,' as though that bypassed all historical questions. The point about new creation is that it is the renewal of *this* world, not the substitution of another one. Good history will explain this and outflank the normal objections.

Dismantling the Distortions

But that doesn't mean, 'Well, we've got rid of the nonsense; let's go back to believing what we've always believed'. If history can defeat the defeaters, it can also dismantle the distortions, challenging ordinary Christian misconceptions. When we do the history better we glimpse forgotten dimensions of what the Gospels were trying to tell us.

The obvious, and telling, example is 'the kingdom of God'. Jesus was perceived as a prophet announcing God's reign. We know plenty about what that meant to his contemporaries, and which scriptural texts they would have associated with it. We know, too, that Jesus appears to have been *redefining* what 'kingdom of God' meant—doing so *around himself and his own strange vocation*. He was not simply *describing* God's kingdom; he was claiming that in his words and deeds, and then vitally in his forthcoming death, he was bringing it about and thereby subtly redefining it, offering a fresh exegesis of the ancient kingdom-promises in the Psalms, Daniel and Isaiah, an exegesis which partly meshed with and partly challenged the other interpretations on offer in his day.

But from at least the third century onwards, much church tradition has not taken seriously either the Jewish context of Jesus' kingdom-proclamation or the content of his redefinition. Most Western Christians have assumed that 'kingdom of God' meant 'going to heaven when you die'. This is flat wrong, just as Schweitzer's idea that the kingdom meant the end of the world was flat wrong. But if we get it right (sharing Jesus' vision of God's kingdom 'on earth as in heaven'), this revolutionises how we read the Gospels, how we understand Jesus and how we imagine the church relating to Jesus and his story today. This historical core is not simply a matter of clarifying what Jesus was talking about. It is the mandate for the necessary vocation of history itself. Once we allow history on stage to defeat the defeaters we must be prepared for it to dismantle the distortions as well.

There will be enormous resistance to this in both church and theology. Theology has regularly said, 'You historians are wolves in sheep's clothing, and we're not going to listen to you'. People have assumed that appealing to 'history' means smuggling in eighteenth-century reductionism. But that is simply scaremongering. In any case, we have no choice. The Word became *flesh*. Avoiding history is the first step to Gnosticism. As I have tried to argue in various places, history will show, not that Christianity is based on a mistake, but that the ways we have perceived and re-expressed what we thought the central texts were all about have indeed *introduced* mistakes, precisely by not paying attention to the historical setting and meaning. That is why it simply will not do to appeal to tradition, whether dogmatic or pious. Dogma and piety alike need to submit—as the Reformers would insist, and as even Aquinas might agree—to the original meaning of scripture itself.

Directing the Discussion

If history can defeat the defeaters and dismantle the distortions, it must then also *direct the discussion*. We dare not start somewhere else, even with copper-bottomed orthodox statements like that of Chalcedon, and try to move forwards while ignoring what the early texts were saying. Chalcedon was an attempt to recapture, in fifth-century idiom and for particular purposes, something central in the early texts. But the mode, manner and content of its retrieval left much to be desired, as even the cautious and orthodox Henry Chadwick acknowledged in a seminal article.[149] It screened out several dimensions of the original historical context and meaning, which, had they been retrieved, would have provided a more robust account of Christology and of other themes too. If theology is to be true to itself it must not simply snatch a few biblical texts to decorate an argument mounted on other grounds, excusing the procedure by referring to great theologians of the past who have done the same thing. It must *grow out of historical exegesis of the text itself.* Where those texts intend a reference to 'history' as *events*, that too must be taken fully into account.

I understand the resistance to historical exegesis. Many theologians experienced undergraduate biblical studies as the dry, lifeless rehearsing of Greek roots and reconstructed sources. That too was always a way of avoiding genuine history, of pretending that digging the soil was the same thing as growing the vegetables. When done properly, historical exegesis (the *task* and the *narrative*) ought to be producing the plants themselves (true knowledge of *events*) and letting them bear their own fruit (*meaning*). But it will only do this if it is allowed to be itself; if the historical task can be pursued without people looking over its shoulder and warning it about the shifting sands or telling it that it's safer to play the violin without the bow. Back to the Petrine temptations once more.

I issue a plea at this point, therefore, to the larger world of theology: do not fear or reject history. You have nothing to lose but your Platonism. Of course, for the last 250 years people have said 'history, history' when there was no history, when all they were doing was using Hume and Troeltsch to undermine Christianity (not least by de-Judaizing it). The slippery phrase 'historical-critical', as we have seen, has often given good exegesis a bad name. Theologians who are used to rejecting the would-be historical critique of Reimarus, the liberal anti-dogmatism of Harnack and the ultra-reductionism of the 'Jesus Seminar' have in effect borrowed Lessing's ugly ditch as a moat to defend their citadel against any historically based critique which might say, not that Christianity itself was based on a mistake, but that some of Christianity's Great Traditions have slipped their moorings and floated off into the blue sky of speculation. But supposing there was an important difference between Christian truth and Lessing's 'necessary truths of reason'?

Reimarus was right, then, to say that the Western church needed to be confronted with history; he was wrong to suppose that this would falsify Christianity itself. Rather, it would remind the Western church of the core kingdom-message which came true in Jesus' life, death and resurrection and the sending of the spirit. Adolf von Harnack was right to say that the third- and fourth-century Fathers changed the shape of the early teaching, but wrong to suppose that the change was from an early 'low' Christology (or Pneumatology) to a later 'high' one. The Jesus Seminar was right to say that Jesus had to be studied in his historical context but quite wrong in the way they went about that task.[150] The challenge of the Gospels remains: to hold together the kingdom and the cross, with Jesus inaugurating the first by suffering the second. To embrace a high Christology and forget the kingdom is as bad as insisting on the kingdom and assuming a low Christology: the divinity of Jesus is the key in which the Gospel music is set, but it isn't the tune that is being played. This results in the irony of people invoking 'scriptural authority' to support various styles of modern Western Christianity, perpetuating Platonic theories which historical exegesis of scripture actually undermines.

Jesus' kingdom-announcement itself therefore commits his followers to the task of history: to the research and careful reconstruction of what Jesus did and what he meant by it, and also what his first followers understood at the time and came to understand shortly afterwards as they wrote the initial history. The *task* of history will then be to produce further *coherent narratives about the past* through which the reader will gain a better insight into *what actually happened* and *what it meant to the key players at the time*. As we grapple with this through the ongoing task, we reach out towards wider meanings, not to collapse the project into subjectivism or to relativize the intermediate tasks but to display the full historical picture and allow the theology to emerge from it. When we examine the events concerning Jesus of Nazareth, in their first-century Palestinian context, as part of the 'natural' world, we discover that they are pregnant with theological meaning. It will not do for the sceptic to play heads-I-win tails-you-lose at this point—to say either, 'You cannot refer to Jesus because he is part of your "special revelation"' or 'We have looked at Jesus and he is just an ordinary Jewish teacher/revolutionary/failed Messiah'. Jesus himself matters for 'natural theology'.

THE TASK OF THE CHRISTIAN HISTORIAN

So what is Christian historiography all about, and how can it contribute to a project that might claim the title of 'natural theology'? As we have seen, it is important to notice that the task of history itself is, for the Christian historian, a kind of *kenosis*, an 'emptying'.[151] The Christian historian is not called upon to abandon belief in divine sovereignty or providence, as is sometimes imagined by those who fear 'methodological naturalism'. Belief in divine sovereignty does not tell me, in advance of historical research, *what it is that has happened in the real world over which I believe God is sovereign*. As soon as someone says, 'Because God is sovereign, because Jesus is Lord, such-and-such *must have happened*'—or alternatively '*cannot have happened*'—I know I am listening to a spurious kind of 'historicism'. One cannot do history 'from above'. The historian has to plunge into the real world, to follow the Jesus of Philippians 2 into the messy and risky sphere of events themselves in order to find out *what it is in fact that God has sovereignly done.* We do not know this in advance: no-one has ever seen God, declares John, but the only begotten God has unveiled him (1.18). Not to do this is to reject the God of John's Gospel, or of Philippians 2. It is not enough to say, 'Yes, we believe in history', meaning simply the bare acknowledgement that Jesus really existed, that God incarnate walked the earth. *We don't know who God incarnate is until we look at the incarnate God.* Without that, our reconstructions of meaning risk becoming circular, self-serving, missiologically futile.

We must, I would stress, beware of imagining that we can produce a new kind of salvation-history, reading divine intention and action off the all too ambiguous pages of even the best history. Just because we believe in divine providence we cannot copy the inspired writers of scripture and leap straight to a God's-eye view of events. Hegel saw history as inexorable progress; we beg to differ. Martin Luther saw the mediaeval period as the Babylonian Captivity of the church: well, perhaps. But perhaps not. As with the depths and ambiguities in our own lives, divine order is seldom perceived all at once, and perhaps that's just as well. Even St Paul, musing on the meaning of Onesimus's conversion, used that word, 'perhaps', to introduce his suggested interpretation (Philemon 15). Back to humility, patience, penitence and love.

And so back to Jesus. He remains central to theology, which means that theology needs history—in all four senses. We dare not embrace methodological Docetism (a Jesus who looks historical but isn't really). That means we must not, for fear of modernist prejudice, invoke something called 'the supernatural' to 'explain' everything. That would merely perpetuate Lessing's false either/or. It would fail at the hermeneutic of love in which we allow the past to be itself, since it would be collapsing the ways in which (some) first-century people thought into the ways that (some) post-Enlightenment people have thought.

Historical study of the early Jewish and Christian world thus itself sets the hermeneutical parameters for the task. As we study that period, as we shall in more detail in the next two chapters, we discover people who did not suppose the world to be divided into nature and supernatural, and whose beliefs cannot easily be captured within the modern Epicurean worldview. Their understandings of reality were Temple-shaped: heaven and earth overlapped and interlocked. Their understanding of time was Sabbath-shaped: God's future was not alien to the present time but could and did appear within it. Sometimes, to be sure, things happened which took them by surprise, so that they said things like, 'God has visited his people!' (Luke 7.16)[152] More often than not, though, their response to events was dismay and puzzlement, particularly when Jesus went to his cruel death.[153] The fact that one cannot (as is often said) 'prove the divinity of Jesus' by history alone is part of the point: we don't even know what 'divinity' is until we discover who Jesus himself was, as all four Gospels insist. The early Christians themselves insist that one cannot start with a picture of God and then try to fit Jesus into it. That didn't work in the first century, and it won't work now. The Gospels insist that one should approach the question the other way around. Nor can we simply declare Jesus to be 'divine' on the basis (say) of his resurrection (though resurrection by itself would not in fact make that point; the Maccabean martyrs, affirming that God was going to raise them from the dead, were not suggesting that this would make them 'divine') and then, assuming we know what 'divine' means, proceed from there while ignoring what the Gospels actually say. That, I think, is what has often happened within would-be orthodox Christianity. That is what has invited the protests, from Reimarus to the 'Jesus Seminar' and beyond.

Rather, when with historical tools we look both *at* and *through* the story of Jesus—at the outside and the inside of the total event—we discover *vital and unavoidable questions*. These turn out to be cognate with the great questions we shall study in chapter 7, the questions that arise within human life as a whole, across time and culture. And, to anticipate our argument there, the point is not that we can deduce 'God' from those questions. History alone cannot form the foundation for an old-fashioned rationalist apologetic. A true apologetic includes the larger 'history' which is the spirit-filled life of the church, the story-telling and symbol-making through which new creation brings healing to the present world and points on to God's ultimate heaven-and-earth future.

Commitment to the historical task obliges us to make a determined effort to reframe our great theological questions in terms of the actual life of first-century Palestinian Jews. Many branches of Christian theology have remained content with looking at Jesus, and at the Gospels, through spectacles manufactured in later centuries. They have tended to seize upon small selections of Jesus' deeds and words to illustrate later theological formulations, without paying attention to the proper setting, and in particular to what 'the kingdom of God' (by all accounts, Jesus' central theme) would have meant there. But only when we attempt this task—when we look at Jesus in his own context—will we discover what the four Gospels were trying to tell us: that by getting to know this resolutely human person, his vocation, his fate and its surprising aftermath, we discover that the questions raised by human life in general (chapter 7 below) and the questions raised by Jesus' own life, public career and death are answered in such dramatic and coherent fashion that we have a strong case for saying that they were the right questions to be asking.

I propose, therefore, that to study first-century history with Jesus and his first followers in the middle of it is a necessary part of healthy Christian life, theology and witness—and that this witness, rooted in this historical study, can and should form a vital part of a refreshed 'natural theology'. History studies events in the 'natural' world, events which have an 'inside' as well as an 'outside'. Jesus can and should be studied that way.

CONCLUSION

I have proposed in this chapter that, once we clarify the different meanings of the word 'history', we can understand the ways in which confusion has arisen because of the different frameworks and agendas within which people have attempted not only to 'do history' but to use the results of their work within larger schemes of thought, all the time either appealing to or dismissing 'history' as though the meaning of the word was unambiguous.

The task of history is thus not unlike the task of Elijah, rebuilding the altar of YHWH which had fallen into disrepair (1 Kings 18.19–46). The priests of Baal—the self-appointed leaders of secular Western culture—have danced around, cutting themselves with their own theories, dreaming dreams of progress and/or revolution, and still the kingdom has not come. Many of the faithful YHWH-scribes have retreated into caves, safe in their private worlds. Taking Elijah's story as a metaphor, it is now time for the historians to reassume the task (taking up the stones that speak of the ancient past, the foundational evidence) and with them to build an altar (a narrative which genuinely points to real events), laying upon it such invocation of 'meaning' as emerges from that work. The altar will, of course, be surrounded by a broad and ugly ditch, full of water. It may look impossible for the sacrifice ever to catch fire. That is not our business. Our job is to build the altar, the public truth which emerges from responsible and careful historical work, displaying as best we can the meanings which make deep, rich first-century sense. Then, and only then, we pray for the fire to fall.

If that sounds like 'apocalyptic', perhaps that is appropriate. And it points us forward to the next chapter.

4

The End of the World?

Eschatology and Apocalyptic in Historical Perspective

INTRODUCTION

Anyone who argues, as I have now begun to do, that Christian theology must be anchored in the historical situation and beliefs of Jesus and his first followers, must expect a standard response. 'You surely don't mean,' people will say, 'that we should all pretend to be first-century apocalyptists, going around thinking the world is about to come to an end?' And anyone who argues, as I have done and will do here, that actually Jesus and his first followers were not expecting the imminent end of the space-time universe, may well meet the puzzled riposte I received from the late Eric Franklin, one of my Oxford colleagues, when I published *The New Testament and the People of God* in 1992. 'So, Tom', he began, 'now that you've abandoned eschatology . . .'

I do not think that to follow Jesus we have to imagine that the world is going to end tomorrow. Nor have I 'abandoned eschatology'. But, as with 'history' and 'historicism' in the previous chapter, we have to address head-on the difficult task of untangling the several different senses those words have had in theological and historical discussions over the last century or so. And, in particular, we have to give a historical account of the first-century 'eschatology' which Jesus and his first followers really did believe. That combination of tasks forms the agenda for the present chapter.

I have argued so far that the question of 'natural theology' meets us in the modern period from within the larger parameters of the revived Epicureanism which has been the assumed theology of the 'secular age'. And I have suggested that the question itself has been thereby twisted out of shape. The overall question of the relationship between God and the world—and indeed the meanings of 'God' and 'world' themselves!—depend on the framework within which we place them, and that framework has been the turbulent modern Western culture. Moreover, as we saw in the last chapter, the Epicurean split of heaven and earth was matched by the Enlightenment's split between past and present, generating further confusions around 'history' itself. It is clear that the ongoing discussions of Jesus and his first followers must be situated in the same swirling cultural context. Pretence to 'neutrality' or 'objectivity' is just that, pretence. However, as I argued earlier, that doesn't exclude, but rather calls the more urgently for, a critical realist approach to historiography, recognising that an idea like 'critical realism' is itself situated within the same modern debates. The results of such an approach will then remain in dialogue with the larger theological questions. Theology, after all, has still invoked Jesus—or at least 'Christ', with various meanings!—even if it hasn't known what to do with him, still less what *he* might do to *it*. The result has been that theology, including 'natural theology', has marginalized any first-century understanding of Jesus himself and his kingdom-message.

This has particularly affected those blessed words, 'eschatology' and 'apocalyptic'. We have all complained at the imprecision of these words, but we've all gone on using them. I here propose some clarifications so that we can then address the question arising from chapter 2: if Schweitzer and Bultmann were wrong about the end-of-the-world Jesus, what about the sayings which seem to point in that direction? This is the necessary route back to our main topic. The texts themselves, read historically, will show that the Enlightenment's radical splits of cosmology and history are bound to produce false readings. Bultmann's Giffords were, I think, caught in this trap: if we think of 'history' within a 'closed continuum' of Epicurean world-development, then anything to do with 'God' must by definition be entirely separate. That is why the word 'apocalyptic' has been taken out of its most natural use, to denote a literary genre, and made to serve as a label for a kind of worldview in which God breaks in from the outside (producing one-way traffic only, i.e. with no possibility for the inference of a 'natural theology').[1] This is one reason why Bultmann turned 'eschatology' into a metaphor for private spiritual experience.

ESCHATOLOGY AND APOCALYPTIC

Introduction

I believe the whole discussion to be ill-founded. But before I turn to the textual argument, we need to lay out the different senses in which these key terms have been used.[2]

Eschatology

On 'eschatology', I follow and develop somewhat George Caird's analysis in his still important book *The Language and Imagery of the Bible*.[3]

We start with the traditional meaning: 'the last things', namely death, judgment, heaven and hell. The word was first used in Germany in the early 1800s and was imported into the English-speaking world later that century, with that meaning. Many dictionaries still give this as the only meaning.

Second, there is the 'historicist' belief, as explained in the previous chapter: 'history' itself is 'going somewhere'. By 1900 the word 'eschatology' was being used to indicate this kind of predictive historicism. Events were progressing towards some kind of a goal, whether that of Hegel, or then of Teilhard de Chardin, or of a more biblical retrieval of something called 'salvation-history'.

This was eclipsed, third, by the *Konsequente Eschatology* or 'consistent eschatology' of Albert Schweitzer, who used the word in the sense it still bears for many: the imminent end of the world.[4]

Fourth, we have C. H. Dodd's 'realised eschatology' response to Schweitzer. Jesus was announcing that the kingdom *was already present*, that it had been 'realised'.[5] Dodd either eliminated future-oriented sayings or flattened them out into present meanings. Dodd later modified his stance, under the influence of Jeremias, who spoke of 'eschatology in the process of being realised'. That still left open what exactly the kingdom might be.

Bultmann then introduced the 'existentialist' meaning, expounded not least in his Giffords. This was a conscious 'demythologising' of Schweitzer: yes, the language used may have meant an actual end of the world (which Jesus and his followers still believed in), but they translated it into meaning something like what English speakers mean by 'spirituality', with 'horizontal' or 'temporal' expectation transformed into vertical inbreaking hope. Like Dodd, this turned the apparently future into the supposedly present. For Dodd, this boiled down to a new ethic; for Bultmann, a new 'authentic existence'.[6] The Lutheran Bultmann, always suspicious of 'works', replaced them with an experience not too different from Gnosticism.[7]

Caird then describes, but does not label, the two meanings which we can confidently identify historically, on which, I suggest, research should concentrate. There is, first, a quite widespread Jewish view of 'two ages', the 'present age' and the 'age to come'. This two-age theory is not, as is often imagined, characteristic of a so-called 'apocalyptic' worldview to be differentiated from other forms of Jewish beliefs. It was widespread, continuing into the much later Rabbis, long after the dangerous kingdom-dreams of bar Kochba, and the books like Daniel that had seemed to give them support, had been abandoned.[8] The two-age scheme summarizes the historical and political hope for the real 'return from exile', the 'new Exodus', and so on. To speak of these 'two ages' is not, as people often suppose, dualistic (though it can be combined with forms of dualism in which a godforsaken 'present' will be superseded by a god-filled future, and some Jews, perhaps some in the little sect at Qumran, may have taken it in that direction). The present world, after all, is itself supposedly the creation of the One God and is under his providential control—with various theories being advanced as to why he keeps delaying ushering in 'the age to come' in which all things will be put right.[9]

Where does this sit in relation to the other meanings? The traditional one is hardly in sight. Most Jews believed in some kind of afterlife theory but not in those terms.[10] Nor does the Jewish two-age scheme yield a predictive historicism, let alone a smooth development (with the Age to Come being simply a polished prolongation of the Present Age).[11] Nor does it support the end-of-the-world idea, which as I suggested in chapter 2 and will underline in the present chapter is simply a modern misunderstanding. Nor does the two-age scheme allow for a fully 'realised eschatology' in either the Jewish texts or the Gospels. Even when Jesus was doing exorcisms, declaring that 'if I by the finger of God cast out demons, then the kingdom of God has come upon you',[12] most of the signs of the 'age to come' (overthrow of wickedness, universal justice and peace) were not present. Likewise, this Jewish two-age view would reject the existential interpretation. An existential sense of the divine presence might perhaps be thought a *necessary* condition for recognising the arrival of the age to come, but it could never be a *sufficient* condition. As Jewish critics have always insisted, the coming age was to be firmly this-worldly: a new political and social order. It would be more than an idea in people's heads or a warm feeling in their hearts.

There is, finally, a seventh meaning: the early Christian version of this Jewish hope, explicit in the Gospels and Paul, claiming that 'the age to come' *has already been inaugurated* through the death of Jesus and his resurrection. He had won the victory over the dark powers; he had dealt with sin and launched the new creation. Anticipations of this view are found already in Qumran and in some other pre-Christian Jewish texts which believed that events had *already* occurred which were to be understood as genuine anticipations of the final day. This view contains within it the promise that all things will be put right at the last, as in Romans 8, 1 Corinthians 15 or Revelation 21 and 22. This includes what we moderns think of as 'social' or 'political' effects. The promises of Psalm 72 are not merely metaphors for spirituality, or distant signposts to a non-spatio-temporal 'heaven'. They are real pointers to actual justice and mercy.

Apocalyptic

I have elsewhere discussed 'apocalyptic' extensively. The Swiss scholar Jörg Frey has recently accused me of 'neutralizing' apocalyptic, a charge I rebut.[13] For Frey, and others on the continent, the word 'apocalyptic' still means what Schweitzer and Bultmann were both talking about, and any denial of the 'end-of-the-world' meaning is seen as a cop-out. More importantly, though, in America and one or two parts of the UK—but nowhere much else—'apocalyptic' is now often used in a specialised sense associated with J. Louis Martyn and his followers, denoting divine invasion 'vertically from above' and allowing no room for earlier stories of the world in general or Israel in particular. This sense of 'apocalyptic', as Frey rightly sees, does not belong at all in the first century. It is a twentieth-century polemical invention, retrieving some features of the early Barth, flying under the false colours of a term from first-century *Religionsgeschichte*. When theologians attempt to retrieve Martyn's meaning as though to give biblical validation to such a scheme, all they are doing is seeing the reflection of a pale Barthian face at the bottom of a muddled exegetical well.[14]

Let us once more clarify meanings. I start with the view of Martyn and his small but vocal group of supporters: 'apocalyptic' is about divine disclosure and/or victory, with no visible antecedent. History has failed; we need a new Word. Galatians 1.4 speaks of being 'delivered from the present evil age'. Adherents of this sometimes cite Walter Benjamin without irony. I have argued elsewhere that this does not describe any recognisable first-century views. Barth himself, certainly the mature Barth, would have rejected it.[15] Martyn's exegesis of Galatians is fatally flawed.

Second, there is the view we associate with Weiss and Schweitzer: that 'apocalyptic' refers to the actual and imminent end of the world. When the text says, 'the stars will fall from heaven', it means that the stars will fall from heaven. Anyone looking up at the sky could see it happening.

Third, there is a focus on the second coming, the *'parousia'* of Jesus. This functions as an extra detail within the idea of an imminent End. This is what Käsemann had in mind when he said that 'apocalyptic' was 'the mother of Christian theology'. For him, the earliest Christians lived on the imminent hope of Jesus' return. The next generation, disappointed, reframed everything differently.

Fourth—the position Käsemann was resisting—we have Bultmann's demythologised reading: 'apocalyptic' in terms of existential experience. Here, Jesus borrowed the *language* of an imminent end, which his followers continued to use in a literal sense; but he did so in order to refer to the timeless (and non-political) existential challenge to every person at every moment.

Instead of this interior struggle, Käsemann saw a cosmic battle. This produces a fifth meaning for 'apocalyptic': the language denotes the struggle in which non-human powers wage war against God and his people. This is where J. L. Martyn diverged radically from his teacher. For Käsemann, the *parousia* would be the final victory; for Martyn (who made the idea of cosmic powers central to his meaning of the word too) the battle had already been won on the cross.[16]

The sixth position is Caird's (supported by many today, e.g. Christopher Rowland), which I follow. The word 'apocalyptic', I suggest, is best used to denote a *genre*, or at least a *literary form and use*, where the writers intend to *denote* what we call this-worldly realities and to *connote* theological meaning. Thus a 'monster' or 'beast' in Daniel 7 or Revelation 13 would *denote* a pagan empire or emperor and *connote* the dark anti-God forces that 'come up out of the sea' (the place of chaos and evil).[17] This is seen in Jewish writing from Daniel to *4 Ezra*, and in early Christian writing including Revelation, Paul and the Gospels.[18] The so-called 'apocalyptic discourse' in Mark 13 is ostensibly about the fall of the Temple which symbolized and effected the joining of heaven and earth. Its destruction could hardly be described except—as Jeremiah already knew—in terms of cosmic collapse.[19]

My specific debate with Jörg Frey is perhaps important enough to summarize here. I hold to the position I have outlined above, while Frey, who seems to hold a version of 'final end' and '*parousia*' meanings, seems to think that my position can be attacked in the same way as Bultmann's existentialist reading. But we both reject, on historical grounds, the view of J. L. Martyn and his followers, which is currently popular in some quarters in America. Frey, seeing my rejection of this view, has reacted as though I were rejecting the idea of an End, or perhaps demythologising it like Bultmann. But *decoding, as in the view I have outlined, is not demythologising*. It is recognising, as a matter of history, the socio-political referent of the language and giving full weight to the writers' belief that the events thus denoted should be seen as the battle-ground of cosmic powers. I am thus, *pace* Frey, neither modernizing, nor taming, nor neutralizing 'apocalyptic'. I am reading it in its historical context. Indeed, to read 'apocalyptic' *without* its political dimensions, as Bultmann did, would be the real 'neutralisation'.

THE HISTORICAL HOPE

What matters throughout is historical exegesis, as explained in the previous chapter: the constant effort to understand texts in their contexts. The Jewish and early Christian writings towards which Weiss and Schweitzer gestured were emphatically to do with this-worldly realities, interpreting those realities, past, present and future, within an integrated cosmology of which the Temple was the effective symbol. The writers in question were not dualists, not Epicureans or Deists, and certainly not Platonists.[20] The Jews and early Christians believed in the cosmology reflected in Temple and Sabbath: heaven and earth, future and present were designed to go together, to overlap and interlock. We shall explore this further in the next chapter. There never was a particular first-century sect or school of 'apocalypticists'. Josephus never mentions such a thing. It is a modern invention. Perhaps quite a variety of groups *used apocalyptic forms* from time to time (as did Jesus himself, in Mark 13 but also for instance in the parables) to express their particular varieties of hope. But none of them could appropriately be defined as 'apocalyptists'.

I agree of course with those who call Jesus an 'eschatological prophet' or even an 'apocalyptic prophet'.[21] But what might that mean? The debates go to and fro, often masking the historical truth. If the choice is between Schweitzer and Wrede, I have always chosen Schweitzer. If the choice is between Bultmann and the 'German Christians', with their historicist 'progress'-agenda, we must choose Bultmann. If the choice is between Käsemann's proposal that 'apocalyptic is the mother of early Christianity' and some non-apocalyptic, steady-state view of Jesus and his followers as teaching merely a new social ethic—a chastened Ritschlianism, as it were, however radical—we must choose Käsemann. But at every point in this hundred-year discussion the appeal has been to *history*, not in the historicist sense of an immanent progressive movement but in the sense of *what the first-century texts were actually talking about*. And at that point we must protest. Neither Schweitzer, nor Bultmann, nor Käsemann got the history itself right.

Jesus' proclamation was indeed about *something that was happening and that would happen*, as a result of which the world would be a different place. If that is what is meant by 'eschatology', then the word is undoubtedly correct. This hope was often expressed in the Second Temple period in scriptural language, not least with echoes of Daniel. If this is what we mean by 'apocalyptic', that too is undoubtedly correct. Jesus was not simply a great moral or social teacher. He was not offering either a new spirituality or a new way to 'get to heaven'. He was talking about something that was happening, and that would happen, once and for all 'on earth as in heaven'. He was using language that would invest that 'something' with its theological significance. But what was that 'something'?

'Apocalyptic' literature, to repeat, uses the *language* of cosmic catastrophe to refer to *actual political events*. Isaiah spoke of sun and moon being darkened to refer to the fall of Babylon, and to give that event its cosmic significance.[22] Jeremiah, referring to the fall of Jerusalem, warned that the world was heading for its chaotic pre-creation state.[23] Having prophesied the return to chaos, he worried for a long time that he might be a false prophet—not because the world had not ended, but because Jerusalem had not fallen. First-century Jews knew that this was how the language worked. Josephus regards Daniel as politically subversive; *4 Ezra* reinterprets Daniel with the messianic lion attacking the Roman eagle. No serious scholar today, and nobody at all in the first century, thought that Daniel's four sea-monsters were the sort of things David Attenborough might display on *Blue Planet*; so why assume that 'the son of man coming on the clouds' would refer simply to a human being flying around in mid-air? Nobody reading *4 Ezra* 12 imagined an actual lion attacking an actual (if unconventionally feathered) eagle. The post-Enlightenment world, having never really engaged with ancient Jewish thought, inevitably understood divine action in the world within the prevailing Epicurean worldview, and so took such language to denote 'intervention from outside', resulting in the present world coming to an end. Since the Enlightenment also understood time to be broken (so that the past was now inaccessible, breaking links with the ancient world which had hitherto been assumed) and was offering its own version of inaugurated eschatology in which Jesus was at best an early teacher of an acceptable 'religion', it was deaf to first-century Jewish notions of both space and time. When Weiss and others declared that the ancient cosmology was not available to the modern world, what they should have said was that they had not bothered to investigate the ancient literary convention. In any case, the Enlightenment was offering, and continues to offer, its own version of inaugurated eschatology, in which Jesus, at best, would have to be an early 'religious teacher'.

In particular, it was deaf to the main themes of Jewish hope: for the 'new age' to arrive, with YHWH himself returning in visible glory, and Israel rescued at last from ongoing exile. This brings us at last to the actual texts at the heart of the debates.

HOPE REIMAGINED: JESUS AND HIS FIRST FOLLOWERS[24]

Those who have insisted that Jesus and his first followers believed in the imminent end of the world have regularly turned to Mark 9.1 and parallels: 'Some people standing here won't experience death before they see God's kingdom come in power'. Closely allied with this is Jesus' answer to Caiaphas (Mark 14.62), where Mark reads, 'You will see "the Son of Man sitting at the right hand of Power, and coming with the clouds of heaven"'.

Many other early Christian passages link to these. There are various sayings about 'the end', such as 1 Corinthians 15.24 ('then comes the end') or Matthew 28.20 ('I am with you, every single day, to the very end of the age'). It is usual in this context to discuss a potential development in Paul: in his earlier writings he clearly expected 'the end', including the general resurrection, within his own lifetime (1 Thessalonians 4.15; 1 Corinthians 15.51–52). However, after the terrible time he had in Ephesus (2 Corinthians 1.8–10) he recognised that he might well die before 'the day' arrived, and was figuring out how to think about the consequences (2 Corinthians 5.1–5; Philippians 1.20–26).[25] But the difference here has to do with Paul's personal perspective, not with a change of belief about the End. It might come *at any time*; originally, he assumed this would be in his lifetime, but he subsequently realised it might well not be. At no point in the earlier period does he suggest that it must be 'within a generation'; at no point in the later period does he express an anxiety that the End itself is 'delayed'.

When it comes to reading the Gospels, we should note a distinction between events referred to as future *from the perspective of Jesus' public career* and events seen as future *from within the perspective of post-Easter Christian life*. Of course, the former were 'written up' within the post-Easter world. But, as with many other aspects of the Gospels' portrayals of Jesus, they are imagining themselves within a world which would have made sense in Jesus' own time.[26] As is well known, some key features (kingdom of God, 'coming of the Son of Man', and so on) are tagged with a time-constraint, the lifetime either of some bystanders (Mark 9.1) or of the present generation (Mark 13.30 and its parallels). Attempts to find such definite short-term indicators elsewhere, however, often involve special pleading, as with *ho kairos synestalmenos estin* in 1 Corinthians 7.29, which NRSV translates as 'the appointed time has grown short' but which, in the light of 7.26 which refers to 'the present difficult time' (referring, some have suggested, to a current famine), I have translated as 'the present situation won't last long'.[27] The *only* points in the whole New Testament at which we find explicit mention of a puzzling 'delay' are the notorious 2 Peter 3.4–10 and the gentler John 21. I have discussed both briefly in chapter 2.[28]

This leaves us with two main questions. First, do any early texts speak of an actual cosmic catastrophe? Second, how did the first Christians themselves understand the sayings which *did* have a specific time-limit, such as Mark 9.1 or Mark 13.30?[29]

Some have cited Romans 8.18–25 as predicting a cosmic convulsion; the passage does indeed envisage the transformation of the present creation. Paul uses Exodus-language: what God did for Israel, liberating them from Pharaoh's Egypt, and what God did for Jesus in raising him from the dead, God will do for the whole creation in the end, setting it free from its 'slavery to decay' (8.21). Paul links this closely to the final resurrection, envisaging an actual event (not something that could be demythologised into an existential experience) in which the cosmos will be transformed. This is presumably why Bultmann could make nothing of the passage.[30] We will shortly correlate this to 1 Corinthians 15, 1 Thessalonians 4–5, Philippians 3.20–21 and 2 Corinthians 5.1–10. As with other parallels, Paul can describe the same event in different ways, drawing on biblical imagery to invest the future event with theological meaning.

Romans 8 does not, however, describe a cosmic *catastrophe* or 'disaster'. This is not 'the end of the world' in the normal sense. The present creation will not be destroyed; rather the reverse. It will be *set free* from destruction, from the severe limitation imposed by *phthora*, 'decay'. It will be more truly itself when, in the end, God will be 'all in all' (1 Corinthians 15.28). All this is guaranteed, in Romans 8, by two things: the death and resurrection of the Messiah, and the power of the spirit. Something *has happened* in the past—the death and resurrection of Jesus—as a result of which something else *will happen* in the future. There is all the difference between a cosmic catastrophe, in which the present world will cease to exist and a new purely 'heavenly' reality will take its place, and a cosmic Exodus in which the whole creation will be liberated from decay. The same principle underlies the arrival of the 'new heavens and new earth' in Revelation 21. In any case, *Paul says nothing in Romans 8 or elsewhere about the predicted cosmic transformation necessarily coming to pass within a generation.* Like the thief in the night, it could come at *any* time.

The point is made graphically in Second Thessalonians 2. Here we don't see exactly what 'the day of the Lord' actually means, but we see plainly what it does *not* mean:

> Please don't be suddenly blown off course in your thinking, or be unsettled, either through spiritual influence, or through a word, or through a letter supposedly from us, telling you that the day of the Lord has already arrived. (2 Thessalonians 2.2)

If 'the day of the Lord' meant 'the collapse of the space-time universe', this sentence would be nonsense. One would not expect to be informed, via the Roman postal service or through one of Paul's messengers, that the world had just come to an end. All that follows in the chapter (the prediction of 'the lawless one' who will be destroyed by the breath of Jesus' nostrils' [2.8, alluding to Isaiah 11.4] and will be destroyed by 'the unveiling of his *parousia*') comes under this rubric. These will be *transformative events within the ongoing space-time world*, not the destruction of that world and its replacement with a 'purely supernatural' existence.

So what did the earliest Christians believe about Jesus' promise of an imminent kingdom? Supposing we showed Mark 9.1 and its parallels to Paul, or the question of Mark 13.30 concerning 'this generation' not disappearing; what would he have said? And supposing we then asked *the writers of the Gospels themselves* to explain what was meant, what might they say?

One of the best-known answers to these questions is that the early Christians developed a 'now-and-not-yet' approach. Something *had happened* to bring the expected kingdom to birth, and something *was yet to happen* through which that already-inaugurated kingdom would reach its ultimate goal. Many have taken this two-stage eschatology for granted in the last half-century. Some, however, still attack it as a modern apologetic invention, or at best the invention of a later first-century Christian mindset once the first generation had died out.[31] The case must be made again.

EARLY TRADITIONS OUTSIDE THE GOSPELS

Paul, as I just pointed out, never changed his mind about the coming 'end', only about whether he would live to see it.[32] But Paul is important in this discussion for many other reasons. In particular, he appears to use what most have seen as early formulae which summed up what most Jesus-followers believed in the 50s and perhaps earlier still. We may note in particular the opening flourish of Romans, not often invoked in this connection. There Paul affirms, as thematic for the whole great letter to come, the fact that Jesus has already been marked out as 'son of God in power' by his resurrection:

> . . . the good news about his son, who was descended from David's seed in terms of flesh, and who was marked out powerfully as God's son in terms of the spirit of holiness by the resurrection of the dead: Jesus, the king, our Lord!
>
> Through him we have received grace and apostleship to bring about believing obedience among all the nations for the sake of his name. (Romans 1.3–5)

'Marked out powerfully as God's son' here translates *tou horisthentos hyiou theou en dynamei*, literally 'marked out as God's son *in power*', and the following verse indicates that this 'power' refers not simply to the power which effected his resurrection but to the power with which the 'son' is now invested, as in the enthronement scene in Psalm 2.8 ('ask of me, and I will make the nations your heritage, and the ends of the earth your possession'). The 'power' in question is now manifested in Paul's commissioning to summon the nations to a new loyalty, 'believing obedience' or 'faithful allegiance'. The addition of 'for the sake of his name' looks across to another bit of early tradition, Philippians 2.10, which would make the same point.

This language, echoing Psalm 2 and 2 Samuel 7, and probably already traditional (and therefore perhaps to be dated at the latest around AD 50), gives a decisive answer to the question of Mark 9.1: yes, the kingdom *has already* come with power, when Jesus was raised from the dead and sent out his messengers to the nations.[33] This doesn't rule out the future tense from Paul's theology, as in Romans 2, 8 and 13. Paul does not suppose for a moment that the ultimate 'end' has already come. Nor do those three chapters, with their future orientation, say anything about 'within a generation' (13.11 is often taken in that sense, but it is in fact vague, perhaps deliberately so). Past and future then frame present obligation: to *implement* the 'already' through apostolic work and thereby to *anticipate* the eventual future.

This notion of God's already-launched kingdom appears explicitly in Romans 5.12–21, the foundation for the climactic chapters 6, 7 and 8. The reign of the Messiah, and of God through him—and, with him, of his people!—are here *present* realities with *future* consequences. This is picked up again in the final theological climax of the letter in chapter 15.7–13, where the resurrection has already constituted Jesus as the ruler of the nations, not least through the quotation from Isaiah 11.1, 10:

> The Messiah became a servant of the circumcised people in order to demonstrate the truthfulness of God—that is, to confirm the promises to the patriarchs, and to bring the nations to praise God for his mercy . . .

> There shall be the root of Jesse,
> The one who rises up to rule the nations;
> The nations shall hope in him. (Romans 15.8–9, quoting Isaiah 11.10)

For Paul, Jesus is *already* enthroned as the world's true Lord, in explicit fulfilment of the kingdom-vision of the Psalms and Isaiah. Without that, the Gentile mission, at least as Paul conceives it, makes no sense. It is because Jesus has claimed world sovereignty that non-Jews can rightfully be summoned to allegiance. This is one vital meaning of his resurrection (he 'rises up to rule the nations'); and this is the ground of the *still-future* hope. *The belief in a now-and-not-yet inaugurated kingdom, through the exaltation of the human being Jesus, Israel's Messiah, is not, then, a clever piece of apologetic invented in the late first century, let alone the mid twentieth century.* It was part of the early apostolic gospel itself.

We see the same in 1 Corinthians 15. The opening gospel summary declares that the Messiah's death and resurrection mean what they mean 'in accordance with the scriptures', and the scriptures which Paul then quotes, or to which he alludes, invest Jesus' resurrection with *messianic* and *kingdom*-related meaning. This is clear in verses 20–28, expounding a clear now-and-not-yet kingdom-teaching. The Messiah *has* been raised; he *is already* reigning; his reign will be complete only when all enemies, death included, are conquered. Paul distinguishes the present messianic reign from the clearly future time when God will be 'all in all'.

Throughout that chapter, Paul is expounding Genesis 1, 2 and 3. His reference to Adam is foundational. The Messiah is the new and generative model human, through whom other 'new humans' will be brought to life from their present mortal state (15.48–49). In particular, the Messiah's *present reign* is to be seen as the fulfilment of two vital and interlocking Psalms: 110 and 8. As in the Synoptics and Hebrews, these two Psalms speak of the coming King (Psalm 110) as also the truly human one (Psalm 8).[34] In both cases the psalm envisages 'enemies' being subdued by the royal/human figure. Paul seems to intend the statement of this in Psalm 8 to be the paragraph's main theme. Psalm 8.7b states that God has put all things under his feet. In the LXX this reads:

Panta hypetaxas hypokatō tōn podōn autou

—and Paul obviously has this in mind, making its main verb thematic in his repeated statement of everything being 'put in order' under the Messiah. The point is that when Paul cites Psalm 8.7b he evokes not only Genesis 1 and 2 but also Daniel 7. In Genesis 1 and 2, the image-bearing humans are put in authority over the plants and animals. In Daniel 7, just as in Psalm 8, we find 'the one like a son of man', who in Psalm 8.7b has been made lower than the angels, now 'crowned with glory and honour'. First Corinthians 15.20–28 as a whole, focused in the psalm text Paul quotes and expounds over and over in this passage, has to do with *the present exaltation of the 'one like a son of man' to a position of world dominion.* With that, even without an explicit quotation from Daniel 7, we are in Synoptic territory. If we ask Paul whether the scripturally promised kingdom has come with power, *and if we ask him whether 'the son of man' has already been exalted to worldwide authority,* the answer is Yes.

This would be true even if 1 Corinthians 15 did not refer to Daniel 7. But it does.[35] In 15.24 Paul explains that the present reign of the Messiah is designed to continue until he has disempowered 'all rule and all authority and power'. That will be 'the end' (*to telos*). Daniel 7.27, where the 'one like a son of man' is given royal authority, is the only other place known to me where a substantially similar set of ideas occurs.[36] The 'one like a son of man', interpreted as 'the people of the saints of the Most High', now has all authority and power subject to him. In other words, when Paul expounds Psalm 8 in relation to his new-Genesis vision of the Messiah's rule, he has Daniel 7 in mind as well, as hints elsewhere in the letter suggest. *The powerful kingdom of God is already in operation*. He says much the same in 1 Corinthians 4.19–21: the kingdom has already come in power, and Paul is prepared to exercise that power, delegated to him from the Messiah (though he will have to spend most of 2 Corinthians redefining more carefully what 'power' actually means). Thus, faced with the prediction of Mark 9.1, Paul would say, 'Yes; it's happened. God's kingdom has come with power. That is why I do what I do'. One could infer the same point from 1 Corinthians 6.2–3: The Messiah's people ought *already* to be qualified to anticipate their role as eschatological judges—including of angels!—by being competent to try earthly cases. In other words, for Paul, *new-creational eschatology has come to birth within history*.[37]

Similar themes, and similar scriptural echoes, are plentiful in Philippians. Here we find the best-known example of what many regard as pre-Pauline fragments, the poem of 2.6–11. The links here with Romans 5 and 1 Corinthians 15 are well known. Though some still dispute whether any reference to Adam is intended, it seems to me clear that Paul is drawing on the same stock of themes as those other passages where the Adam-link is explicit. There are few verbal links with Psalm 8, but the sequence of thought is the same.[38] The human figure is made a little lower than God (or the angels) and then crowned with glory and honour, with all things put underfoot. The emphasis in the poem then falls on the *name*:

> And so God has greatly exalted him,
> And to him in his favour has given
> The name which is over all names:
>
> That now at the name of Jesus
> Every knee within heaven shall bow—
> On earth, too, and under the earth
>
> And every tongue shall confess
> That Jesus, Messiah, is Lord,
> To the glory of God, the father. (Philippians 2.9–11)

The emphasis on the *name*—which is either *kyrios* itself or the combined *Kyrios Iēsous Christos* of verse 11—joins up with the narrative of humiliation and exaltation to make a powerful link to Psalm 8, whose opening and closing lines (vv. 2, 10 LXX; vv. 1, 9 EVV) read:

Kyrios ho kyrios hēmōn, hōs thaumaston to onoma sou en pasē tē gē.
(O Lord our Sovereign, how majestic is your name in all the earth!)

The *name* of *Kyrios Iēsous* is thus already, one might say, *thaumaston*, a name to be marvelled at. One way or another, it is clear that the poem itself, and Paul in his fresh use of it (supposing him to have borrowed it from elsewhere, which I regard as moot), see Jesus as *already* the exalted *kyrios* of Psalm 8. The undoubted future element in verse 11 (every tongue *shall* confess) refers, not to the Lordship itself, which Jesus already possesses, but to its universal acknowledgement.[39]

It therefore seems to be the case that, across these three books (Romans, 1 Corinthians and Philippians) and the early traditions which they may well incorporate, the early Christians who knew these traditions would join with Paul himself and declare both *that the kingdom had already come with power,* even though the power was paradoxical, made perfect in weakness (2 Corinthians 12.9), and that *the Son of Man of Psalm 8 and Daniel 7 had already been exalted.* This belief can therefore be dated to the 50s at least and to the 40s by implication. There still remained, of course, a coming day when Jesus would return to be acclaimed by all. But the prediction of the exaltation of the Son of Man had been fulfilled.

We are here, obviously, at the same point as we were in 1 Corinthians 15.23–28. Indeed, the same Christological puzzle emerges here as there: the son will be subject to the father, and now, when every tongue confesses Messiah Jesus as Lord, this will be 'to the glory of God, the father'. The early church does not seem to have been as worried about that as some subsequent theoreticians have been. Our purpose here, though, is not to go deeper into the Christological question but simply to note that in all these passages we have classically Pauline inaugurated eschatology, related specifically to the *present and future kingdom* and also to the *exaltation of the Son of Man* as something which has already taken place and whose implications are being worked out through the apostolic mission against the day when every tongue will confess him as *Kyrios.*

This is why Paul can call on similar scriptural texts when looking to the future, as for instance in 1 Thessalonians 3.13 or 2 Thessalonians 1.3–10. The present exaltation ('already') and the future *parousia* ('not yet') are mutually supportive and explanatory. The echoes they set up, not least of passages such as Zechariah 14:5 which speaks of YHWH himself 'coming with all his saints', are to be expected. They do not indicate that for Paul or other early Christians such language could *only* refer to the still-future event.[40] We could back up the point with detailed studies of the other letters and indeed of the Letter to the Hebrews. But we have said enough to point us back to the Synoptic Gospels themselves, where the heart of the problem lies.

THE GOSPELS, THE KINGDOM AND THE SON OF MAN

What might the Gospel writers themselves have replied to our question, whether the kingdom had indeed come with power in the events which followed Jesus' death? No surprises here: I shall argue that they would have agreed with Paul.[41]

All four Gospels frame the story of Jesus in terms of the long-awaited return of Israel's God. Matthew and Mark introduce John the Baptist by reference to Isaiah 40, where the herald announces YHWH's return.[42] Mark adds Malachi 3.1, with the extra echo of Exodus 23.20.[43] The idea of John as the 'Elijah' figure, preparing for Israel's God himself, is emphasized in Matthew 11, where Jesus himself quotes the relevant texts. Luke does the same thing in chapter 7 and elsewhere: for him, Jesus' journey to Jerusalem is the actualisation of God's return. This results in the dire 'apocalyptic' warnings about the coming destruction 'because you didn't know the moment when God was visiting you' (Luke 19.44).[44] John has his own way of saying the same thing, but it *is* the same thing. The Gospels do not 'contain' apocalyptic; in the first-century sense I have been outlining, they *are* apocalyptic. That is to say, they are describing this-worldly events and doing so in such a way as to claim that in these events the 'revelation', the unveiling, the visible coming of God, took place. Of course, as with other kinds of 'revelation' and 'apocalypse', many would look and look and never see. The written Gospels thus share, to this day, the paradox of Jesus' own public career. They are written with post-resurrection hindsight, a hermeneutical position we will explore in chapter 6. But the point remains that they are not written as 'private truth' for a secret group. The new creation which they see opening up is the new public world.

Thus, as far as the Gospel writers were concerned, YHWH had returned to his people. The story of Israel's returning God had taken the form of *the messianic career and death of Jesus of Nazareth*. So far as we can tell, Jesus' contemporaries had had no thought that a coming 'Messiah' (should such a figure appear) would be the personal embodiment of Israel's God. The way the evangelists told the story of Jesus, however, was as the story of a potential messianic claimant *in whose actions and ultimate fate they discerned, in retrospect, the presence of Israel's God.*[45]

This has long been overlooked both in Christian tradition and in biblical scholarship. The liberal Protestantism of Weiss and Schweitzer had no idea of the synoptist's incarnational Christology; the British writers who appropriated their work wanted a form of incarnation but never saw it in terms of Yhwh's return. But this puts everything in a different light.[46] The 'return of God' had taken the form of *a human story* in which there was now a sense of something already done and something still to be done.

The messianic narrative, however, mattered in itself. Actual would-be messianic movements in the period always had a now-and-not-yet element. After all, as long as we think in nineteenth-century categories, asking whether a 'supernatural' event has occurred through which the 'natural' world has been 'obliterated', we already know the answer: either it's happened, or it hasn't, and since the world is still going on the answer is that it hasn't. But supposing we take the two most obvious movements, those of Judas Maccabeus roughly two hundred years before Jesus and of Simeon ben Kosiba roughly a hundred years after him. Here is the central figure, leading a brave, determined little group. Judas is commissioned by his father to take the fight forward (1 Maccabees 2.66). Ben Kosiba is hailed by Akiba, the leading Rabbi of the time, as the true king, 'the son of the star'.[47] Bar-Kochba, as he thus becomes, mints coins with the year '1', then '2'. The kingdom of God, in other words, *has already been launched*. But if someone were to suppose that there was therefore no 'future' element, he and his followers would have laughed, perhaps bitterly. They had an urgent and dangerous agenda. They had to defeat the Romans—to rebuild the Temple. The ancient stories of victory followed by temple-building would have to be fulfilled. That's what the Maccabees had done, but it had proved a false dawn. Herod's similar attempts were worse. Now (they believed) they would have the real thing.

It didn't happen. The bar-Kochba revolt went into a third year. The coins, instead of a number, carried the words 'Freedom of Jerusalem'. Then the Romans closed in, and the inaugurated eschatology came to a swift and sad end.

Anyone who wants to propose that Jesus and his first followers were disappointed, because they expected something to happen which then didn't, should look closely at bar-Kochba and the aftermath of his movement and contrast it with early Christianity. This comparison does not seem to have occurred to most end-of-the-world scholars, which merely shows that they have not been thinking in terms of the actual Jewish history and culture of the period. Reimarus was right to this extent: Jesus' kingdom-announcement was indeed to be understood historically within the 'apocalyptic' *and therefore political* aspirations of the time, though the 'and therefore political' was ignored by Weiss and Schweitzer even though the latter made Reimarus his hero. *What Reimarus said about Jesus applies exactly to bar-Kochba*, except that his followers never did what Reimarus said Jesus' followers did (inventing stories about him to support a continuing though changed movement). What made Jesus different, in his own public career, was his radical redefinition of what the kingdom would actually mean. What made the early church different from any who survived the bar-Kochba revolt has to do with what the whole early church said had happened next. The two on the road to Emmaus were of course bitterly disappointed, but they didn't stay that way. But if you deny the resurrection of Jesus—as did Bultmann himself—what are you left with? Some Jewish thinkers, after the bar-Kochba disaster, began to explore Gnosticism. That is more or less what Bultmann did. He invented a hypothetical pre-Christian Gnosticism out of thin air, to give him apparent grounding for his interpretation of early Christianity. Anything, it seems, rather than do business either with the real first-century Jewish world or the real first-century Christian claim about Jesus' resurrection.

There is of course a further wrinkle in this argument. After Jesus' resurrection and ascension, and the gift of the spirit, the church, as reflected in the New Testament, was aware of having entered a new type of now-and-not-yet time. The 'now' was more emphatic by far than during Jesus' public career: something had happened as a result of which the whole world was a different place and was to be seen as such. The gospel had already been preached, as Paul puts it with breathtaking theological reach, to every creature under heaven (Colossians 1.23). But Paul wrote that letter, and other similarly celebratory ones, from prison. The 'not yet' was just as real, and any attempt to suggest otherwise had to be confronted with warnings against complacency.[48] What is striking is that, despite all the 'not yet' signs—suffering, persecution, apparent failure, internal division, and so on—the dominant note of earliest Christianity was not 'hope' (though there was plenty of that) but 'joy'. Something had happened that made everything different.[49]

Jesus' own redefinition of 'kingdom of God' is at the heart of the parables, though remarkably they are seldom seen this way. One Gospels scholar even suggested that Jesus did not try to modify what 'the kingdom' meant in his world.[50] The kingdom-parables all assume a meaning of the kingdom *and then explain that in fact the kingdom is indeed coming, but in a different, subversive fashion.* The hope of Israel is being fulfilled, but not in the way people had thought—a theme which permeates the texts. It is of course possible to suggest that all this is a later Christian interpretation—in other words, that Jesus really did share the normal 'kingdom'-aspirations of his contemporaries, but that the early church hushed this up after his death and made it all mean something different. But there comes a point beyond which such arguments begin to eat their own tails. How do we know the evangelists have readjusted the picture if our only evidence for the picture itself is what they tell us? Or, to put it another way: if our evidence for what Jesus himself said is contained in these four books, and if these books have themselves carefully readjusted what Jesus meant, we have no access to the first term in the comparison. Better to press on with the main evidence.

The messianic theme in all the Gospels reaches its height in Jesus' crucifixion. All four Gospels, fully aware of the shocking paradox, see this event as Jesus' royal enthronement. That is the point of the *titulus* ('King of the Jews'), and all that leads to and surrounds it. For Matthew, this is how 'the Son of Man' is humiliated in order then to be glorified (see below). For Mark, it encapsulates Jesus' paradoxical redefinition of power itself (10.35–45). For Luke, the powers of darkness do their worst and Jesus defeats them (22.53). For John, 'the ruler of the world' is cast out so that Jesus, his being 'lifted up', will draw all people to himself (12.31–32). This is the real victory over the real enemy.[51] The evangelists knew perfectly well that they were living in a 'not yet' time. But as far as they were concerned, the cross—with its meaning disclosed and discerned in the resurrection, ascension, and subsequent spirit-led scriptural reflection—was one vital element within the 'already' which they were celebrating. Weiss, Schweitzer and their followers were right to criticize attempts to 'spiritualize' the meaning of Jesus' message, turning the 'eschatological' or 'apocalyptic' original meaning into a teaching of piety, morality and social conformism. What they never realised, despite their admiration of Reimarus, was that Jesus was not depoliticizing the kingdom. He was redefining power and politics themselves.

Within all this, all four Gospels indicate, in different though converging ways, that Jesus was constantly warning that the Temple in Jerusalem was under divine judgment. We shall return to this presently when addressing Mark 13 and its parallels.

This now-and-not-yet theme could be pursued through Acts, though there is only space here for a brief summary. The strange events of Acts 1 and 2 appear to have to do with the joining together in a new way of earth and heaven—with, in other words, the replacement of the Jerusalem Temple, the current heaven-and-earth establishment, with a new kind of link, formed by Jesus on the one hand and by his spirit-filled people on the other. That is why so many of the crucial and dangerous points in Acts have to do with temples in general (Athens, Ephesus and so on) and with the Jerusalem Temple in particular (thinking of Stephen's speech and Paul's trials). All this comes under the rubric of Acts 1.6–8, which offers one of the classic statements of the New Testament's now-and-not-yet. The disciples ask Jesus if this is the time when he will restore the kingdom to Israel. Jesus' answer—exactly as with the Gospel parables—is, 'Yes, but not in the way you imagine'. That is why the disciples, faced with persecution, invoke Psalm 2, which speaks of their belief that Jesus is *already* enthroned as the true king, having drawn on to himself the wrath of Herod and Pilate, representing the evil powers of the world, and having overcome them (Acts 4.23–31). For Luke, Jesus is already reigning. He has already fulfilled the promises of establishing his kingdom.

We return, then, to the central saying, Mark 9.1: some standing here will not taste death until they see the kingdom of God come with power. Luke (9.27) shortens this to 'until they see God's kingdom'. Matthew (16.28) has Jesus saying that 'some of those standing here will not taste death until they see "the son of man coming in his kingdom"'. This is a composite quotation from bits of Daniel 7.[52] How did Matthew, at least, understand this vital clause? Did he think it was to be 'taken literally', as a prediction of Jesus flying about in mid-air on a cloud? Did he think—at the time of writing his Gospel—that this was still a prophecy awaiting fulfilment?

Emphatically not. The howls of protest that will meet this answer must not get in the way of exegesis—our exegesis of Matthew, and Matthew's exegesis of Daniel. Matthew is clear. He frames his entire passion narrative (26.2) with the prediction that 'the son of man' is going to be crucified, and when it is all over he has the risen Jesus declare that *Daniel 7 has now been fulfilled*:

> Jesus came towards them and addressed them.
>
> 'All authority in heaven and on earth', he said, 'has been given to me! So you must go and make all the nations into disciples . . . and see, I am with you always, to the end of the Age'. (Matthew 28.18–20)

The echo of Daniel 7.14 is unmistakeable:

Matthew has

edothē moi pasa exousia en ouranō kai epi tēs gēs;

Daniel has

edothē auto exousia, kai panta ta ethnē tēs gēs . . . auto latreuousa.[53]

In the same way, the final words of Matthew's Jesus (about his being with the disciples until the *synteleia tou aiōnos*, the 'completion of the age') answer to Daniel's emphasis that the *exousia* in question will be *aiōnios*, 'of the age' (Matthew 28.20; Daniel 7.14).[54] As far as Matthew is concerned 'the son of man' *has* now been exalted into his 'kingdom'. Of course the eschatology is a long way from being finally 'realised'. But it has been well and truly inaugurated.

This is confirmed by Matthew's account of Jesus' hearing before the high priest. Jesus has been accused of saying that he can destroy the Temple and rebuild it in three days. The high priest puts him on oath to declare if he is 'the Messiah, God's son' (Matthew 26.63). Jesus' reply brings together two vital early Christian texts, with the quotation from Psalm 110 held between the two parts of the quotation from Daniel 7.13:

> 'You said the words', replied Jesus. 'But let me tell you this: from now on you will see "the son of man sitting at the right hand of the Power, and coming on the clouds of heaven"'. (Matthew 26.64)

The key phrase here is 'from now on', *ap' arti*. Caiaphas will not have to wait long. Jesus will be vindicated, will be enthroned as the true priest-king of Psalm 110, will be exalted as the 'son of man' of Daniel 7—and indeed of Psalm 8, since Matthew has carefully woven that 'son of man' passage, too, with Psalm 110 and with the prediction of the Temple's destruction.[55]

Luke agrees. The main difference is that he has *apo tou nyn* instead of Matthew's *ap'arti*, but aside from that the sense is the same. Matthew and Luke both have Jesus speaking of a *new and lasting state of affairs*. This, to be sure, will have been inaugurated by the single (if complex) event of Jesus' death, resurrection and ascension, but the relevant sentence in both Matthew and Luke is not about that event but about the ongoing kingdom which it will launch. 'From now on he will be reigning'. We see the same in Peter's Pentecost sermon in Acts, declaring that Psalm 110 is *already true* of Jesus. As in the psalm itself, there is still an 'until', in this case 'until he has put his enemies under his feet' (Acts 2.32–36).[56] A new kind of 'now and not yet', in fact. This cannot be a Lukan invention. It corresponds to what Paul says in 1 Corinthians 15 and also to Matthew and indeed to the psalm itself.

What then about Mark himself? Did he think, in writing the regularly cited key texts, that Jesus had been predicting an imminent cosmic catastrophe? The main answer is found in Mark 13, but this is prefaced by Mark's placing of the discussion of Psalm 110 in 12.35–37, where Mark, like Paul and Luke, sees Jesus as *already* fulfilling Psalm 110. When we meet this Psalm in Mark 14.62 we might expect it to refer to the enthronement which is about to take place.[57]

This is what we then find in chapter 13. Since my earlier contributions,[58] the upsurge of interest in Temple-theology (see chapter 5 below) has strengthened my view, first, that the discourse is primarily about the fall of the Temple, and second, that, since the Temple was the heaven-and-earth place, the *microcosmos*, its imminent destruction was bound to mean more than the mere failure of national hope. It was, from the Jewish point of view, *the collapse of the space-time order itself*—not in the sense that the literal space, time and matter would suddenly cease to exist, but that the created order of 'heaven and earth' had lost the linch-pin which held it together. This line of thought goes back to Jeremiah, for whom the destruction of the Temple meant the return of creation itself to primal chaos.

As with Jeremiah, this was the event Jesus predicted would happen within a generation. With hindsight we see his death, resurrection and exaltation, the fall of the Temple, and the still-future consummation of all things, as separate events in a way which could not be seen when Pontius Pilate was governor and Caiaphas high priest. But Mark indicates that a nexus has been established between Jesus and the Temple, more specifically between Jesus' kingdom-claim and his warnings against the Temple. Mark is just as clear as John, though in different ways: the implicit claim made by Jesus leaves no room for the Temple. With the hindsight that John makes explicit, the Temple has done its forward-pointing work.[59] Now a haunt of brigands,[60] it was ripe for destruction.

That meaning would have been obvious from the start of Mark 13, were it not for verses 24–27 in the middle. These verses have been seen by many as such an obvious reference to 'the end of the world' that it has been almost impossible to read them as referring to anything else:

> 'The sun will be dark as night
> And the moon will not give its light;
> The stars will fall from heaven
> And the powers in heaven will shake.
> Then they will see "the son of man coming on clouds with great power and glory".
>
> And then he will dispatch his messengers, and will gather in his chosen ones from the four winds, from the ends of earth to the ends of heaven'.
> (Mark 13.24–27)

And this, says Mark's Jesus, is the event which will take place 'within a genera-tion' (13.30)—in other words, the event spoken of in 9.1—even though the precise hour is known to none but the Father alone (13.32).[61] However, everything we have seen so far from Paul, from Matthew and from Luke insists that we should read this language in terms of the death, resurrection and ascension of Jesus on the one hand and the fall of the Temple (the heaven-and-earth place) on the other.[62] The crucial arguments come from the allusions to Isaiah 13 and 34 and Daniel 7, though there is no space here for the details.[63] The language and imagery had been in regular use for a long time to refer to (what we call) socio-political events and to invest them with (what we might call) their 'cosmic' significance. What-ever Daniel 7.1–14 may have meant in some earlier literary setting, it is absurd to think that a first-century reader would have taken literally the monsters emerg-ing from the sea, or that anyone interpreting verses 13 and 14 would have ignored the interpretations given in the passage itself, in verses 15–27.[64] Mark has here presented a construct, retrospectively of course but quite carefully, of *how it all may have appeared from within Jesus' public career*.[65] Mark's Jesus believes on the one hand that he will die and be raised, as the climax of his kingdom-bringing vocation, and that these events will be the reality towards which the vivid imag-ery of Daniel 7 (interpreted with the help of the Psalms) had been pointing. Mark's Jesus believes, too, that he is called to pronounce the Temple's doom, so that when the Temple is destroyed he will be vindicated. The two go together. The Gospel writers agree with Paul. Jesus' death and resurrection constituted his powerful, scripture-fulfilling inauguration as king. The world had changed; Israel had changed; history itself had changed. The early Fathers agreed. Had there been a 'problem of delay' in the second and subsequent generations, you might suppose they would address it. They do not.[66]

Here, then, is the irony of today's invocations of 'apocalyptic'.[67] As soon as you say that 'apocalyptic' now makes sense to us, since we too live in turbulent times, you show that you have not grasped what the early Christians were say-ing. Jesus was not teaching general truths—not even a 'general truth' about 'dis-ruptive events'! As the Reformers insisted, he was doing something *ephapax*, once and for all. 'Apocalyptic' *was not a general principle about the way things happen in the world*. It was biblical language to convey the meaning of a one-off, unique event, the meaning which belonged to its *unique* and *disruptive* role *within* the narrative of creation and covenant. The words 'unique', 'disruptive' and 'within' in that sentence are all vital. If, however, you say that 'apocalyptic' must mean 'vertical revelation from above with no horizontal connection', you rule out not only all the Jewish 'apocalyptic' texts which give the term such historical anchorage as it claims to possess. You rule out, also, the interpretative frameworks evoked by Jesus, Paul, the evangelists, and, not least, the book of Revelation itself, the ultimate 'apocalypse'.

Of course, from the mid-nineteenth century to our own day we have seen enormous social, cultural and theological turbulence. If that calls for a more revolutionary form of Christian discipleship, fine. But let us not imagine that that is what Jesus was talking about. The real 'apocalyptic Jesus' believed, prior to his death, that in that death, and the resurrection that he believed would follow, he would accomplish the work of inaugurating the kingdom of God. His first followers, including the writers of epistles and gospels, believed that he had done so. This belief, I shall argue in the next chapters, gives us a new basis for considering the larger questions of God and the world.

CONCLUSION

I have argued that the modern 'dogma of delay' is seriously flawed. Jesus and his first followers, including the New Testament writers, did not expect the world to end, either during his public career or shortly thereafter. The early Christians knew that Jesus might return at any time; but their richest emphasis lay elsewhere, in the claim that he had already been enthroned as the world's rightful lord. There was no crisis of confidence, or grinding of theological gears, when, after a generation, Jerusalem was destroyed and Jesus had not reappeared. The modern mistake emerged, by a typical projection of contemporary concerns onto a fictitious historical screen, from modern disappointments with, or disapproval of, the modern idea of 'progress', a disappointment and disapproval variously expressed by writers from Kierkegaard to Nietzsche, from Barth to Walter Benjamin, and many besides. Some Anglo-Saxon scholarship welcomed the idea of the 'delay' as an indication that Christian origins were culturally relative and that major revisions (desired for reasons that had nothing to do with historical study) were therefore justified.[68]

The underlying problem, of course, is that to suggest that something happened in the first century which is to be seen as the climax of world history flies in the face of the normal claim of the Western Enlightenment, that the real climax of world history took place in Europe in the eighteenth century. That is the real challenge.

All this indicates three things. First, a fresh understanding of Jesus as a genuinely first-century Jewish apocalyptic or eschatological prophet is overdue (and will require much more precise and careful use of those two adjectives). Second, such a historical task must take seriously the Temple-theology in which heaven and earth are not separated by a great gulf, as in Epicureanism, but gloriously and powerfully joined. Third, exploring Jesus—and supremely his resurrection—in the light of this worldview ought to open new possibilities for speaking more largely of God and the world, and hence of Jesus himself as the starting-point and clue to the questions that concern 'natural theology'. All that sets the agenda. We have now staked out the territory, in particular in relation to 'history' and 'eschatology'. In the next chapter I shall start to build my main argument.

III

Jesus and Easter in the Jewish World

5

The Stone the Builders Rejected

Jesus, the Temple and the Kingdom

INTRODUCTION

We have now arrived at the turning-point of the argument. We have seen that the cultural, political and social context of Western thought in the last three centuries has embraced (among many other things) one particular philosophical standpoint, namely a modern variation of ancient Epicureanism. This has then had a damaging effect on several crucial theological enquiries, including not least 'natural theology'. Further, it has pulled out of shape some crucial moves in biblical studies, particularly the question of early Christian eschatology. Behind this again the notion of 'history' has been shaped by the same cultural pressures; underneath that the question of knowledge itself has been wrongly framed. So, to work back through this sequence: epistemology has tried to do without the notion of 'love', producing in historical study a false antithesis of rationalist certainty-hunting on the one hand and scepticism on the other; Jesus and his first followers have been portrayed as holding an 'imminent-end-of-the-world' belief which has distorted other features; and the question of God and the world, of which 'natural theology' is one aspect, has suffered. Our task now, in the second half of this book, is to articulate and argue for a transformed vision all through, and in the process propose that there are ways, in the light of Easter, of bringing the question of Jesus and the question of 'natural theology' back together again, to the mutual benefit of both.

In the present chapter I will sketch the worldview, that of many Second Temple Jews, within which Jesus and his first followers lived and in terms of which they prayed, thought and taught. This worldview, which in itself is radically unlike all forms of Epicureanism and indeed Stoicism and Platonism, is not an 'ancient' worldview to be written off as unavailable in the 'modern' world. It offers itself as a way of making sense of things, as a 'social imaginary' to use Charles Taylor's term. Then in the following chapter I will propose that the striking central claim of the early Christians—that Jesus of Nazareth was bodily raised from the dead—invites and encourages both the ordinary type of historical investigation, in which as I have suggested the 'epistemology of love' plays an important part, and a deeper variety of historical epistemology, a further depth of love-knowledge. This kind of knowledge does not cancel out or bypass real knowledge of the real world. Rather, it opens up a vision of new creation which precisely overlaps with, and radically transforms, the present creation—as, according to the story, Jesus' dead body was itself transformed. Then, just as Jesus' resurrection shed a flood of light back on his public career and horrible death, explaining meanings that had previously been puzzling even while the things he did and said had been exciting and evocative, so, in chapter 7, we will see that the resurrection-shaped vision of new creation enables us to see that the signals of divine presence and power within the present world—the raw matter of 'natural theology'—were telling a true story, were asking the right question, were doing their best to point in the right direction. This is where the story of Jesus offers a promise of a new kind of 'natural theology', even if it doesn't fit with the culturally shaped way that question has normally been posed in modern times. All then depends, as in the final chapter, on the larger circle of argumentation to be provided by the eschatological vision of a completed new creation and by the mission of the church which brings that hope into the present.

What our study so far has done, in fact, is to challenge the assumption that the modern discussions of 'natural theology', including the normal terms of debate, are fixed forever in the form they have taken within the dominant Epicurean worldview. Epicureanism is neither an automatic default mode nor the assured result of modern science. It is a particular worldview which cannot assume pre-eminence but must make its way in the implicit market-place. Thinkers from many contexts, assuming many different worldviews, have puzzled over these questions, and it will not do for the Epicurean to insist that all possible opponents must play the game on the Epicurean home ground (studying the world without reference to God, and thinking about God without reference to the world), with the home team always playing with the wind, the slope and their own cheering crowd.

To make this point is quite different from saying, as many conservative modernists have done, that they are opposing something called 'naturalism' by arguing for something called 'supernaturalism' instead. That move might then appear to 'prove' any and every Christian conclusion in advance. It would by implication accept the Epicurean's split world and then claim that the apparently absent divinity does nevertheless sometimes act in the world, however illogically. Equally, to challenge an Epicurean framework does not precipitate us merely into a choice between Plato and Aristotle, or their various Christian retrievals (Augustine and Calvin going with Plato; Aquinas with Aristotle; and so on). There remains a significantly different way of conceiving the three main areas of interest, cosmology, eschatology and the human condition. This way has a *prima facie* case for being considered vital for understanding Jesus and the first Christians. This is the great ancient Jewish tradition, involving various retrievals of the Hebrew scriptures in the Second Temple period and then framing the radical mutations we find in the New Testament. This tradition, like the stone rejected by the builders in Jesus' parable, presents itself as the appropriate foundation for fresh cultural, political, ideological and above all theological construction.

This is all the more important because, as the subtitle of this book indicates, throughout my argument I am homing in, from different angles, on Jesus himself. There is, as we have seen before, an obvious irony here. The normal 'natural theology' of the last two or three centuries has insisted, almost by definition, on keeping Jesus out of the picture. Bringing him in (as we saw at the start of this book) looks like cheating: he counts as 'special revelation'. But actually the charge of 'cheating' would rebound on those who would object, since—on their own premises, emphasised all the way from Reimarus and his predecessors to the 'Jesus Seminar' and their ilk—Jesus was a genuine human being, to be understood, as are other human beings, within the 'natural' world, the historical parameters, of his place, time and culture. And if Jesus was every bit as much part of the 'natural' world as anyone else—as so many of the 'historical Jesus' portraits, produced precisely within Epicurean modernism, were eager to show—then one cannot rule him out *a priori*. A similar response, of course, could be made to those Christians who, for apologetic reasons, bracket Jesus out of their initial theological arguments (prove 'God' first, and fit Jesus in afterwards). Setting 'Jesus' to one side, for whichever reason, might seem to imply that the word refers to a being or construct significantly different to the actual man from Nazareth.

But if we are to speak of Jesus, we must do so precisely in relation to *his own* cultural and ideological context, not (first and foremost) our own. That, again, would be something the good modernist ought to insist on, though that project has then been derailed, as we have seen, by the end-of-the-world theory. However much we may sense their first-century Jewish cultural context to be alien to our own (with our implicit divisions, both of heaven and earth on the one hand and of past and present on the other), this is where the sympathetic imagination necessary for the historical task (similar, *mutatis mutandis*, to the sympathetic imagination necessary in the hard sciences) comes into play. It may be difficult to understand Jesus, to see him as his contemporaries saw him or even as he saw himself. But we will make it not just difficult but downright impossible if we pretend that they, and he, were addressing the same issues as we do—only in a muddled or mistaken way. We need to make the genuinely historical effort, as required by an epistemology of love which insists on allowing the 'other' to be genuinely different, to see Jesus and his followers, and to understand their aims and intentions, within their own world.

Avoiding this challenge has been endemic in much writing about Jesus in the last three hundred years. Such a move is sometimes excused, by Christian thinkers, on the grounds that the gospel was new wine, so we don't have to bother studying the old wineskins. Behind this there may lie a darker hint: that the old wineskins were *Jewish*, and we know, *a priori*, that the gospel message of grace and freedom was diametrically opposed to the Jewish world of law. But if we know anything about Jesus' public career, we know that he announced God's kingdom, a notion widely current in the Jewish world of his day. To understand what it meant, and then to understand the new spin he seems to have put on it, we need to get inside that Jewish world. Likewise, more broadly, *the idea that the early Christian message was radically new doesn't absolve us from understanding the setting in which that radical newness meant what it meant.* Still less does it give us the lazy licence to ignore history and assume we know, by some other means, what Jesus and his first followers 'must' really have been talking about. I therefore want to argue now for a fresh retrieval of key elements in the Second Temple worldview, within which the strikingly new things the early Christians were saying about cosmology, eschatology and what it meant to be human had their intended resonance.

Let me once more head off one obvious objection, only now more explicitly. Surely, someone will say, you don't expect us to adopt a first-century worldview? We live in a new day; we have electric light and modern medicine; we are post-Copernicus, post-Darwin, the poster children of the postmodern world. To this we must reply: No; we live within a revived (and no doubt modified) form of ancient Epicureanism, conditioning us to think in terms of a split world in which the gods have nothing to do with us, nor we with them. The only 'modern' thing about this is that it is so widespread; the worldview itself is no more 'modern' than that of the Dead Sea Scrolls. Forget the modernist rhetoric, the chronological snobbery which assumes that all who went before us were epistemological thieves and robbers. Nothing that Galileo spotted through his telescope, nothing that Darwin found crawling or squawking in the Galapagos, has anything to say here. We must not caricature ancient Jews and Christians as though they were naïve cave-men, believing in a three-decker universe with 'supernatural' upstairs, 'natural' downstairs and something nasty down in the cellar. That shallow cosmological sketch is like the early maps that tried and failed to capture the globe on a sheet of paper. Perhaps some did 'take it literally', but that is not the main point. The main point is that Second Temple Jews assumed that heaven and earth were intended to overlap and did in fact overlap in certain contexts. Our modern assumption of a split world does not mean that we understand cosmology and they didn't—much the same way as, just because we've invented mechanical clocks, we mustn't assume that we understand time and the ancients didn't. The modernist protests are trying to distract our gaze from the pink nakedness of the Enlightenment's Emperor, strutting down the street.

The way forward once more is through *history*, that is, the task of paying attention to ancient evidence in its context, aiming at a larger description of what words meant and what actions intended. Here we live in exciting times. New studies have highlighted what we may loosely call 'Temple-theology', generating fresh ideas about Jewish cosmology. They have also highlighted the way in which the weekly Sabbaths enabled a particular kind of eschatology. These are the co-ordinates for all sorts of things, not least *anthropology*, what it means to speak of humans within *this* cosmos and within *this* idea of time. Epicurean anthropology sees humans as autonomous accidents, formed at random, ultimately disposable. Jewish anthropology sees humans as image-bearers: God-reflectors, standing at the dangerous threshold of heaven and earth, of present and future. That (more or less) is how the early Christians saw Jesus. With that vision, they offer us a way of seeing, *through* him, how the world of 'earth' might all along have been telling us the truth about 'heaven'; how the present age might all along have been speaking the truth about the Age to Come.

I propose, then, that Second Temple Jews in general, and the early Christians amongst them, assumed an integrated cosmology of heaven and earth, within which there was always the possibility and hope of new creation, not as abolition and replacement but as redemptive transformation. They lived, that is, within a world of story, symbol and praxis in which it made sense to think of some kind of commerce between heaven and earth, and of the possibility of new creation arriving—however dangerously and disturbingly!—within the present world. This general way of putting it needs teasing out into its different Jewish and early Christian expressions, but for the moment the point will stand.

The two central Jewish symbols which anchored and explained this world-view and its attendant narrative, then, were the Temple and the Sabbath. Both of these could be, and in some traditions were, linked directly to the story of creation in Genesis 1, offering a symbolic rootedness to any potential narrative of 'new creation'. The combination of Genesis, Exodus, Temple and Sabbath can be seen in the implicit controlling narrative which emerges in many biblical texts as indeed in parallels from the ancient Near East: victory over dark forces; divine enthronement in the newly built world or house; and, not least, the role of the human king within both victory and building. This narrative maps on to the story I and others have told often enough, the story of Israel's long exile, of the longing for a properly rebuilt new Temple to which YHWH would return at last in visible glory and victorious, rescuing power.

I should say right away that the evidence for something like this construct as a widely available and easily recognised first-century worldview is contested. The evidence normally cited is from the Pentateuch, particularly from the supposed 'P' source, and the question always presents itself as to how many people, and in what contexts, would have read it like this and made these connections. However, the Psalms offer rich multi-layered support at several levels; the interpretation of the Tabernacle and Temple by Philo and Josephus gives strong first-century support at least to an outline proposal; the apocalyptic literature, from Daniel onwards, draws on the same symbols and narrative; and there are some important references in the Rabbis, though as always that evidence must be used with care.[1] Above all, the early Christian movement provides a great deal of evidence that this combination of symbol and story was basic to their life, faith and hope, even though it had been reshaped in ways nobody had anticipated. The apparently confused state of the evidence has led some into what seem to be considerable overstatement, and others (perhaps by reaction?) into denying or at least ignoring the presence of these themes entirely.[2]

The point of all this should be clear. Jesus and the early Christians were not Epicureans, taking for granted a cosmos in which 'heaven' and 'earth' were radically separated. Nor, for that matter, were they Stoics, seeing the presence of divinity within all things. Nor, certainly, were they Platonists of whatever sort; like Israel's scriptures, they celebrated the goodness of creation and looked for its renewal. They believed, in other words, in a cosmology where heaven and earth, though very different, were made for one another and were able, under certain circumstances, to come together—the circumstances in question having to do, normally, with the Temple, and then with Torah.

Jesus and his first followers, as Second Temple Jews, believed as well in an eschatology of new creation. This did not involve the abolition of the present world and its replacement with a totally different one. Nor did it imply the steady evolution-from-within of the Stoics, let alone the escapist 'eschatology' of the heading-for-heaven Platonists. They believed in the *redemptive transformation* of the present world into the new one. They lived, that is, within a world of story, symbol and praxis in which it made sense to think of (a) commerce between heaven and earth and (b) the possibility of new creation arriving—however dangerously and disturbingly!—within the present world. This potentially integrated cosmology and overlapping eschatology converged on the idea of (c) humans, and perhaps one in particular, as the Image of the God. This triple framework contextualizes the central proposal of the present chapter: that the New Testament view of Jesus himself, though shocking and unexpected in its own world, meant what it did precisely *in* that world, the world within which Jesus and his contemporaries were making fresh retrievals of ancient scriptures, including sometimes finding unexpected meanings within them. Jesus himself finely expressed this balance of the unexpected new element which makes fresh, disturbing sense within the old world: the stone which the builders rejected has become the head of the corner. That serves both as metaphor for our overall task and as metonymy for its central focus. This in turn will compel us to reframe the question of God and creation, which flows one way into Christology and in another way into 'natural theology'.

If we were to ask early Jewish Jesus-followers how they knew this worldview to be the right one—always supposing they would have understood the question!—they might have spoken of their existing worldview as having been reshaped around the Messiah. If we were to ask early non-Jewish Jesus-followers the same question, their obvious answer would have focused on Jesus himself and on the new worldview they had learnt in 'knowing him'. They had been drawn by what they called 'love' into a place of 'knowledge'. The epistemology of love, we might suggest, is the correlate of the Temple-based cosmology and the Sabbath-based eschatology. That, they would say, is how they were discerning the dawn, recognising that the new day had begun. We will explore this in more detail in the next chapter. And those who looked and looked but could not see were incurring the rebuke which Jesus borrowed from Psalm 118: the stone the builders rejected has become the head of the corner.

This works at both levels. By rejecting Jesus, his contemporaries (Jew and non-Jew alike) were missing out on the new creation. By ignoring the Temple-imagery, foundation stone and all, the philosophy and theology of our own day have found it hard to speak coherently of Jesus himself. By marginalising the idea of the Sabbath, and failing to see its eschatological potential, exegetes and theologians have robbed themselves of an obvious answer to some of the strange proposals about 'eschatology' and 'apocalyptic' on offer in the last two centuries. By putting Temple and Sabbath back in place, as interpretative grids, and by exploring the question of the human 'image' within that picture, we have a chance to understand a great many things a lot better—not least the ways in which we ourselves, looking at real evidence in the real world, might learn to 'discern the dawn'.

TEMPLE, SABBATH, IMAGE: ELEMENTS OF A COSMIC NARRATIVE

Filling the Earth, Filling the Temple: From Creation to Tabernacle

We begin with some scriptural highlights. Psalm 72 prays that Israel's king will fulfil God's purpose by doing worldwide justice and mercy, particularly for the helpless and vulnerable. The Psalm ends:

> Blessed be Yhwh, the God of Israel, who alone does wondrous things.
> Blessed be his glorious name for ever; *may his glory fill the whole earth.*
> Amen and Amen. (Psalm 72.18–19)

This theme is echoed in Isaiah 11 and Habakkuk 2, which speak of the *knowledge* of Yhwh, or the *knowledge of the glory* of Yhwh, filling the whole earth (Isaiah 11.9; Habakkuk 2.14).[3] In Isaiah, as in the Psalm, this is the result of the Messiah's wise and just rule. In a similar way, the promise and warning in Numbers that 'all the earth shall be filled with Yhwh's glory' is responding to the people's rebellious panic over the report of the spies (Numbers 14.1–25).[4] Yhwh is angry: he has promised to go with them; his glory appears at the Tent of Meeting; but they need to know that this present glory is simply one stage on the way to a larger worldwide glory-filling. The spies are implying that the promised land is unattainable; Yhwh replies that it is only a step on the way to a much greater promise. We are reminded of Solomon's statement: the highest heaven cannot contain God, how much less this little house (1 Kings 8.27).

That link between the divine glory filling first the Tabernacle and then the whole earth is echoed in Isaiah's vision in chapter 6. In verse 1, the hem of Yhwh's robe fills the Temple; in verse 3, the Seraphs sing that his glory fills the whole earth; in verse 4, the house is filled with smoke. The immediate and present 'filling' of the Temple thus indicates a larger 'filling' of the whole earth. We might have figured this out from Psalm 72, Isaiah 11 and Habakkuk 2, where the promise of cosmic glory-filling reflects the notion of glory filling the

Wilderness Tabernacle, Solomon's Temple and Ezekiel's new Temple. Israel's God promises to do in and for all creation what he has done in Tabernacle and Temple (though how precisely this might happen is never clear in these vivid but momentary scriptural glimpses). Again, we note, this makes no sense within split-level Epicurean cosmology. Nor would it appeal to the Stoic, for whom divinity permeates everything anyway. It wouldn't be welcome to the Platonist, for whom earth, however fine in its own way, is ultimately a disposable shadow of the true reality and the hoped-for goal.

These ancient Israelite references to glorious filling, however, are the tip of the iceberg. They point to other aspects of the remarkable new wave within biblical studies which is now exploring the connection between cosmos and cult, creation and shrine: between Genesis 1 and 2 on the one hand (at least as they were being understood in the Second Temple period) and Tabernacle and Temple themselves on the other. Here we must be careful, partly because we do not know in what sequence the texts were written or edited, so that we cannot easily track influence and dependence, and partly because it would be easy to miss the all-important sense of *narrative* in the way the whole picture was subsequently read. Genesis 1 and 2 appear as the start of a *project*. Eschatology, or at least a *telos*, a goal, is in the reader's view from the start. What matters, then, is how reflective Second Temple Jews might have thought about the relevant texts, and then how the radically new proposals of the early Christians resonated within that world.

The central proposal, explored by many today, is that the Pentateuch offers what Harvard's Jon Levenson calls a 'homology' between the creation-story in Genesis 1 and the construction of the Tabernacle in the closing chapters of Exodus. For Levenson, this goes both ways: the sanctuary is depicted as a miniature 'world', a *microcosmos*; while the creation, at least in Priestly circles, was seen as a macro-Temple, God's palace.[5] Some have cautioned that we should only see one-way traffic: Tabernacle and Temple may be seen as small working models of creation, but that doesn't necessarily mean that creation itself was seen as a temple.[6] Here we meet the question of *Urzeit* and *Endzeit*. Are the shrines trying to go back to the original creation or on to a supposed cosmic goal?

From a Second Temple perspective, we should stress two things (without prejudice, by the way, as to decisions on when Genesis reached its final form or its final canonical placing). First, all these sources would be read within the well-known forward-moving implicit narrative, new elements being added to an existing picture without needing to suppose that everything was present in code, or in hints, in Genesis. Second, those who knew the texts would easily make inferences in both directions whether or not the original text was intended like that. Once you glimpse a family likeness in a child, you may find that the grandparent can remind you of the child as well as the child of the grandparent. You might even see things in the grandparent which you hadn't noticed before.

The detailed echoes between Genesis and Exodus, creation and Tabernacle, have been laid out in various ways, with obvious points such as the Menorah in the Tabernacle reflecting both the Tree of Life in Genesis 2 and the seven heavenly bodies in Genesis 1. Second Temple writers like Philo, Josephus, Jubilees and the Enoch literature (in very different ways) see the Tabernacle and/or the Temple, and/or its furniture or priestly robes, as the representation of the cosmos. The theme continues into the Rabbis where, as Jacob Neusner wrote, it is assumed that the Tabernacle 'stands for the cosmos'.

Close readings of relevant texts, especially within the wider ancient Near Eastern context, make the same point.[7] The seven 'days' of creation have been linked to the seven stages of the Tabernacle's construction and also the seven years of building Solomon's Temple. The Tabernacle instructions conclude with a reaffirmation of the Sabbath commandment, reflecting the close of the Priestly creation account. Many have seen the parallel between the Holy of Holies (as the focus of the Tabernacle) and the Sabbath (as the focus of time), the day which the creator 'blessed' and 'made holy'. Sabbath is to time, it seems, what the Holy of Holies is to place.

All this makes sense within wider ancient culture, where temples were regularly understood as meeting-points between heaven and earth.[8] Temples were often seen as symbolic mountains, perhaps reflecting ancient beliefs (as with Olympus in Greece, or indeed Sinai) that the mountain-top, swathed in cloud, would be the likely divine dwelling place. Thus Mount Zion, the location of YHWH's Temple, is spoken of as a high mountain despite being only a small hill, overshadowed by an immediate neighbour.[9] If you didn't have a mountain, you could substitute pyramids or ziggurats. Noah's Ark, the Tower of Babel, and Jacob's Ladder all fit here in different ways.[10] The question of how far ancient Israelite symbolism reflected wider ancient culture and how far it protested against it is not important at this point. What matters is that the wider context makes it natural to see all kinds of parallels between (as in the title of Morales's helpful collection) 'cult and cosmos'.

The wider parallels emerge in the prophets and the Psalms as they echo versions of a well-known ancient Near Eastern narrative. The creator overcomes the forces of watery chaos. The cosmos then emerges, like Mount Ararat as the Flood recedes. The shrine is constructed either (like the Ark) on top of the waters or replacing them altogether.[11] This narrative enters historical writing in the stories of the Tabernacle and Temple. God defeats the waters of the Red Sea, with the Exodus seen as a microcosmic enactment of the original act of creation. The waters, in both stories, are driven back by a wind; Yhwh overcomes the enemies, presumably including the sea-god as in Isaiah 52. In the narrative, this leads to the building of the Tabernacle. In the song of Moses and Miriam, it points further—to Solomon's Temple on Mount Zion.[12]

In each case the context is 'rest'. The divine presence finds its 'rest' by filling the tent. God then gives David 'rest' from his enemies, whereupon he decides to build God a house.[13] Solomon is given 'rest' from *his* enemies;[14] he can then go ahead with the great project, constructing the 'house', with the brazen 'sea' as part of its furniture, representing the chaos-waters now overcome, into which the divine glory comes to 'rest', as in Psalm 132.[15] Psalm 2 tells the same story: God laughs at the raging nations and installs his king ('his son') on the holy hill of Zion, summoning the nations to allegiance. This Psalm remained massively important in early Christianity and in books such as the Wisdom of Solomon.[16]

All this Temple-building constitutes the *enthronement* of Yhwh: once the waters are overcome, he will reign for ever and ever (Exodus 15.18). Temple and earthly kingship are two parts of the same reality, both reflecting and bringing to actual expression the one kingdom of the one God. This depends on the link of microcosmos and macrocosmos; without that, the god of a particular temple would just be a local deity. The narratives and poems which state all this, constructed piecemeal over many centuries, come together in the functional canon of the Second Temple period. Cosmos and Temple are mutually interpretative.

This does not mean, to repeat, that the *Endzeit* will exactly match the *Urzeit*. The story which the scriptures appear to tell, variously and as a whole, is not going around in a circle and ending up where it began. The narrative is aiming towards an end which, though contained *in nuce* in the beginning, is the fulfilment of a project. What is to come will be modelled on, and fashioned out of, the good creation, but it will not stay the same. Furthermore, the disaster of Genesis 3 demands that for the project to reach its goal the human agents need rescuing. Israel's history, from Abraham onwards, comes under this rubric: the *covenant* will restore *creation*, just as the call of Abraham promises to undo the *problem* of Adam and thus to restate, in a new mode, the *vocation* of Adam. Within this larger covenantal narrative, the destruction of the first Temple is seen by Jeremiah as creation reverting to chaos. If Solomon's Temple had been a forward-looking new-creation promise, that hope was now gone. Ezekiel, however, then envisions the divine glory, which had abandoned the old temple to its fate, returning to fill a newly built house. It's the same story: the Babylonian chaos has been overcome; the Temple is constructed; the people's sins are purged; the glory can return. Instead of the waters of chaos, living water will now flow from the sanctuary to make even the Dead Sea fresh.[17]

All this offers, therefore, a kind of inaugurated eschatology—not the same as the early Christian variety, but not so different either (once again, these differences will become more apparent in the next chapter). The Tabernacle and Temple, situated within and reflecting the present creation, are already, for the writers of certain evocative passages, effective indications of the divine intention to renew heaven and earth and fill them with glorious presence. It will have been easy for Second Temple Jews, under pressure about so many things, to ignore or forget these scriptural hints and with them the reminder to see their God as the creator of the whole world, not just of Israel. That is a point to which the early Christians return eagerly. But the hints were there. Solomon was aware that his Temple was only a small working model of a much vaster reality.[18] But, so many believed, Israel's God graciously deigned to dwell there and to use it as a base of operations, a new global centre towards which prayer would be directed and from which divine power and rescue would go out.

The difference between this worldview (of special places where worlds overlap) and our prevailing Epicureanism are obvious. No wonder we have found it difficult to understand early Christian language about heaven and earth and their mutual relation—the question of which 'natural theology' ought properly to be seen as a subset.

The dangerous fusion of heaven and earth is matched with the overlapping eschatology of the 'present age' and the 'age to come'. This points to our second theme. *Just as ancient Israelites believed that heaven and earth were not far apart, but overlapped and interlocked, so some of them seem to have believed that the age to come might be anticipated during the present age.* The Temple was the place on earth where you would find yourself in heaven. The Sabbath was the moment in ordinary time when God's new age would arrive in advance.

Sabbath and the Age to Come

Sabbath was thus to time what Temple was to space.[19] It was 'a tabernacle in time'.[20] Just as Jewish views of the Temple cannot fit within the split cosmos of Epicureanism, so Jewish views of the Sabbath cannot be fitted into the Enlightenment's sharp break between past, present and future. The Temple spoke of the life of heaven present in the midst of 'earth'; the Sabbath, of the Age to Come inserting itself into the rhythms and sequences of present time.

In both cases what counts is the divine presence; discussions in Western scholarship of both Temple cult and Sabbath-keeping have been hamstrung by the many years of protestant prejudice which (framed by the various unhelpful philosophies of the Enlightenment) has seen nothing but 'legalism' in formal or sacrificial worship and in the careful guarding of the seventh day. That was never the point. Temple and Sabbath belong together as forward-looking symbols. The new age towards which they gesture is the new creation, the *completion* of the *project* of Genesis 1 and 2, accomplished through the *redemption* of the *disaster* of Genesis 3. On both counts, biblical eschatology resists the idea that if the kingdom of God were to arrive it would mean obliterating the present world, or at least shoving it to one side.

This close link of Temple and Sabbath is the more striking in that, whereas the ancient Near East offers parallels for Temple-ideology, the Sabbath institution appears distinctive. Brought together in Israel's life, they framed the idea of the divine *kingdom*: the Temple was the *place where* God was enthroned; the Sabbath was the *time when* it happened.[21] The Temple was where YHWH would find his sabbatical, his 'rest'—not a time for doing nothing, but the moment of his inaugurated reign.[22] The Sabbath was blessed and holy, just like the inner sanctum. This explains why (at a later date, of course) the Mishnah gives instructions to read Psalm 93, celebrating YHWH's victory over the waters, on Fridays, and then Psalm 92, celebrating God's enthronement, on the Sabbath itself.[23] This is further explained in a reported saying of Rabbi Akiba: Psalm 93 is about how God finished all his works 'and reigned over them as king'.[24] Here is the point. Sabbath-references in early Christianity are few, though important. But *any claim that Israel's God has become king, or is becoming king, carries the implication that the true Sabbath has arrived, and the true Temple is being built.* This offers, to say the least, a striking contrast with the nineteenth-century idea that the arrival of God's kingdom meant the end of the world.

Other evidence indicates that for some Jews at least the weekly Sabbaths were seen as foretastes of, and hence pointers towards, the coming 'great Sabbath', the eternal 'rest' of the Age to Come.[25] Some have seen this in the description of the new world (after a waiting period of seven days) in *4 Ezra* 7.26–44, the new creation which will last for 'a week of years' (7.43), and which is described at 8.52 in the language of perpetual Sabbath, the gift of 'rest'.[26] In the *Life of Adam and Eve*, the archangel Michael tells Seth not to mourn for more than six days, 'because the seventh day is a sign of the resurrection, the rest of the coming age; and on the seventh day the Lord rested from all his works'.[27] The world to come will be a kind of perpetual Sabbath: 'the delight and joy that will mark the end of days is made available here and now by the Sabbath'.[28] Some later Rabbis retrospectively interpreted Shammai's strict Sabbath-teaching in terms of his attempting to make the weekly Sabbaths resemble as closely as possible the life of the world to come. Thus, in Tosefta Shabbat 16.21, one must not kill even a moth, because in the world to come all creation will live in harmony.[29] Mishnah Shabbat 3.4 declares that one must not carry a weapon on the Sabbath, because in the messianic age swords will be beaten into ploughshares. This is in fact a powerful and pervasive theme in the Rabbinic literature, explaining (according to some) why the Sabbath-regulations are so detailed: if 'the Sabbath is the anticipation, the foretaste, the paradigm of life in the world-to-come', it is vital to keep it properly.[30] The link of Sabbath and Temple (in both, one is brought into the divine presence in a special way) is demonstrated in the way in which some early Sabbath rules echo Temple-based purity codes: the laws relevant for the Temple must apply to the Sabbath as well.[31] The Sabbath thus looks *back* to creation, *across* (as it were) to the Temple, and *forward* to the Age to Come.

Much of this evidence comes from the period after the destruction of AD 70. In earlier material, the Scrolls insist on rigorous Sabbath-observance but do not so obviously interpret it in relation to the coming Age.[32] It seems unlikely, though, that this Sabbath-focused eschatology was a post-70 innovation; it emerges quite naturally from scripture itself. Levenson argues that, for Jews prior to as well as after the destruction, the Sabbath possessed 'cosmogonic significance'; on the Sabbath, creation is 'completed, consummated and mimetically re-enacted', so that 'the annual renewal of the world has become a weekly event', as well as a re-enactment of the Exodus.[33] The Sabbath thus became 'a *weekly* celebration of the creation of the world, the uncontestable enthronement of its creator, and the portentous commission of humanity to be the obedient stewards of creation'.[34]

This vision of the Sabbath can be expanded to include the great festivals, most notably of course Passover.[35] They, too, look back to foundational events in Israel's story (which, in turn, are as we saw closely linked to creation) and at the same time look on to the promised completion, the ultimate 'rest', the Great Sabbath, signalled by the Sabbatical Year and the Year of Jubilee.[36] And among signs of a longer back story to the idea of the Sabbath as an eschatological marker are the larger proposals about long Sabbath-shaped periods of history, all pointing forwards to the coming eschaton. This is clear, as one might expect, in *Jubilees*, which envisages the Lord telling Moses of what will happen 'throughout their weeks of years according to the jubilees forever, until I shall descend and dwell with them in all the ages of eternity', with these years and jubilees inscribed on tablets detailing the full number 'from the day of creation until the day of the new creation when the heaven and earth and all of their creatures shall be renewed according to the powers of heaven and according to the whole nature of earth, until the sanctuary of the Lord is created in Jerusalem upon Mount Zion'.[37] These jubilees will pass until Israel is finally purified from sin and able to dwell in the purified land.[38] Similar ideas are found elsewhere, with speculation that the 'days' of creation will represent a thousand years, giving six thousand years of world history before the Great Sabbath to come.[39]

This idea of a six-thousand-year creation is one way of expressing it, one which was picked up in some early Christian writing.[40] Another way of saying something similar, which seems to have been extremely popular in the Second Temple period, is the idea of a great Jubilee: not just seven times seven, resulting in the sabbatical year as in Leviticus 25, but *seventy times* seven:

> Seventy weeks are decreed for your people and your holy city: to finish the transgression, to put an end to sin, and to atone for iniquity, to bring in everlasting righteousness, to seal both vision and prophet, and to anoint a most holy place.[41]

I and others have argued at length elsewhere that this is the passage referred to by Josephus, in his explanation of the uprising of AD 66, as 'an oracle in their scriptures' which predicted that 'at that time a world ruler would arise from Judaea'.[42] One Qumran passage links this text with others from Leviticus, Deuteronomy and Isaiah, forming a composite of 'sabbatical' eschatology and messianic prophecy.[43] And this anchors the broader theme of the Sabbath as eschatological marker firmly into the Second Temple Jewish world, producing a particular and obvious focus when Jesus declares that 'the time is fulfilled, and the kingdom of God is at hand'.

Temple and Sabbath, then, go together; and together they can be seen as pointing forward to the divinely intended goal. They can be glimpsed as gifts from God's future, like the fruit which the spies brought back as a literal foretaste of the promised land.

I am not, of course, suggesting that 'all Jews', in Jesus' day or at any point, saw things like this. My point here is twofold. First, this way of construing Temple and Sabbath explains why the Enlightenment's approach to both place and time was bound to misunderstand and then misrepresent what the New Testament was saying. This is not because the early Jews and Christians lived in the ancient world and we in the modern. It is because Epicureanism, in both its ancient form and its modern retrieval, rules out both the Jewish and the early Christian view on philosophical grounds. Second, however, this helps us to understand more fully why the early Christians said what they did about

Jesus' resurrection—the topic of our next chapter—and how that can lead to a new view of 'nature' on the one hand and a new understanding of the questions surrounding 'natural theology' on the other.

Our more immediate concern now is with the framing of *anthropology* within this Temple-cosmology and Sabbath-eschatology. Here again we face the contemporary challenge. Epicureanism now, as before, sees humans as both autonomous and perishable: eat, drink and be merry, for tomorrow you die. Platonism, invoked by many Christians to relieve their Epicurean plight, answers, 'Ah, but I have an immortal soul, and it will leave this world and go home to heaven'. Other contemporary proposals, such as cynicism or existentialism, belong with these too. The early Christians, however, spoke of being 'renewed in knowledge according to the image of the creator'. The role of humans in general, and one in particular, is thus radically different from what our culture, including our would-be Christian culture, has imagined.

The Image-Bearing Vocation

There is still more to be gleaned from Genesis 1, read in the way I am suggesting. In particular, there is the place of the human beings, 'made in God's image', in Genesis 1.26–28. As many writers have stressed, over against the thousand years of speculation about which aspect of humanness is thereby singled out as sharing the divine likeness, this must be interpreted within the notion of Genesis as Temple: the 'image' of the deity is the final piece of equipment, placed within the inner sanctum.[44] So strong is this point that even without the parallels with ancient Near Eastern temple-building one might suppose that the mere idea of a heaven/earth structure with an 'image' in it would already tell us that Genesis 1 was describing some sort of a Temple.

But, if this is so, then when we read the chapter against its Near Eastern background two things are particularly striking. First, the notion of 'being made in the image' is *functional* or *vocational*—not that ontology doesn't matter, but that the stress and weight of the 'image' language here is on the tasks which the humans are called upon to do, a vocation re-emphasized in Psalm 8 and evoked, in that sense, in the New Testament. The point is that the image-bearers are there to implement the intentions of the creator; they are God's vice-gerents, summoned and equipped to take forward the creator's purposes. This reflects as much about the creator as it does about this particular creature. The picture is of a creator who determines to work *through humans*, not as a whim or occasional hobby but as a general rule. He is a 'working-through-humans' God. He delights in delegated authority. What needs to be done within his world will be done through humans. In retrospect (in other words, with the hindsight that comes through resurrection and cross, as in our next two chapters), it is easy to see this in proto-trinitarian terms. And if the Temple is the place of God's 'rest' (see above), then the image-bearing human beings are called to share that divine Sabbath.

Second, and following from this, the ancient Near Eastern parallels noted by the various writers on whose work I have been drawing so far suggest that the role of humans in Genesis 1 is the role regularly given to kings. One can see this either way: either the democratization of kingship or the ennobling of humans. Or perhaps both. This royal theme can still resonate in Jewish tradition, as we see in various retrievals of Psalm 8 where what is said there of humans in general is applied to a coming king: if humans are the royalty within creation, then within Israel royalty can take on the vocation of humanity.[45] That takes us back once more to Psalm 72: the king will do justice for the poor and the oppressed, so that the divine glory can fill the whole world, and when the king builds the Temple it is so that the divine glory can dwell in it as an advance sign of that purpose. God's purposes in general are to be taken forward by humans in general; the restoration of creation and of human society is taken forward by the justice-bringing king. With the Image in place and working properly, the heaven/earth Temple can be filled with divine glory. It is not difficult to see lines of thought moving forward from this point to (among many other texts) John's Gospel or Paul's Letter to the Ephesians.

The kings are not, to be sure, the only humans through whom the cosmic Temple finds completion. In Exodus 25–40, as the narrative of covenantal rescue reaches its height and the Tabernacle is completed, it is Aaron the High Priest, and his sons, who (despite the sin of the Golden Calf!) minister before the dangerous divine presence. Aaron is the one who goes in to the innermost sanctum on the Day of Atonement. With this we are brought into the next range of themes which, it may be supposed on the usual theory, were dear to the heart of those who composed or compiled Genesis 1. If the Tabernacle of Exodus 40 is (at last!) the new microcosmos, the 'little world' which declares that the creator is restoring his creation after the failure of the original humans, then we should not be surprised that, in the shaping of the Pentateuchal canon, the book of Leviticus follows at once. If the divine presence has come to dwell with the people of Israel, the people need to know how to cope with its dangerous presence. To a later generation, especially to those not accustomed to complex rituals and purity-codes (though our own modern constructions of ordinary rules for hygiene, and indeed 'health and safety', may form something of a secular parallel!), it is easy to be bewildered by the range of themes and regulations in Leviticus. Whole libraries have been written to expound it all. But certain things stand out for our purposes.

At the heart of it is the recognition that in Israelite faith and cult what matters is not the possibility that humans might leave 'earth' and go to 'heaven'. That has been the assumption of most Christians, certainly most Western Christians, from quite early times, due, I think, to the powerful influence of Platonism. This has systematically distorted every other aspect of theology, not least in relation to the notion of sacrifice. Rather, the point has been that the creator God has always intended that his glory would dwell with humans, so that the glory of heaven would live on the earth and indeed fill it. It is impossible to exaggerate the difference this makes to virtually every other topic in theology, and I shall be following it up in the final chapter in particular.[46]

It may help to explore further just how this worked. Cities in Paul's world competed for the privilege of hosting an imperial temple and counted themselves specially favoured if this was granted. Ephesus was proud of being honoured in this way not just once but twice.[47] So the ancient Israelites, and those who collected and edited their traditions to give shape to post-exilic reconstruction, saw their task as being to play host to the single shrine of the true God, the creator. Jerusalem celebrated its status as 'the city of the great king'.[48] Granted the utter holiness of the life-giving creator, and the impossibility of his coming into contact with anything to do with death, whether ordinary impurity or actual sin, a great deal of the Levitical cult was aimed at the careful and regular purgation of the shrine itself (always in danger of being polluted by the people's uncleanness) and then of the people, with the annual 'day of atonement' as its climax.[49] At the same time, however, there is the weekly and annual round of festivals, from ordinary weekly Sabbaths to the great festivals such as Passover. And, in a kind of climax, there is the Sabbath of Sabbaths, with the week translated into years and the years multiplied again, producing the 'sabbatical year' when Jubilee will be proclaimed and freedom celebrated. The sabbatical symbolism indicates what this means: this is a sign of creation renewed, of justice and mercy becoming realities in the life of the nation, of the living and liberating God dwelling with his people. This is then focused, in Exodus and Leviticus, on Aaron and his successors. They can be seen, by any reader following this line of thought, as playing, within the Tabernacle, the role of Adam in the original 'temple', the heaven/earth creation of Genesis 1.[50]

When we put all this together within a possible historical reconstruction of the Second Temple Jewish worldview, we find striking results. For a start, there is the Jewish version of the wider cross-cultural sense of *the king as temple-builder*. David had planned the Temple; Solomon had built it; Hezekiah and

Josiah had restored and cleansed it; Zerubbabel had been supposed to rebuild it, but that had been ambiguous at best. Judas Maccabeus had cleansed it after the Syrian desecrations, and even though he and his family were priestly, not from the tribe of Judah or the house of David, that had been enough to constitute them as kings for a century. Herod's massive rebuilding programme seems to have been designed to present himself and his family as the true 'kings of the Jews'. The would-be Messiahs who emerged at the time of the great revolt had the Temple as their focus; bar-Kochba, the one hailed as Messiah in the final revolt, put a picture of the (then ruined) Temple on his coins, as an obvious statement of intent. He would re-enact the old myth, slaying the dragon and restoring the cosmos: that is, he would defeat the Romans and rebuild the Temple, so that the divine glory could dwell there at last. It would be a new creation, a new Genesis. Psalm 72 would come true at last. King and Temple went hand in hand.

At the same time, and for the same underlying reason, the ongoing tradition of 'wisdom' teaching means what it means within a Temple-cosmology. The book of Proverbs links the figure of 'Lady Wisdom' to creation itself, so that 'wisdom' is seen to be what humans need if they are to live appropriately as image-bearers. But as the tradition develops one strand insists that this figure of 'Wisdom' has come to live in the Temple in Jerusalem, thus apparently fusing together 'wisdom' with the glorious divine presence. Ben-Sirach envisages 'wisdom' dwelling in the Temple in the form of Torah; since the priests in this period were the teachers of Torah, Wisdom and Torah seem at least to be held together, and together to represent that divine presence and glory.[51] All this is then focused, one way and another and in one Psalm after another, on Jerusalem itself, lauded with language appropriate for the 'cosmic mountain', the high hill from which the rivers will flow down, the 'rock' where God's house has been built.[52] Jerusalem is spoken of as the new Eden, the Lord's garden.[53]

The point of all this, to spell out what we hinted earlier, is that in the underlying implicit narrative of Israel's scriptures the living God desires to dwell with his human creatures and to accomplish his purposes within the world through their agency. Of course, granted the sorry story of Genesis 3 and all that follows, these humans need rescuing and redeeming, and their vocation renewing. But the divine purposes—to work *through* image-bearers to bring order and wisdom into the world, to work through the king to build the Temple on the one hand and to bring justice and mercy to the world on the other, so that the divine glory would come to dwell there, and to work through the priests to maintain the purity of the shrine—these things are not put on hold until all is accomplished. As with the weekly Sabbaths, one might discern *advance anticipations* of this divine purpose. Temple-and-cosmos theology belongs within an eschatological narrative. The Sabbaths bring that narrative to life. Kings, priests and ordinary humans have a central role within this story, which is all the more powerful for remaining mostly implicit.[54]

The resultant inaugurated eschatology therefore offers, within an ongoing interpretative tradition, a *vocational* and indeed *political* emphasis—certainly also an *ecological and aesthetic* emphasis. Genuine science belongs here, too: the Solomonic activity of research and classification, delighting in the wonders of creation and developing technology to use it appropriately.

This theme of image-bearing is not simply an eschatological goal to be anticipated in present creation-care and scientific endeavour. The human image-bearing task, seen within the Temple- and Sabbath-framework we are attempting to discern, turns out to include not only organisation but imagination, not only labour but also love. (The 'hermeneutics of love' is not simply about discerning the rich depths of truth; it is also about responding appropriately.) Once you grasp the idea of the image within the Temple, and of humans sharing the 'rest' of God, you find the human vocation of *interpretation*: the human and humanizing task of hermeneutics as a rich and multi-layered truth-telling, discovering and displaying 'meaning' by articulating, in symbol, story and song, the many levels of significance in God's world past, present and future, and particularly in human life. Discovery and display of 'meaning' is about discerning the larger story within which events and ideas, actions and artefacts, words and worship, are what they are, mean what they mean, and require what they require in terms of continuing human involvement. This is a never-ending task: a gift that keeps on giving, a vocation that keeps on calling. The summons to glimpse the new creation *and, on that basis, to discern and respond to the meaning in the old* rather than retreating from it or letting it go to wrack and ruin is one central focus of what it means to be human. It includes the task of history, as I explained earlier. It is the call to a form of knowledge for which the ultimate word might be 'love'. It is, in fact, the foundation for a biblical approach to the questions of the world and God which might yet—as I shall argue in the next chapters—reshape something we could still call 'natural theology'.

All this we have said through an initial and highly compressed exploration of the possible links of world-creation and temple-building, bringing together Genesis 1 and various Temple-related passages. It is important to stress that this is very much a big-picture construct, a putting together of implicit symbolic narratives which, whether speaking of texts or of archaeology, stretch across wide reaches of time and space. We certainly cannot infer from these interlocking points that any particular Jewish thinker held all of them in a coherent whole at any one time. What we can suggest, though, is that even laid out in this minimal way they bring to possible expression *a worldview in which heaven and earth are designed to belong together*, and in which, under certain circumstances, they can and do come together in fact, not in a clashing category mistake—as would be the case within Epicureanism—but with a natural fit. My main underlying point is that it has been too easy for theologians and philosophers, glancing back at bits and pieces of Israel's scriptures, to fit those bits and pieces into the framework of contemporary Epicureanism or its variants, rather than allowing them to bring on to stage a very different contender for a framing cosmology, eschatology and anthropology. I am suggesting all through that the question of 'natural theology', of the possible ways in which human beings can learn to think wisely about God through contemplation of his creation, has been seriously distorted by being placed in its normal Epicurean framework and should be given the chance of being explored in a framework which would make more sense to a first-century Jew or Christian—and which might encourage Jews and Christians today to re-appropriate that framework for a new generation.

Within such a framework, the 'earthly' dimension of the cosmos could not be a mere secondary phenomenon, a distant and distorted reflection of the heavenly one, as in some kinds of Platonism.[55] When the Letter to the Hebrews speaks of the earthly Tabernacle being a 'copy or shadow of the heavenly one', this is not to say that the earthly one was bad, only that it was temporary, a signpost to what was to come (Hebrews 8.5). Creation was and is 'very good'; to distinguish between a signpost and the building to which it points is not to say anything derogatory about the signpost. The point of the life of heaven being brought into conjunction with earth is not to abolish earth, or to snatch humans away from it, as has routinely been assumed in the last two centuries, but to fill the earth with divine glory, or at least to give advance indications of that eventual intention. And the conjunction and the advance glory-filling are to take place through the work of the image-bearers, specifically the priests and the kings. This is the combination of roles ascribed to Israel itself in Exodus 19 and reaffirmed in relation to Jesus' followers in 1 Peter and the book of Revelation.[56]

The result of all this is that even if some of the details are controversial, even if we cannot demonstrate that a majority of Jews in the Second Temple period would have recognised this summary of their supposed worldview, there are enough lines all converging on the same point to make it possible to say with confidence that not only were first-century Jews not Epicureans in their view of heaven and earth; they were more or less the opposite. They believed that heaven and earth were made to work together, to dovetail, to cooperate, and at the last to be joined together; that the tabernacle and the Temple were advance signs of a new creation; that the weekly Sabbaths were in some sense foretastes of a coming New Age which would be in some sense continuous with the present time, however much radically transforming it; and that humans, or at least some humans, however sinful and corrupt, were still summoned to stand in the middle of this picture, to take up the vocation of kings and priests. All this contributes, I suggest, to *the implicit cosmology of the Second Temple period and, with it, to that of Jesus and his early followers.*

How much of all of this was glimpsed by how many people it is impossible to say. But my point is that when people in that world thought about these things at all, this is the set of parameters within which we might expect them to be working. We must avoid any insidious suggestion that, because 'not all Jews', or indeed 'all early Christians', will have thought exactly like this, they must instead have embraced the normal modern default mode, seeing 'heaven' and 'earth' as two utterly different and incompatible spheres of existence, as in Epicureanism, and in a sense as also in Platonism. They will have assumed, to the extent that they thought about such things, that these dimensions of reality were made to live and work together, and that this kind of glad symbiosis was symbolized dramatically in the Tabernacle and then the Temple. And they will have seen the present time and the promised future, not as separated by a great gulf, nor yet with the one needing to be abolished to make room for the other, but as strangely overlapping at the key point which itself spoke of creation's completion. If we reframe the questions about 'natural theology' (and many other theological topics as well) within this context, everything will look different.

SPACE, TIME AND HUMANS: JESUS AND THE EARLY CHURCH

As we move towards the end of this chapter, and begin to look ahead to the proposals for which we will argue in chapters 6 and 7, we turn to the New Testament with this complex of ideas in our heads: Temple, Sabbath and Image, with their associations of creation and new creation, of royal and divine enthronement, of the divine glory coming to dwell. As we do so, many passages, and indeed whole books, spring into new life. Obvious examples are John's Gospel and the Letter to the Hebrews. In the Pauline corpus, Ephesians and Colossians cry out for fresh related treatment. But it is striking to look first at the Synoptic tradition, still sometimes ignored in the search for rich theology.[57] It is here, not least, that the stone which the builders refused—the builders in question being the broad historical-critical tradition—turns out to be the head of the corner.

Again, a preliminary note. We cannot simply reconstruct a Second Temple worldview and find Jesus comfortably within it. One thing we certainly know about Jesus was that his compatriots found him extremely uncomfortable. (That is why, in case the point needs making again, I am not portraying Jesus as the easy culmination of a steady historical 'development' or 'progress'. The continuity between Jesus and what went before is to be discerned, as Richard Hays has insisted, by 'reading backwards'. This will be important in the next chapters.) But, again, the fact that Jesus was a radically disturbing presence within his own culture is no excuse for doing what many have done, namely, ignoring history and recontextualising Jesus somewhere else—whether in the orthodoxy of the fifth century or the unorthodoxy of the nineteenth. What Jesus did in the Temple and on the Sabbath, and how he explained those actions—these events were earth-shattering. But the earth they shattered was the first-century Jewish earth. And the purpose of this shattering was not to destroy but to fulfil.

Perhaps one or two thought experiments in Gospel exegesis would help to make the point. Take Mark. His landscape is dominated by Jesus' Temple-action in chapter 11. But the Gospel opening already evokes the ancient Near Eastern cultic and creational narrative. Jesus emerges from the water, is anointed with God's spirit/wind, and the divine voice addresses him with echoes of Psalm 2 and Isaiah 42. This is new creation and new Temple, with the Messiah in the middle of it. Mark frames this story with quotations from Malachi and Isaiah, both of which are from passages which focus on the long-awaited return of Israel's God to his people, with all that this will mean in terms of sins forgiven, exile finished, the heavens torn open, and the divine glory returning. This is the moment of enthronement, of the Great Sabbath. When Mark's Jesus then declares that the time is fulfilled, and God's kingdom is at hand, the reader should think, 'Of course! That's what it all means'. First-century Jewish assumptions are the natural context for Mark's opening, and when we pay attention to them all sorts of things look different to our normal current understandings. At a stroke one would have to reframe all those modern discussions, for instance, about Jesus' 'miracles', in which the sceptics have said that it was impossible for a god to invade the world like that and in which the defensive orthodox have said that perhaps he might after all. Those were the wrong terms for the debate.

Similarly, the idea of the Gospel Sabbath-controversies having to do with a legalistic Judaism objecting to a libertarian Jesus is embarrassingly anachronistic. What we have, rather, is the striking claim that the Age to Come is being inaugurated in powerful acts of new creation. Mark's Gospel continues almost at once by emphasizing not only what Jesus did on the Sabbath but his claim that 'the son of man' is 'lord of the Sabbath'. Well yes, we think: the kingdom has arrived, the signposts are now irrelevant. You don't put up signposts to 'Edinburgh' in the middle of Princes Street. The appropriate echo-chamber for the startlingly new message both *of* Jesus and *about* Jesus is, as before, the Jewish assumption of a heaven-and-earth *cosmology*; of an *eschatology* in which the end is anticipated in the present; and now with the addition of an *anthropology* in which humans, particularly the king, reflect God into the world in wise, sovereign, self-interpreting action. This applies as much to the parables as to the passion.

Faced with this kind of interpretation—which I throw out as a suggestion, not a fixed conclusion—you might want to invoke Lessing once more and say that these mythical truths need no anchorage in contingent historical events. This might then seem to threaten the whole argument, like the grinning serpent who waits on the penultimate square of a snakes-and-ladders game. Perhaps after all Mark is offering interpretation without event. But the roll of the dice to get us home is the narrative of creation and new creation. The point of Mark's whole story, just like those of John or Paul, is that it has to do with real things that happen in the real world. It is not an Idealist's dream. To approach these narratives within alien philosophical frameworks, whether ancient or modern—as though there were any neutrality here!—is to fail to pay attention. The New Testament's claims about Jesus, and about what Israel's God was accomplishing in and through him, mean what they mean, not within some other framework, certainly not within the modern 'discovery' of Epicureanism as though it were the newly demonstrated 'modern' worldview which had relativized all 'ancient' ones!—but within the robust, complex but coherent world where Jesus and his first followers lived. The attempts to avoid this, for instance by picking up the idea of a failed 'end-of-the-world' hope or by then demythologising that into a mixture of neo-Kantian Idealism and Heideggerian existentialism, are like putting a dolphin into a field to see if it will eat grass. Mark is telling us, from the start, that Jesus is the true king, the truly human one, the one who will defeat all enemies of the new-creation project and so construct, on earth as in heaven, the holy dwelling place of Israel's God, thereby inaugurating the endless Great Sabbath. All the '-ologies'—Christology, pneumatology, soteriology, eschatology and many more—mean what they mean (if they are to be genuinely Christian) within this worldview, this view of space, time and the royal human vocation. Philosophers sometimes justify their adoption of a non-biblical metaphysical framework by saying that, since the Bible contains various different cosmologies, we can use not only them but also others that may come to hand. I remain to be convinced that the cosmology brought to light through the events concerning Jesus is inadequate or insufficient for theology today.

Meanwhile, back in Mark's Gospel, opposition to Jesus mounts, seen by Mark (and I believe by Jesus too) in terms of the dark forces which, embodying themselves in human adversaries, are to be discerned (as in Daniel and similar books) as the satanic monsters from the abyss. If even Peter can be rebuked as 'Satan', how much more the implacable opponents of this sudden and disturbing manifestation of God's ultimate reign![58] Pharisees, Herodians, shrieking demons, muddled disciples, and ultimately the Chief Priests and Pontius Pilate are all subsumed under this category. Hence the evocation, at various points, of the cryptic 'son of man' tradition: Daniel 7 is a fantasy-version of Psalm 2, or indeed Psalm 110, with the dark forces massing themselves against the royal representative of God's people and being overthrown by his victory.[59] Mark sees the crucifixion in terms of royal enthronement, the fulfilment (in other words) of the cosmic victory enacted in advance in Jesus' baptism, and not least *the establishment of the true Temple*. In terms of ancient Near Eastern culture as a whole, Mark's narrative may be hinting that the cross would now be the dangerous location where heaven and earth would meet, thus taking the place of the ziggurat, of Noah's Ark, of the Tower of Babel, of Jacob's ladder—and now also of the wilderness tabernacle and the Jerusalem Temple whose destruction Jesus had announced in symbolic action and apocalyptic prophecy. The crucified Jesus (then to be raised from the dead; but Mark highlights the cross) is himself the place where heaven and earth now meet, where the long-awaited victory is won so that the already-inaugurated great Sabbath can be celebrated, where the image-bearer truly reflects the creator. He is the stone rejected by the builders, now become the head of the corner. Temple-cosmology, Sabbath-eschatology and messianic anthropology formed a comprehensible whole. When reworked around Jesus and the spirit they made the fresh sense that the early Christians grasped.

It is of course impossible here to follow this theme through the whole of the New Testament. Some crucial points will be picked up in the next chapter as we focus on the new creation launched in the resurrection. But we may at least glance at three key texts, showing slightly more fully some ways in which the early Christians were at home within the worldview I have been sketching, before we move to a conclusion of the present theme.

First, consider Matthew chapter 11. After the transitional verse 1, the chapter opens with John the Baptist sending messengers to Jesus to ask if he is, after all, 'the one who should come', *ho erchomenos*. Jesus answers with a demonstration of healing and the accompanying words of Isaiah 35: new creation, in other words, is happening right here, for those who have eyes to see.[60] Jesus then quizzes the crowds about John and declares that John is the one spoken of in Malachi 3.1 (echoing also Exodus 23.20): he is the preparatory messenger. He is 'Elijah who was to come' (*ho mellōn erchesthai*). The implicit Christological claim is massive. In both Exodus and Malachi, the advance messenger, the angelic or Elijah-figure, was not preparing the way for Israel's Messiah. He was preparing for the long-awaited arrival of Israel's God himself. Thus, if John is Elijah, Jesus can only be YHWH in person. Somehow the coming king and the returning God turn out to be one and the same, though this seems not to be anticipated in Jewish speculations prior to Jesus himself.

It might then appear that Matthew 11 takes a different turn, as Jesus solemnly denounces the towns where he had done so much and where he had had neither response nor repentance (verses 16–24). But if we are thinking in terms of the larger narrative of enthronement, with its overtones of Temple and Sabbath, then this passage can be seen as part of the denunciation of the 'enemies', as in Psalms 2 or 110, or indeed Daniel 7. Whether or not that is correct, the chapter then reverts to the larger question of Jesus' identity and mission. Jesus prays with thanks that the Father 'has hidden these things' from the wise and understanding and has revealed them to babies; and he declares that within the new world he is launching there is *a new mode of knowing*, in which the Father himself enables people to 'know the son', and the son himself enables people to know the father. Jesus' answer to John, then, is about *discerning the dawn*, recognising the new creation in the midst of the old: about the way in which people are now enabled *to look at events in the present world, the world of space, time and matter, and to see in them the light of the dawning day.*

In distinguishing between (a) people being 'enabled' to know things and (b) people being 'able' to know the same things without external aid, I may appear to have parted company with the rules laid down by the strict modern gatekeepers of 'natural theology'. As I shall argue in the next chapter, however, the force of the argument may run in the other direction. We warned earlier that the way 'natural theology' has been pursued in much of the last two or three centuries ought not to be regarded as a fixed, unalterable starting-point. It too was shaped, and I believe distorted, by the Enlightenment proposals, even when it was doing its best to resist the modernist pressure towards functional atheism. When operating under those implicitly Epicurean principles, such 'natural theology' may sometimes have supposed that it could operate all by itself, from some kind of *a priori* or philosophical intuition, without acknowledging the appropriate and necessary place of the retrospective revelation which enables one to 'see' Jesus himself as the unveiling-in-person of the One God. Such an epistemology would be no less 'natural' for being retrospective. Part of the point of the resurrection, as we shall see in the next chapter, is the opening up of a whole new public world, a whole new, true 'nature', not the invitation into a new private one. The dawn of the new day allows us to understand the present age itself in a new light. The tradition of the modern 'natural theology' at its best ought then to be seen as a gesture towards a more complicated, and ultimately more interesting and fruitful, set of questions. By starting with Jesus himself (instead of trying to get straight about 'God' first, and then to force a 'Jesus'-figure into the picture), such questions might answer the longings of the heart as well as the enquiries of the mind, and do so in a way which, transforming heart and mind in the process, retrospectively validated the questions and longings themselves, and thereby concluded that *the longings and the questions were themselves part of a good creation now confirmed as such*, rather than part of a meaningless creation, now obsolete and to be discarded, within which something quite different had appeared.

This dawning day is the new, true Sabbath. Jesus' invitation to 'take his yoke' (Matthew 11.29) has regularly been interpreted in terms of the 'yoke of Torah', but though that is important the underlying point should not be missed. 'I will give you rest', he says (11.28); literally, 'I will rest you', *kagō anapausō hymas*. Jesus will, in other words, give people the true, ultimate Sabbath as opposed to the long, hard working days that have preceded it. And the echo of the promised 'rest' in Exodus 33.14 is rich in meaning: that is when God promises to Moses that, despite everything, the divine presence will go with the people and settle them in the promised land.[61] Jesus' messianic role is thus displayed: his 'yoke' is 'easy', for which the Greek is *chrēstos*, probably indistinguishable in pronunciation from *christos*, 'anointed'. And, lest we might think that this Sabbath-interpretation was overdrawn, Matthew presents us in the next chapter with a Sabbath-related controversy in which the question of Jesus' identity as Davidic messiah is in question, and the real battle (against the prince of demons) is unmasked: the son of man is Lord of the Sabbath (12.8). All this makes very good sense within the cosmology and eschatology we have outlined.

Once we grasp the eschatological significance of the Sabbath, aligned with the cosmological significance of the Temple, the similar controversies elsewhere, not least in John, fall into place.[62] They are part of the Johannine announcement of creation and new creation, and of Jesus himself as the one who, like the Temple, embodies the holy presence of the creator within the midst of creation, revealing the Father in real space, time and matter within the scandalous particularity of historical events; and who, like the Sabbath, launches new creation as a present reality even while the old creation continues on its regular way. These are precisely the options that are ruled out by definition in the modern and postmodern worldviews we studied in the first two chapters. Now, with the help of historical reconstruction of the cosmology and eschatology known to at least some ancient Jews, and clearly retrieved by Jesus and his first followers, we are able to see what kind of claims are really being made. The stone the builders had rejected can be used as the chief corner-stone.

The other obvious passages we could draw into this discussion are Ephesians and Colossians on the one hand and Hebrews on the other. The Temple-theology of Ephesians is on the surface of the text: God's plan was always to sum up in the Messiah all things in heaven and on earth (1.10); this was the divine plan 'for the fullness of the times', the great sabbatical moment. In Jesus' enthronement (1.15–23) this plan has gone forward, resulting in the creation of a new Temple consisting of the Jew-plus-Gentile family indwelt by the spirit (2.11–22). Unity and holiness are therefore mandatory (chapters 4 and 5); the dark powers will strike back, but they can now be defeated (6.10–20). In the great poem in Colossians 1.15–20 the mutually interpretative themes of creation and Temple are replayed in the messianic key: the Messiah is the one in, through and for whom all things were made (1.15–18a), and he is now the one through whom the new creation has come to birth, since in him all the divine fullness was pleased to dwell (1.18b–20, esp. 19).[63]

The Letter to the Hebrews is perhaps the most explicit about these themes. Jesus is the truly human one, on the model of Psalm 8 (2.5–9); he is the one who has fulfilled the divine promise to give 'rest', the great 'sabbatical' which had remained to this point in the future (2.7–4.13, focused on 4.9–10). He is also the royal high priest, fulfilling both the Davidic promises of Psalm 2 and the 'Melchizedek' promises of Psalm 110, and joining heaven and earth together in presenting his blood in the heavenly tabernacle.[64] The result is the establishment of the 'new covenant' promised by Jeremiah, the new dispensation in which the Levitical cult itself is rendered redundant, as Psalm 40 had indicated (8.7–10.18). The result is that those who belong to Jesus and follow him faithfully are welcomed into the heavenly sanctuary (12.18–24).

All this striking evidence in the New Testament provides part of the argument that ideas such as I have listed briefly were, to put it at its weakest, not unknown in the Second Temple period. As with other large themes, we should not claim that 'all Jews believed' this or that. But the early Christian evidence suggests that, even if only some circles in the Jewish world were thinking about a Temple-cosmology and a Sabbath-eschatology, these ideas were available and comprehensible and would have made the fresh sense that the early Christians envisaged when rethought around Jesus and the spirit. Though, as we have seen, radical innovation did occur, it would be strange to suggest that nobody up to the time of Jesus had been thinking like this at all and that suddenly, with the messianic and kingdom-bringing events of his death and resurrection, an entire Temple-and-creation theology, and an entire Sabbath-focused eschatology, should spring up without antecedents, replete with complex and interlocking echoes of Genesis, Exodus, the Psalms and the Prophets. Of course, Jesus and his first followers do seem to have found things in the scriptures which others had not (though our scanty evidence means we must say that sort of thing with due caution; it is quite possible that the archaeologist's spade may turn up more previously unsuspected evidence). But all the signs are that they were bringing into fresh focus biblical themes and ideas which were already current, rather than drawing attention to those biblical themes and ideas in a way which had no parallel or forerunner.[65]

There is of course a sharp difference between this way of approaching a Christian assessment of Jesus and the kind of thing we find among the Fathers of the third or fourth century. It seems to me that the worldview, thought-forms and implicit narrative embedded within what I am calling a Temple-cosmology and a Sabbath-eschatology were not so much rejected by the later church as simply not grasped. The music of the scriptures was being played in a different echo-chamber. Different resonances were being set up.

If that was so in the third and fourth centuries, how much more was it the case in the middle ages, and then at the time of what we now call the rise of historical exegesis in the eighteenth and nineteenth centuries. Within on the one hand mediaeval Aristotelianism and on the other hand the Epicureanism that was coming into its own with the Enlightenment, the whole idea of a temple as a place where heaven and earth would be drawn together was straightforwardly incomprehensible. And the idea of a 'present age' and an 'age to come', with the latter being anticipated in the Sabbath and then realised in the launch of new creation through Jesus, was doubly incredible. First, as we saw in the second and fourth chapters, it made no sense within the Epicurean worldview where 'heaven' and 'earth' were incompatible polar opposites. New creation could only mean the abolition of the old. Second, as we saw in the first chapter, the claim that in Jesus the new creation had come to birth, once and for all, flew directly in the face of the Enlightenment belief that the world was turning its great corner at last through Descartes and Kant, Rousseau and Voltaire, Jefferson, Hegel, Schopenhauer and Marx. Finally, the suggestion that human beings were two-way reflectors, projecting the image of a god into the world of creation and summing up creation's praise before that god, made no sense, either to the strict Epicureans for whom humans were simply random accidents or for the believers in 'progress' who supposed that humans had finally come of age.

Thus the powerful Enlightenment agenda, producing as it did cosmologies and eschatologies of its own, and reliant on the rival epistemologies of rationalist induction on the one hand or Idealist intuition on the other, was bound to reject the early Christian claims. Its invitation to Christian apologists to play the 'natural theology' game on its own sloping pitch and with its own local rules and referees was never going to end well. But the fatal chink in the Enlightenment's armour always was its appeal to 'history'. Rather than refusing this challenge, as many have done, I have argued that the real knowledge gained through the application of a critically realist epistemology of love to the questions of history must pose the challenge afresh. The first-century Temple-cosmology, Sabbath-eschatology and image-anthropology are not, after all, 'ancient' worldviews which we 'moderns' must reject. They are non-Epicurean worldviews which the prevailing Epicureanism has done its best to dismiss, and which now need to be thought through afresh. They need to be given their chance to set up a better framework for considering the major questions of theology.

By themselves, of course, these ancient Israelite, Jewish and early Christian worldviews, focusing on an overlapping cosmology of heaven and earth, an overlapping eschatology of the present age and the age to come, and the two-way anthropology of humans as image-bearers, simply pose the question: how might we judge? Do these ways of thinking, of telling the great stories, make sense? This is where the early Christian claim comes into its own: the biblical cosmology and eschatology are no longer 'by themselves'. They have appeared in human form, in the form of an image-bearer who announced God's kingdom, challenged the Temple and the reigning high priest, and was executed as a would-be king. The overlap of heaven and earth, and the interlocking present and future, have presented themselves in a historical, visible form, though the 'visibility' of that overlap and interlock would depend on seeing and understanding the entire story of Jesus' kingdom-launching public career and its unexpected climax. Eschatology has come to life, say the first Christians, in the person of Jesus, and we know it because when we look at him we discern the dawning of the new day in a way which makes sense of the old, and of the questions it raised. New creation has been launched in and through him, they claim, and they know it both because of what they know about Jesus—which, despite prejudice to the contrary, they invite us to investigate for ourselves—and because of what they find to be true through living as the 'new Temple'. They do not simply assume a particular cosmology, eschatology and anthropology and then locate Jesus in the middle of them. They present a Jesus who makes the sense he makes as the explosive presence who makes retrospective 'sense' of *them*. As Jesus explained to the two puzzled disciples on the road to Emmaus, when you look back at Israel's scriptures it all fits together, even though nobody had seen it like that before. So, too, when you look back at Israel's cosmology, eschatology and anthropology. So, too, I shall suggest, when we look back at the questions and promptings which humans of all sorts have discerned within the 'natural' world.

What all this means, and how it might reshape the tasks of theology in general and 'natural theology' in particular, will be the subject of the remaining three chapters.

6

The New Creation
Resurrection and Epistemology

INTRODUCTION

'It is love that believes the resurrection'.[1] That famous quote from Ludwig Wittgenstein sets both the goal and the puzzle for this chapter. One can imagine Wittgenstein's own hearers rolling their eyes and wondering whether this was another Zen-like Koan from the master of dense paradox—wondering, too, what exactly he meant both by 'love' and by 'resurrection', and indeed by 'believe'. I do not know whether Wittgenstein himself ever unpacked this statement at any length. The paragraph where it appears pops up in his writings, like Melchizedek, without father, mother or genealogy. There might be, as we shall see, an appropriateness to this, an orientation to the subject-matter. The resurrection of Jesus is presented in the early Christian texts not as something in a series, not as a comprehensible part of a larger comprehensible whole, but as something which is what it is, means what it means, and is known as it is known, primarily within the new world which it launches. It brings its own world with it. The resurrection of Jesus is presented in the New Testament as, more specifically, an event which brings its own ontology and epistemology with it—which regenerates and redirects the ancient Jewish cosmology, eschatology and anthropology we were looking at in the last chapter. Wittgenstein, however, frames his proposal by distinguishing sharply between the 'certainty of faith' and the 'speculative intellect', the 'soul' from the 'abstract mind'; and there, while borrowing his slogan, I shall part company with him. 'It is love that believes the resurrection', I shall argue, because love is the most complete form of knowledge, *including* not bypassing historical knowledge in particular; and

187

the resurrection is the most complete form of event, not simply a random 'fact' but an event which conveys both meaning and power.

The problem with speaking about 'love' as the ultimate mode of knowing, of course, is that this line of thought appears to back itself into the very corner from which 'natural theology', as normally conceived, was supposed to escape. Does it not sound like the worst kind of special pleading, the most blatant confession of a 'private knowing', a sheer subjectivity with no possible purchase on ordinary reality? After all, to the hard-nosed left-brain rationalist 'love' is precisely the fluffy, romantic rose-tinted view of things which makes you feel happy but won't stand up in the light of day. But that perception of 'love', as I have argued earlier, is itself symptomatic of a major problem in Western culture, the culture within which the question of 'natural theology', and the questions of Jesus and history which refuse to be separated from that question, have been shaped for the last two hundred years.

This cultural shaping has not been so much a matter of actual scholarship. It has happened through the questions being asked within the atmosphere of implicit Epicureanism, sometimes modified with forms of Idealism. That atmosphere is precisely where 'love' is discounted: because, within Epicureanism, it gets in the way of a severely rational approach to the world; because, within Idealism, it belongs in the upper world of Ideas rather than in the lower world of space-time events. It takes us to the wrong side of Lessing's ugly ditch. It is the quality that our culture, like Faust, or indeed like Wagner's Alberich, has had to foreswear in order to gain power over the worlds of science, technology and empire.

These examples tell a dark and important story. The model of 'knowledge' which has been privileged in Western culture is certainly focused on the left brain, as has been brilliantly argued by the brain scientist and cultural critic Iain McGilchrist in his ground-breaking book *The Master and His Emissary*.[2] But it is also (and perhaps the reasons for this are the same) an attempt at a *controlling* epistemology, a 'knowing' in the service of power. Nietzsche and Foucault were truly on to something, even if their critique only really found an appropriate target precisely in the models of knowing that had come to dominate the culture. The desire for the particular kind of knowledge that would confer power is analogous to the request of James and John in Mark 10.35–45, wanting to sit at Jesus' right and left in his coming kingdom. Jesus' response is to replace their love of power with the power of love. He was bringing to birth a different kind of kingdom, in which 'the son of man came to give his life as a ransom for many'.

We might, through a similar transposition, propose an 'epistemological' reading of Romans 8—in line, to be sure, with the notion of the 'mind of the flesh' and the 'mind of the spirit' (the *phronema tes sarkos* and the *phronema tou pneumatos*) in 8.5–8. It is perhaps too easy to read these simply in terms of ethical behaviour, though Paul does of course speak of 'living' according to the 'flesh' or the 'spirit', and then of 'putting to death the deeds of the body'. But my point—in line with one reading at least of the famous 2 Corinthians 5.16 ('we don't regard anybody from a merely human point of view')—would then be that he is advocating a new mode of knowing. Some have suggested that this would mean a kind of 'apocalyptic' knowing, a fresh revelation which actually cancels out 'ordinary' modes of knowledge. That, however, capitulates once more to the either/or learned from the Epicurean split. What is envisaged is indeed a new mode of knowing; but the larger context of 2 Corinthians 5, which has to do with the *redemption* of the created order and also of the human body, indicates that this fresh revelation does not rule out ordinary knowledge, but takes it up to a new level, providing it with a fresh perspective, a new dimension of meaning. Paul's argument in this whole passage (actually, from 2 Corinthians 2.14 to 6.13) is precisely to frame the apparently puzzling and ambiguous apostolic life within the larger vision of the divine purposes, focusing on Jesus' resurrection and the promised resurrection of his people.[3] The resurrection *interprets* the present situation, rather than ignoring it and offering a quite different sort of reality.

The insidious and powerful effect of the split-world assumption within our culture is why I have attempted, in this book so far, a slow, outflanking strategy. I have tried, as it were, to come around the back of our assumed Epicureanism with its heaven/earth split, its divided time, and its random and meaningless humans. I have proposed instead that there might be another way, a Jewish and then early Christian way, of understanding space, time and human beings. The knee-jerk response one might anticipate to this kind of proposal is that it is 'unacceptable in our modern critical world', but that is pure smokescreen. There is nothing 'modern' about Epicureanism. The ancientness of the early Jewish and Christian worldview cannot properly be used as a rhetorical scare-tactic to stop the message of new creation infiltrating tomorrow's world. What matters, once again, is history: not historicism, not reductionism, but patient attention to evidence, abductive essays in hypothesis, and verification through narrative proposal. History is not the only tool in the box. But, as I argued in chapter 3, it is very good at defeating defeaters, dismantling distortions and redirecting discussion. That is where we shall presently begin.

To that extent, we are simply talking once more about 'critical realism', as opposed to the *un*critical realism (positivism) which ignores its own prejudices and assumes it can get to the 'facts', to a kind of 'knowledge' which is really a self-aggrandizing project—back to James and John, in fact. We are also opposed to the critical *un*realism of the sceptic who, wary of being taken in by other people's power-plays, refuses to believe any evidence at all. A genuine 'critical realism', operating with the ordinary 'epistemology of love' as outlined in chapter 3 above (the eagerness that the evidence should be itself, should not be distorted to fit one's own previous guesses or fantasies) will always be open to the radically new, to something which, as in Thomas Kuhn's famous work, demands a complete 'paradigm shift'.[4] That happens again and again in all kinds of serious research. I have lived through two such shifts in my own field, the 'new perspective' on Paul and the 'third quest' for Jesus, both much misunderstood but still important.[5] But at exactly that point there opens the fresh possibility to which we shall return later in this chapter. What if the new paradigm, driven by the new evidence, was all about a revelation of love itself? Then the 'epistemology of love', which is normally (at least in my work) a shorthand for saying 'a mode of knowing that takes with utter and delighted seriousness the distinct otherness of the thing known', would acquire a double meaning. The normal critical realist imperative would find itself transcended, translated, transposed into a different mode. That, I shall argue, is what happens with Jesus' resurrection. And this is what I mean by saying that the resurrection brings its own ontology and therefore epistemology with it, without ever risking a collapse into the fantasy-world of private or 'purely subjective' ideas or apprehensions. The world opened by Jesus' resurrection is the *real* world in its new mode: the new creation which recontextualises and reinterprets the old.

All this talk of resurrection and consequent alternative epistemologies is bound to seem opaque, or worse, within other philosophical paradigms, not least the ruling frameworks of Western culture. Paul declared that the gospel was foolishness to the Greeks and scandalous to the Jews. We might expand this: the resurrection is impossible for an Epicurean, undesirable for a Platonist, unnecessary for a Deist, meaningless for a Pantheist and scary for an emperor.[6] But within the world we sketched in the previous chapter—the world shaped by a Temple-cosmology, a Sabbath-eschatology and an image-bearing anthropology—the resurrection of the crucified Messiah is the new microcosmos through which the new, great Sabbath is launched. It is the declaration that the new world has been born in the midst of the old *and that this makes sense of the old world like nothing else could or would.* The resurrection is simultaneously the foundational and paradigmatic event of the new creation and also, on that basis, a very strange though actually sense-making event within the present creation. Temple, Sabbath and the 'imaged' anthropology help us to understand how this works, even though nobody had seen it coming. This is where the question of the resurrection addresses directly the question of natural theology, though we will only get to that conclusion in the final two chapters.

Today's sceptics and today's conservatives both get it wrong, because the modern Epicureanism within which both live has flattened out the antithesis. Most people today agree with the ancients: resurrection doesn't happen in the 'natural' world, so it can't have happened.[7] The apologist who then says it *did* happen, invoking something called 'the supernatural' to explain it, is simply leaping across Lessing's ugly ditch. But Lessing's ditch is still there. Worse, this makes the resurrection an *example* of something else, 'the supernatural' (whatever that is), rather than itself being the starting-point, the new reality that brings its own ontology and epistemology with it.

Similar anxieties are raised when we investigate the resurrection historically. Theologians worry that if we elevate something called 'history' as the benchmark, that becomes the ultimate reality, and 'resurrection' has to fit in—or, more likely, finds itself ruled out by the sleight of hand which equates 'history' with Humean scepticism. This, too, reflects the wrong approach. Perhaps heaven and earth really are mutually porous. Perhaps it is possible for the future to arrive, in some sense, within the ongoing present. Maybe humans really are God-reflectors. Note again: you can't start with 'Temple, Sabbath and Image' and deduce Easter. If you could, the two on the Emmaus road wouldn't have been so worried. But if you start with Easter and look back, you see, not something called 'the supernatural', but a classic Jewish philosophical framework within which, however unexpected, the event might make new and compelling sense.

In other words: if by 'natural theology' we refer to the question, 'Can we, *under the intellectual conditions of modernity*, start with the natural world and reason our way up to the God of the New Testament?', the answer must be No. You might, of course, reason your way to an Epicurean divinity, aloof, detached, uninvolved. You might, as many have, reason your way to the 'Unmoved Mover' or the gods of pantheism and panentheism. You might well end up with some kind of Platonic divinity, though the question of whether this being is really 'God' or something less personal—'the divine', perhaps—would remain open. But the italicised clause within the question shows what is going on. The question is slanted from the start. Enlightenment Epicureanism hands the theologian a microscope, designed to see the smallest atom, and challenges the theologian to see the morning star. It can't be done. But the theologian should then suggest a telescope.

And one component of the telescope—surprisingly enough, to many—is history.

RESURRECTION AND HISTORY

I have written at length elsewhere about the ways in which historical research challenges the easy-going proposals which have often been advanced for disbelieving in Jesus' bodily resurrection.[8] In our present topic, this comes under the category of 'defeating the defeaters', using historical research to address, and in these cases to render highly improbable, the various alternative proposals that have often been advanced as supposed explanations for the rise of belief in Jesus' resurrection. Thus, for instance, the idea that his followers suffered from 'cognitive dissonance' is historically incredible: many other Jewish movements ended with the founder's violent death, and in no case did people claim he had been raised from the dead. The frequent suggestion that Jesus' followers suffered from what we today call mass hallucination, or that they experienced the well-known phenomenon of 'sightings' of a person who had recently died (and who in fact stayed dead), simply doesn't work. People in the ancient world knew about these things as well as we do. The suggestions that the women went to the wrong tomb, or that they met Jesus' brother James in the half-light and mistook him for Jesus himself, or that the surface inconsistencies in the Gospel accounts mean that they were all invented later, have again and again been shown to be trivial and irrelevant. More seriously, the suggestion that the idea of Jesus' resurrection was generated by reflection on scripture fails to take account of the remarkable absence of scripture from the stories in the four Gospels.[9] This relates to another regular proposal, that the four accounts were composed (along with the Gospels in which they are contained) a generation or more after the event and so cannot serve as the eyewitness testimony they seem to claim. This is straightforwardly falsified by other significant features: the striking role of the women in the narrative (contrasted with the 'official' summary in 1 Corinthians 15.3–8), the absence of reference to the future hope of believers, and the strange portrait of Jesus himself.[10] Another major misunderstanding relates to Paul's use of the phrase *sōma pneumatikon* in 1 Corinthians 15.44–46; this has regularly been taken to mean 'spiritual body' in some kind of platonic sense, implying that for Paul the 'body' was not what we would call 'physical'. But this has again and again been shown to be seriously misleading. The adjective *pneumatikos* does not tell us what a body is *made or composed of*, but what it is *animated by*.[11]

At this point the task of 'defeating the defeaters' has merged into the second historical task, that of dismantling the distortions. Among these one of the foremost is the word 'resurrection' itself. I was struck forty years ago by the conversation with Karl Barth that T. F. Torrance reports in *Space, Time and Resurrection*. Torrance had commented that some scholars thought of resurrection in a docetic way, 'lacking concrete ontological reality'. He describes how Barth leaned over to him and 'said with considerable force, which I shall never forget, "*Wohlverstanden, leibliche Auferstehung*"—"Mark well, bodily resurrection"'.[12] That was a fine moment in the history of modern theology. But my point is that *it should never have been necessary*. The reason for agreeing with Barth here is not a theological *a priori*, the rejection of Docetism,[13] but a matter of history. In the first century, a *non*-bodily 'resurrection' would have been a contradiction in terms. *Resurrection meant bodies.* To think otherwise is to fail on your linguistic homework. Yes, the language of resurrection can be used metaphorically. Yes, from the late second century Gnostic writers began to use the word to mean Platonic soul-survival.[14] Jews or Greeks who wanted to say that sort of thing had perfectly good language to do so, and the word 'resurrection' would have made exactly the wrong point. The home base for the metaphor, and for the gnostic mutation, was that 'resurrection' always meant some kind of new bodily life.[15]

Another distortion is the long-standing proposal, associated with Rudolf Bultmann but widely held still, that when the early Christians said Jesus had been raised from the dead what they really meant was that his death had caused their sins to be forgiven.[16] The attraction of this in a modern, Epicurean framework is obvious. No sacred cows get harmed in the making of this movie. But it raises insuperable textual and historical problems. Paul—our earliest witness—is clear: the resurrection demonstrates *that* sins have been forgiven; the two are not the same thing (1 Corinthians 15.17). Without the belief in resurrection as something out beyond the crucifixion, the note of new creation which permeates the New Testament is inexplicable.

Similar misunderstandings and distortions occur among theologians who want in some sense to affirm Jesus' resurrection. Thus Robert Jenson, for example, cautiously suggests that the tomb had to be empty because otherwise it would have become a shrine, whereas now Jesus became 'available' to his followers.[17] But this is grossly inadequate as an account of the role of Jesus in the apostolic preaching. There is no reason to suppose that the Sadducees of Acts 4 would have been angry with Peter or that the Athenian greybeards in Acts 17 would have mocked at Paul, if they had said that Jesus was now 'available to them'. What the authorities objected to, for reasons we would call 'political' as well as religious, philosophical or cultural, was the announcement that new creation had been launched and that the signposts of Temple and Sabbath had finally led Israel and the whole of creation to the new reality, the new Image in whom the One God was personally establishing his kingdom on earth as in heaven.

Another distortion that has to be dismantled is the idea that people in the ancient world were ready to believe all kinds of strange things, including bodily resurrection. The evidence is massively to the contrary: everybody in the first-century world understood what 'resurrection' meant, and everybody except the Pharisees and other Jews who thought similarly firmly believed it was impossible.[18] From Aeschylus to Marcus Aurelius this is clear. Philosophically and politically, we can see why. Resurrection doesn't fit. In the great set piece in Acts 26, Paul explains himself before the Roman governor Porcius Festus and the current 'king of the Jews', Herod Agrippa, emphasizing the resurrection of Jesus as the event which has fulfilled the ancient scriptural promises. At the end of the speech, as he presses the point home, Festus shouts at Paul, telling him he is mad. Herod Agrippa, however, knows Paul is not mad, but he sees only too clearly what the social and political consequences might be if the ancient hope of Israel (as expounded by the Pharisees) were to come true in this way. It would mean, for a start, that Jesus of Nazareth was the true 'king of the Jews' and that he, Herod, was not.[19] This double reaction persists. Enlightenment Epicureanism is nothing if not a project of Western imperialism. It has developed Festus-like reactions to Jewish and Christian claims, perhaps for Agrippa-like reasons.

The mirror-image of this distortion is the idea that because many, perhaps most, Jews believed in resurrection, it was easy for Jesus' followers to grasp on to that and imagine that it had actually happened. This too can be easily dismantled. Not only were there many other failed messianic and prophetic movements in the centuries before and after Jesus, none of which claimed that the dead founder had been raised. The early Christian resurrection-belief, though clearly belonging within a Jewish frame of reference rather than a pagan one, very quickly developed several significant mutations, none of which is explicable in terms of uncaused theological speculation. I have listed these, summarizing wider arguments, in *Surprised by Hope*.[20] One might easily compile another list, of the unprecedented combination of features in the early Christian movement which are only explicable if we assume that Jesus' first followers really did believe that he had been bodily raised, not simply (as in the usual alternative) that they had had a new 'spiritual' or 'religious' experience.²¹ They lived, spoke and wrote with the presupposition that an event had occurred through which Israel's God, the creator, had returned at last and had, through his chosen Messiah, won the decisive battle against the real enemy—even though this 'return', and this 'battle' and 'victory', were now seen quite differently to what we find in earlier Jewish expectations. They believed that, through this messianic achievement, the long exile was over, the great Sabbath had dawned, the 'new Temple' had been built (consisting of Jesus and his followers) and the creator God, through Messiah Jesus, had established his sovereign rule over the world, however paradoxical this might seem in terms of continuing persecution and struggle. The young Christian movement was recognisably Jewish. It pressed all the buttons, though in a totally unexpected way: the royal leader had won the decisive battle; the Temple was destroyed and rebuilt; Daniel's long exile was over; freedom and forgiveness had arrived in the present; the covenant had been renewed, creation itself was restored, and the One God had returned in a shockingly new kind of glory. Those were the major themes of early Christian belief—though you wouldn't know it from those schemes which project backwards the belief-structures of the fourth, the sixteenth or the nineteenth century. This again is a failure of *history*, an attempt to make the past in one's own image. We know that those were major elements in Second Temple Jewish practical eschatology, and we know—from careful historical exegesis—that they were major themes in early Christianity. *But they now appear in a completely different guise.* You could not have predicted early Christianity from the Jewish matrix, but that's where it belongs, albeit in revolutionary mode. Everything we know of various movements within the Second Temple world indicates that these things would not have happened simply through the death of the movement's founder.

Nor do these things constitute the early Christians as simply a 'new religious movement', in either the ancient or the modern sense of 'religious'. They were, from the start, a distinctive *community*.²² We notice in particular that the post-Bultmannian proposal, as might be expected granted its genealogy, shrinks the meaning of the whole movement into what we would call 'religion', disengaged politically and philosophically, concerned with 'salvation' or 'forgiveness' only in some Idealist or platonic sense. But that was never the point either of 'kingdom'-movements or of 'resurrection'; and it was never the point of real early Christianity. The early Christians were indeed concerned with 'forgiveness of sins', but in the holistic, indeed socio-political as well as theological sense we find in Isaiah, Daniel and elsewhere, retrieved powerfully in the New Testament. Israel was in long exile because of ongoing 'sin', so that 'forgiveness' would mean the overthrow of Babylon—in first-century terms, Rome—and the rebuilding of the Temple ready for the glorious return of YHWH. Something must have happened to make people say *both* that these expectations had been fulfilled *and* that they had been translated into a new mode.

This is where the dismantling of distortions joins up with the third historical task, directing the discussion: because these features of early Christianity demand a serious historical explanation. These features, to repeat, make sense within the Jewish world, but it is a shocking, unanticipated sense even there. We need both halves of that claim. These features do *not* make that much sense within fifth- or sixteenth-century theology, which is why they have been ignored or roughly reinterpreted. We cannot use the fact that they were new and shocking in Jesus' day as an excuse for saying that we will therefore ignore the historical context and substitute our anachronistic ones instead. And these features then pose the obvious question: how can we explain the sudden emergence of a movement at the same time so very Jewish and so very unlike anything known there before? The early Christians say with one voice that it was because a crucified messianic pretender was raised bodily from the dead and that in him they glimpsed God's glory. The historian must ask how they came so quickly to this rich combination of inaugurated-eschatological conclusions—not just a new set of ideas, but practical conclusions about ordering their common and personal lives and launching an outward-looking movement we loosely refer to as 'mission'. Can it really all have happened simply because they had new internal religious experiences?

This is why, in various earlier works, I have set out the case for affirming that on the Sunday after his crucifixion, and for some while thereafter, Jesus of Nazareth was found to be bodily alive again, leaving an empty tomb behind him, even though the body which he now had seemed to be strangely different from his previous one—though with continuity literally etched into it by the mark of the nails and the spear. The early accounts show every sign that for the writers then, as for us today, this was shocking and puzzling at several levels. I recall Professor Ed Sanders once saying that, from the accounts we have, it looks very much as though the early Christians were struggling to describe something they knew had happened but for which they were aware that they didn't have good language. That seems to me pretty much on target. But what then emerges is that the early Christians spoke, taught and lived on the basis that in Jesus something had happened through which the cosmology symbolized by the Temple, and the eschatology symbolized by the Sabbath, had attained a new kind of fulfilment. And they coupled this with the remarkable claim that in his human life he had fulfilled, again in a new way, the 'anointed' vocation of Israel's king and, in some traditions, Israel's High Priest. Though this is not the place to pursue this insight, I regard it as very telling that one of the characteristic activities of the early church was to tell the *human* story of Jesus *as the story of how Israel's God had returned to fulfil his ancient promises.*[23] When followers of Jesus told and wrote stories about him, and when four of them wrote 'the story of Jesus' as a whole, they were not simply collecting personal reminiscences. Still less were they merely projecting backwards the various situations and controversies in the early church. They were saying, in a thoroughly Jewish way, that the symbols and stories of Israel had been fulfilled in a shocking and decisive manner; that in this all too human story—hence the choice of the biographical genre, however modified—not only the promises of a coming Messiah but also the promise of the returning creator and covenant God had been realised. Temple and Sabbath had come true in a new way. Jesus had truly joined together God's space and human space, heaven and earth. In him God's planned future for the whole cosmos was truly anticipated in the present. In him, so the early church claimed, we see revealed the true Image of God.

None of this in itself—to the disappointment of some, perhaps—is intended to serve as a knock-down argument for the historicity of Jesus' bodily resurrection. We have done, in outline, what we argued in chapter 3 'history' can and should do. Using the 'epistemology of love' by which we make the delighted effort to think into the minds of people who think differently to ourselves, and recognising that this 'difference' between us and them is not, as used to be supposed, that between an 'ancient' pre-scientific and a 'modern' scientific worldview but between an assumed Epicureanism and a Jewish or Christian view of space and time, we are proposing an understanding of what the early Christians said and thought which considerably clarifies the discussion. From here we can then move forwards in a different direction.

It is, after all, open to anyone to propose a puzzled agnosticism at this point. Once clarity has been attained, and spurious 'defeaters' seen off, the choice is clear. All the signs are that the first disciples really did believe that Jesus was bodily alive again—albeit in a new body which seemed to possess properties for which were quite unprepared—and that easily the best explanation for this is that they were right.[24] But since accepting this conclusion involves some theory about the way the world is which cuts clean across the normal assumption, from Homer to the present day, that dead people stay dead, many will naturally hold back. Some, indeed, may attempt other theories, perhaps that Jesus had become such a remarkable human being that, uniquely so far, he managed to survive death by the sheer force of his own character. (In other words, there might be ways of saying that he really was in some sense alive again which do not involve ascribing this event to divine action.) Others will prefer to say that since they hold an *a priori* belief in the non-existence or non-intervention of a deity—in other words, some variation on Epicureanism or Deism—they believe that there must be some other explanation for the rise of early Christianity even though they are unable to say what it is.[25]

At this the discipline of history can have nothing more to say. If it cannot be invoked in aid of a Humean reductionism ('scientific history shows that resurrection cannot happen'), nor can it be invoked in aid of a rationalistic orthodoxy such that to refuse to believe would be an admission of intellectual incompetence or wickedness. But what the task of history can do, as part of drawing attention to all relevant evidence, is to point out that the beliefs which humans hold about what can and cannot happen in 'real life' are always a function of larger worldviews or unspoken philosophical assumptions. History thus tells a story about how and why humans come to believe what they believe, a story in which History's own role is necessary but by itself insufficient. It can lead us to the water but cannot make us drink.

What makes the difference in this case—and here we turn the corner of this chapter, and thereby of the present book—is an understanding of what it is that Jesus' resurrection unveils. This remains hidden in much reflection on the subject because the Epicurean context of modern scholarship, and the often-rationalist response from the would-be orthodox, have tried to conduct the conversation in terms of whether or not one believes in 'miracles' or 'the supernatural'. That implies a split-level ontology which then demands a kind of rationalistic epistemology. As I indicated at the outset of this chapter, the resurrection of Jesus of Nazareth offers itself as the centre of a new kind of ontology, inviting a new kind of epistemology.

This 'newness', though, is not mere novelty. The whole point of new creation, at least within the perception of the early Christians, is that it is about the redemption and renewal of creation, not its abolition and replacement. Here the stories of Jesus' bodily resurrection serve as model as well as source. And with this redemption and renewal there goes the reaffirmation of the original creation. The resurrection of Jesus declares that 'God so loved the world'; and this declaration constitutes a summons to an answering love. The renewal of creation therefore demands a renewed version of knowledge, including a renewed version of 'the epistemology of love'. It is in this sense that I want to reappropriate (whether against his intention or not) the saying from Wittgenstein with which we began. It is *love* that believes the resurrection.

RESURRECTION AND THE VINDICATION OF CREATION

How then might the resurrection of Jesus of Nazareth open up new pathways to some kind of 'natural theology'? The revisionist proposals we have examined provide no clue. But if we take the witness of Paul and the Gospels seriously, on the grounds that what they say provides an unparalleled historical explanation for the rise of early Christianity, then a new line of thought emerges. The resurrection *reaffirms the goodness and God-givenness of the original creation*, the true 'nature' so to speak, including all the apparent signposts and question-marks within that original creation. The resurrection provides food and clothing for the hungry and naked arguments that might have tried to make the case for 'natural theology' from within creation as it was. The resurrection, precisely by its redemptive transformation of creation, reaffirms the goodness of the original—and, hence, the appropriateness of recognising the signs and signals that function as 'signposts' within the original, in the paradoxical senses we shall explore in the next chapter.

After all, the resurrection of Jesus, comprehensible as the fresh apocalypse within the Jewish world we have studied, announces itself as the new creation, *not as a replacement for something now thrown away but a rescued and renewed version of the old.* This unveils not only the creator's power but the creator's *love*. The lavish, generous love exhibited in the original creation, which had seemed to be an idle dream—even a cruel fantasy—in the light of the harsh realities of the world, summed up in the horrible execution of a young prophet whose eager followers believed he was bringing about Israel's redemption—this creational love, focused in scripture on the divine covenant love for Israel, is astonishingly and powerfully reaffirmed. As in the covenant language of Deuteronomy or Isaiah, the resurrection reveals that the cross was the supreme act of love, and the resurrection itself declares that the creator loved the old creation itself and had all along been determined to rescue it. The signs of that love within the old creation were not a sick joke. They were telling the truth. If of course we were to understand 'resurrection' merely in a Platonic sense, with Jesus' soul going to heaven, the world of space, time and matter would not be ultimately important, and we shouldn't try to deduce from it anything about God's ultimate truth. You won't find Gnostics doing natural theology.[26] But if Easter was the start of *a new creation* which is a *creatio ex vetere* and not a fresh *creatio ex nihilo*; if the resurrection was therefore an act of love, God's love for the old world and its image-bearing inhabitants, then the 'old' creation, as it plays host to the new, is itself validated. Its silent witness to the creator (as in Psalm 19) is retrospectively reaffirmed. And, as I shall draw out presently, this ultimate and utter love generates in response *a new mode of knowing*, a mode which itself is the redemptive renewal of the other modes to which we are more easily attuned. The 'love' element within 'critical realism'—the insistence on respecting and admiring the 'other' for and as itself rather than either dismissing it or collapsing it into the shape demanded by fantasy or 'projection'—this 'love' is itself shifted into a different gear.

Before we get to that, two analogies suggest themselves for the underlying point I am making. First, the story of Israel. The New Testament is emphatic that with Jesus and his death and resurrection the covenant with Abraham has been fulfilled, the 'old covenant' with Moses on Mount Sinai has been transformed into the 'new covenant' promised by Jeremiah, and the long, dark and winding narrative of Israel's story with God—anything but a smooth, steady progress or 'development'!—has reached its surprising and indeed shocking goal.[27] Each of the canonical Gospels opens, in its own way, with a strong evocation of the ancient story of Israel, presenting Jesus as the fulfilment of the original intention. John takes that back to Genesis 1 itself. And each Gospel, again in its own way, presents the entire narrative as the fulfilment of Israel's scriptures.[28] The high point of all this, though again inevitably controversial, is in Romans 9–11. The result is that, for the early Christians, the resurrection of the crucified Jesus did not mean that Messiahship, the calling of Israel, the scriptures and the symbolic world of Temple and Torah—and especially Sabbath—had been a mistake and should now be forgotten as a quite different new movement made its way in the world. Rather the reverse. The death and resurrection of Jesus have *retrospectively and transformatively validated* what was there before. 'Abraham rejoiced to see my day', says John's Jesus; 'he saw it and was glad' (John 8.56). The resurrection reaffirms the goodness of the ancient purposes. Those who, in earlier centuries, had looked at creation, at Torah, at the Temple, and had believed that the God who was strangely made known there was the true God and would one day be known as such, were vindicated in that earlier belief, though at the same time we must note the warnings expressed in various places by both John the Baptist and Paul (e.g. Matthew 3.9; Romans 2.17–29). In Romans 10, Paul declares that Israel's 'zeal for God' (he is referring not least to his own former self) was 'not according to knowledge', since the true 'knowledge' was now revealed in the Messiah and in the covenant renewal, fulfilling the promise of Deuteronomy 30, which opened up heart and voice to a new level of faith, and which opened up the community of God's people to all who shared that faith, Gentile equally with Jew (Romans 10.1–13). This analogy between the reaffirmation of creation in the resurrection and the reaffirmation of the story of Israel is not, in fact, simply an analogy.

Part of the point is that Israel was always the bearer of the divine promise to the world, to the whole created order, as in Psalm 72 and elsewhere. And this close connection may explain why some who have in other respects been channelling the early Barth (whether or not they were arguing about 'natural theology') have been, Marcion-like, resistant to any idea of continuity between the story of Israel and the dramatic 'apocalypse' of Jesus, Israel's Messiah.[29]

The second analogy is that of 'moral order', as in Oliver O'Donovan's famous argument.[30] We do not and cannot simply learn 'moral order' from creation in its present state. All sorts of things—natural disasters, animal cruelty, human moral chaos—forbid us straightforwardly to infer a 'natural law', any more than we can retrieve a Butler-like 'natural theology'. People sometimes try, as for instance when it is implied that since humans are merely 'naked apes' there is no good reason, aside from local convention, why we should not behave like the regular variety. But the Gospel events, revealing the new way of being human, do not sweep away creation's inbuilt moral structures. They reaffirm them. As Jesus insists in Mark 10.2–12, God's kingdom *at last fulfils the creator's long intention*, even if until then this seemed difficult or impossible—even if, as in the case under discussion in Mark 10, the Torah itself gave permission for a lesser standard. And, as the gospel story unwinds to its conclusion, we discover how this happens: the creator's intention is fulfilled through the Messiah's death and resurrection. Paul applies this to Jesus' followers by insisting that they are 'in the Messiah' and that this means they have died with him and been raised with him. But this argument, so clear in Romans 6, does not mean that creation—the present world, the present human life—is irrelevant. The new bodily obedience of Romans 8, and the bodily suffering that the Messiah's family share with him, belong on the map of the rescued and transformed new creation which forms the climax of that chapter.

We do not, in other words, arrive at 'moral order' by simply trying to 'top up' the old world. Grace cannot simply 'perfect' nature as it stands. That would be like trying to build a solid house on top of a sand-castle. But nor does the resurrection mean that we can then ignore the created order and start the new world, and the new life, with a blank sheet. Resurrection *redeems* and so *retrieves* and now *firmly establishes* the goodness of the original creation. The launch of new creation reaffirms the God-given order of the old, including perhaps paradoxically the sense of dis-ease, of out-of-jointness, which humans in all cultures and at all times have felt with 'the way things are'. This points ahead to the argument of the next chapter.

As we reflect on these two analogies, certain things become strikingly clear. In the first, the story of Israel, the new gospel imperative seemed nonsense.

We only have to think of Galatians to make this clear. Welcoming non-Jews into the community of Abraham's family on equal terms, without the normal 'works of Torah', was almost literally unthinkable for many. How could the people of God be defined without the focus of the Promised Land and its holy city and shrine? How could they live as a multi-ethnic family? How, in particular, could they find their way without the Mosaic Torah to fence them in? Paul and the other early teachers articulated and emphasised the fresh reading of scripture—much as with Jesus himself on the Emmaus Road—in which it all *did* make sense. The new event was not after all a mere *novum*. It was, they argued, what Moses, the prophets and the psalms had always envisaged, though it would require a radical transformation in the ways they were to be read. In the second, moral order, the new-creation behaviour now required was previously thought either impossible or undesirable. The absolute demand for forgiveness, humility, chastity, patience, for the care of the poor, appeared quite out of reach.[31] These (as people quickly discovered) made no sense in the world the way it was. But when Jesus' followers began to live like that they displayed a way of being human that proved self-authenticating. It really was the genuinely human way to live, though nobody had seen it like that before. These virtues seemed to offer keys to open doors which people knew existed, but which up to that point had appeared to be locked tight forever.

In both cases—Israel's way of life suddenly expanded to include Gentiles, moral possibilities previously unimagined—the new pattern was at one level shocking and disruptive, but at another level fulfilling and empowering. Paul explains: *The Messiah's love leaves us no choice* (2 Corinthians 5.14). The creational love now revealed in the gospel launched the new world of ecclesial and moral possibility. Earlier longings and puzzles were not, after all, illogical or unwarranted sensitivities. They were genuine signs, from within the present creation, that something more was not only required but also promised.

So it was with the resurrection of Jesus. *It was simultaneously a shocking event within the 'old' world and the foundational and paradigmatic event within the new.* Like the idea of Jew and Gentile forming a single family, or the new styles of behaviour, it was of course unthinkable in the 'old' world. Everybody from Homer and Seneca to Hobbes and Hume—let alone A. J. Ayer or Richard Dawkins!—has known that dead people do not rise to new bodily life. But, like the new family and the new ethic, it quickly made sense. It was not just a matter of *credo quia impossibile*, as Tertullian grandly said—though he himself, in his day, did as much as many to show why in fact that faith did make new and vivid sense. It was a matter of recognising that, once the sun was up, one could see everything else clearly as well. Discerning the dawn enabled you to discern lots of other things, too; and the coherent sense which those things now made indicated that they *had* made sense all along, even though one could not, until now, see that sense clearly.

In earlier writing I illustrated this with a parable. A College receives from a rich donor the gift of a magnificent, priceless painting. There is no room in the existing buildings to display it properly; so the decision is taken to make drastic alterations to the College so that it can be seen to best advantage. When this is done, all sorts of things previously irritating or not quite right with the old building are at last sorted out. With this new, unexpected gift in place the College is as good as new, indeed better.

That is what happened when the early Christians were faced with the resurrection of Jesus. They interpreted the event in terms of the existing Jewish framework of space, time and the human being—the framework, in other words, which we set out in the previous chapter. But this framework itself did not remain unchanged. As I have argued in detail elsewhere,[32] the first followers of Jesus very rapidly made several significant modifications to that framework—but they are clearly modifications *from within*, not a new framework which has abandoned the stories and beliefs of Israel and borrowed others from elsewhere (as Bultmann and others would have wanted).

Some worldviews, clearly, needed more 'modification' than others. Faced with Platonism, the early Christians insisted on bodily resurrection, and the rescue and renewal, not the abandonment, of the present created order. The mainstream Jewish view, in fact. Faced with Epicureanism, they again agreed with a normal Jewish view: creation is not random; there is one God who is both the transcendent Creator and actively pursuing his long-promised rescuing purposes in the world. Faced with Stoicism, they once more agreed with the Jews: God and the world are not the same thing. Faced with ordinary-level paganism, they insisted that there was One God who had made the world, namely the God of Abraham, Isaac and Jacob. In each case, the resurrection of Jesus was seen to affirm a basically Israelite and Jewish worldview over against all comers. It made the sense it made there and nowhere else.

At the same time, there were radical modifications to be made within the Second Temple Jewish worldview. Eschatology is perhaps the most obvious of these. What Israel had hoped for in the future had happened in the present—only, instead of all God's people being raised from the dead, one person, seen already by some as Israel's Messiah, had been raised ahead of everyone else. This was a complete *novum*, expounded as such by Paul in a central passage, 1 Corinthians 15.20–28.[33] The future had come forward into the present, just as some Jews then, and many more later, would say about the Sabbath and *a fortiori* about the great festivals, not least Passover, which Jesus had made thematic for his last great vocational actions. The resurrection announced that 'new time' had arrived in the present: a permanent Jubilee, the fulfilment of Daniel's 'seventy weeks of years', and hence the time of liberation, of forgiveness, of endless Sabbath. That was why the keeping, or the not keeping, of specific holy days ceased to matter (as Paul argues in Romans 14): every day was now a kingdom day, and the first day of the week especially captured the mood and the theme of new creation.³⁴ *But all this meant that the earlier sense of a story, the long Jewish narrative of promise and hope, was retrospectively validated even while being radically modified.* Most of those who told that Jewish story in Jesus' day, and the centuries either side of it, could not and did not see the idea of a crucified and risen Messiah as in any sense the fulfilment of the story they knew. Certainly nobody was understanding that story as a narrative of 'progress', a plot-line like that envisaged by Pierre Teilhard de Chardin. The retrospective validation of the story did not make it look like that either. But it remains the case that when the shocking and unexpected thing happened, and a so-called Messiah was raised from the dead, people were able to look back and see that, however stumblingly and with however many missed opportunities and false starts, a dark and twisted narrative had nevertheless arrived at its proper goal.

If this was true in relation to eschatology, it was also true in relation to cosmology. Just as the Tabernacle and then the Temple, a tent and a building made by human hands with real curtains and poles, real stone and timber, existed within the present world, and yet were the place where the living God made his glorious presence to dwell, so the first Christians quickly came to believe that the resurrection had revealed Jesus to be indeed what he had implicitly claimed throughout his public career: the human equivalent of the Temple, the place where, in Pauline language, 'all the fullness of deity dwelt bodily'. Heaven and earth were indeed meant to come together, to dwell together in unity, and both John and Paul saw this in terms of Jesus as the new Temple (and then, to be sure, of the church also as the new Temple, indwelt by the spirit). Just as the Tabernacle and Temple functioned as 'little worlds', buildings which symbolized the creator's intention to fill the whole creation with his glory at last, so Jesus and the spirit now became advance signs and foretastes of what God would do for the whole creation. This was simultaneously the *radical reaffirmation* of a mainstream Jewish worldview and its *radical transformation*—particularly because at the heart of the revelatory events there stood the *scandalum crucis*, the shocking and unimagined fate of Israel's anointed king. Romans 8 then looks ahead to the ultimate fulfilment of Israel's hope for the whole cosmos, with God doing for the cosmos as a whole what he had done for Jesus in his resurrection, and all because of the creator's unshakeable love for his world and his people. Not for nothing is John 20 set in a garden, with Jesus mistaken for the gardener. The point, once again, is that through all the radical transformations, all the unexpected and shocking events, this totally new event of Jesus' resurrection retrospectively celebrates the garden itself and declares, for those who can now hear it, that the apparent promise of spring was not just imagination. The old creation really had been, all along, pointing forward to the long-intended ful-filment.[35] If it is love that believes the resurrection, it is because the resurrection reveals the Creator's sovereign love for creation and the utter lengths to which he would go to rescue and restore it and to fulfil its age-old purpose. And with all that we remind ourselves—against the obvious sneer that 'love' takes us into a private world of pure subjectivity—that all this means what it means in rela-tion precisely to the *real public world*, not to a 'spiritual' or gnostic realm, and not to a world of personal fantasy.

Again, as with cosmology, so with anthropology. Nobody, so far as we know, was imagining that heaven and earth would come together in a single human being—let alone that this human being would display that union at the moment of shameful death. The closest one might come to the idea of a heaven/earth anthropological union might be the persons of an anointed High Priest or Davidic King, and of course in retrospect we can see the early Christians picking up hints that Jesus was in some senses fulfilling both roles. You could read or sing Psalm 8 every day for a year and not realise what was to come, but when it came you could look back and see that it had always been intended. Lower than the angels, but now crowned with glory and honour. This is what it means to be image-bearers; and the Image-bearer himself has now shown the way. With the resurrection of Jesus the hidden promise latent all along in Genesis 1 and 2 was held up to the light and gloriously affirmed. Again, once you discern the dawn, you realise that even the darkness of the night had been secretly full of hope and longing.

RESURRECTION AND THE EPISTEMOLOGY OF LOVE

Thus Jesus' resurrection, by unveiling the creator's rescuing and transformative love for the whole creation, opens up the space and time for a new holis-tic mode of knowing, a knowing which *includes historical knowledge of the real world* by framing it within the loving gratitude which answers the creator's own sovereign love. The way stands open for an account of 'knowledge' itself in which 'love' can be understood, not as the opposite to 'reason' (as perhaps Wittgenstein was thinking), nor simply as subjective fantasy, but as the larger framework within which both reason and subjectivity can play their appropriate roles. Here we must be careful. I have already insisted that knowledge in general, and historical knowledge in particular, must include an element of what I have called 'love', the delighted affirmation of the otherness of that which is known. I now want to propose that with Jesus' resurrection this 'love' is shifted into a new mode in which the earlier modes are themselves redeemed, taken up and transformed. In each case the initial stage is something that would probably be affirmed by many epistemologists. It is the second stage that takes us to a different place—though my point is that this different place is, as it were, directly cognate with the first, if anything made more explicit and concrete.

'Knowing' is, to begin with, *a whole-person activity*. All human knowing, as we are now aware, involves the body and the emotions, not just the senses and the brain. If we try to detach the different aspects of the person from the act of knowing, we end up, like the logical positivists, with supposedly 'scientific' knowledge being 'objective', 'ethical' knowledge being merely 'emotive' or subjective, and theology or metaphysics being simply nonsense.[36] This is precisely where modernity's Faustian pact has made its point, detaching itself from the creator, rejecting love itself, and instead grabbing at a 'knowledge' which is part power and part pleasure.

What happens when we remember this principle and approach the resurrection? Here we tread carefully on a narrow path. On one side, we have the rationalist temptation: let's try to *prove* the resurrection with a resounding QED, compelling everyone to accept it. On the other side, we have the romantic temptation: this warms our heart so much that we are going to pretend it's true. ('You ask me how I know he lives? He lives within my heart!') The first tries to yank everyone into faith by the scruff of the neck. The second leaves faith as a private world, a fairyland where escapists will mutter to themselves that the heart has reasons which reason ignores. Neither pays sufficient attention to the possibility that when heaven and earth really do overlap, when the Age to Come really does break into the present Age ahead of time, a new image-bearing possibility is awakened, a kind of whole-person knowledge we didn't know was possible, a knowledge shaped by and responding to the object of knowledge rather than using its own private method as a Procrustean bed. *And in this case 'the object of knowledge' is precisely the unveiling of the Creator's unbreakable love for his creation.*

The point of the Temple-shaped cosmology, the heaven-earth overlap, is after all that *things happen on earth* which are true signs of the presence of heaven and which can therefore be discussed historically, not just in a private sphere called 'faith'. The point of the Sabbath-shaped eschatology, the overlap of the ages, is that *things happen in the present time* which are true anticipations of the ultimate future. In this world of doubled space and doubled time we are talking about the public world, but a larger public world than that envisaged either by Cartesian induction or by Kantian deduction. To know this world with our whole image-bearing selves then means opening up, in answering love, to the revelation of the creator's lavish and generous love. It means coming out from our sheltered epistemological 'safe zones', the over-bright light of a spurious and supposed 'objectivity' and the comforting glow of private subjectivity, into a new, multi-layered form of knowledge. This new mode finally tears up the Faustian pact, saying to the risen Jesus (like the two at Emmaus) *Verweile doch, du bist so schön*—finding in that moment that Mephistopheles has been defeated, that forgiveness of sins both moral and epistemological is now a reality, that the College is being rebuilt with the masterpiece at its centre and that we are members of it. And the College in question is, to say it once more, not a private club for those who share a particular fantasy, but the real world, the world of new creation *and therefore the world of creation itself*, rescued and transformed but still the true creation as the Creator intended it to be. And with that we open up at last the fresh possibility of natural theology: of a celebration of creation which is also a celebration of God the creator and redeemer.

Once more, faced with this epistemology of love, the suspicion may arise that it will all collapse into mere subjectivity. But something deeper is going on. Rationalism and romanticism are the epistemological twin daughters of modern Epicureanism, trying to make sense of things after humans have been downgraded into random atomic accidents. Platonic answers don't help either. But in the New Testament, love is not just an ethic, nor just an emotion, but the highest mode of knowing, including all others within it. 'If anyone thinks they know something', says Paul to the Corinthians, 'they don't yet know as they ought to know; but if anyone loves God, *they are known by him*' (1 Corinthians 8.2–3). The real knowledge isn't your knowledge of the world or God, but God's knowledge of you. Your answer to that 'knowledge' is first and foremost love, because the revelation is itself love. That's why loving God and neighbour are the greatest commandments, overtaking all sacrifices and burnt-offerings. That's why faith, hope and love are the greatest, love above all, not just as virtues but again as modes of knowing. Faith is love reaching out to heaven, only to discover that heaven has come to earth and is busy repairing it. Hope is love reaching out to the future, only to discover that the Age to Come has arrived, Sabbath-like, in the present, giving rest and refreshment to the tired old working world. It isn't just that love transcends the objective/subjective divide, though that is true too. Paul draws together Romans 8, his new-Temple chapter, his resurrection-chapter, his new-age chapter, by insisting that God works all things together for good *for those who love him*. And they are further described as being 'conformed to the Image of the son', or, as in Colossians, 'renewed in knowledge according to the image of the creator' (Romans 8.29; Colossians 3.10). The new kind of knowledge is not a secret *gnosis* for the initiate. Paul's vocation is that by the 'open statement of the truth' he will declare the light of the knowledge of God's glory in the Messiah's image-bearing face.

This leads to a further dimension of the epistemology of love, in its new manifestation: that *all knowing is communal knowing*. Pretend otherwise, and you land up in solipsism, the phenomenalist's trap, only knowing your own sense-data.[37] We all rely on a wider community of some sort to help us with the project of knowing. Abduction itself is regularly a communal activity. This is why the Enlightenment's new epistemologies produced different kinds of revolution: different 'communities of knowing' came into direct conflict, having (as in other areas) left Love out of the equation. Descartes split the epistemological atom, and Marx provided the resulting explosion.

What happens to this principle when confronted with the evidence which points to Jesus' resurrection? Part of the answer may be that, though shared knowledge may provide confirmation in many settings, the shared knowledge of the Creator's love, grasped with answering love, generates a different kind of community: precisely a community of love. Paul, writing to the young church in Colosse, celebrates the fact that Epaphras has told him about 'your love in the spirit': there is in Colosse a group of people who, despite being from different cultures and of different social status, love one another, in other words, treat one another as 'family'. This is itself, for Paul, powerful evidence that the gospel has been at work (Colossians 1.6–8). This is one of the many reasons why he highlights love as the first characteristic of the 'fruit of the spirit' and as the 'greatest' of the trio of virtues, surpassing even faith and hope (Galatians 5.22; 1 Corinthians 13.13).

This expansion of the ordinary 'epistemology of love' into the world of new creation, of a renewed human life, moves outwards into the wider world. All human knowing presupposes views of space, time, matter and what it means to be human and to engage in knowing itself. Thus all knowing is *engagement and involvement and not merely detached observation*. Knowing is *relational*, having to do with the to-and-fro between the knowing subject and the 'object', whether it's a mountain, a mouse or a movement in a symphony. The relation is always two-way. To pretend otherwise—whether to claim passivity ('I am just letting the facts speak to me') or to claim to be in charge of the data ('Take it from me, I know the truth')—is either naïve or a cunning power-play. To recognise the necessary two-way nature of *engaged relational knowing* is to recognise the epistemology of love.

This, too, is part of what I have sketched as a wise 'critical realism'. The difference in kind between the ordinary 'critical realism' involved in normal observation of the world and the new mode opened up by Jesus' resurrection is that the 'relation' in question becomes not merely personal (with Jesus himself as a living presence to be 'known') but the direct result of Jesus' own act of love: 'the Messiah's love makes us press on' (2 Corinthians 5.14). Thus believing in the resurrection *includes*, though cannot (as with Bultmann and others) be reduced to terms of, the belief that in his crucifixion Jesus has overcome the power of evil and death. 'If the Messiah is not raised, your faith is futile and you are still in your sins' (1 Corinthians 15.17). Nor can this simply be wish-fulfilment, another trick of a self-interested subjectivity. The convergence of the personal knowledge with the historical evidence does not provide (to say it once again) the kind of 'mathematical certainty' coveted by those who want the James-and-John kind of knowledge, the kind of 'knowledge' that would put us in charge, that would enable us to wield our certainty with power. If any theologians are still looking for that kind of thing, they are hoping for a self-contradiction, asking for something which would undermine the very truth they want to commend. Does this then mean giving up 'natural theology'? By no means. It merely means repenting of the attempt to grasp at such a thing within the split-level Epicurean framework of modernity. It means being open to the possibility that the divine being revealed in this way may be significantly different from some other views of 'god'; may be, in fact, a lot more like the crucified and risen Jesus of Nazareth.

The same is true when we consider the ways in which, as Francis Bacon declared, knowledge is power.[38] Our modern world is characterized by claims to knowing which can be unmasked as claims to power. That is the point made by Nietzsche and Foucault. This fits exactly with the Faustian pact, with empires that claim to 'make their own truth', with Pilate's cynical question. Within the truncated modern view of being human, our world is basically competitive, a zero-sum game for power. All our claims to knowledge can then be construed as attempts to gain mastery over one another, and ultimately over space, time and matter themselves, rather than seeing them as gifts of the creator's love.

That, too, could be agreed by many who would still balk at the resurrection itself. But the specifically Easter-shaped version of this aspect of the 'epistemology of love' is then that the 'power' in question, as Paul makes clear throughout 2 Corinthians, is the power that is found paradoxically in weakness. The attempt to use knowledge—any knowledge, but especially knowledge of the risen Jesus!—as a claim to any sort of mastery will at once falsify and undermine itself. That has come true with tragic frequency in the history of the church. The new world that is presented to the astonished and bewildered followers of Jesus is indeed under the lordship of Jesus, as Jesus himself declares in Matthew 28.18. But this lordship is defined by (among other things) the Sermon on the Mount. It is precisely not the kind of masterful power that James and John were hoping for. The love that believes Jesus' resurrection is the kind of love that seeks to follow the Son of Man in serving rather than being served. That, too, is a 'mode of knowing', as the story of the 'sheep and the goats' in Matthew 25 makes clear, with Jesus promising to be 'known' in the persons of the poor, the helpless, the prisoners and so on to whom his followers will minister.

My argument has therefore been that the element of love needs, first, to be restored within 'ordinary knowing'. Our day-to-day epistemology needs thereby to be rescued from the Epicurean instinct we find from Machiavelli onwards, the instinct that was unmasked but ultimately shared by Nietzsche with his will to power. Reflective persons of all sorts, Christian or not, might well agree with this point. But the more they contemplate this possibility, the more they might recognise that the point to which they have thereby been led possesses a strange congruence with the curious claims of Jesus' followers. In other words, reflecting on ordinary knowing might point on to the extraordinary knowing of faith.

This is why, it seems to me, it is love that believes the resurrection. The ordinary love which conditions wise knowing in the regular world respects, and responds appropriately to, creation as it is. (Where creation is dark and broken, that appropriate response would include lament, prayer for healing, and such practical help as can be offered.) The transformed, upgraded love that manifests itself as faith in Jesus' resurrection is responding to the divine declaration, in the Easter events, that our sense of being at home in the present creation is reaffirmed as God rescues and remakes the world rather than abolishing it. Within that there is the astonished and delighted discovery that the power of evil has been broken: that the cross was itself the victory of the creator's love over the destructive powers of darkness. Again and again in Paul and John this comes across as deeply personal. Paul's statement, 'the Son of God loved me and gave himself for me', and John's statement that Jesus loved his people 'right through to the end' sum it all up (Galatians 2.20; John 13.1). This love-based knowledge of the resurrection (against what Wittgenstein seems to have meant!) shares much with ordinary knowing, since the ontology to which this epistemology gives proper access is the place at which heaven and earth overlap, not a secret place where heaven does its own thing away from earth. That, to say it again, is part of the point of the bodily resurrection.

To believe this, then, includes the elements of ordinary knowing, particularly ordinary historical knowing, and in transcending them it continues to affirm them. Such belief takes a whole transformed person, not just a convinced mind. It takes a new kind of community to confess it properly, not a bunch of isolated individuals. In this sort of knowing one is fully involved with the drama of the reality which is known, in this case the person of the crucified Jesus himself. It involves humility, recognising that all knowing involves us small short-sighted creatures engaging with a wide and complicated world, and gratitude, recognising that the resurrection is above all the genuine foretaste of that new creation which, like the original creation only so much more, is the fruit of the Creator's self-giving love. Instead of trying to grasp it or master it, we are grateful for it, and turn that loving gratitude into vocation, the image-bearing vocation once more.

All this explains why belief in Jesus' resurrection has appeared so impossible in the Western world of the last few centuries. It isn't just that 'science' has shown that resurrections don't happen. That was always a trivial objection, partly because the permanence of death has been common knowledge as far back as we can trace, and partly because 'science' studies the repeatable, whereas the Christian claim always was that what happened to the dead body of Jesus was precisely a one-off—though to be repeated on a grand scale in the end. No: the reason why Jesus' resurrection was unbelievable was, in general, that if true it would mark the true turning-point of history, whereas modern Western culture is built on the premise that the true turning-point happened in the eighteenth-century Enlightenment. The more specific point, within this, is that *modern Western culture had screened out 'love' itself*, or at least reduced it to irrelevant sentimentality or romantic subjectivity. Love is the quality which, carefully avoided in the Faustian Enlightenment, addresses, contextualises, makes sense of and enriches all other modes of knowing, while rescuing them from Nietzsche's power-trap. The love that believes the resurrection is thus the foundation for a proper awareness of the goodness of the present creation, as well as the motivation to take part in the *missio Dei*. 'The Messiah's love', to quote Paul once more, 'leaves us no choice'.

Love, therefore, the love that discerns the dawn in the resurrection of Jesus, is not something detached from the other types of knowing. Precisely because it is love, it is open to genuine historical investigation. The new creation has arrived, inconveniently and unexpectedly, in the middle of the old, and in its light we can ask perfectly good questions about the old, about an empty tomb, a broken loaf on the table at Emmaus, footprints on the shore after a Galilean breakfast. The false modesty that has made some theologians shy about such questions is the same withdrawal that has made them anxious about 'natural theology'. But love remains at the heart of a Christian 'knowing', not only of the new creation but also of the old. And it is that love, not least in its mode of grief, that meets us in every aspect of the human vocation, as we shall see in the next chapter.

The resurrection of Jesus, therefore, is the beginning of creation's renewal. That is why it also looks back, affirming the goodness of the original creation and retrospectively validating the signs of the Creator's power and handiwork within it. The resurrection, in fact, assures us that all that we have known in the present creation, all that we have glimpsed of glory and wisdom and creational goodness, will indeed be rescued from corruption and decay and transformed into the new mode the Creator always intended. As a gift of love, of course, the resurrection can always be refused, whether through pride or pique. Gratitude and humility do not come easily, especially in the modern world. But when the historical evidence which points to Jesus' resurrection joins hands with the recognition that in this event we are witnessing the ultimate affirmation of the Creator's love, and when with Christian hindsight we reflect on the promised work of the Holy Spirit, love revealed gives birth to an answering love, a love which is both faith and knowledge, knowledge of the creation as the work of God, and knowledge of God as the maker and redeemer of creation.

CONCLUSION: KNOWING AND LOVING

This, then, is where the either/or of Epicureanism, summed up in Lessing's broad and ugly ditch, is transcended. The resurrection is the reaffirmation, through redemptive transformation, of the old world. That redemptive transformation does not leave the original creation behind or pretend it is irrelevant. As with the Exodus, the slaves are freed, not by forgetting the promises to Abraham but by fulfilling them. Love in creation and redemption closes the gap from God's side; love as the ultimate mode of human knowing reaches out in response. In Jesus himself *both of these come true*: that is the mystery of Christology, and the clue to its proper integration. In the new creation there is 'no more sea' (Revelation 21.1), and no more 'ugly ditch' either. 'The Messiah being raised from the dead will never die again; death has no more dominion over him'. The divide between eternal and contingent, as also between past, present and future, is overcome by the Image-bearer himself, bringing Love to birth in the world, and then by those who, in response, are renewed in loving knowledge according to the creator's image. 'Simon, son of John', says Jesus, 'do you love me?' (John 21.15–19). Once the Petrine failures, moral and epistemological, are forgiven, love believes and goes to work. And that work, as we have seen, includes the task of a rejuvenated history.

This is why—though the fuller case must wait for the last two chapters—the argument from Jesus' resurrection to a refreshed form of 'natural theology' cannot collapse into mere subjectivism. What counts is the epistemology of love, the love which our Faustian culture has tried to rule out in order to master the world by sheer power, a power which brings its own nemesis in every domain of life. Love, as *historical epistemology*, opens itself to first-century Jewish modes of thought and refuses to slap them down as 'ancient worldviews' which we 'moderns' have left behind, to be replaced with a heavy-handed assumed Epicureanism or Platonism. Love, as *theological epistemology*, finds itself drawn to explore the ancient Israelite, and then Second Temple Jewish, Temple-cosmology and Sabbath-eschatology, focusing both on the one true Image-bearer, discovering through both a worldview in which not only the resurrection of Jesus but, through it, the reaffirmation of creation's goodness makes (so to speak) a sense that goes on sensing. Love itself, knowledge itself, are thereby renewed, so that by responding to the creator's love revealed in the resurrection a new mode of knowing is born to greet the new mode of reality to which Temple and Sabbath had all along pointed. Love, as *vocational epistemology*, discovers like Peter a fresh calling to tend the flock, to feed the sheep, to be for the world what Jesus was for Israel. 'As the Father sent me, so I send you' (John 20.21). The commission of love, including the commission to speak new-creational truth and to celebrate its foretastes in the original creation itself, will retrospectively illuminate every earlier glimpse of reality.

All this alerts us to the possibility to be explored in the next chapter: that the strange signposts we find in the present world, though in the dark of midnight they may seem to point nowhere, or even to be some kind of sick joke, are after all true, if broken, signposts to the ultimate realities of God and the world. Once you start to discern the dawn, you may come to realise that the signposts you had tried to follow in the darkness were after all telling the truth, even if in their brokenness we could not always go where they were pointing.

In the light of the resurrection, the first thing to be rethought in our backward look is the cross itself. Nobody on Good Friday evening saw the cross as anything other than as what it actually was, the ugly symbol of imperial oppression, the cruel death of a wonderful dream. Of all the events in Jesus' life, his death is the most 'natural' and indeed historically demonstrable feature: if Jesus is to be brought together with 'natural theology', this would be the most obvious place to begin—except that by itself it might seem to lead nowhere, precisely because of its apparent denial of any God-related meaning. The positive meaning emerges, of course, in the light of the resurrection, which is why we have approached these central events this way around. The resurrection compelled Jesus' followers to ascribe fresh retrospective meaning to his crucifixion. As we already see in the early formula alluded to by Paul in Romans 1.3–4, the resurrection was seen by the first followers of Jesus to be telling the world-shaking truth: that his crucifixion was to be understood in terms of his subsequent public revelation as Israel's Messiah. And, before too long, the confession that he was the very embodiment of Israel's God.

Thus the signpost of a broken human being, in whose fate the horror, shame and injustice of the world seem to be drawn together, sums up the problem of natural theology. The resurrection, however, compels us to look back at that symbol, and that problem, and see them differently. When love believes the resurrection—when the historical hermeneutic of love grasps the eschatological truth of new creation—that love will discover its own true identity. It is the grateful response to the love displayed, in action and passion, on the cross. This new-creational perspective compels us to look back on the world of creation in general, but also on the events concerning Jesus himself, and supremely his crucifixion, as the place where, and the means by which, God's creational and redemptive love might be known, calling forth from us a love which is also genuine knowledge, a knowledge which is also love.

George Herbert's poem 'Love' can perhaps, with due temerity, be translated into epistemological mode:

> Love bade me welcome; yet my mind drew back,
> Eager for fact and proof;
> But quick-eyed love, observing my sad lack
> Of larger modes of truth
> Drew nearer to me, sweetly questioning
> Why I stayed wondering.
>
> Knowledge I need, I said, worthy the name.
> Love said: it shall be yours.
> I, the perverse, the 'objective'? I, the same
> Who thought to grasp at powers?
> Love touched my eyes, and smiling did reply,
> Who made the mind, but I?
>
> 'My mind is hostile, crushed beneath the load,
> A stranger and to blame'.
> Come then, said Love, the Stranger on the road.
> Why then, my heart will flame.
> You must sit down, said Love, and hear my voice.
> Knowledge and Love rejoice.

IV

The Peril and Promise of Natural Theology

7

Broken Signposts?

New Answers to the Right Questions

INTRODUCTION

'You are so senseless!' said Jesus to the two disciples on the road to Emmaus.
'So slow in your hearts to believe all the things the prophets said to you! Don't
you see? This is what *had* to happen . . .'

That is, of course, the turning-point in one of the best-loved of all biblical passages (Luke 24.25).[1] It sums up the theological perspective not only of
Luke but, as I have argued elsewhere, of all the early Christians.[2] Some have
thought that Luke was out on a limb in this respect, in that a supposed 'Pauline' gospel might be thought to reject as irrelevant any 'back story', especially
the story of Israel, whereas Luke clearly wants to see the cross and resurrection as the long-awaited fulfilment of Israel's whole scriptural narrative.[3]
But a strong case can be made for understanding the whole New Testament,
and indeed the mind and message of Jesus himself, in this light. The present
book is, in one sense, simply drawing out what is implicit in this passage and
applying it to the larger issues which have been raised in recent centuries
about the world and God, and about the modes of knowing through which we
can speak wisely and truthfully about them. About (in fact) something which
we may still want to call 'natural theology', albeit with the qualifications and
nuances for which I argued in the previous chapter.

The present discussion, like the one in the final chapter of the book, shifts
the argument into a different mode, as explained in the Preface. Up to this
point the argument has been made step by step, in dialogue with many conversation partners. From here on I am putting forward a new proposal. Though

it would be possible at every point to provide 'annotation' for those who want to follow up particular issues, my case does not depend on the arguments of others, and I shall mostly leave such questions to one side.

What after all (to sum up earlier discussions) is the task summarized in the phrase 'natural theology'?[4] Is it the attempt to provide a 'neutral' argument, acceptable to all, irrespective of presuppositions, leading to the existence of God and perhaps to more specific Christian claims, in such a way as at least in principle to convince the sceptic? Is it the attempt to sketch, from a Christian point of view, what such an apparently 'neutral' argument might look like? Or might it be a Christian account, 'reading backwards', like Jesus retelling Israel's story on the road, to show how the 'natural' world had in fact been pointing, however brokenly, to the truth? It might try to be all of these. But something like the last of these has, to my mind, most coherence, and that is what I shall be trying to sketch in the present chapter.

What then might 'natural theology' be *for*, anyway? I think Lord Gifford, in establishing his Lectures, was hoping to scare up lines of thought that would glue together the new things the world was finding out, particularly through scientific investigation, with the old things the church was supposed to be teaching. It was no good the church claiming divine inspiration for its texts and traditions and holding them out as an *a priori* to an increasingly sceptical world. That merely, to the popular view, pulled up the battered old drawbridge across something like Lessing's ugly ditch: we have our eternal truths, and nothing can touch them. Lessing's 'eternal truths' were of course different from the supposed 'truths' of Christian theology, but the idea of a ditch works in both contexts. The 'special revelation' claimed within Christianity was seen by Christian and sceptic alike as firmly detached from the 'natural' world. Within the revived forms of Epicureanism, there was no desire to cross that ditch in any case: the world does its own thing, and the only eternal truth is that there is no eternal truth. Lord Gifford seems to have been hoping that there might be an *apologetic* case to be made: if not actually for the *truth* of Christianity, then at least for its plausibility. One might, perhaps, show that it was at least not unreasonable. There was also an *explanatory* case, more for internal consumption, enabling believers to rest content knowing that new discoveries might sit happily alongside, and even illustrate, traditional teaching. Those aims may be all very well in their way. But I want to argue a different and perhaps paradoxical point.

THE THREE WAYS

I have argued so far that modern theology and exegesis have been shaped by the Epicurean heaven/earth split; by the post-Renaissance chronological split between past, present and future; and by understandings of human nature shaped by those two. I have proposed an alternative perspective, rooted in Israel's traditions, seeing the Temple as the *microcosmos* disclosing God's ultimate purposes for the heaven/earth world; the Sabbath as the advance foretaste of the Age to Come; and humans as constituted by the Image-bearing vocation. These are then reshaped, quite drastically and in unexpected ways, around Jesus and the spirit. But the new shape still presupposes an integrated cosmos, a purposed new creation already tasted in advance, and a vocational anthropology.

Only in the broadest and most general terms do these correspond to the three broad approaches to 'natural theology' over the last three hundred years, as for instance in Paley's *Natural Theology* of 1802: cosmology, teleology and the human moral sense.[5] However, there are (as it were) shadowy parallels. The cosmological argument proposes that the existence of the world points to a Creator. Israel's central institution, the Temple, looks back to an original heaven/earth creation, even as it claims to house the Creator himself, and points on to a heaven/earth renewal of creation in which the Creator will be gloriously present. But no-one, neither Israelite nor Gentile, was expected to *infer* the existence of Israel's God from these symbols of creation and new creation. It begins to look as though the 'cosmological argument' is trying to get at something—a God/world nexus—which in Israel's institutions is approached by a very different route. The closest one might come to the 'cosmological argument' from within the Hebrew scriptures could be Psalm 19. In Joseph Addison's version, to which we referred in chapter 1, the stars give *information* about their maker and invite the reader or singer to draw an inference about the Creator, in other words, to make a 'natural theology' move: 'the hand that made us is divine'. But in the original the heavenly bodies are simply praising God, and it is the Psalmist who has to inform reader or singer of what is in fact going on. Psalm 19, which moves from the all-penetrating heat of the sun to the all-penetrating wisdom of Torah, was written by one who already knew what he wanted to say about Torah and was using the sun as an illustration. I do not think the Psalmist had been contemplating the sun's effects and deducing that Torah functioned similarly. It was the other way around. This might then correspond, not to the supposedly *apologetic* task of 'natural theology'—trying to convince the sceptic without appealing to 'inspiration'—but to the supposedly *explanatory* task, drawing out ways to hold together the truth of God and the truth of the world. The important point was that Israel's God was the Creator of the actual world, not a private or tribal deity, and that, conversely, the Creator of all things was in covenant with Israel. Israel needed regular reminders of being part of that larger world.

The 'teleological argument', looking at 'design' in the world and inferring a Designer, has to do with the purpose or goal of creation. But again, in Israel's traditions, and in their Christian retrievals, the purpose is glimpsed in the future and in the anticipations of that future both in the Temple and in the Sabbath. There is an analogy: an inference is drawn from the completed work to the intention of its original Maker. But the work is not complete until the ultimate *telos*. Again, it might look as though traditional 'natural theology' has got its finger on an important point—the glimpsing of the Designer from that which appears to be designed—but the modern versions of 'natural theology' have tried to make that argument 'work' within a framework which explicitly excludes the possibility of a worldview other than that of Western modernity—particularly the worldview brought to birth in Jesus' resurrection from the dead.

What then about the argument from moral intuition, which has sometimes tried to build on the idea of humans being made in God's image? Immanuel Kant argued in the *Critique of Practical Reason* (1788) that 'the highest good in the world is only possible insofar as a supreme cause of nature is assumed, which has a causality corresponding to the moral disposition'[6]—in other words, our moral sense implies a Supreme Moralist, an ultimate Lawgiver. Kant could also use teleological or cosmological arguments, but he believed, as a recent commentator says, 'that the inherently moral capacity of the human mind offered the strongest proof of God's existence'.[7] This was rejected by sceptics like John Stuart Mill on the grounds of evil and suffering in the world—the long aftershock of the Lisbon earthquake—and by theologians like James McCosh who were suspicious of Kant's moral intuitionism. McCosh, like Paley, preferred the more 'rational' arguments from cosmology and teleology. This is where we rejoin the story set out in the first two chapters of this book, with the First World War confirming Mill's scepticism and with Schweitzer and the early Barth rejecting the Hegelian 'progress' theology of Ritschl and Harnack. And this, too, is where the well-known question of a 'point of contact' between God and humans (is there something in humans which provides a link to the divine?) has been foregrounded in much discussion, however misleading it may be to use that language.

As with my overall critique of the Kantian tradition, I believe that the 'moral' argument has gotten out of focus. I have argued elsewhere that the Platonic eschatology of Western Christianity ('souls going to heaven') has generated a moralistic anthropology ('my problem is sin'), which has then produced a pagan soteriology ('God so hated the world that he killed Jesus'), so that in order to retrieve the biblical theology of the cross we need to unpick and rework each stage, not merely the final one.[8] The problem comes when anthropology is reduced from *vocation* to *ethics*—from calling to behaviour. Of course behaviour matters. I am sometimes accused of not caring about sin or not seeing 'sin' as a power. That is ridiculous. No: the primary vocation, to love God and neighbour, must constantly be encoded in motives, decisions and actions; and idolatry hands over our human powers to whatever it is we worship, so that we 'miss the mark' (i.e., 'sin') by our humanness being fractured and misdirected. But to be an image-bearer is more than simply right behaviour. Otherwise we put the knowledge of good and evil before the knowledge of God. Indeed, the 'moral' version of the natural-theological argument might be thought to be running that risk *ab initio*. The moral sense which Kant intuited, from which he thought to derive God as the ultimately moral being, is only part of a larger whole. And to treat the part as the whole is distorting as well as deficient.

I propose therefore that we avoid the traps of the older construals of the 'image' in terms of the human imagination or even 'moral sense'.[9] I start from my earlier argument: the 'image' has to do, primarily, with *vocation*. This (by the way) already draws the sting of any suspected methodological works-righteousness: a calling presupposes a caller. I offer here seven aspects of the human vocation. These do not form an exact replacement for Kant's 'moral' theory; I suggest that they straighten it out, giving it a full-bodied sense of possibility which Kant's theory lacked.

We could sum it up like this, anticipating the whole argument I shall present. To begin once again with the Emmaus Road scene: first, the disciples had been living in a story which they hoped was leading to the redemption of Israel; they had seen Jesus as the leading edge of the story within which they believed themselves to be living. Second, however, the story had rather obviously run into a stone wall. Messiahs are supposed to rescue Israel from the pagans, not to get themselves crucified by those same pagans. Third, however, the resurrection of Jesus—still unknown to the two on the road but built into Luke's narrative so his readers already know what's going on—sheds a radical new light both on the devastating event of the cross itself and then on the entire back story, the biblical narrative, which the disciples had been invoking.

This was after all what the biblical narrative had been about, though until Easter Day it could not be seen as such. Luke says that 'their eyes were prevented from recognizing him' (Luke 24.16); they embodied, at that moment, the wider epistemological problem. And that problem was resolved not simply by the information which the risen Jesus would then supply but by the person of Jesus himself, as the end of the story makes clear.

The tensions some have perceived between Luke's integrative approach to the story of Israel-and-Jesus and the supposedly 'apocalyptic' view some have ascribed to Paul—which I have discussed in the fourth chapter and elsewhere[10]—are symptomatic of the problems which were faced by 'natural theology' in the first half of the twentieth century. One of the fixed points in the debate is of course the clash between Barth and Brunner in 1934. The loud 'Nein!' which Barth pronounced at that point, though most of us would say it appeared necessary and urgent in the context of the times, owed a bit too much, in my view, to the early Barth's insistence on what has later been retrieved under the misleading slogan 'apocalyptic': the view that nothing before or alongside Messiah Jesus can serve as an index to reality, as a starting-point for discovering who God is and what he's up to. Over against all attempts (which are still widespread, even among those who should know better) to say that we must simply observe what God is doing in the world and then join in, Barth declared that outside of faith in Messiah Jesus it is impossible, starting from within the world, to discern God in general or God's actions in particular. Precisely because I think that lesson is still well worth repeating I find it important, in this chapter particularly, to explain why I think that by itself it can in turn become a dangerous half-truth. The risen Jesus did not say to the disciples, 'How senseless you are! Don't you see that all that long story from Abraham to the Maccabees was just smoke and mirrors, and that you can forget it all because God has now done something completely different?' That is, in effect, what some of the over-eager 'apocalyptic' school have done. But, as I and others have argued elsewhere, the Jewish apocalyptic literature which contextualises the New Testament is not about the *abolition* of the hope of Israel, the hope rooted in that great two-millennia story. It is about the shocking and unexpected way in which that story has in fact been fulfilled. All the central 'apocalyptic' texts we have, from both the Jewish and the early Christian worlds, emphasize precisely the sense of a great story reaching a startling denouement.

The clash between Barth and Brunner has been written up from various angles.[11] Even those who want to stand up for Brunner as offering a nuanced position may admit that in the political circumstances of the time he should have known his position would be abused, that his apparently theologically detached position would be seen as supporting the Nazis.[12] There are other internal dynamics at work, as we see from Barth's positioning of himself as the champion of a supposedly 'Protestant' theology over against Roman Catholics on the one hand (Catholic theology, always anxious about ontological dualism, continued to advocate some variety of 'natural theology') and what he called 'neo-Protestantism' on the other, referring to the liberal tradition from at least Schleiermacher to at least Harnack.[13] The whole struggle through which Barth had lived in the first two decades of the twentieth century, climaxing with his Romans commentary as a massive, though exegetically wobbly, protest against Harnack and Hermann and the socio-political outworking of their easy-going liberalism, had prepared him for this clash with Brunner. But, like the early Romans commentary itself, this should not be taken either as an exegetically warranted larger theological position or as Barth's last word on the subject. By the 1950s many things looked different, and in the third and fourth volumes of the *Church Dogmatics* we see a more nuanced, and much more exegetically sensitive, position. My point now, however, is not to enter into those details but to let them stand as a reminder, as I have noted on and off throughout, that the pressures of the times have often affected quite sharply both the way the theological questions are addressed and the way the relevant biblical texts are read. That, once again, is why genuinely historical exegesis remains vital. Without it, the texts can be pulled and pushed around to suit the scheme.

My proposal in the present chapter, then, is that when we examine the wider world, the perceptions and aspirations of human beings across different times and cultures, we find a situation we can compare with that of the two on the road to Emmaus. They had followed the signposts of their own history, their scriptures, and their culture—insofar as they had understood them. But the narrative as they had read it, the signposts as they had seen them, had led them to a hope which was straightforwardly falsified by the crucifixion of their would-be Messiah. However, the resurrection of the crucified Jesus compelled a fresh telling of the narrative, a fresh glance back at the signposts. And with that glance, in the light of the newly discerned dawn, the story turned out to be completed in a whole new way. *The signposts were vindicated*: Israel's story had after all pointed in the right direction. It has often been said that the resurrection compelled a fresh understanding of the cross; indeed, as we saw in the last chapter, some have reduced the resurrection itself to nothing more than a fresh evaluation, so that the sentence 'Jesus was raised from the dead' becomes simply a metaphor for saying 'he died for our sins'. I am suggesting that this needs radical extension—in line, in fact, with the larger meaning of 'dying for our sins' for which I have argued elsewhere.[14] Just as the history of Israel was, in retrospect, full of forward-pointing signs, yet all of them together led devout people to conclusions that the cross appeared to falsify, so the world in general, and human life in particular, is full of signposts which seem to be pointing to some kind of deeper meaning; yet all of them together will not lead the unaided mind to the God who is the Father of the crucified and risen Jesus. The resurrection compels the fresh evaluation of the stories and signposts, leading to the shocking conclusion that the place above all where the true and living God is revealed is actually in the event which appeared to destroy hope and falsify the story.

This, however, at last uncovers the true paradox of natural theology. Precisely in their brokenness, the stories and signposts were gesturing toward the truth all along. This, I suggest, is why the crucifixion of Jesus—both the event and the story of the event—carries such power. To explain this, we need to examine the signposts more closely.

THE VOCATIONAL SIGNPOSTS

There are seven features of human life which can be observed across different societies and times. I name these 'vocations' as a shorthand for 'vocational signposts', though they are often present as inarticulate aspirations and impulses; they are all, I suggest, different aspects of the overall vocation to be genuinely human. We know them in our bones. The seven are a somewhat odd assortment. The loose labels I assign provide enough for the ongoing argument. They take us to the heart of traditional questions about 'natural theology', but what we find at that heart may be unexpected.[15]

The seven are Justice, Beauty, Freedom, Truth and Power, Spirituality and Relationships. These are not all the same kind of thing, and exact classification is in any case not my point here. Our modern word 'religion' doesn't get near this complex of categories, which may be why many today leave 'religion' alone. The point about all seven, to put it crudely, is that we all know they matter but we all have trouble with them. I am not claiming that everybody everywhere thinks the same about all these—far from it. What I am suggesting is that these seven broadly name areas of life which confront more or less all humans, and all human societies, and that each of them presents us with puzzling questions. We know they're important, but we can never quite grasp them the way we feel we should.

In an earlier work I discussed four of these (justice, spirituality, relationships and beauty) and argued that in each case when we study the phenomenon in question what we find are puzzling echoes: echoes of a voice, perhaps, calling us from just out of sight, telling us of meanings at which we grasp but which always just elude us.[16] What then happens is disturbingly interesting: that, in attempting to grasp them, we easily distort them, and in so doing distort the meaning of our humanness itself and—as I shall suggest—the meaning to which they were pointing all along and which we are, it seems, attempting to grasp in the wrong way. In each case, I shall now suggest, the echoes can be interpreted in the light of the newly told story opened up by the resurrection of Jesus. In that reinterpretation we can see why the echoes were real echoes, why we were bound to misinterpret them, and what would happen as a result of that misinterpretation. But the underlying point is that, just as Jesus' fresh telling of Israel's story on the road to Emmaus was a *retrospective validation* of that story, even as it was correcting the inevitable misunderstandings, so the resurrection points to a *retrospective validation* of the signposts which have been there all along in human culture. They were real signposts. Insofar as they were asking questions, those questions were the right ones to ask. Insofar as they were 'broken signposts', they were pointing all the more exactly, if paradoxically, to the ultimate broken signpost, the cross itself.

I shall unpack each of the seven in a minute, but two more introductory comments are in order. First, I am not saying that any or all of these seven constitute what has been called a 'point of contact', the point in human life where there is 'contact' with the divine. That might or might not be true, but I don't find it a helpful way in. Indeed, the very idea of a 'point of contact'—a metaphor, I think, taken from travelling in strange lands and needing at least one phone number to be sure of finding what's what—is itself misleading, implying that what one might be looking for in 'natural theology' would be a tangential meeting, the touching of two circles at a single point on the rim. That already concedes, I think, far too much to the split-level world against which I have been arguing in this book so far. Nor do I think that 'intersection' is going to be exactly right either.[17] The model of cosmology and eschatology I outlined in the fifth chapter offers a much richer, more complex integration. Once we propose the Temple-based interlocking model of God's space and ours, and once we grasp the Sabbath-based overlap of God's future and our present, then all sorts of possibilities emerge.

But whatever image we use—point of contact, intersection or (as I would prefer) complex integration—we are still looking, in all the seven 'broken signposts', at features of *human* life and thought. I am not starting with the starry heavens above or the universe around us as described either by evolutionary biology or contemporary physics. Even if I were competent to do that I do not think it would be the right starting-point, and in any case whatever observations are made, and conclusions drawn, from the material cosmos, they are made and drawn *by human beings* coming with particular questions and filtering the data through their own system-building activities. I will return in the final chapter to say a little about the world of science—it might be odd, in a book on natural theology, not to mention it at all!—but here I am going straight for what seems to me the heart of the matter.

I argued in the fifth chapter that the ancient Jewish world which contextualises Jesus and the early Christians offers two models. First, there is the model of cosmos and Temple, of Temple (in other words) as microcosmos. Second, there is the Sabbath, seen as (so to speak) microeschaton. In the middle of this picture, as we saw, is the human being as *image*; and the image-bearing vocation means what it means within the cosmos-as-Temple. Humans are called to exercise the *royal priesthood*, summing up the praises of creation before the creator and exercising a delegated authority within the created order. The 'royal' bit of the vocation relates directly to the first five of my seven broken signposts: humans are called (and humans know they are called) to do justice, to celebrate and foster the beauty which is built into creation and to make more and more of it as co-creators, to live freely and to foster freedom, to speak truth, bringing the creator's true order into the world (this last, I suggest, is where scientific investigation belongs), and to exercise power wisely. The 'priestly' bit of the vocation relates, I suggest, to the last two. Humans are called to live at the overlap of heaven and earth, which is what we loosely call spirituality. And, above all, we are called to love, to love God and to love one another.

These seven are not in fact separable. They modify and contextualize one another. As I said, they are not exactly the same *kind* of thing. Love in particular belongs with, and shapes, the 'royal' vocation as much as the 'priestly'. Spirituality—I deliberately use a word with wide, even vague, reach—might be said to contextualize all other vocations, though people who ignore spirituality are still aware of the others. But even this compressed proposal already indicates, I think, that if there are signposts in the world, albeit broken ones, they are to be found—as we should expect if humans are indeed in some sense made in the divine image!—within human life, human perception and (not least) human puzzlement.

Justice

Take Justice. We all know that some things are fair, and some are not. Children know this without studying moral philosophy. When a country signs a treaty and then breaks it, we know it matters. If people think a criminal has 'got away with' a ridiculously light sentence, the hunger for justice may lead to vigilantism. Yet we are all prepared to bend or even ignore justice when it suits us. A good lawyer may get you off, however guilty you are. Countries with military or industrial muscle force unjust trade deals on weaker partners. People say 'there's no justice' as a complaint against 'the system'—unless, like Machiavelli, you accept the Epicurean premise and know that this is just a game and you'd better learn how to play it. Philosophically, never mind theologically, that is a counsel of despair. Here is the paradox: how can something we all know matters so much be so hard to attain? We can't do without justice, but enacting it on a small or a large scale is harder than we might imagine.

Nor is this just a matter of how society should respond to criminal behaviour. It's about constitutions themselves, the way societies are organised, and indeed about independence or protest movements seeking to reform them. Justice requires that someone, or the representative of some system, should decide on policy, authorize it, implement it and deal properly with dissent (which might mean negotiating amendments and the like). Though we all know this matters, we all find it difficult—sometimes, it seems, impossible. Is this not paradoxical?

Beauty

The same paradox occurs with Beauty. We all know that beauty is a central and vital part of life, whether in nature, art or music. Some of the earliest signs of *homo sapiens* are the remarkable works of cave art which indicate much more than a functional interest in the world. Some of the oldest works of literature are stories which, by their form and style, do much more than merely tell 'what happened'. But what is that 'much more'? What is beauty, and why does it matter?

Whether it's a sunset or a symphony, the smile of a child or a bunch of spring flowers, beauty makes us more alive. We know it matters. If you live in a prison cell, or the corporate prison cells of the brutalist buildings in old Eastern Europe, the stripping away of beauty is dehumanising. But, as with justice, even when we celebrate and relish beauty, it doesn't last. The sunset fades. The smiling child becomes a bitter adult. The flowers wither. The music stops. The darkness closes in, making us wonder if what we thought was delight was merely the accidental by-product of our evolutionary history, a vestigial memory of hunting prospects or mating opportunities. Would we still find it beautiful if we knew that to be true? Or perhaps, still worse, Sartre was right and the whole thing is a sick joke at our expense. We are drawn to beauty as to a magnet, but it disappears like a mirage. Why? These questions haunt us and are not easy to answer.

Among the curious aspects of post-enlightenment modernity is the origin of the term 'aesthetics'. The word was coined in Germany in the mid-eighteenth century and first used in Britain in the nineteenth. Up until then beauty was woven tightly in with other aspects of life, not least what then came to be called 'religion' or 'spirituality'. The 'sacred', as we have noted elsewhere, was replaced by the 'sublime'. You can see this going on in German Romanticism. Beethoven knows about 'the sacred'. That is clear in the *Missa Solemnis*. But what really fires him is the sublime. The 'Ode to Joy' is the new secular hymn.

The Bible, interestingly, doesn't say much explicitly about beauty. This is not because it's unimportant but because it is part of what is going on all the time, particularly in the making and use of the Tabernacle and the Temple, its architecture, design, liturgy and music. In the Psalms and the prophets, and in those other astonishing books, Job on the one hand and the Song of Songs on the other, we find some of the most hauntingly beautiful writing from any culture anywhere. The Temple-focused vision of beauty was very practical; as we might say, very incarnational. Part of the sense of 'seeing the glory of God' in the Temple was the overwhelming experience, for anyone coming in from the wild and arid lands around, of a stunningly beautiful building filled with colour, light, movement and music. Looking from Temple out to creation as a whole, when the Psalmist says that God makes the morning and evening to praise him, I take for granted that he is referring to the peculiar quality of light around sunrise and sunset, clothing the landscape and even mundane objects with a sense of 'more than', of wonder, mystery and glory (Psalm 65.8). But, as with all other beautiful things in the world, it came to an end. The Temple was destroyed. The night is dark.

Freedom

The paradox repeats when we consider Freedom. We all know it matters; we all want it for ourselves and for those about whom we care. But freedom is surprisingly difficult to define or defend, to get or to keep. We all want it, though we're not sure what it is or what to do with it if we had it. One person's freedom often comes at the cost of another person's slavery. Does it have to be a zero-sum game? Is our instinct for freedom merely a delusion? Rousseau's version of Genesis 1–3 ('Man is born free but is everywhere in chains') catches the paradox. Quarter of a millennium later we are no closer to resolving it.

Philosophers still debate whether we humans really have free will itself or, if we do, whether that means we are simply random particles whizzing around deluding ourselves that we are making real choices. In any case, does 'freedom' mean freedom *from* or freedom *for*? Empires promise freedom to their subjects and just as frequently take it away again. After Cicero's banishment from Rome, they put up a statue of Liberty on the ruin of his house, something not always noted by those who only know the somewhat larger version that greets you as you sail into the port of Manhattan. But for many in the Roman empire, just as for many in the more complex American empire, the slogan meant one thing for the imperial power and another for its subject peoples. Social and political freedom is as elusive as ever. New forms of slavery emerge just when we thought we'd got rid of it. Moral freedom collapses into license, which is again a form of slavery. We all believe in freedom; politicians promise it; but it slips through our fingers.

Freedom was of course written in to Israel's long narrative. The Exodus is the classic historical example of slaves being freed. Yet the prophets tell the story of how Israel then wanted freedom *from* Yhwh's rule as well as from Egypt, a recalcitrance that landed the people in another long period of slavery, under Babylon, Persia, Greece, Egypt, Syria and finally Rome.[18] Every would-be prophet or Messiah in the first century promised the people a new Exodus, freedom at last. That was the slogan on bar-Kochba's last issue of coins as the Romans closed in for the kill. So was the dream an illusion?

Truth

Or take Truth. The Enlightenment boast of objectivity has been deconstructed by the postmodern assertion that truth-claims are power-claims in disguise and that what seems to be true for me may not be true for you. But, like people drinking poisoned water, we may suspect it's bad for us but we're still thirsty. We still want the truth. We don't want to be surrounded by liars or to live in a hall of distorting mirrors. So, being anxious about fraud (with good reason), we want more paperwork for everything: more modernist 'truth'-markers to stave off postmodern suspicion. As in warfare, alas, we throw heavy modernist solutions (tanks and bombs; official enquiries) at postmodern problems (terrorism; deconstruction) and things just get worse. We demand more truth just when it is becoming more elusive.[19] We need truth and were made to tell truth, but we live in a world of lies. Often enough we add to them ourselves. We even tell lies about telling lies (being 'economical with the truth').

At a simple, everyday level, we all live with a correspondence theory of truth. But its problems are well known. The regular alternatives, some kind of coherence theory on the one hand or the various pragmatic theories on the other, may have their uses, but they can all quite easily collapse into mere subjectivism.[20] Is there then such a thing as 'truth'? If so, why is it so hard to come by?

Power

All this leads to Power. Power has been a dirty word in some circles particularly since Francis Bacon (knowledge is power), Friedrich Nietzsche (claims to knowledge are claims to power) and Lord Acton (power tends to corrupt and absolute power corrupts absolutely). But we can't do without it. Reformers and visionaries, realising that evil thrives when good people do nothing, have grabbed the levers of power only to discover that either they don't work or they work backwards. Some have therefore suggested that power is straightforwardly bad, a view which sits easily alongside arguments for political anarchy. But, as world-weary commentators know, anarchy is the most unstable of all political situations and always generates new forms of power which are regularly worse than what the anarchists were trying to replace. If nobody is in charge, the loudest voices, the biggest muscles and the most unscrupulous bullies will win, and everyone will be the poorer. No society, then, can survive without someone exercising power, but the world has known for a long time that power needs to be exercised wisely and held in check. That's what Magna Carta was about. Nor is violence the answer; if you fight fire with fire, fire always wins. We humans, being image-bearers, know we are supposed to exercise God's delegated rule in the world (not that unbelievers would see it like that), but we regularly make matters worse.

Since the Enlightenment, however, many have seen 'power' as automatically corrupt and to be suspected—and, if possible, to be resisted or overthrown. All revolutionaries, of course, want power for themselves, assuming that because their ideas are superior to those of the rulers they replace they will not fall into the same traps . . . and the cycle repeats itself. Modern political history is the story of how this naivety has received the exposure it deserved, and yet continues unchecked. Similar puzzles, by the way, await anyone who tries to over-define 'violence' so that it includes anything you do or say to me which I perceive as invading or violating my space or even my opinions. You can't actually live like that, though people try. Generation after generation of politicians have gone into public life in the hope of gaining power to make their world, their country, their region a better place, but this always proves more elusive than they had supposed. At the very moment when you think you are using power altruistically, you may simply be implementing your own ideological agenda. And when push comes to shove, well, push comes to shove; and sooner or later countries find themselves locked in high-octane arm-wrestling, which does neither them nor the world any good. Power seems necessary within human societies, but there is no agreement in sight as to what it consists of or how to regulate it and use it wisely.

These first five—justice, beauty, freedom, truth and power—are all, I suggest, *vocational signposts*. They are part of the basic kit of what it means to be human. They include moral intuition, but they go beyond: they aren't just about our behaviour but about the difference we are supposed to make in the world. The last two take us into a different register. 'Spirituality' and 'relationships' are slippery words, but something needs to be said about each.

Spirituality

I grew up in the world of the 1960s where secular modernism seemed rampant. Compulsory worship in schools gave an outward form of spirituality. But this—certainly for the pupils, and I suspect for the teachers too—was a socially conformist exercise with little inner content. Within that context, those of us who for whatever reason found ourselves gripped by the message of Jesus were easily nudged towards colluding with split-level philosophies: let the world go its own way, while we celebrate our private secret. But now things have changed. After the years of arid secularism, society in general knows once again that spirituality matters. But that same society, perhaps more in Europe than America, doesn't expect to find spirituality in the church and official Christianity. People contrast being 'spiritual' with being 'religious': Oh, they say, I'm not *religious*—by which they mean they don't go to church or read the Bible—but I am a 'very spiritual person'. The search for a dimension to human life that goes beyond material and bodily needs and wants continues unabated, as witnessed by the bookshop sections called 'Mind Body Spirit' and the like. Despite the sneers of the fashionable atheists, all kinds of 'spirituality' flourishes: straightforward and unashamed paganism, odd mixtures of astrology, semi-scientific suggestions like biorhythms, revivals of ancient philosophy, and so on. These easily mix together in undemanding forms of syncretism where the main aim seems to be the discovering a true (if normally hidden) personal 'identity'. Thus forms of Gnosticism are rampant, though not usually the ascetic kinds. There is a reason why Dan Brown sells so many books, and it's not just because of the cliff-hanging chapter-endings. People who go that route sometimes proudly declare that they have found some kind of 'religion', as though, from a standing secular start, this puts them on the same map as Christianity.

There is, in fact, a strong sense in the late modern or postmodern world that there are other dimensions to life than what you can put in a test tube or a bank balance, and that these other dimensions are not just a bit of added value or decoration around the side but rather make a vital contribution to the whole of our life, personal and corporate. When the subject of spirituality comes up in unguarded conversation, many people will tell of uncanny or mysterious phenomena, of experiences of what seem to be dimensions of life that go beyond the obvious material world. But few today have any frame of reference within which to make sense of such things, and thus either shrug their shoulders or fall prey to whichever strange cult offers a solution. Even where people have embraced some form of Christianity, this is often conceived within a mixture of Deism (with a distant divinity who might still be interested in our moral behaviour) and Platonism (where we have a 'soul' that's destined for a distant and non-spatio-temporal 'heaven'). Christians face an ongoing problem: we have conceived of Christian spirituality in terms of humans somehow making our way towards God, or heaven, whereas the Jewish and early Christian worldview focused on the promise that *God* would come, has come, will come again, *to dwell with us*. So new forms of spirituality let us down. And even when we embrace the incarnational gospel itself, there are dark nights of the soul when it all goes blank. Yet another paradox.

So what is 'spirituality', and how do you acquire or retain it? Is there a difference between healthy and unhealthy spirituality, and if so what is it? Some, faced with the rise of militant Islam, and with memories of Christian fundamentalisms of whichever sort, use that as an excuse to suggest that religions are dangerous and abusive, and that the only safe spirituality might be pure aestheticism. We all know spirituality is important, but it remains an elusive and perhaps even a risky part of human life.

I argued in the fifth chapter that for many Jews of Jesus' day all this would have been interpreted within the assumed overlap of 'heaven' and 'earth', an overlap which was focused on the Temple. The Psalms remained both a repository of such spirituality and a resource for its regular regeneration. It could easily hold together the glad awareness of God's presence and power in the created order alongside the personal challenge of faith and obedience, as we see in Psalm 19 with its parallel between the sun in the sky and the Torah in the heart. That tradition contained a robust realism: there are times when God seems totally absent and heartless, and it's better to say so than to pretend all is well. The narcissistic tendency of any privatized spirituality is held within a much larger implied narrative: how *you* feel today is not as important as what God is doing, and will do, with his creation as a whole. There might, too, be signs of a refreshed future, even in the midst of horror. The Sabbaths were regular reminders that God's time was linear, not circular, and that the promised 'rest' was coming—that, as Walter Benjamin picked up from a strand of Jewish mysticism, every moment might be the little door through which the Messiah might enter.[21] But this, too, seemed to have proved illusory when the Romans closed in in AD 70 and again in 135. That was, at least in part, why many seem to have turned to forms of Gnosticism in the later second century. The 'spirituality' they knew had let them down. There are many parallels in our own day.

Relationships

Finally, 'relationships': again, an appropriately slippery word, because my point is not that there is something called 'love' which we can first analyse accurately and then ascribe to God but that all of us know we are made for relationships of one sort or another. All of us are formed, for good and ill, by our relationships, whether supportive or abusive, healthy or unhealthy. Often the abusive or unhealthy relationships are the ones to which we return like an addict. Here, then, is the paradox. As Pannenberg argued, humans are exocentric creatures, becoming the people we are through the relationships we have outside of ourselves.[22] Yet we mess up those relationships and are messed up by them. The very best still end in death itself.

I argued in the first chapter that modern Western society has been haunted by the Faust myth, in which the diabolical pact includes the prohibition: *You must not love.* Love is already seen in that myth as the window through which, even in the darkest night, one might just discern the possibility of dawn. And love therefore does what justice, freedom, power, truth, beauty and spirituality all do in their own ways: it raises questions, questions which point beyond themselves and demand that some story be told which will provide the larger meaning for which they all long. The cynical answer, that there is no larger story and no greater meaning, is always possible. Epicurus and his followers have done their best to make it seem a dignified, even noble, position to hold. But love will re-emerge, in one form or another. I argued in the previous chapter for a particular view of how 'love' works within different levels of epistemology.

There is, to be sure, a small minority of humans who seem to have little or no need for relationships. But Sartre's line about 'hell' being 'other people' is too cynical for most of us. We would go mad without human contact, or at the least contact with one or more animals. For most of us, a loving relationship, or a set of loving relationships, is what makes life worth living. We would rather be poor and loved than rich and unloved—and most people would regard us with pity if we disagreed with that verdict. Love, friendship, companionship, collegiality: all these and more bring not only a sense of fulfilment but a sense of self-discovery, of growing into more than we are when left to ourselves, recognising who we really are not by tortured introspection or narcissistic mirror-gazing but by the response and prompting of those around us. We are, in short, exocentric creatures, designed to be centred not within ourselves but outside of ourselves.

But relationships are really hard, whether at the personal, societal or international levels. A few of us are blessed with unproblematic and supportive friendships, neighbourhoods, families and spouses. Many of us have to work hard at some of those some of the time; some of us have to work hard at most of those much of the time. Even then things can fall apart. The best friendships, the best marriages, have many moments of mystery, surprise or even alarm, and often disappointment as we come to terms with the fact that we may have projected our own hopes and needs on to someone else who is in fact significantly different from the image of them we have allowed ourselves to construct.

This happens globally as well as personally. Political leaders imagine that their opposite numbers in other countries are like themselves only with different languages and eating habits; they then discover misunderstandings, threats, broken relationships and ultimately hostility, as the deep assumptions and hidden story-lines in different cultures end up in dangerous collision. World peace and prosperity, we all believe, are better than world war and devastation; but though we can make expensive weapons to wage war and wreak havoc we haven't invented even cheap ones that will make peace or build wise community. The world is capable of growing enough food for everyone, but we still haven't figured out how to share it properly. And so on. Relationships matter vitally, but they remain a serious problem at every level.

The Hebrew scriptures tell the story of creation and covenant, and the point of the covenant is love: love with a purpose, a plan and a promise. That is so in the garden; it is so once more in the calling of Abraham. Right from the start, though, the relationship between the creator and his creation is fractured, and the fracturing continues down the line, with the sons of Adam, Noah, Abraham and Isaac showing all the signs of brokenness, pointing on to the extreme dysfunctionality of Jacob's family which seems to come to an end with Joseph enslaved in Egypt. The remarkable reconciliation of Joseph and his brothers then points forward, in the implicit eschatology of the book of Genesis, to the larger covenant purpose of God for Israel and *through* Israel to the world.[23] The relationships, however, continue to be strained at every level, with the subsequent disruption of the Babylonian exile merely the low point in a long and sad story. But the rumour of love will not go away. The prophets speak of covenant restored. Is this just a dream, the theological equivalent of a romantic fantasy?

WHERE MIGHT THE BROKEN SIGNPOSTS LEAD?

These seven, then, I see as signposts. As they stand they are broken signposts, promising much but failing to deliver.

We might, of course, try to argue from them all up to some sort of 'natural theology'. One might suggest that the passion for justice and the love of beauty make sense within a world which God has promised to put right, a world he will fill with his glory. Our longing for freedom could be said to resonate with scripture's Exodus-theme. We could rightly say that the creator God is the God of truth, of reality, who calls his human creatures as Image-bearers to be truth-tellers, so that his wise order may come, through wise human words, into his world. Human puzzles about power might be seen to reflect the constant biblical theme of God's power. The human quest for spirituality, in all forms, points to Augustine's line that God has made us for himself and our hearts are restless until they rest in him.[24] Finally, our need for multi-levelled relationships might be seen as a window onto the pluriform interrelationships within the Trinitarian Godhead, and on our ultimate vocation to love God and love our neighbour. From all this, as a kind of refreshed version of Kant's moral argument, we might hope to argue our way up to God. Perhaps even to the Father of Messiah Jesus. And, working out from there, we might then hope to incorporate some version of the cosmological and teleological arguments. Our own creativity might be seen as a mirror of the Creator's own original creativity. Our own planning and projects might reflect the sense of purpose built in to the world we know.

We might think all this, but we would be walking out on a frozen lake with no realistic prospect that the ice would hold. One can imagine Richard Dawkins, in his usual response to a post-Paley natural theology, dismissing it all as projection: your 'God' is rather like you, only bigger. Throw in some Freud, Marx and Nietzsche, and the ice cracks. However deeply rooted these 'vocational signposts' may be, they may just be 'memes' transferred across cultures and time. And that's not all. Deeper than the cynic's sneer is our own analysis: that we have failed, individually and corporately. We have turned justice into oppression, beauty into kitsch, freedom into licence, truth into fake news, power into bullying. We have turned spirituality into self-exploration or self-gratification. We have made the calling to relationships the excuse for exploitation. All these, from a Christian point of view, have the word 'idolatry' hanging over them.

It gets worse. Even when we haven't got it wrong, when we really have done justice, loved beauty, given and sustained freedom, told the truth, exercised power with wise restraint, and sought the true God with all our hearts and loved our neighbour as ourselves—why, then entropy kicks in. This is John Stuart Mill's response to Kant. However much you puff up the human moral capacity—and, in my version, however much you emphasize vocational qualities common to all humans—events in the world, from Lisbon to Auschwitz, events in our hearts and lives, and the harsh fact that we all die and life seems a cruel joke, suggest that any new version of the 'moral' argument will fail the test of 'theodicy'. The moral argument, even in my new form, falls through the ice and drowns.

The seven 'vocations', then, are at best broken signposts. They appear to be pointing somewhere, but they lead into the dark, or over a cliff, or around in circles to where we began. Were they just wraiths, the ghosts of our own imaginings? Were they just random impulses in a late-developed evolutionary pattern? Were they, after all, the wrong questions to ask? Should we simply have capitulated to the cool Epicurean cynicism: yes, we feel these things, but they don't really mean anything, and we should silence such irrelevant voices and pursue the placid pleasures available to us here and now? Or should we smile an early Barthian smile and say, Well, there you are, nothing good was ever going to come from all that?

Is there a way forward from this apparent impasse? I think there is, but only if we move the argument forwards in an unexpected way.

BROKEN SIGNPOSTS, BROKEN STORIES

Our discovery that the apparently promising signposts were broken takes us back to where this chapter began, with Jesus' teasing rebuke to the two disciples on the road to Emmaus. You are so senseless: this is how it had to happen . . . What was going on?

Richard Hays has reminded us that the early Christians read Israel's scriptures 'backwards'.[25] They didn't start with the Bible, figure out an Identikit portrait of a Messiah, and discover Jesus of Nazareth. They had plenty of scripture-based messianic portraits, and Jesus didn't fit them. But notice, as we said before, what Jesus does *not* do. He does not say, 'Why were you bothering with those scriptures? They just led you into trouble, into wrong views of God and salvation. Throw them away and trust me for the brand-new thing I'm offering!' No: 'beginning with Moses and all the prophets', says Luke, 'he interpreted to them in all the scriptures the things concerning himself'. Here is the truth which cuts across the different philosophical and theological movements that have tried to do 'natural theology' on the one hand and historical studies of Jesus and the Gospels on the other. When you look back from the resurrection of the crucified one to the hopes and aspirations of Israel—and, as I shall now argue, to the seven vocational signposts we have briefly noted—you do not see a void. You see a broken, desolate story limping along, faint but pursuing, stumbling into the ditch here and there, taking wrong turnings, grabbing at false solutions and hanging on to empty hopes. But still it comes, in tears like the women at the tomb, in sorrow like the two on the Emmaus road. And behind that broken and bleeding story we glimpse the *narrative of Israel's vocation*: Abraham's call and covenant, Moses' Exodus and Tabernacle, David's and Solomon's victories and Temple, the catastrophe of exile and the long, dark time of waiting. When you read backwards from cross and resurrection, you see muddle, failure and mistake, but you also see the divine promises and vocations to which Israel kept returning, however partially and fitfully. And you now see, in a way you couldn't before, that *this was the right story to be telling*, that these were the right signals if only you could have steered by them, that what Israel's God has now done has as it were *retrospectively validated* the genuine forward-pointing signposts that went before. The so-called 'apocalyptic' rejection of any 'back story', reflecting in would-be exegesis the Kierkegaardian and Barthian rejection of Hegel, throws out the tea-pot with the tea-leaves. Israel's story is the story of God's faithfulness; and, as Paul rightly saw, the very brokenness of the story magnifies that faithfulness.[26] To say otherwise lands you in the arms of Marcion, where you will find many friends ancient and modern. Nor will you worry about any normal kind of 'natural theology' there: Marcionites, like Gnostics, don't want to be told that the story of Israel, having snapped in two like a dry twig, nevertheless still pointed in the right direction. When you learn to 'read backwards', you will glimpse, like the Father seeing his bedraggled son limping over the horizon, the story that got it all wrong yet found its way home at last. The father's words of welcome—'This my son'—reaffirm the truth that had seemed to be obliterated by the son's earlier behaviour.

So it is with the 'broken signposts' we have noted. By themselves, they do not point upwards to God; or, if they seem to, they might simply be building a new Tower of Babel. They can be deconstructed, interpreted otherwise. And yet. *At the very moment of their failure, they point to the ultimate broken signpost, which turns out to be the place in real life, in concrete history, where the living God is truly revealed, known and loved.* Each of the signposts leads to the same place.

The cry for justice is central Israel's to prayer life; the boast of justice was central to Imperial Rome. But it didn't work when Jesus stood before Pilate. Everybody knew Jesus was innocent. Pilate washed his hands. His wife had nightmares about 'that just man' (Mathew 27.19). The irony is that God's justice-bringing action—as Paul sees Jesus' death—is carried out by means of a flagrant and shameful miscarriage of justice. Jesus, in his prophetic words, had announced God's reign and denounced the wickedness of his world. But he refused to be 'a judge or divider' when it came to property rights (Luke 12.14); and, at the end, he was himself the innocent victim of scheming, plotting, false testimony and flawed trials. The Roman governor, servant of an empire which prided itself on its own *Iustitia* and on bringing that justice to the world, looked the other way. Jesus went to his death as the silent embodiment of the cry for justice which arises from the world. If the notion of justice is indeed supposed to be a signpost to God, set up gloriously within the present world, it looks (to put it mildly) as though someone has tampered with the sign. It is pointing the wrong way. It is broken.

Beauty is elusive in the Bible. Like the Old Testament, which as we saw describes beautiful things rather than commenting on their beauty, the New Testament does not often mention beauty itself. Instead, it tells a story which retains its evocative power and haunting mystery even in unpromising contexts. It is not accidental that among the most frequent subjects for art and music in the mediaeval and baroque periods was the crucifixion of Jesus. But we should not therefore forget the shocking paradox. In ordinary human terms, Jesus' crucifixion was not only ugly and horrifying in itself.[27] When we say the phrase 'the crucifixion', we think of course of Jesus, but in the Roman world where crucifixions were two a penny Jesus' execution was just another young idiot getting what was coming to him. It was banal. At the time, Jesus' death didn't even have the dignity of uniqueness. And yet within twenty years people were writing poetry in which that death held together not only the drama and meaning of Jesus' life but the beauty of creation ransomed, healed, restored and forgiven. The slaughtered lamb joins the One on the Throne, surrounded by a jewel-like rainbow, with seven burning lampstands and a sea of glass like crystal, and angels playing trumpets. What seemed to be the very denial of beauty, the quintessence of our cynical disappointment with its promise and allure, turns out to be the generating source of a beauty through which the whole creation is renewed and throbs with praise. That is how the signpost of beauty is retrieved by the early Christians. But at the cross of Jesus it had seemed a mere deceitful mirage. As Jesus died, there was no beautiful twilight, just darkness. And in the morning, only horror.

Jesus chose Passover, the freedom-festival, to do what had to be done. And the Romans stamped on freedom as only they knew how. Paul, looking back at Jesus' death and resurrection, speaks with Exodus-echoes of the ultimate liberating victory over the ultimate Pharaoh. Jesus himself had joined the other prophets of the day in promising freedom, but his particular message resulted in confrontation and redefinition: the real slavery, he insisted, was slavery to sin, the destructive power that takes people captive and warps their genuine humanness out of shape all the way to death. Yet here again we have paradox. The very events to which Paul refers, Jesus' execution and burial, embodied and enacted the classic Roman squashing of the Jewish cry for freedom. The Jews had made many bids for freedom throughout the two centuries from Pompey's invasion to the fall of bar-Kochba, and the heavy-handed Romans had done what they always did, no doubt explaining to one another that this was the only language these Jews would understand.[28] The execution of Jesus fitted exactly into this pattern. The longing for freedom, the puzzle over what it might mean, and the pain of having it denied, reached a climax as Jesus went to the cross. If freedom is a signpost pointing beyond itself from within the present world, it appears to be pointing the wrong way. It points to a promised land, but experience suggests that it leads only to Egypt; to Babylon; to Rome. To a cross.

What about truth? Pilate asks Jesus if he is a king, and Jesus answers that he has come to tell the truth (John 18.37–38). That isn't changing the subject. Part of the way the kingdom of God operates is precisely through the wise and obedient words which bring God's order into the disordered world. But when Jesus expands this to comment that everyone who belongs to the truth listens to his voice, Pilate has had enough. 'Truth!' he snorts. 'What's that?' The only 'truth' Pilate knows, as Foucault recognised, is the truth of naked, violent power. Empires make their own 'truth'. So Jesus' death, in John's Gospel at least, is seen as the direct clash of two different notions of truth. By Friday evening it looks as though Pilate's truth has won. If truth is a signpost telling us something important from within the midst of the world, then Pilate the proto-postmodernist turns out to be right. Truth is what the powerful make it to be. Truth, the first casualty in war, is perhaps the central irony of the crucifixion.

So too with power. The good news announced by Jesus was all about power. 'The kingdom of God' was about God becoming king, which meant that God's kingdom was arriving and that his will would be done on earth as in heaven. Some of Jesus' followers seem to have assumed that this would mean, once Jesus had been established as the rightful king, that they would exercise the normal kind of power, sitting at the new king's right and left hands (Mark 10.37). Jesus quickly disabused such notions, not that his followers got the message. The rulers of the nations do it one way, he said; we're going to do it the other way round. That is then picked up by Paul, who weaves the redefinition of power into the heart of his theology. He sees 'the word of the cross' as the rescuing power of God, even though pagans think it's crazy and Jews think it's blasphemous. The kingdom of God, he said, doesn't consist in talk but in power. Paul does allow (as part of his overall creational monotheism) that the ruling authority has a God-given role, though it is limited and will be held to account.

The same point is actually made by Jesus himself in John's Gospel, in one of the most remarkably ironic claims. Pilate chides Jesus for not answering his questions: don't you know, he asks, that I have the authority to let you go, and the authority to crucify you? Jesus answers, astonishingly, that this authority has been given to Pilate 'from above', referring not just to Pilate's actual boss, Tiberius Caesar, but to God himself. And Jesus points out that this means a holding to account for those who misuse that authority. Thus, as with justice and freedom, the irony of power in the gospel story, and then in Paul, Revelation and elsewhere, is that Jesus' crucifixion is presented *both* as the archetypal misuse of imperial power *and* as the secret launching of a different kind of power altogether. But on Good Friday this secret is unimaginable. Even if we acknowledge that some kind of power is necessary, the cross indicates that once more absolute power has corrupted absolutely and that Jesus has taken its full force. If power is a signpost from within an otherwise chaotic world, the only thing it points to is the reality that abusive tyrants seize power for themselves and trample on those who get in their way. The only 'god' then involved is the one the chief priests shockingly invoke at the end of Pilate's hearing: 'We have no king except Caesar!' (John 19.15). Jesus had announced a new kind of power, but it seemed that the old kind had won after all.

Spirituality? The realism of ancient Jewish spirituality seems to have reached its peak with Jesus himself. To speak of his own 'religious experience', as some have tried to do, is to enter the realms of psychological speculation, often framed in distorting modernist categories. But what shines out from the texts is that when people were with Jesus they were aware of a power, a joy, a forgiveness and healing that seemed to flow out of him; and they were aware that he was aware of it and that he was in constant personal touch with its ultimate source. He was acting, and was eventually perceived to be acting, as if he was a Temple-in-person, a place where heaven and earth interlocked; as if the time of his public career was a perpetual Sabbath, a time of fulfilment, a time when God's promised future had arrived in the present. But the vividness of all this, which shines out of all four Gospels in their different ways, serves then as the bright frame within which the darkness of the Psalms, the despair of Jeremiah, the years of weeping by the waters of Babylon, all come rushing together. The Gospels hold together 'Come to me, and I will give you rest' with 'My God, my God, why did you abandon me?' (Matthew 11.28; 27.46).[29] As some of the greatest saints have discovered, the quest for authentic spirituality will regularly end at the foot of the cross. If spirituality is a signpost towards God from within the present world, it seems to lead, quite literally, to a dead end.

Relationships? Judas denies Jesus; Peter betrays him; the rest run away. 'He saved others; he can't save himself' (Matthew 27.42/Mark 15.31).[30] We meet the paradox for the final time. The story of Jesus, explicitly in John and implicitly in the other three, is a love-story: having loved his own in the world, says John, 'now Jesus loved them right through to the end'. But, just as in its Hebrew antecedents, this story reaches its climax precisely through the *failure* of love. Jesus' own family misunderstand him and think he's mad (Mark 3.21). The villages where he did his early work refuse to accept his message. He comes to his own and his own do not receive him. Even those who do receive him then betray him, deny him and abandon him at the last. The puzzle of love—we can't live without it, but it seems to be much harder than we thought—is exposed in all its bewildering terror at the cross. As in all the other cases, so too in this: it looks as though, with Jesus' death, the signpost of love, planted tantalisingly in human hearts, is broken beyond repair.

When we stand at the foot of the cross, all seven signposts appear to be not only useless but utterly deceitful. We have been tricked. The crucifixion story confirms the cynic's view. There is no way 'up to God' from there.

But when we 'read backwards' we discover that *this was after all the means by which the true God was revealed*. If we thought that the seven human vocational signposts would lead along a noble upward path to God, we were gravely mistaken. Perhaps all along we were really wanting—as perhaps Kant was wanting?—to find the God of the 'omni's—the omnipotent, omniscient, omnicompetent deity, the celestial CEO of much Western imagination. Instead, the four Gospels tell us of the God who suffered the ultimate injustice, the God with no beauty that we should desire him, the incarnate God denied freedom, whose fresh truth was trumped by the empire's truth-making machine. The Messiah who healed by the power of love was crushed by the love of power. The one whose own rich spirituality bound him in intimate relationship to the Father found himself abandoned.

Here, then, is the point. The early Christians all insist that the divine revelation took place neither simply *before* this, in Jesus' public career, or *after* it, in the resurrection, but, as John makes clear, in the crucifixion itself. That was when they 'gazed upon his glory, glory as of the Father's only son, full of grace and truth'. The point is that if we go looking for a god who matches our culture's expectations, or indeed the expectations of some philosophical theism, we may get the wrong one. There is only one God like this. As the First World War poet Edward Shillito wrote in his best-known poem:

The other gods were strong; but thou wast weak;
They rode, but thou didst stumble, to a throne.
But to our wounds, only God's wounds can speak;
And not a god has wounds, but thou alone.[31]

Of course, none of this was apparent at the time. Nobody in the hours immediately following Jesus' death was saying, 'Well, that was very unpleasant, but at
least now we have seen God's glory'. Jesus' followers were hiding in fear, shame
and grief. But the resurrection compelled them to look back and retell what
had happened, drawing out the way in which not only Israel's broken story
but the broken signposts from the entire human world turned out after all,
precisely in their brokenness, to be pointing to the ultimate broken signpost,
the cross itself.

READING THE SIGNPOSTS BACKWARDS

So what kind of 'natural theology'—if any!—might now emerge from our
investigation of the broken signposts of the human vocation? Perhaps the first
and in some ways the most important thing to say is that, unlike a great deal of
'natural theology' from the eighteenth century onwards, we are driven from this
enquiry to focus not on the first person of the Trinity but on the second—and
at the point which the four Gospels highlight as the dark climax of his short
public career. These failures, in other words, point not to the Creator, specially not to the Deist divinity of much eighteenth-century thought, but to
the crucified Jesus. This, one might say, is a kind of 'Holy Saturday' version of
natural theology, a moment which the Psalmists would recognise: the time
when everything wrong with the world seemed to gather itself together into
one moment of utter, bleak disaster and horror. That, I suggest, is why the
crucifixion of Jesus has exercised a strange power on the human imagination,
whether or not people have seen it in the light of the resurrection. When the
resurrection then enables a backward look at the same story, this power is not
undermined, but set within a larger context.

So what then can be said about the ways in which these 'vocational signposts' function, in retrospect, within some kind of refreshed 'natural theology'?

First, *the early Christians made these signposts thematic for their own ongoing
life*. They looked back, in the light of the new day whose dawn they had discerned, and they declared that God *had* established his justice in the world and
would complete this task at Jesus' return. Their visions and poems, their common
life and shared love, radiated a beauty which turned into world-transforming art
and music, poetry and drama. They embraced the freedom of the new Exodus

and lived in it. They spoke a lot *about* truth, and through their words the truth of new creation spread into the world. They spoke and acted with a healing, restorative power. They practiced a spirituality that could cope with the darkest night of the soul while being open to rich, multi-layered experiences of the God in whose image they found themselves remade.[32] Above all, in their rich relationships they turned the ancient rumour of love into practical policy, caring for one another and for anyone their outstretched hands could reach.

All this was the common coin of early Christian life. The Enlightenment has done its best to rubbish church history, to see it as part of the problem. And of course the church has failed, sinned, used violence, colluded with wickedness; but at the same time the ordinary life of ordinary Jesus-followers is still the principal way people are drawn to faith, not least because these seven signposts are in the process of being repaired. *Things are happening in the real, 'natural', public world which function as genuine signposts to the God of creation and new creation.* Huge problems of course remain; the church still makes serious mistakes; but new life has happened and is happening. When, in other words, we look back from Easter and Pentecost, we see with hindsight that the vocational questions raised in the 'natural' world *were the right questions to ask.* The Epicurean cynicism of a Machiavelli or a Nietzsche is answered. The signposts may have been broken but they were doing their best to tell the truth. You cannot start with them and argue your way up to God's existence or character. If you try, you may well end up with a God significantly unlike the incarnate, wounded God of the New Testament. But when you discern the dawn of new creation you see that the signposts were gesturing toward something true, even if that truth was only visible through a glass, darkly. *Now that we have the new answers, we see that those were the right questions.* They were not simply the frantic ravings of random desires. The signposts were intending to point to a country where, astonishingly, we are now welcomed as citizens.

Second, we have a new angle on *the 'point of contact' between God and the world.* The phrase is itself unfortunate, suggesting a merely tangential meeting, almost an accidental or misleading concession. To be sure, if by 'point of contact' we were thinking of an upward ladder of divine revelation, a movement of intellectual or human progress by which humans could climb up towards the knowledge of God, a kind of mental or spiritual Pelagianism, we find that the ladder has no rungs. As we have seen, when we look at each of the seven signposts in turn, the story the Gospels tell us, the story which ends with Jesus on the cross, simply highlights the problem. Justice is denied as Jesus is condemned; the hope of freedom is quashed; the only effective power is violence; truth is swallowed up in *Realpolitik*; beauty is trampled underfoot;

spirituality ends up in dereliction. Love itself is betrayed, mocked and killed. The Gospels show us an event within the public world, the 'natural' world of history, of human beings, of politics and power-games and kangaroo courts. They make no attempt to suggest that the crucifixion itself consisted of a divine 'intervention' that might be visible only to the eye of an already-attained faith. Jesus refused to summon twelve legions of angels. Elijah did not come to save him from death. *The cross of Jesus, precisely as a 'natural' event in the real public world of human affairs and history, is already on Holy Saturday the quintessential moment of meaningless horror. Seen retrospectively from after Easter, it becomes the ultimate true signpost to God, to God's work in the world, to God's purposes for the world.* And, indeed, to God's ultimate dealing with evil in the world. The trail of broken signposts leads to the broken God on the cross.

Nor is this, as in Bultmann, a bare fact, a mere *Dass*.[33] The cross, planted in the solid ground of human history, in the 'natural' world of human life and land, is the signpost that simultaneously says 'no' to all human pride and folly and 'yes' to all the vocational longings. The Temple veil is torn. In the light of what happened next, we can see that the healing and forgiveness of the future came forward into the midst of the present time, ending with the silent Sabbath of Holy Saturday when God lay buried in the heart of the earth. *God was reconciling the world to himself in the Messiah*; Paul, as often, says it sharpest (2 Corinthians 5.19). 'Nobody has ever seen God', comments John in his matchless poetry. 'The only begotten God, who is intimately close to the father—he has brought him to light' (John 1.18). All four Gospels are telling us, in language more familiar to first-century Jews than to third- or thirteenth-century theologians, that here heaven and earth overlapped entirely. If the modern discipline calling itself 'natural theology' is looking for a god other than the one nailed to the cross, it is looking, however accidentally, for an idol and needs to be reminded that our knowledge of God, if it is to be genuine knowledge, is the reflex of God's knowledge of us and that this is to be energised by love.[34] The cross of Jesus belongs totally within the 'natural' world, the world indeed of nature red in tooth and claw—including human nature, where Orwell's terrible image, of a boot stamping on a human face for ever, sums up the world. But when we look at this event from the angles we have now explored we can say with trembling but grateful confidence that here the living God is truly revealed. When we look at the cross and see there the failed hopes and despairing cries of history, we discover the deepest truth: that the meeting point is not somewhere to which humans can raise themselves up on tiptoe while God stretches down for a brief moment. *The cross is where the downward spiral of human despair meets the love which was all along at the heart of creation.*[35] There lives the dearest freshness, deep down things.

That is why, I believe, paintings and other depictions of the cross retain, even to the cynical and doubting, a pre-articulate and sub-rational power, which our investigation can bring to rational articulation. That is why hard-boiled atheists will still turn out to listen to, or even to sing in, performances of Bach's great Passions. As the theatre director Peter Sellars explained, in relation to his choreographing of the St Matthew Passion, in this story more than anywhere else in the world all human beings are confronted both with the utter darkness of human life and with the possibility of finding the way through, through inhabiting that story for oneself.[36] Sellars said this without any preliminary statement of faith. He was not invoking a secret 'supernatural' interpretation. He clearly saw the event of Jesus' crucifixion, brought to life first by the evangelist Matthew and then by J. S. Bach, as a kind of 'natural' revelation of God. Perhaps the only true kind.

This was apparent in two incidents I noted near the start of my book *The Day the Revolution Began*.[37] First, in 2000 the National Gallery hosted an exhibition put on by its then Director, Neil McGregor. It was called 'Seeing Salvation', and it consisted mostly of old paintings depicting Jesus' death. The newspapers and critics rubbished it: why, in our bright late-modern world, do we need to stare at these grisly old pictures about someone being tortured to death? But the general public ignored the experts and came in their droves, over and over again. The power of the cross still speaks across cultural barriers.

Or take the example of the former Cardinal Archbishop of Paris, Jean-Marie Lustiger.[38] He told the story of three young lads in a provincial town who decided to play a trick on the priest. They went into the confessional and 'confessed' all kinds of sins they'd just made up. The first two ran away laughing. But the priest, having heard the 'confession' of the third, gave him a penance to perform. He had to walk up to the great crucifix at the east end of the church; to look at the figure on the cross; and to say, 'You did all that for me, and I don't give a damn'. He had to say it three times. So the lad went off—it was all part of the game—and, looking at the crucifix, said, 'You did all that for me, and I don't give a damn'. Then he did it a second time. And then he found—that he couldn't do it a third time. He left the church changed, humbled, transformed. And the Archbishop, telling this story, added, 'And the reason I know that story is—that I was that young man'. The cross—or perhaps we should say the one revealed in depictions of the cross—can speak to the hardest heart.

In both these cases—the exhibition and the young French lad—there is no suggestion of a 'supernatural' element. Of course, the paintings, and the crucifix, are contextualised within the larger story which the church has always told, of how this crucified man was raised from the dead, of how his transformative spirit is let loose in the world and in human hearts and lives. But the visitors to the National Gallery, and the young Frenchman, needed to know none of this. They were confronted (in the way that art can and does confront, by making present to us a multi-layered reality) with an event that precisely *belongs in our natural world of broken signposts.*

One response to all this might be that I am substituting a 'romantic' train of thought—or at least 'feeling'!—for a 'rational' one. Those who listen to the *St Matthew Passion*, who view the great paintings, who stand shocked into silence before a solemn crucifix, may indeed be moved towards contemplation of, and perhaps faith in, the God revealed in Jesus; but this hardly constitutes anything that could be called 'natural theology'. As I have said before, neither in method nor in results does my proposal align with what has come to be seen as traditional 'natural theology'. But it raises the question to which the central argument of this present chapter can provide, as a response, a genuine form of Christian 'natural theology', doing in a different framework something distantly related to what Kant was trying to do with the 'moral sense' (and avoiding Mill's objection), focusing now on an analysis of human *vocation*. In this argument, I am proposing that within the 'natural world' of human aspirations and unfulfilled longings—'broken signposts' as I have called them—we find the crucifixion of Jesus as the strongest and strangest 'signpost' of them all, making sense of the others, drawing them to a point which poses the question: can you not see that all these 'vocations', precisely in their brokenness and paradoxes, converge? And when we then ask the question: What is this story about? And why did people tell it this way? We find that the answer lies in the ancient Jewish vision of an earthly world in which heaven might after all be at home, of a dark present which might yet be shot through with light from an ultimate future, of a human vocation to reflect the world's Creator into that world. The 'vocational' variation on the 'moral sense' argument leads to the cross; but the crucifixion of the risen one then invites consideration of the kingdom of God. That is the point at which the epistemology of love, after which we enquired in the previous chapter, comes into its own.

First, then, the early Christians made these 'signposts' thematic in their common life; second, this offers a new perspective on the question of a 'point of contact'. Third, the perspective I have offered provides a fresh way back into *a new-creational viewpoint of which the traditional teleological argument might be seen as a radical distortion.* Paley, famously, spoke of a watch and an implied watchmaker. We might want to speak of new creation, of 'discerning the dawn', as seeing a broken watch repaired, and telling the new time demanded by the new world which had been born. Part of the point here is that the restored creation is precisely restored *creation*; it is not a matter of deleting or forgetting all that had gone before and simply receiving a fresh gift from the future. When the future gift arrives, it makes retrospective sense of the earlier signposts, in the way that a repaired watch makes retrospective sense of the broken one we had discovered: *this*, we might think, this telling of the true time, *is what it was there for in the first place.*

The power of the argument will then depend on the extent to which the new time makes sense in the lives of puzzled onlookers. That points to the final chapter, where the church's mission in the world—in the 'real, natural world'!—must form part of the overall argument. Once again, if a 'natural theology' thinks that it can run on 'reason' alone, detached from the larger communal life of those who tell and live the story, it is simply playing along with a form of modernist rationalism. True, the car cannot run without petrol. Reasoned argument is vital within the larger whole. But trying to argue up to God—especially the God of creation and new creation!—on reason alone is like buying a can of petrol and hoping that it will, all by itself, somehow get you home.

Fourth, and picking up where this book began, *the focus on the cross addresses the question of theodicy in a fresh way.* Ever since Lisbon the so-called 'problem of evil' has been split off from 'atonement' theology, as though the cross, central to the latter, was irrelevant to the former. I have suggested that a 'vocational' focus, doing the job that Kant thought to do with the 'moral' argument, brings us back after all to Jesus' crucifixion. It is time for the two questions to be reunited. The three basic questions of 'natural theology'—God's action in the world, arguments for God from within the world, and the problem of evil—return to, and are reshaped by, the cross itself.[39]

Fifth and finally, *we return once more to epistemology.* If, as I explained in the previous chapter, it is love that believes the resurrection, it is love itself (in Christian terms, the love of God poured out into our hearts) that enables us to see the larger picture as well. Love, in believing the resurrection, discovers with it that the signs of the creator's presence in the old creation really were true pointers to the new. Love is the mode of knowing which includes, though it transcends, the others (and, where they are inherently faulty, as with rationalism or romanticism, it either displaces them or transforms them). And with this we note a particular twist. When we look back at the broken story and the broken signposts, and at those who have struggled and puzzled to make sense of it all, we remind ourselves that grief, too, is a form of love and so shares its epistemological possibility. Mary Magdalene saw the angel, and then the risen Jesus, through her tears. Those who have loved justice, beauty, freedom and the rest, and have grieved over their denial, have had unawares, all along, true knowledge of the true God who gave us these vocations. Blessed are those who mourn, said Jesus; they shall be comforted. I think that works with epistemology as well.

CONCLUSION

I have implicitly rejected the working assumption behind some attempts at 'natural theology': that, from within a Faustian world, one could by reason alone storm the heights and reach the citadel. That, of course, is what Barth was reacting against: a 'natural theology' achieved with force and power that would sustain a political system based on force and power. Instead, I am suggesting a 'natural theology' of *weakness*, corresponding to Paul's theology of weakness in 2 Corinthians. Barth's alternative, a revelation 'vertically from above', was itself potentially problematic, with its implication of powerful preaching from a high pulpit. Paul's apostolic preaching was framed by apostolic weakness, embodying the Gospel in apostolic suffering. The 'natural theology' revealed when we read backwards to the cross and thence to the broken signposts can never be a rationalist's triumph. It is known by love, and love must be its *modus operandi*.

That is why the early Christian new-creational eschatology, rooted in the actual events concerning Jesus, must issue in the flesh-and-blood *missio Dei*. That is part of the argument. The signposts must come to life afresh. When we fight for justice and stand up for the oppressed, we are knowing God, making him known, demonstrating by the spirit his own passion for justice. When we delight in beauty and create more of it, God the glad creator is displayed and honoured. When we cherish freedom and share it; when we speak truly, and especially when we speak new creation into being by articulating fresh truth, the God of Genesis and Exodus is present, celebrated and known. When we exercise power humbly and wisely, and hold to account those who do otherwise, we are living out publicly the power of the cross and demonstrating that the innate human vocation, given in the creation of image-bearers, was a true signpost to the reality of God and the world. When we worship and pray, and above all when we enter into wise, self-giving and fruitful relationships, we are knowing and honouring the God of creation and making him known. There will be grief in all this. There will be love in all this. There will thus be knowledge: we will be engaged in the true, image-bearing 'natural theology'. Those who discern the dawn must awaken the world.

Such an image-bearing 'mission', shaped by Temple-cosmology and Sabbath-eschatology now refocused on Jesus, will be oriented towards the ultimate goal, when the earth shall be full of the knowledge of the glory of the Lord, as the waters cover the sea. 'Natural theology' has sometimes tried to gain that goal without going through the dark valley. It sometimes looks as though traditional 'natural theology' has operated, unknowingly it seems, with an over-realised eschatology (as though what in fact can be known only through the resurrection is able to be known already in creation) and an under-realised theology of the cross (imagining that the 'signposts' were all in good shape all along). But when the epistemology of love gives birth to the missiology of love, even the broken signposts will laugh and sing for joy. And that points us to the final chapter.

8

The Waiting Chalice

Natural Theology and the *Missio Dei*

INTRODUCTION

The world is charged with the grandeur of God.
It will flame out, like shining from shook foil;
It gathers to a greatness, like the ooze of oil
Crushed.[1]

Gerard Manley Hopkins's extraordinary sonnet manages to pack into fourteen lines almost the whole of what I now want to say as I draw the strands of my argument together. The poem not only articulates the theology of creation and new creation, the latter winning the victory over the desolation of the former; it *embodies* that victory by its art, creating a fresh beauty that symbolizes the beauty it describes. That too will be part of the point.

Let me offer a bird's-eye view of where the argument is now going. I have described the social and cultural context of the modern quest for 'natural theology', and the modern study of Jesus and the Gospels, showing how this context has distorted both questions, not least by holding them apart from one another. In particular, the modern neo-Epicureanism has split heaven off from earth and has likewise separated past, present and future from one another. It has then understood what it means to be human within that split world and that fractured time, so that the 'modern' human now stands in a strange and disorienting isolation. Instead of all this, I have proposed historical arguments for a fresh understanding of Jesus and the Gospels in the Jewish world where the Temple stood for the *coming together* of heaven and earth, the Sabbath stood

252 // HISTORY AND ESCHATOLOGY

for the long-promised future *arriving already in the present*, and humans were seen as *Image-bearers*, as God-reflectors, standing at the threshold of heaven and earth, of past and future.

In that light, I argued in the previous chapter that the three main lines of modern 'natural theology' are shadowy, quite distorted forms of this triple understanding of the world, time and humanness. The cosmological argument knows that there is something to be said about the world and its implied Creator, but it tries to make its case (for inferring the Creator from the creation) without seeing how, in biblical theology, heaven and earth are designed for one another. The teleological argument recognises 'design' and looks back to a 'Designer', but without recognising the biblical insight that the ultimate design looks forward to the still-future world. The argument from the human moral sense—that our intuition of good and evil must come from somewhere—might be more promising, but only, I have insisted, when it is replaced with the richer and more multi-layered category of *vocation*. In short, all three traditional arguments are dead ends. I then went on to suggest that our vocational senses—to do justice, to love beauty, to seek freedom and so on—all appear to fail, to let us down, but that their very failure points to the broken figure on the cross (whose depiction can therefore still speak powerfully even to those who know nothing of Easter), who in the light of Easter is revealed as the wounded God of the Gospels. In that light, they invite us to start with the 'natural' world of failed human aspirations and see, in the cross—the 'natural' manner in which Jesus was killed!—the moment that makes sense of all the other moments, the ultimate broken signpost to which all the others were pointing. Of course, within the framework of the Enlightenment's Epicureanism such an insight could only be seen as a rather overdrawn coincidence, irrelevant for any ultimate issues. But that is precisely to beg the question: to treat as the absolute and 'given' frame of reference for the investigation something which itself ought to be on the table for critical discussion.

Neither in method nor in results, then, does this proposal follow the footsteps of an older 'natural theology'. When that question was raised, not least by Lord Gifford himself, the context of the times (sketched briefly in our opening chapters) introduced distortions. Even if we can't help introducing new ones ourselves—Heisenberg's principle of uncertainty works in theology and philosophy as well as physics!—we ought still to try to address the ones we see. I have argued throughout that part of our problem, in our contemporary Epicurean atmosphere, is to have banished from our agenda the one thing which makes us truly human and grounds all true knowing, namely love itself. Correcting this will necessarily result in a deeper and richer 'natural theology', which must involve praxis. If we renounce Platonic escapism (a favourite nineteenth-century strategy for dealing with the Epicurean challenge), we must embrace *mission* at every level.

The fact that this is not how 'natural theology' has usually been done does not trouble me. I take that phrase in the wider, new-creational sense, not simply of the experiments which have been made under that title in the last two hundred years but of the challenge of the larger implied question itself: are there ways in which we can look at the 'natural' world, the 'real' world—including the 'real' world of history and human life—and see there the plausibility of faith, faith in the God who in the New Testament is revealed as the father of Jesus? I have been arguing towards the conclusion that the answer to this question is Yes. I will now attempt to bring out this positive response in further fresh ways.

I will do so, particularly, by filling in the picture from the previous chapter, in which the seven 'broken signposts' all point to the cross—even though that pointing is only discerned for what it is in the light of Easter. I will integrate that discussion with the historical and eschatological vision I sketched in chapters 4, 5 and 6, rooted in the clarifications of historical method in chapter 3 as then further explored in chapter 6. This will enable us at last to move from the natural order, in the sense of real history in the real world, grasped with a critically realist epistemology, to address the puzzles laid out in the first two chapters, puzzles we find within the real world of 'natural' history.

By and large—these generalities are always subject to qualification, but they are important none the less—the Western churches in the nineteenth century had colluded with the Enlightenment agenda, backing off from engagement with the world of politics, economics and empire. This resulted in a shrinking of vocation, away from the biblical vision and towards a Platonic eschatology and spirituality. I think that was one of the reasons why the question of 'natural theology' became prominent just then, which may well be why Lord Gifford decided on that as the topic for his endowment. Faced with a new, hard-nosed and largely Epicurean world, which ruled out any appeal to 'special revelation', what could now be said? The task of 'natural theology' might then be conceived as the attempt to speak about God outside the private world of the church. But the church's world should never have been 'private' in that sense. The kingdom of God is not *from* this world, but it is emphatically *for* this world.[2] What the church *says to* the world is one part of what the church *does within* the world. Rational argument about God and God's world (the kind of thing for which I was arguing in chapter 3, where responsibly studied history can 'defeat the defeaters' and so on) is one important facet of a larger whole, and isolating it under the imperative of an artificially truncated question—which is what, I think, some 'natural theology' has effectively done—does little good to anyone. The biblically rooted mission of the church, in other words, is necessarily a larger and more many-sided task than was often envisaged in the nineteenth century, including both reasoned argument and practical work. Part of my point in this final chapter is to recover those biblical roots and to re-establish that multi-layered public discourse.

What counts for the whole argument—the whole biblically based, theologically oriented argument—is *new creation*. Not sceptical historiography, not existentialised eschatology, but a new creation, a rescued, renewed and transformed creation in which the first creation, the 'natural' world, is not cancelled out, as though by (in the modern sense!) a 'supernatural' irruption or invasion, but rather rescued, put right and transformed. The point is precisely that, as well as the discontinuity implied by all those adjectives, there is also substantial and vital continuity. Whatever the Creator will do in the end, this will not cancel (so to speak) the first article of the Creed. The new creation will reveal, fully and finally, that he always was, is and will be 'maker of heaven and earth'. And with that continuity, ultimately to be established in the final consummation, comes the possibility, and now indeed the promise, of a new kind of 'natural theology'.[3]

This new creation, displayed in both continuity and discontinuity with what went before, is rooted in, and modelled upon, the resurrection of Jesus himself. That is the paradigm for all eschatological thinking. This extraordinary event makes the sense it makes, including the disruptive sense, within the ancient Israelite and early Jewish worldview. In some varieties of this worldview, as sketched in the fifth chapter, the cosmos and Temple were seen as mutually interpretative, with heaven and earth overlapping and interlocking. Sabbath and eschaton were likewise seen to be mutually interpretative, so that the future was seen as coming forward into the present with genuine foretastes of the promised goal. Why (one might ask) should we give house-room to such strange ideas? Here, to say it again, there is no neutral ground, no still epistemological point within the whirling hypotheses. We must dismiss the easy criticism that such worldviews are 'ancient' and therefore now redundant in our 'modern' world. As we saw in the first chapter, what thinks of itself as 'modern' in that sense is basically the addition of some scientific footnotes to a well-known, and inherently problematic, ancient worldview. Epicureanism (within, to be sure, a world in which many were exploring different combinations of philosophies) has had the field largely to itself, risking a situation in which the rich, integrated sense of an epistemology of love could be reduced to the arid inductions of a left-brain rationalism or the fluffy deductions of a right-brain romanticism. It is time for the debate to move into more holistic and fruitful modes.

From the perspective of new creation, already launched in Jesus and awaiting its ultimate future, we can look back in the power and fresh understanding of the spirit and see, in reflex questioning, how and why certain aspects of the present world do in fact point forward to that future. This conversation about the relationship between present and future, I suggest, is a more biblically grounded and hence (we may hope) more theologically fruitful way of approaching 'natural theology' than stripping out the eschatology (or distorting or demythologizing it as has been done over the last two centuries) and turning it into a vertical axis. Whenever the conversation is trapped within the 'vertical' debates between 'nature' and 'grace', one is forced to operate on the assumption that Jesus' resurrection—along with the eschatological ontology and epistemology that it brings to birth—simply has no role to play in these discussions. Of course, if one were forced to operate in such an eschatologically deficient framework, we would have to conclude that any attempts to work our way up from 'nature' to 'grace' in order to prove God's existence would constitute an epistemological version of Pelagianism. But if instead we employ the eschatological framework we have outlined in the previous chapters, then a whole new world—literally!—opens up for the questions surrounding 'natural theology'.

After all, we do not control our future any more than the disciples, disappointed beyond belief after Jesus' crucifixion, 'controlled' his resurrection. We can as little infer the incarnation from the 'natural' state of Mary's virginal womb as we can infer the resurrection from the 'natural' state of Jesus' dead corpse in the tomb. Incarnation and resurrection are gifts of grace; but, as with other gifts of grace, they are to be perceived and received precisely as gifts of love and with that to be recognised as possessing genuine continuity with what went before. Once again 'love' becomes the appropriate mode of knowing. It is neither to be mocked by rationalism nor subverted by romanticism. It must hold its nerve and, in parallel with the historical task of reaching out to the key events of the past within the natural world (the 'love' element in 'critical realism'), must reach out also into the future in hope and trust.

The question of natural theology is thus realigned, poised between history and eschatology—with what I have called 'vocation' as part of that poise, that balance. The spirit-led mission of the church includes the task of always being ready 'to make a reply to anyone who asks you to explain the hope that is in you' (1 Peter 3.15). But the wider context of that command is not that of an isolated rationalism. It is that of the whole life of the church in the midst of a potentially hostile world. And, in First Peter (the letter from which we just quoted), the life of the church is seen in terms of a new Temple: 'Like living stones yourselves, you are being built up into a spiritual house' (1 Peter 2.5).

This points us back, for the main theme of this final chapter, to the notion of the cosmic Temple we studied in chapter 5.

FULL OF GOD'S GLORY: THE PROMISE
OF THE COSMIC TEMPLE

How then might a Second Temple Jewish worldview re-contextualise our question?[4] To summarize the point: creation itself was seen as a vast Temple, a heaven-and-earth structure in which God would dwell and in which humans would reflect his image. The Tabernacle in Exodus and the Temple in 1 Kings and 2 Chronicles were built as pointers to the larger heaven-and-earth cosmic reality and, for those who knew Israel's God and his purposes for the world, as foretastes of its future realisation. They were signposts to new creation, confirmed as such when they were refashioned around Jesus' resurrection. When the Babylonians destroyed the Temple, and when the prophets declared that it would be rebuilt, this promise resonated with new creation. Not only would there be a divine House in Jerusalem to which the divine presence would return, but there would be an entire new creation in which Israel's God, the creator, would come to dwell and 'rest' for ever. Thus, though there is sometimes in Israel's scriptures an occasional suggestion that creation is already full of the divine presence (Isaiah 6.3; Jeremiah 23.24),[5] what is promised now is a new kind of filling, a saturation or soaking with divine presence, glory and knowledge, 'as the waters cover the sea' (Isaiah 11.9; Habakkuk 2.14). How do the waters cover the sea? The waters *are* the sea.

This can be given as an assurance in the midst of dire circumstances, as in the rebellion in Numbers 14, at which we glanced already in chapter 5. In this story, it looks for a moment as though the divine presence will not go personally with the people to the promised land. No, says God to Moses, judgment will fall on the rebels, but the divine purpose will stand:

> Then YHWH said, 'I do forgive, just as you have asked; nevertheless,—as I live, *and as all the earth shall be filled with the glory of* YHWH—none of the people who have seen my glory . . . and yet have tested me these ten times . . . shall see the land. (Numbers 14.20–23)

The point seems to be that the glorious divine presence, currently filling the wilderness Tabernacle, fully intends to dwell in the land of promise which the faithless people are spurning—but that this dwelling will itself be simply a foretaste of the Creator's ultimate intention, which is to fill all the earth, not just the 'promised land'. The people are turning away from what is after all only the first phase of the divine intention. But that intention will be carried out with or without their co-operation.

But the promise can also be made in happier circumstances. In one of the most majestic of the royal Psalms, the psalmist prays for the king to bring God's justice to the poor and God's help to those in most need—seeing the king, in other words, as image-bearer, reflecting God's love and care for his world.[6] When this is the case, then God will be praised, and his glory will fill the earth:

> Blessed be YHWH, the God of Israel,
> Who alone does wondrous things;
> Blessed be his glorious name for ever;
> May his glory fill the whole earth.
> Amen and amen. (Psalm 72.18–19)

Solomon builds the Temple which is then filled with divine glory, but the coming king of Psalm 72 will do justice and mercy for the poor, the widow and the helpless, so that the divine glory may fill *the whole earth*. It is not, of course, exactly clear what this will mean; nor is it clear that when the early Christians envisaged the renewal of all creation (as in Romans 8, for instance) they were thinking of exactly the same thing as these earlier texts were envisaging. But at least we must say that in all such passages the present mystery of divine hiddenness in creation, and the obvious pains, disasters and death itself within the world as it presently is, will finally be dealt with. That, it seems, is how the implicit promise of Genesis 1 is to be fulfilled. This joins up, as I argued before, with the idea of the regular Sabbaths, and particularly the great festival and the multiple Sabbath of Jubilee, as advance foretastes of the final promised state. Sabbath, we remember, is to time what Temple is to place. The Temple-promise and the Sabbath-promise, as we saw earlier, converge at the notion of 'rest'. God will be at home in his creation; his people, reflecting his image, will be at home with him. This is the promise of new creation, *in which the promises inherent in the original creation will be realised.*[7]

What might this biblical vision of 'new creation' have to say to the various projects covered by the broad category of 'natural theology'? It shakes things up, for a start. The risk with some attempts at 'natural theology' is to settle too readily for a starting-point within a supposedly static world and to aim too readily for a theology which, if not actually Deist, is leaning that way. Start with the world as a machine, and you will end with God as a celestial Chief Engineer, whose being and operations can be deduced from the way the world currently is. Such a project would then be in the service, we may suppose, of convincing sceptics so that they, coming to faith, could share the hope of 'going to heaven when they die'—the Platonic escape-hatch out of the otherwise closed this-worldly continuum. Such a 'natural theology' might well collapse back into pantheism or panentheism, with an epistemology that would be unable to glimpse the truth within the present world, let alone the further truth to which, precisely at its points of brokenness, the present world points forward (though that forward glimpse is only validated and explained in the light of Easter). If you agree too readily with Hopkins that 'the world is charged with the grandeur of God', you may find you can get rid of a transcendent God and still enjoy the grandeur . . . as long as you don't notice what comes next. One of the problems with pantheism and panentheism is that they cannot really admit, let alone deal with, the problem of evil. Such schemes want the first three lines of Hopkins's poem without the next four: the fact that

> Generations have trod, have trod, have trod,
> And all is seared with trade; bleared, smeared with toil,
> And wears man's smudge and shares man's smell; the soil
> Is bare now, nor can foot feel, being shod.

You have to overlook that if you want to say that the world and God are the same thing or at least that everything is 'in God', panentheism. The alternatives are bleak. Once you eliminate the biblical eschatology of new creation, you are left with an escapist 'eschatology' to be activated in the present by existentialism (Bultmann), or with the depressing theory that we live in the best of all possible worlds (Leibniz), or with a shoulder-shrugging Epicureanism, or with Sartrian despair.

My sense, in fact, is that if a 'natural theology' is seeking to find the building blocks for a doctrine of God from within the present creation, then—in terms of the model I am outlining—such an attempt must be seen as trying to have the full eschaton in advance. It is attempting to leap forwards to the final moment when God will be 'all in all', but without going by the cruciform route the New Testament takes to get there. Cognate with this problem is the possibility of a 'natural theology' trying to discern the being and activity of God by rational inquiry alone, screening out once more the epistemology of love which, as I have insisted all along, belongs at the heart of true knowledge. Thus not only will rational, left-brain knowledge not be able to grasp what is already true or to see the significance of the 'broken signposts' we explored in the previous chapter. It will also, certainly, be unable to glimpse the eschatological promise of new creation.

In response to this, a biblically and eschatologically informed natural theology must proceed, I suggest, by way of exploration of new creation, and of the light it sheds back on creation itself. The promises of the Temple-like 'filling' of creation with the divine presence enable us to postulate an appropriate answer to the old question, as to why a good God would make a world that is other than himself. The answer seems to be that he intends to dwell in it as a house—to fill it to overflowing with his presence and his glory. This will not mean obliterating it, as Schweitzer and others imagined, with a 'supernatural' takeover that would leave no room for the original 'natural' world. Nor will it mean any diminishing of creation's creatureliness and peculiar identity and meaning. Rather, God's intention is to enhance and celebrate it. It is not only human beings who might say to God, 'You have made us for yourself'. This is part of what is meant by God's *love*: the delighted creation and celebration of creatures other than himself yet made 'for himself'. And that 'for himself' has to do with the glad, non-obliterating union with that which is other than himself. The union thus envisaged is one in which every creature, and especially every image-bearing creature, will be more truly and uniquely and gladly itself, and the Creator will delight in its being so. And this love then calls forth an answering 'love', the larger category of which 'knowledge' is a key component.

So how will the creator fill his creation with his own presence? One answer, hinted at already in Genesis 1, is 'with his wind or his spirit'. This leads directly to the proposition that the God of creation is already to be known as the God who sends the spirit into the world; and this is at once complemented by the creation of humans in the divine image, a sign that the God of creation is already to be known as the God who intends to work in his world *through obedient humanity*. This is where the promise of new creation and the vocation of the king come together, as we already saw in Psalm 72. And this is part of the root of the church's vocation to mission, as the 'royal priesthood' taking forward the original creational mandate as included within, albeit transcended and transfigured by, the fresh, transformed mandate of new creation.

With this, we have an alternative to the famous proposal of Jürgen Moltmann, that we should adopt the Rabbinic theory of *zimsum*, in which God retreats into himself so that there may be a space in the cosmos for a creation which is other than himself.[8] This, it seems to me, is the wrong way round. Much better to suggest that, out of sheer exuberant creative love, God creates a world that is other than himself in order eventually to be 'all in all', allowing creation still to be itself while becoming, through being filled with his glorious presence, more than it could ever be by itself. It may be that Moltmann's way of putting it and mine are in the end compatible. Certainly we converge in terms of the ultimate goal. But though there is something attractive about the humility of God in retreating to make space, it seems to me that the glad out-flowing of creativity in the great creation-texts from Genesis through Psalms 103 and 104 all the way to Colossians 1 and Revelation 4 might emerge more clearly by putting it as I have.

The key Genesis-based roles of the spirit and the image-bearing human are of course central in the New Testament. Jesus is 'the image of the invisi-ble God' (Colossians 1.15). The spirit is the *arrabōn*, the down-payment, of the 'inheritance', which is not simply our own future resurrection bodies but 'the inheritance' as a whole, the entire renewed cosmic order of Romans 8.[9]

Once we recognise the centrality of the Temple/cosmos nexus for early Jewish and Christian thought, several passages offer themselves for particular consideration. High on the list is Paul's discussion of apostolic ministry in 2 Corinthians 2–6, particularly in chapters 3 and 4. Paul is rebutting criticisms of his apostolic style. To do so he sketches the line from new covenant to new creation, and locates within the story of Moses and the Tabernacle the relationship he has with the cantankerous Corinthian church. This is hardly a flattering comparison. If Paul is parallel with Moses, his hearers are compared with the Israelites who had made the golden calf. Nevertheless, Paul's argu-ment hinges on the difference between his hearers and those of Moses. Moses' hearers were hard-hearted; Paul's, he insists have been transformed by the spirit, so that all of us with unveiled face—unlike Moses—can now gaze at the glory of God. *The church is thus the pilot project for new creation: ei tis en Christō, kainē ktisis,* he says in the later summary: literally, 'If anyone in Messiah—new creation!' (2 Corinthians 5.17).[10] What the spirit now does within Jesus' follow-ers will be done for the whole creation. The presence of the spirit within Jesus' people is the sign and guarantee of the same renewing presence within the whole of creation. Exactly as in the Temple/cosmos picture we have invoked, in 2 Corinthians 4 Paul locates the sharply focused point of chapter 3 on the cosmic map with his reference to Genesis 1. It is the God who said 'let light shine out of darkness' who has now shone in our hearts to give the light of the knowledge of the glory of God in the face of Jesus the Messiah (2 Corinthians 4.6). And that key passage is set precisely within the mystery of Paul's apostolic apologia, his explanation of why he does what he does and how the spirit works through him. 'We speak the truth openly', says Paul, 'and recommend ourselves to everybody's conscience in the presence of God' (2 Corinthians 4.2). Unbelief, then, is not a matter of bad arguments on the part of the apologists, but the result of a kind of spiritual blindness. It is, however, a blindness that can be overcome when, through the announcement of the gospel, people discern the dawning of the new day and find that it makes sense of everything else. That is where the step-by-step argument and explanation come in: not to use rationalism as a means of bludgeoning people into faith, but to clarify and explain how the larger picture fits together and makes sense.

The closer you get to that vision, the more Paul emphasises suffering. The dark powers, though defeated on the cross, will not give up without a struggle. But that, too, is part of the point. The 'signs of an apostle' are the cruciform life which bears witness to the cross itself.[11] The broken signposts are still, in that sense, telling the truth.[12]

THE WAITING CHALICE

Here I want to introduce the *Leitmotif* for this chapter: the waiting chalice. Supposing you had no knowledge of the Christian tradition or its characteristic symbolic actions. Supposing you then, in a museum or antique shop, came upon a beautiful silver chalice, elegant yet powerful in form, delicately etched with the motifs of the cross, the tree of life, and perhaps of Passover, or the Last Supper, or the heavenly messianic banquet, or some combination of these. You would know it was important, and full of meaning. People don't make beautiful things like that, with carefully chosen decorations, just on a whim. Someone took thought and care over it. Someone paid a lot of money for it. And you might know enough comparative anthropology to know that in many societies a large and important vessel like that might be used for some ceremony, some binding together of a family or clan. There would be enough clues to point you in the right direction.

The question raised by the very existence of such an object is then not unlike the question raised in the previous chapter by the seven 'broken signposts' (justice, beauty and the rest). (Like all analogies, the parallel is not exact, but the point should be clear.) They are important, but by themselves they do not suggest answers to the questions they raise that might enable one to discern fully what it is they point to or why. They might actually lead to frustration or even despair. But when we look back at them in the light of Jesus' crucifixion, we might 'get it'—and when we looked back at them, and at the crucifixion, in the light of Easter, we would 'get it' in a whole new way. There is a multi-layered fit. The same answer applies here too: when we hear the story of Jesus' crucifixion—and in particular when we find that in giving his disciples the clue to what his death would mean he didn't give them a theory, he gave them a new kind of Passover-meal focused on bread and wine—then we discover, looking back on those events in the light of the resurrection, that the things the beautiful chalice had been saying were true, were genuine pointers to a unique event, and to a unique ritual which recalled that event.

For a follower of Jesus, then, the empty chalice has a complex beauty. It is beautiful in itself; a complete outsider might recognise that and respect it. But for a Jesus-follower it is many times more beautiful *because we know what it is to be filled with, and why*. The wine which will fill it and be shared among Jesus' followers will convey his death, and the personal meaning of that death, to the worshippers. As they drink it, they will say, with Paul, 'The Son of God loved me and gave himself for me'. (This is so whatever sort of Eucharistic theology you employ, though as we shall see my argument will point towards one particular type.) This action, and this meaning, do not detract in any way from the beauty the chalice had when empty on the altar, or indeed when on display in a museum or even when wrapped up in the vestry safe. Those who know the ultimate intention will appreciate that beauty all the more.

All this is metonymy as well as metaphor. It is both an analogy for the point I want to make and a quintessential part of the point itself. As it stands, the present creation has a power and beauty, a strangely evocative quality. 'The world is charged with the grandeur of God', like the empty chalice inviting a measure of awe and respect even from the outsider. The presence of horror and suffering and apparent futility in the world, however—the brokenness of the signposts, in my previous illustration—has led some, including sadly some Christians, to suppose that the beauty and power is a mere illusion or distraction. 'Generations have trod, have trod, have trod:' we are in a world full of idols and must renounce the seductive power and beauty. We must escape. Plato stands ready to help us, to explain that the beauty and power of the present space-time world were the play of shadows cast by a different light, and to show us the way to reach their source. Much Western Christianity has gone that route without questioning. But the biblical eschatology of new creation which I have been expounding will resist that tempting option. The outpoured blood is the sign that the idols have been defeated, that the suffering of the present time is not worth comparing to the glory that is to be revealed, and that creation itself is to be set free from its slavery to decay to enjoy the freedom that comes when God's children are glorified. Creation itself is to be filled with the divine glory. That is why it is beautiful; that is why it is powerful; that is why, as it stands, it is puzzling and incomplete. The rejection of 'natural theology' in some quarters—thinking obviously of Barth in the 1930s—is a reaction against those who, seeing the beauty of the chalice, want to use it, in pagan style, as a means to acquire wealth, power or privilege. But the answer is not to throw away the chalice but to celebrate the Eucharist. The wine itself joins heaven and earth, denying Plato his easy victory.

We should perhaps say more about the kind of 'filling' of creation that the New Testament envisages. I have mentioned Romans 8, and that passage remains at the heart of this vision. It is no surprise that Bultmann underestimated the importance of the whole-creation horizon of Paul's thought (as his student Käsemann rightly pointed out) and that he found the supposedly 'apocalyptic' passage in Romans 8 so impenetrable. In that passage Paul envisages God doing for the whole cosmos at the last what he did for Jesus at Easter. The 'Temple'-overtones in the passage are powerful: Paul's language about the 'indwelling' spirit echoes the idea of YHWH's dwelling in the Temple, and the promise of resurrection is then to be understood as the promise of the ultimate rebuilt Temple. But the 'inheritance' motif, too, carries Temple-overtones, since the Temple was the focal point of the promised land, the inheritance gained after the divine victory over the sea-monster.[13] At the heart of the passage Paul speaks of prayer, the prayer of unknowing, inspired by the spirit and understood by the Father, constituting those who pray as the younger siblings of the Firstborn Son through their sharing of his suffering and glory. They are thereby 'conformed to his image', enabled to be the genuine human beings at the heart of the cosmic Temple, reflecting the creator's 'glory', as in Psalm 8, in their stewardship of creation, and summing up the priestly intercession of all creation through the High Priest himself, Jesus (Romans 8.18–30, 34).[14] Cosmology, eschatology, and image-bearing anthropology; heaven and earth together formed in the pattern of the crucified Messiah; glory in the midst of suffering: no wonder Romans 8 is so powerful. And so relevant to the argument of this book.

A similar result—the new creation as the new Temple, with renewed humans playing their part in it—is offered in Revelation 21 and 22. The echoes of Genesis 1 and 2 are obvious. It has not always been so obvious that the vision of the New Jerusalem is conceived in terms of an enormous Holy Place, the city being a giant cube which mirrors, on a vast scale, the construction of the inner sanctum in the tabernacle or Temple.[15] The 'new heavens and new earth' are thus the new Temple itself, and the city is its innermost shrine, its Holy of Holies. That, of course, is why there is no Temple in the city (just as there is no Sabbath in the new world, and indeed no night either); the whole new creation is the Temple, and the city *is* the inmost sanctum. The divine presence ('God and the Lamb') is there, and in this new creation that presence replaces even the need for sun and moon, reflecting perhaps the otherwise strange point in Genesis 1 that 'light' itself is created before the two 'great lights'. This is the final realisation of the original creative purpose. What went wrong with the original creation has been put right; what was preliminary and pointing forward in the original creation has now reached its goal. (Discerning which of those is which is itself part of the challenge.) The redeemed human beings are now at last enabled to be what they were made to be: the true image-bearers, the 'royal priesthood' (Revelation 20.6).[16]

We see the same picture in John's Gospel, particularly granted the overtones of Genesis and Exodus in the Prologue itself and the way the Temple-imagery of incarnation in that passage is then developed through the Gospel's pneumatology. 'The word became flesh and *tabernacled* in our midst, and we gazed upon his glory': this imagery from Exodus 40, though with the whole people (not just the High Priest) now able to gaze upon the glory, is the proper fulfilment of the echoes of Genesis 1 planted at the very start.[17] Heaven and earth come together throughout the narrative, with Jesus' own body being explicitly designated as the new Temple, the one that will be destroyed and raised up (John 2.21). The contextualising of this narrative by the Prologue with its cosmic reach prevents any suggestion (as in Bultmann's 'gnostic' interpretation) that what we are being offered is a private sphere, away from the world. This is the story of how the whole creation is redeemed, and hence of how everything within that creation that had pointed forward in whatever broken manner was in fact reaffirmed when refashioned around the resurrection. That is part of the point of John's Easter story, framed in a garden but with the outflowing water of life expressed through the commissioning of the disciples by the spirit. This in turn echoes the promise in John 7.38, that 'rivers of living water' would flow out of the believers' hearts.[18] The echoes of the Prologue in John 20 indicate strongly that the whole gospel is about creation and new creation, with that new creation the fulfilment, not the abolition, of the old, once the 'ruler of this world' has been 'cast out' (John 12.31).[19]

That, in fact, gives us a clue as to what may be going on in some of the normal debates about 'natural theology'. The problem with trying to start with this present world and argue up to God is that the present world still reflects, from the Johannine point of view, the fact that it has been taken over by 'the ruler of this world'. (Here there is of course a tension, since in the Gospel Jesus appears to claim that the ruler will be cast out' through his death, but in the First Epistle we are firmly told that 'the whole world is under the power of the evil one' [1 John 5.19]. This appears to be more 'now-and-not-yet'.) The world has then been shunned as a possible source: nothing good can come from there.

> All is seared with trade; bleared, smeared with toil;
> And wears man's smudge and shares man's smell; the soil
> Is bare now, nor can foot feel, being shod.

But that is not John's last word, just as it is not how Hopkins's poem ends. Nor could it be Paul's last word, though some might suppose that he would want to denounce the present world and leave it at that, believing only in a fresh revelation coming from somewhere else. There is a grain of truth in that, but it is mainly wrong. In the very passage where Paul most obviously reflects and draws on what might be called 'apocalyptic' imagery (1 Corinthians 15) we see precisely the vision of Psalm 72 writ large. The rule of the Messiah, already inaugurated through Jesus' death and resurrection, has launched the new creation in which he is the image-bearing new Adam, fulfilling the Psalms which speak of the king and the Image and fulfilling, too, the Danielic picture of the exaltation of the 'son of man' over the monsters.[20] In a passage we looked at earlier, 1 Corinthians 15.20–28, the different elements of the whole picture come rushing together, and, instead of a supposed 'apocalyptic' *abolition* of the world, we have the genuinely 'apocalyptic' *fulfilling* of it—literally, a filling full, completing the Genesis project, celebrating the Davidic purpose and echoing the Isaianic hope:

> The Messiah rises as the first fruits; then those who belong to the Messiah will rise at the time of his royal arrival. Then comes the end, the goal, when he hands over the kingly rule to God the father, when he has destroyed all rule and all authority and power. He has to go on ruling, you see, until 'he has put all his enemies under his feet'. Death is the last enemy to be destroyed, because 'he has put all things in order under his feet'. But when it says that everything is put in order under him, it's obvious that this doesn't include the one who put everything in order under him. No: when everything is put in order under him, then the son himself will be placed in proper order under the one who placed everything in order under him, *so that God may be all in all*. (1 Corinthians 15.23–28)

The last couple of sentences have often drawn commentators' attention away from the final line (here italicised), since later discussions of Christology were much exercised with the question both of the subordination of the son and of the extent of his reign. But this means that, not for the first time, anxiety about later dogmatic puzzles, trying to tidy up the supposedly loose phraseology of the New Testament, has distracted theologians from seeing the real point of the passage.[21] The point is that God, the one God, will be 'all in all'—and will arrive at that goal, as we would expect from Genesis 1, through the work of the Image-bearer, the true Adam, the ultimate King who comes to the help of the poor and needy. Heaven and earth will be one; the future will have arrived at last; the True Human, already enthroned, will have completed his task.

What Paul offers us, in fact, is a vision which seems not to have a name, but really deserves one. Instead of *panentheism*, the idea that everything is 'in God', we might propose *the-en-panism*, the view of God being 'all in all'.

Panentheism, like its tired old cousin pantheism itself, has glimpsed a truth but has seen it the wrong way round and tried to arrive at it by a shortcut, without going the only possible route. Seeing the danger of various forms of dualism, panentheism has insisted on putting God and the world together, with 'God' as a kind of general receptacle 'into' which all else is fitted. What's more, it affirms this as being true *already, in the present time*. Paul's vision is altogether subtler. It requires an implicit Trinitarian theology (that is, a theological understanding for which the later doctrines provide a conceptual analysis), since it appears from various passages (though admittedly not this one) that the mode of union of God and the world will be that of the divine spirit indwelling, infusing and irrigating the cosmos. And it requires an eschatological perspective: this 'filling' is not yet a reality, but it is assured by the Messiah's victory over the powers of evil and by the sovereign rule in which that victory is being implemented. We are therefore speaking of an *eschatological* the-en-panism, a final God-in-all moment and lasting reality. In terms of our *Leitmotif*, this will amount to the ultimate filling of the chalice with the rich wine of divine love, the powerful messianic love which has already resulted in his inaugurated rule and which will go on loving and ruling until all enemies, including death itself, are put under his feet. Pantheism and panentheism offer, from a Christian perspective, an over-realised eschatology which does indeed partially reflect the creator's eventual intention. This is why they are often popular with those who are escaping from types of Christian dualism. But they cannot offer a meaningful way of acknowledging the ongoing reality of evil, perhaps because, whether consciously or not, they want to avoid the drastic solution to that problem, in other words, the cross. That is in fact the only route to the promised glorious goal. Interestingly, they tend as well not to highlight love, whether God's love for us or ours for God.[22]

It is hard to say all these things at once, to put into the same sentence or even paragraph the visions of creation renewed in Romans 8, of the new city in Revelation 21, of the spring garden and the outpoured spirit in John 20, and of the final victory and ultimate 'filling' in 1 Corinthians 15. But it is hard to doubt that in these ways the early Christians were consciously retrieving, in the light of Jesus and the spirit, the biblical theology of cosmos and Temple I have sketched earlier. (They were also retrieving the theme of Sabbath and eschaton; that is perhaps most obvious in John but visible elsewhere too.) And they were doing so with a conscious and biblically rooted vision of Jesus as the truly human one, the true Image, and of his followers, indwelt by the spirit, as themselves 'renewed in knowledge according to the image of the creator', a renewal characterized by love both as ethics and as epistemology (Colossians 3.10). At the heart of early Christian theology we find precisely the cosmological over-lap of heaven and earth, and the eschatological overlap of present and future, both of them focused on Jesus and the spirit and both of them offering a vision of the world and God, and of the relation between them, which enables us to open up the modern questions of 'natural theology' in a whole new way.

The picture is not, however, quite complete. As with my earlier illustration about the College receiving a spectacular gift and having to rebuild to accom-modate it, so the image of the 'waiting chalice' leaves something vital out of the picture. As we have set it out up to this point, the chalice itself remains unchanged throughout. But that is clearly untrue to the promised reality. The present creation is corruptible, subject to decay and death. The promise is that in the end, in the 'new heavens and new earth', death itself will be done away with, not in the spurious manner of the Platonist who escapes corruptible physicality into a world of pure non-physicality (that merely allows death to claim its victory over the created world of space, time and matter) but in a recreation of the material world so as to be itself immortal, incorruptible. That is very clear from Romans 8 (e.g. 8.21: freed from its slavery to decay). In Reve-lation 21.1 the 'old' which has passed away is best taken to be the corruptibility itself; the new world will not be a fresh creation from nothing, but the redemp-tive, transformative new creation made out of the present one. Once again, the resurrection of Jesus himself is the vital prototype: a renewed, immortal body, 'using up' the material of the previous one.

To take account of all this, the picture of the chalice needs to be made more complex. Without getting too fantastic and artificial, we might suggest that the original chalice had some serious defects which the outpoured wine would somehow rectify. It was not, perhaps, merely 'waiting'; it was damaged, and the inner properties of the wine would repair it. Or one could invent other features: perhaps the chalice turned out to be translucent, and the glow of the wine, visible through the sides of the bowl, would bring out curious details in the decoration that had previously been invisible. Or perhaps there were other ways in which repair, transformation and enhanced beauty might be effected. No matter: the point is made, that 'creation itself will be set free from its slav-ery to decay', through whatever image we like to glimpse that promise and hope. And my overall argument remains: that the chalice itself, the image for the entire present creation, genuinely and truly points forward to the ultimate 'filling' for which it was made, and thus also to the Creator whose purpose this was. This image, as will readily be seen, needs a Trinitarian theology and a typically early Christian eschatology to make it 'work'. The question which the discovered chalice poses to the puzzled finder can only ultimately be answered in terms of the Creator himself filling, transforming, repairing and enhancing it with his own spirit. This simply strengthens the point.

NATURAL THEOLOGY AND THE *MISSIO DEI*

This leads us at last to some detailed proposals for taking the argument, and the project, forwards. There would be many possible vistas to explore from the vantage-point we have reached; but I will simply suggest five concrete areas in which the argument, and the project, might be taken further.

The first is the whole notion of the Mission of God, the *missio Dei*, itself. The spirit calls and equips the church to a mission which is aimed at the creator's purpose: to fill his world with his glory, to rest and reign within his proper home. This original purpose, diverted though not thwarted by human idolatry and sin, was redirected into the Abrahamic mission to rescue God's human creatures so that, through them, the creational purpose might be accomplished. (Even saying it like this makes one realise just how distorted most modern Western soteriology and eschatology has become. Instead of a [Platonic] mission aimed at enabling saved souls to leave the earth and go to be at home in heaven with God, what the Bible offers is a mission aimed at transforming rebel idolaters into restored image-bearers through whom God will find his permanent abode among humans, in the 'new heavens and new earth'.[23])

This means that the *missio Dei* is itself part of the overall task of 'natural theology', just as a refreshed and Jesus-focused version of 'natural theology' can be part of the church's mission. To reduce 'natural theology' to rationalistic propositions is, to repeat an earlier metaphor, to assume that a can of petrol will get you to your destination without involving a car. The new-creational task of bringing healing and justice to the world, including not least the holding to account of the powers of the world, is one of the church's powerful ways of saying *that the present creation matters and so it's worth putting it right*, rather than saying, as the church has often done, that the present creation doesn't matter so that we can back off and leave the task of putting it right to others.[24] This is part of the significance of Jesus' healings in the Gospels, not least those that happen on Sabbaths: this is what it looks like, these actions are saying, when the Great Sabbath arrives, the ultimate Jubilee, the release of captives and the forgiveness of debt. Every healing is a *reaffirmation* of the goodness of the currently sick body, just as the resurrection itself is the reaffirmation of the goodness of the original creation. Every time there is a fresh work of justice or liberation, a fresh telling of truth or wise exercise of power, a new glimpse of beauty, experience of spirituality or embrace of love—every time the resurrection reveals the broken signposts to have been telling the truth after all, the quest of natural theology is affirmed. Every time the chalice is filled afresh with the sacramental wine, we see again why it was made so beautifully. We realise both why we found it evocative before and why it was nevertheless incomplete (and, in our artificially developed illustration, damaged) as it stood. Once again, if all you had was the chalice, you couldn't deduce the Eucharist from it (though you might guess, in bare outline, at something like it). Once you know the Eucharist, you see that the chalice was pointing in the right direction all along.

Hand in hand with the tasks of healing and justice, second, goes the artist's vocation. As we saw, aesthetics (itself a new invention) was split off from the mainstream of theological culture in the Enlightenment. Ever since then, Christian artists have laboured under the frustration that many of their fellow believers don't know why their life and work should matter. In church, as in many Western education systems, art and music have been turned into mere decoration, rather than being seen as actually part of an eschatologically informed 'natural theology' itself, a way of responding to the-world-the-way-it-is which can speak, as the broken signposts and the waiting chalice can speak, of the true intention of the Creator. (Here as elsewhere, of course, I do not intend any suggestion that 'the artist' occupies a kind of privileged position in the cosmos, with a direct access to truth which somehow bypasses the brokenness of the signposts, and of the cross itself.)

There are of course many aspects to this. Visual art differs from music, and both from drama or dance, and so on. But they have this in common, that in glimpsing simultaneously the beauty and the brokenness of the world the way it is, and in simultaneously drawing our attention to that combination and making something new out of it, something which has its own beauty and poignancy, the artists' works tell us that the world is indeed charged with the grandeur of God, even though the soil is now bare. It is hard, perhaps, for art to convey the full truth of the eventual hope, to offer the new kinds of beauty and power which will show the present beauty and power to be mere broken signposts. The Hallelujah Chorus has perhaps too much of the early eighteenth century about it, which may be why one might choose instead, as a true glimpse of the world to come, the hauntingly evocative 'I know that my redeemer liveth'. (Whether this has something to do with the difference between D Major and E Major I leave to the theoreticians.) But my point is that in art, which offers the chance to say several things at the same time in a way which ordinary prose finds almost impossible, one has the possibility not only to say, but to express and embody, the truth of Hopkins's poem, *both* the sudden flaming out of glory *and* the tragic disappointment of creation spoiled by 'man's smudge and smell'—*and* the resolution on the further side. Art, as itself a celebration of the created world, offers the chance to do all that, even as it also offers the standing temptation to idolatry.

Similar things can be said, I believe, in relation to my third example, the sciences. Here by contrast with most of my Gifford predecessors, I pretend to no expertise. Science, like art, offers rich prospects both for idolatry and for the kind of celebration of creation which can be taken up within a Christian eschatological perspective.

I have explained earlier why the popular assumptions which regularly emerge under the heading 'science and religion' are based on several interlocking mistakes. You see this at a popular level when someone mentions God in a newspaper article and is then howled down in online responses by people who insist, as though they have been mortally insulted, that modern science has disproved God and established a secular worldview for all time. That is still the widespread Western perception, fuelled of course by the follies of some believers who insist on defending indefensible positions and dying in the wrong last ditch.[25] But it seems to me, as an onlooker and occasional discussion partner, that, when we park the Epicurean assumptions of some scientists since the eighteenth century, we can recover the familiar vocation, happily acknowledged by most earlier scientists, to think God's thoughts after him.[26] This was not, indeed, to imply that one could infer something about God from what one could weigh or measure. It was, rather, to sense the grandeur of which Hopkins spoke: to admire both the flaming from the shook foil and the oozing of the crushed oil, and to see them as pointing beyond themselves.

In particular, as I have argued elsewhere, the use of creational imagery in Jesus' teaching—most obviously in the parables but visible in many other places—might indicate ways forward in some of the painful and often wrongly conceived disputes. If Jesus was correct to insist that the kingdom of God comes like a sower sowing seed, some of which goes to waste, some of which is snatched by birds, some of which is trampled underfoot, but some of which finds good soil and brings forth a great crop, ought we to be surprised if the now common view of cosmic origins is that of an enormous broadcast sowing of life potential, much of which appears to go to waste but some of which takes root and produces life as we know it?[27] There are many other insights to be gleaned by approaching the question in that light, in particular the realisation that the very form and subject-matter of those parables is itself testimony to Jesus' seeing the natural world as full of pointers to the truth of God and God's kingdom, albeit needing to be drawn out by the artistry of the parables themselves as well as by the powerful works of healing which made the same point.[28]

THE WAITING CHALICE // 271

In this light, and thinking through the way my argument so far has gone, I want to question somewhat the common idea of scripture and nature as 'two books'.[29] As a broad-brush Christian approach it will open up the subject in much better ways than any viewpoint which assumes a head-on clash. But in what sense are they 'books'? The danger with using that language is that we come to both expecting them simply to provide parallel information. But that view is too shrunken. It emerges from a world already divided into 'natural' and 'supernatural' in a way which the whole argument of the present book challenges at the core, and it addresses the resultant question within a quasi-rationalist framework. As I have argued, studying history, including the history of Jesus as witnessed by the New Testament, is itself part of the study of the 'natural world'. In any case, the world of creation is not simply a large pile of unsorted information. It presents itself to us, unless we systematically screen our eyes against such an idea, as a waiting chalice, beautiful and powerful yet hauntingly incomplete and perhaps even damaged. It asks questions, setting up signposts which then don't seem to lead anywhere, or at least not anywhere we can see without help. Thus, if creation is a 'book', it is not like a dictionary or a railway timetable. It is more like a great play or poem, or indeed the kind of music—I think of Sibelius's seventh symphony—which is exquisite but leaves us with a simultaneous sense of completion and incompletion, of a signpost reaching out still into the darkness, even while telling us that there, in the darkness, will be the truth which cannot now be spoken, played or even sung. Or perhaps creation is like Wittgenstein's *Tractatus*, with its haunting sabbatical moment at the seventh point: 'Wovon man nicht sprechen kann, darüber muss man schweigen' ('whereof one cannot speak, thereof must one keep silent').[30] Creation is perhaps a book like that—not the kind of book you simply 'look things up in'.[31] After all, the real danger of seeing Bible and 'nature' as 'two books' somehow in parallel is that it could simply increase the tendency, already strong in some quarters, for avoiding the historical task involved in any serious reading of the Bible itself.

As for the Bible itself: if it is a 'book', or even a collection of books, it too must not be regarded, as some rationalist thinkers have wanted to regard it, as the kind of book which is there simply for 'looking things up in'. There are, to be sure, plenty of things to find at that level, plenty of things to look up if that's what is needed at the moment. But to use the Bible in that way and no others would be like trying to understand classical music by listening only to Classic FM.[32] We need the bigger picture—the larger public world opened up at Easter, replete with its eschatological ontology and epistemology. The Hebrew Scriptures tell the story of hope, of creation and covenant and Sabbath and

Temple and promise and exile and hope renewed. The Christian scriptures, picking up that story, are the open-ended narrative of covenant renewed, creation restored, the Great Sabbath and the New Temple and the surprising but joyful reversal of exile, and, yes, the continuing hope for eventual completion. The idea of books you can look things up in is, after all, a stepping back from the epistemology of love. Love invites us not to look at all this from a distance, but to make the story our own, to live within it, to find our place between the 'but now' of 1 Corinthians 15.20 and the 'not yet' of 15.28.

Actually, once we have spelled this out we may nevertheless see the 'two books' converging at a higher level. After all, as millions have found, from atomic scientists to abstract artists, creation itself poses not just a question but a challenge: where do *you* belong in this story? What response will *you* make to the strange combination of glory and tragedy that we find in our world? Creation and scripture (not just 'nature' and 'some old historical texts') thus function as parallel 'books' of a different sort: the kind of books you read to force you to think differently about the world and your role in it. Each offers an implicit challenge, a possibility of vocation. These may converge. If and when they do, we are back with the broken signposts on the one hand and the waiting chalice on the other. Here, I think, is a way of looking at current debates between science and religion which might take us forward.

My fourth point, which deserves far more attention than we can allocate here, has to do with politics. The debates about natural theology, and about Jesus and the Gospels, have been radically shaped by a rich mixture of philosophy, culture and politics, from the French and American revolutions to the turbulent history of Germany, through two terrible wars and yet more horrific acts of genocide and terrorism. It isn't just that these have forced us to think about the great questions afresh, though they have done that. It is a two-way street. People's minds are formed into political will and ambition not least by the ideologies, theologies and philosophies they embrace or reject. I have written about all this elsewhere,[33] but I emphasize here the ongoing importance of Psalm 72, with its vision of the true king doing justice and mercy. This picture was, of course, invoked in England and elsewhere in previous centuries, so that would-be biblical exegesis and preaching was directly linked in to the social, cultural and political turbulence of the times. It was in reaction to this, indeed, that the Enlightenment sought for alternative ways forward, and those who in that new period wanted still to speak of God looked away from the Bible to the world of nature, generating subtly new approaches to 'natural theology' with which we are still living. Our present problems often reflect, more than we realise, the perceived problems of former centuries. If we are to recover a biblical political theology we must learn lessons from the past.

Part of the recovery of such a theology must be the retrieval of the church's central spirit-led vocation as set out in John 16: to 'convict the world of sin, righteousness and judgment'. *Part of natural theology is to affirm the good, and God-given, structures of the world, and to affirm them by support without collusion and critique without dualism.*[34] We all too easily mirror the facile assumptions, either that 'the powers' must be getting it all right or that they must be getting it all wrong. Think of Harnack in 1914 and Barth in 1918. Life is more complicated than that. The church needs to pray for wisdom and discernment to state clearly where the broken signposts are supposed to lead and to speak fresh truth to power even if—especially if!—power doesn't want to hear it, when dark forces in the world are once again doing their worst.

My fifth and final point picks up the image of the waiting chalice and translates it from metaphor into metonymy. If what I have been saying makes sense, then a refreshed Christian sacramental theology (not just theory, but reflection on practice!) ought to belong within the wider picture, and the wider picture ought to make fresh sense in relation to it. I suspect this is one reason why the sacraments have so often been a flash-point for inner-Christian disputes. A great deal hangs on them. Larger issues are focused there, whether we understand them or not. But in particular we ought to approach them, I suggest, in terms of the cosmology and eschatology of Temple and Sabbath which I have been expounding. The sacraments ought to embody a wise, scripturally resourced and Christologically enabled natural theology. In scripture, heaven and earth overlap and interlock; God's future comes to meet us in the present. And the image-bearing humans, the royal priesthood, share in that double overlap and indeed exercise their human vocation in bringing it to birth again and again. This is so partly in the very activities of making grain into bread and grapes into wine, or indeed pouring out water. But these activities are then focused in the mysterious royal priesthood of the people of God, enacted through their representatives, in a drama within which these events and these elements are charged—that word again—with new meaning.

Various works on sacramental theology have, I think, looked in this kind of direction, though as with the other topics raised briefly here there is no space for full exploration. Alexander Schmemann's *World as Sacrament* is pointing the way, though much more could be done.[35] Robert Jenson's *Visible Words*, with its eschatological emphasis, might help—though Jenson's ambiguity about the bodily resurrection raises some doubts.[36] The combination of space, time and image which I have explored might then give birth to the other missing dimension, 'matter' itself: can it be that God's matter and our matter can overlap and share the same space? That, of course, is what the incarnation affirms, and thereby legitimates (I think) a view of baptism and eucharist at least, and perhaps other events as well, as moments when not only space and time but also matter come together. The world is indeed *charged* with the grandeur of God, charged as with a solemn vocation, charged as in a battery, and there really are moments when it will flame out or gather to a greatness.

There is no time or space to explore this further, but once again I glimpse the argument here as a two-way street. The biblically refreshed and eschatologically informed version of natural theology for which I am arguing might give rise to fresh views of the sacraments. The sacraments themselves, which like music form their own unique language to which all theology is mere programme-notes, might help us explore afresh the interface and the inferences between God and creation. They might also point us in fresh ways to what was accomplished in Jesus' cross and resurrection, through which, within a world already charged with God's grandeur, that same Creator God has now dealt with the smudge, the smell and the bare soil.

CONCLUSION: THE FRESH MANDATE

The many-sided argument that has been converging on this point is that when we look back at the whole world of creation, like the disciples on the Emmaus Road looking back to the whole story of Israel, we find that the resurrection of Jesus compels a re-evaluation not only of past history but also of all past observations of the world. It makes sense not least because it explains why the broken signposts seemed so important as well as why and how they were broken—and, in particular, how the reality to which they really were pointing is now opened up in fresh ways. And the reality in question turns out to be, not the God of 'perfect being', nor the prime mover, nor yet the ultimate architect, but the self-giving God we see revealed on the cross.

This explains two things straight away. First, none of this would ever be observable by the Faustian epistemologies that had screened out love itself. In other words, we have explained why a rationalist 'apologetic' could never arrive at its hoped-for goal of a kind of neutral 'natural theology' standing up all by itself. We rule out, that is, any kind of 'natural theology' that would overreach itself and try to lasso the truth of heaven from a fixed point on earth or to gain the eschatological Promised Land without plunging through the river Jordan—to gain the new creation, in other words, without going by way of the cross. Second, the richer, more rounded epistemology of love can not only explain natural theology in retrospect ('yes, the hints and puzzles were true signposts, even if broken'), but they can do so in a way which eludes the subjective trap ('it's true for us but of course you will never see it unless you join the magic circle'). As the *epistemology* of love grasps the *ontology* of love—in other words, recognising and celebrating the ultimate truths of the Trinitarian creation and the promise that the outpoured divine love will at the last suffuse the whole of creation—so this generates the *missiology* of love, which, by the spirit, produces genuine and compelling signs of new creation in the world, opening hearts and minds to glimpse the truth previously invisible to the gaze that had been blinded by idols. Neither rationalism ('Here's an argument you can't refute') nor romanticism ('Here's how to have your heart strangely warmed') will do, though clarity of argument and the warming of the heart are both important. What matters is new creation coming to birth, in whatever form, like the Sabbath coming forward to meet us in the middle of time.

In particular, the work and message of *healing*, at whatever level, remains a vital sign. We need to break free from the false either/or which goes back to at least the eighteenth century, with Christians claiming 'miracles' as evidence of 'supernaturalism' and dogmatic truth and unbelievers citing Hume and others to deny the miraculous, to insist on 'naturalism', and hence to deny the dogmas. That was a parody of the real discussion that needs to be had. In particular, we have to avoid the trap of arguing about 'naturalism' and 'supernaturalism' as though they were the best categories to work with, and as though, once you had proved the existence of something called 'the supernatural', you would have opened the door to Jesus' resurrection, making Easter simply a special example of a larger truth. No: the resurrection of Jesus was a brand-new event, and its preaching was a new kind of claim, to be contextualised, not by the modern appeal to 'the supernatural', but within—and then bursting out from within—the Jewish world of Temple and Sabbath.

Part of the problem with those older debates was that they were carried on with both sides—the sceptics who denied the dogma and the believers who affirmed it—trying to make their points while sidelining the cross itself. The question of 'atonement' had been split off from the larger question which became known as 'the problem of evil', and the cross was addressed to 'atonement' only, playing along with the idea that the gospel was not about new creation but simply about how to escape the old one. Once we reintegrate the questions of evil, sin and death, however, we see that the narrative of Jesus, up to and including the cross, recognised in hindsight as the story of how God became king, was always designed as the true answer to the composite 'problem of evil'—of idolatry and the dark powers that were unleashed through it, resulting in continued sin and death. The cross itself—this was the point of the seventh chapter—declares the resounding 'no' to any kind of epistemological Pelagianism (using that term in a loose, popular sense) that imagines it could start 'where we are' and work up to God. But the fact that the cross is simultaneously the ultimate outpouring of personal divine love—in John, the supreme revelation of divine glory—indicates that when the human 'quest for God' reaches a dead end *it may then discover God as the one who has himself died.* God himself has revealed himself right there, at the dead end, simultaneously unveiling his true character and rebuking any attempt to find it by other means.

History, then—the full-on investigation into the past and the full-on commitment to the present—together frame a vision of a God whose feet are firmly planted in the 'natural' soil of the present world. Bultmann was right to say that one ought not to 'objectify' God (and that any attempt to do so would fail almost by definition) but wrong to imagine that this compelled a retreat into the private, dehistoricized, de-Judaized, world of idealist existentialism. God, we might say, 'objectifies himself' in and as Jesus (and then, through the spirit, in Jesus' followers, though that is another story). The vision of creation and new creation opened up by a fresh historical enquiry into the apocalyptic eschatology of Jesus and his first followers invites a faith ('here is your God!', as in Isaiah 40 or 52) not by trying to provide an 'objectivist' or 'certaintist' account, which would merely encourage a slide back into a trivial and brittle rationalism. Telling the historically rooted story of Jesus *as the story of God*—as the evangelists themselves do, writing of course in the light of Easter—becomes the focus of the church's work in justice and beauty as well as in evangelism, generating an ongoing told-and-lived narrative which, by its very nature, invites new participants and, if it is true to itself, can never collapse into the 'in-talk' of those who have received a private 'special revelation'.

None of this is to imply that history itself can produce primary God-talk.[37] Here we have, I suggest, a kind of kenosis, corresponding to the true meaning of that much misunderstood passage Philippians 2.6–8. Just as Jesus did not regard his equality with God as something to be exploited, but emptied himself to go all the way to the cross, so the historian cannot and must not assume that a faith-stance licenses or encourages what would actually be a docetic account of Jesus in which the answers are known in advance and the full horror of a suffering God on the cross is avoided. The point of the Philippians poem (2.6–11) is that Jesus has himself worn man's smudge and shared man's smell, ending where the soil was bare on the rock of Calvary and the only thing his feet could feel were the nails. Rather, a fully historical account of Jesus and his first followers can and should arrive at the point of the cross, the point where in the poem and in theology the true God is truly revealed, and discover thereby, in the power of the spirit by which new creation is truly anticipated, the necessary conditions for the first-order God-talk which consists not just of words but of actual power: of the works of justice and beauty and the proclamation of the gospel. That is where, as we argued in the sixth chapter, the fuller 'epistemology of love' which believes the resurrection transcends the 'critical realism' required for history: a love which answers the sovereign love unveiled at Easter.

Thus, when the followers of Jesus are obedient to their calling within the larger *missio Dei*, what they say, embody, produce in art, campaign for in the world, and so forth, generates a communal life which becomes a place in real history (events) where God promises to be truly present and where humans can come to know him as whole persons. The community thus formed, as the spirit-enabled 'body' of the risen Messiah energised by the outpoured love of God, becomes a place where new creation, glimpses of the dawn, can be discerned. History (task) then has a vital role to play as a source, and resource, for that mission, not least in recalling the various philosophical and theological frameworks that have developed over time back to the New Testament's vision of the world in which the central event of history (meaning) took place. This will lead, again and again, to a celebration of the coming eschaton, the world of new creation in which the divine love will be fully revealed. That present celebration, in faith, sacramental life, wise readings of scripture, and mission, will constitute the outworking of that divine love, the highest mode of knowing, a self-giving love in and for the world. This will indicate in self-authenticating fashion (though, to be sure, set within the 'not yet' of an ongoing brokenness, as in 2 Corinthians) that the ultimate reality in the world is the self-giving God revealed in Jesus. It will invite us to enter into the larger public world opened at Easter. It will enable us to know him with, once more, the knowledge whose depth is love.

That is how history and eschatology come together at last. That is how the true story of Jesus opens up the promise of a genuine, if radically redefined, 'natural theology'. That is how the dawn of the new creation—and with it, the fresh affirmation of the original creation—is to be discerned:

> And for all this, nature is never spent;
> There lives the dearest freshness deep down things;
> And though the last lights off the black West went
> Oh, morning, at the brown brink eastward springs—
> Because the holy Ghost over the bent
> World broods with warm breast and with ah! Bright wings.

Notes

PREFACE AND ACKNOWLEDGMENTS

1   See my essay, 'Get the Story Right and the Models Will Fit: Victory through Substitution in "Atonement Theology"', in *Atonement: Sin, Salvation and Sacrifice in Jewish and Christian Antiquity* (papers from the St Andrews Symposium for Biblical Studies, 2018), ed. M. Botner, J. Duff and S. Dürr (Grand Rapids: Eerdmans, 2019). See too 'Reading Paul, Thinking Scripture: "Atonement" as a Special Study', in my *Pauline Perspectives* (London: SPCK, 2013), 356–78, and also *The Day the Revolution Began* (London: SPCK, 2017) (hereafter *Revolution*).

2   Karl Barth, 'Nein!' in *Natural Theology: Comprising 'Nature and Grace' by Professor Dr. Emil Brunner and the Reply 'No!' by Dr. Karl Barth*, trans. Peter Fraenkel (Eugene, Ore.: Wipf & Stock, 2002 [1946]), 74.

3   For a historical survey of the development and outcome of the Barth/Brunner debate, cf. J. W. Hart, *Karl Barth vs. Emil Brunner: The Formation and Dissolution of a Theological Alliance, 1916–1936* (New York: Peter Lang, 2001). A helpful discussion is that of A. Moore, 'Theological Critiques of Natural Theology', in *The Oxford Handbook of Natural Theology*, ed. Russell Re Manning (Oxford: Oxford University Press, 2013) (hereafter *OHNT*), 227–44. From a different angle, see A. E. McGrath, *Emil Brunner: A Reappraisal* (Chichester: Wiley Blackwell, 2014).

4   These are only a handful from a wide range of possible definitions. One should at least quote Lord Gifford: '[Natural theologians should] treat their subject strictly as a natural science, the greatest of all possible sciences, indeed, in one sense the only science, that of Infinite Being, without reference to or reliance upon any supposed special exceptional or so-called miraculous revelation' (quoted by Rodney D. Holder, 'Natural Theology in the Twentieth Century', *OHNT*, 118). The Oxford English Dictionary is briefer: 'Theology based upon reasoning from observable facts rather than from revelation'. Other definitions are offered

by, for instance, W. L. Craig and J. P. Moreland: 'That branch of theology that seeks to provide warrant for belief in God's existence apart from the resources of authoritative, propositional revelation' ('Introduction,' in *The Blackwell Companion to Natural Theology*, ed. William Lane Craig and J. P. Moreland [Malden, Mass.: Wiley Blackwell, 2012], ix). Most of these are negative definitions; Alister McGrath offers a positive one: 'Natural theology can broadly be understood as a process of reflection on the religious entailments of the natural world' (*Re-imagining Nature: The Promise of a Christian Natural Theology* [Chichester: Wiley Blackwell, 2017], 7).

5   Christopher R. Brewer, 'Beginning All Over Again: A Metaxological Natural Theology of the Arts', PhD thesis, University of St Andrews, 2015. See also Christopher R. Brewer, *Understanding Natural Theology* (Grand Rapids: Zondervan Academic, forthcoming).

6   McGrath, *Re-imagining Nature*, 18–21.

7   I have discussed Bultmann's work, and particularly his Giffords, in chs. 2, 3 and 4 below.

8   London: SPCK; San Francisco: HarperOne, 2011.

9   In this I have been greatly helped by the 'Logos' Institute in St Andrews, whose staff and students have provided challenge, stimulus and direction.

10 On the varied reactions to Lisbon 1755, see ch. 1 below. The event stands as a telling shorthand symbol for a complex shift of cultural, philosophical and theological mood.

11 See e.g. 1 John 4.2.

12 An important study of this area which reached me after I had worked out what I wanted to say on this is E. L. Meeks, *Loving to Know: Covenant Epistemology* (Eugene, Ore.: Cascade, 2011).

13 See P. G. Ziegler, *Militant Grace: The Apocalyptic Turn and the Future of Christian Theology* (Grand Rapids: Baker Academic, 2018).

14 See 'The Meanings of History: Event and Interpretation in the Bible and Theology', *Journal of Analytic Theology* 6 (2018), 1–28.

CHAPTER 1: THE FALLEN SHRINE

1   For common definitions of natural theology along these lines, see the preface, p. x, with notes at pp. 279–80.

2   On Butler and the Deists see e.g. H. G. Reventlow, *The Authority of the Bible and the Rise of the Modern World* (London: SCM Press, 1984 [1980]), 345–50.

3   See e.g. Iain Murray, *The Puritan Hope: Revival and the Interpretation of Prophecy* (Edinburgh: Banner of Truth, 1971).

4   Addison's father, Lancelot, was Dean of Lichfield from 1683 to 1703.

5   For the singing of the spheres see Cicero, *Rep.* 6.18. On the cosmology of the *Timaeus* see now D. J. O'Meara, *Cosmology and Politics in Plato's Later Works* (Cambridge: Cambridge University Press, 2017).

6   I am reminded of the way some modern hymn-books have altered 'Jesus loves me, this I know,/ *For* the Bible tells me so' to 'Jesus loves me, this I know,/ *And* the Bible tells me so'.

7   A resident of the Durham diocese, Bewick was born just after Butler's death. The irony is that farmers were at that time doing their best to alter 'nature' by different methods of breeding and feeding. On Bewick's religious views—a sort of warm Deism, it seems—see J. Uglow, *Nature's Engraver: A Life of Thomas Bewick* (London: Faber, 2006), 79.

8   For details, see e.g. E. Paice, *Wrath of God: The Great Lisbon Earthquake of 1755* (London: Quercus, 2009) and, more generally, B. Hatton, *Queen of the Sea: A History of Lisbon* (London: C. Hurst, 2018).

9   This has been explored especially by S. Naiman, *Evil in Modern Thought: An Alternative History of Philosophy* (Princeton: Princeton University Press, 2002; repr. with new preface and afterword, 2015). See too D. Fergusson, *The Providence of God: A Polyphonic Approach* (Cambridge: Cambridge University Press, 2018), 124–32. Fergusson twice describes Lisbon as 'a hinge event' (124, 130), and stresses (125) that for Voltaire the event cast serious doubt on the optimistic view of the natural order seen e.g. in Alexander Pope.

10   On the origin of this term, and the difference between the various writers, see T. Zenk, 'New Atheism', in *The Oxford Handbook of Atheism*, ed. S. Bullivant and M. Ruse (Oxford: Oxford University Press, 2014), 245–60. The 'new atheists' are regarded as the least important type in John Gray's recent *Seven Types of Atheism* (London: Allen Lane, 2018), ch. 1: he calls the movement 'a tedious re-run of a Victorian squabble', saying that 'the organized atheism of the present century is mostly a media phenomenon and best appreciated as a type of entertainment' (9, 23).

11   See Fergusson, *Providence*, 127, 162.

12   *Civ.* 1.8–11. A similar response is made by C. S. Lewis in *The Screwtape Letters* (London: Bles, 1942), Letter 24, where Screwtape rebukes Wormwood for getting excited over the number of people killed in bombing raids: 'In what state of mind they died, I can learn from the office at this end. That they were going to die sometime, I knew already. Please keep your mind on your work'. Lucretius, however, already used the apparent 'faults' in the natural world as an argument against divine involvement (*Rer. nat.* 2.180f.).

13   For a brief overview of ancient scepticism see e.g. Jula Annas and Jonathan Barnes, *Sextus Empiricus: Outlines of Scepticism* (Cambridge: Cambridge University Press, 2000), xvi–xix.

14   From the voluminous literature on Descartes see recently H. Cook, *The Young Descartes: Nobility, Rumor and War* (Chicago: University of Chicago Press, 2018).

15   See A. C. Kors, 'The Age of Enlightenment', in Bullivant and Ruse, eds., *Oxford Handbook of Atheism*, 195–211.

16   Voltaire, 'Poem on the Lisbon Disaster: or, An Examination of that Axiom, "All Is Well"' (1756, though apparently composed late 1755: see *Toleration and Other Essays by Voltaire*, ed. and intro. by J. McCabe [New York: Putnam's, 1912]), sourced at https://en.wikisource.org/wiki/Toleration_and_other_essays/Poem_on_the_Lisbon_Disaster. Voltaire possessed at least six copies or translations of Lucretius, the great Roman Epicurean (Peter Gay, *The Enlightenment: The Rise of Modern Paganism*, 2 vols. [New York: Knopf, 1966], 1.99); in one work, he introduced himself as 'a new Lucretius who will tear the mask from the face of religion' (1.104). True, in his post-Lisbon poem Voltaire claimed to reject both Plato and Epicurus, and to prefer Bayle. Perhaps what he was rejecting in Epicureanism, as in the closing stanzas of the poem, was not the idea of absent divinities but the idea that life could consist in 'the sunny ways of pleasure's genial rule'. He was now contemplating a gloomier prospect.

17   See C. Smith and M. L. Denton, *Soul Searching: The Religious and Spiritual Lives of American Teenagers* (New York: Oxford University Press, 2005): they introduced the now-popular term 'moralistic therapeutic Deism'.

18   On ancient Epicureanism see the summary in my *Paul and the Faithfulness of God*, Christian Origins and the Question of God 4 (London: SPCK, 2013) (hereafter *PFG*), 211f.; on Lucretius see now M. R. Gale, *Oxford Readings in Classical Studies: Lucretius* (Oxford:

Oxford University Press, 2007). On Epicureanism in the seventeenth and eighteenth centuries see the older works of T. Mayo, *Epicurus in England (1650–1725)* (Dallas: Southwest Press, 1934) and H. Jones, *The Epicurean Tradition* (London: Routledge, 1989); and, more recently, e.g. W. R. Johnson, *Lucretius and the Modern World* (London: Duckworth, 2000); D. R. Gordon and D. B. Suits, *Epicurus: His Continuing Influence and Contemporary Relevance* (Rochester, N.Y.: RIT Cary Graphic Arts Press, 2003); and particularly C. Wilson, *Epicureanism at the Origins of Modernity* (Oxford: Clarendon, 2008) and S. Greenblatt, *The Swerve: How the Renaissance Began* (London: Bodley Head, 2011) (telling the story of the 1417 rediscovery and its aftermath). Peter Gay's large-scale treatment of the Enlightenment (*The Enlightenment: The Rise of Modern Paganism*) highlights the role of Epicureanism; Gay has been criticized, but I do not think his underlying thesis has been overturned. A set of important in-depth critical studies of the whole phenomenon, resisting oversimplifications but still highlighting my main point here, can now be found in N. Leddy and A. S. Lifschitz, eds., *Epicurus in the Enlightenment* (Oxford: Voltaire Foundation, 2009).

19   On Gassendi see e.g. Gay, *Enlightenment*, 1.305f. He was admired by Locke, Newton, Voltaire and many others.

20   See W. R. Albury, 'Halley's Ode on the *Principia* of Newton and the Epicurean Revival in England', *Journal of the History of Ideas* 39 (1978), 24–43.

21   Wilson, *Epicureanism*, 237; see R. H. Syfret, 'Some Early Reactions to the Royal Society', *Notes and Records of the Royal Society* 7 (1950), 234.

22   Gay, *Enlightenment*, 1.307.

23   See particularly Wilson, *Epicureanism*, 200. Leibniz's first letter to Clarke: see *Die Philosophischen Schriften von Gottfried Wilhelm Leibniz*, ed. C. I. Gerhardt, 7 vols. (Berlin: 1875–1890; repr., Hildesheim: Olms, 1965), 7.352.

24   See Gay, *Enlightenment*, 1.314.

25   This suggestion, which I owe to Prof. Tom Greggs, is fascinating but cannot be pursued here. See e.g. C. Taylor, *A Secular Age* (Cambridge, Mass.: Belknap Press of Harvard University Press, 2007), 284. See also Gillespie, *Theological Origins of Modernity*, 36, stressing that the modern retrieval of ancient atomism and Epicureanism took place within 'what was already an essentially Nominalist view of the world'.

26   Wilson, *Epicureanism*, 6; cf. p. 33 for Richard Bentley's attack at this point. See too p. 28 for Margaret Cavendish, who in the 1640s advocated a form of materialism as offering support for an early version of women's liberation (if the world was now free from the tyranny of the gods . . .). The idea of religion curbing revolution emerges later, of course, in Marx, who wrote his doctoral dissertation on Epicureanism: see below.

27   On Jefferson see below.

28   So e.g. Taylor, *Secular Age*, 367. See too p. 376: in the new 'Epicurean-naturalist' view, 'one can indeed live in a world which seems to proclaim everywhere the absence of God'. In such a world, 'all order, all meaning comes from us'.

29   G. S. Jones, *Karl Marx: Greatness and Illusion* (London: Penguin, 2017), 613 n. 67.

30   Jones, *Karl Marx*, 616 n. 25.

31   Wilson, *Epicureanism*, v, vi. She goes on to suggest that a period of civil unrest and a climate of scepticism created the conditions in which a reworked Epicureanism could 'transform the material world to suit human interests' (2), thus altering 'the assumptions of political and moral theory in ways we now take for granted' (3). We look back on rival theories with a detached interest since 'we are all, in a sense, Epicureans now' (3). Wilson offers an extended

definition of Epicureanism at pp. 37–38, explaining that the retrieval of key elements has radically altered Western intellectual life.

32 See Greenblatt, *Swerve*, 185.

33 Taylor, *Secular Age*, 626.

34 This is the main thesis of Naiman, *Evil in Modern Thought*. See my discussion in *Evil and the Justice of God* (London: SPCK, 2006).

35 On the fascinating complexity of relationships between different thinkers see R. Collins, *The Sociology of Philosophies: A Global Theory of Intellectual Change* (Cambridge, Mass.: Belknap Press of Harvard University Press, 1998).

36 I have been unable to trace any written source for this legend.

37 A. Pope, *An Essay on Criticism* (1711), 2.298. Pope's famous line is itself an example of its own point.

38 On the early reception of Nietzsche see E. Behler, 'Nietzsche in the Twentieth Century', in *The Cambridge Companion to Nietzsche*, ed. B. Magnus and K. M. Higgins (Cambridge: Cambridge University Press, 1996), 282, dividing his impact into before and after the Second World War (before: literary impact; after: philosophical).

39 See e.g. Seneca, *Letters* 8.8. At 2.5–6 he writes, 'I am wont to cross over even into the enemy's camp—not as a deserter, but as a scout'.

40 See Gay, *Enlightenment*, 1.42f., 304f. and (citing Fontenelle as an example) 317f.

41 N. Leddy and A. S. Lifschitz, 'Epicurus in the Enlightenment: An Introduction', in Leddy and Lifschitz, eds., *Epicurus in the Enlightenment*, 1–11 (2). They contrast this complex analysis with the apparently simpler either/or offered by Gay, *Enlightenment*, 1.371 and elsewhere; but Gay's treatment is regularly more nuanced than they imply. D. Edelstein, *The Enlightenment: A Genealogy* (Chicago: University of Chicago Press, 2010), 45, suggests that correction is needed for Gay's thesis of the Enlightenment as a 'new paganism', but he nevertheless admits (4f.) that his own work is informed by that of Gay all through.

42 On the neo-Stoicism of the period see Taylor, *Secular Age*, 115–30 and elsewhere. For Wilson's point see above, pp. 8–9, with pp. 282–83 n. 31.

43 Gay, *Enlightenment*, 1.105, summarizing an important discussion (98–105).

44 On Deism see e.g. J. R. Wigelsworth, *Deism in Enlightenment England: Theology, Politics and Newtonian Public Science* (Manchester: Manchester University Press, 2013).

45 On the problem of the gods' physical structure, and the difficulty of interpreting the relevant evidence, see A. A. Long, *Hellenistic Philosophy: Stoics, Epicureans, Sceptics*, 2nd edn. (London: Duckworth, 1986), 46–49; and J. Mansfield, 'Theology', in *The Cambridge History of Hellenistic Philosophy*, ed. K. Algra, J. Barnes et al. (Cambridge: Cambridge University Press, 2008), 472–75, noting (but rejecting) the variant interpretation of Cicero, *Nat. d.* 1.49–50, according to which the idea of the gods was simply a projection of the human mind.

46 For the question of whether Newton was really a Deist, as most have thought, or whether Voltaire was correct to see him retaining a basic Christian position, see Gay, *Enlightenment*, 1.316f. On the different types of Deism see e.g. Taylor, *Secular Age*, ch. 6.

47 In the *Cyclopedia, or a Universal Dictionary of Arts and Sciences* of E. Chambers (London: Knapton, Darby and Midwinter, 1728), 1.322, the Epicureans are said to think it 'beneath the Majesty of the Deity to concern itself with human Affairs' (cited by J. A. Harris, 'The Epicurean in Hume', in Leddy and Lifschitz, eds., *Epicurus in the Enlightenment*, 161–81 [166]). See Tennyson's portrayal of Lucretius reflecting, albeit with questions, on the gods' 'sacred everlasting calm' (*The Complete Works of Alfred Lord Tennyson* [London: Macmillan, 1898], 162).

48 Lucretius draws attention to defects in the world for which no god could have been responsible: *Rer. nat.* 2.165–183; 5.195–234.

49 See Epicurus, *Letter to Menoeceus* 125.

50 Chambers again (*Cyclopedia*, 1.322): 'Rigid Epicureans' focus on the pleasures of the mind and of virtue, while 'Remiss Epicureans' look for the pleasures of the body (cited by Harris, 'Epicurean in Hume', in Leddy and Lifschitz, eds., *Epicurus in the Enlightenment*, 165).

51 See A. A. Long and D. N. Sedley, *The Hellenistic Philosophers*, vol. 1, *Translations of the Principal Sources with Philosophical Commentary* (Cambridge: Cambridge University Press, 1987), 1.146.

52 Some, ironically, have seen the 'gap' between God and the world not so much in the scepticism of the seventeenth and eighteenth centuries but in the great reformers themselves: see e.g. Edelstein, *Enlightenment*, 34: 'Calvinism introduced such a breach between this world and the next that even Catholics (and particularly Jansenists) came to consider the reality of the divine as inherently separate from the world of humans'. This strikes me as contentious, but worth pondering.

53 Immanuel Kant, 'Beantwortung der Frage: Was ist Aufklärung?' *Berlinische Monatsschrift* 12 (1784), 481–94. See J. Robertson, *The Enlightenment: A Very Short Introduction* (Oxford: Oxford University Press, 2015), 7.

54 *OED* cites J. H. Stirling, *The Secret of Hegel* (1865), xxvii–xxviii.

55 See Greenblatt, *Swerve*, 261f. The seventeenth century saw the rise of great critics of the early Enlightenment such as Vico, Hamann and Herder: see I. Berlin, *Three Critics of the Enlightenment: Vico, Hamann, Herder*, 2nd edn. (London: Pimlico, 2013 [2000]). Gottlieb, *The Dream of Enlightenment*, 39, sees 'a revived materialism', updating Democritus and Epicurus, as 'one of Hobbes's two main philosophical innovations', the other being a novel view of government. Locke, as we saw, was influenced by the followers of Gassendi, who had tried to combine forms of Epicureanism and Christianity (Gottlieb, *Dream of Enlightenment*, 126, 138).

56 See his 'Mock on, mock on, Voltaire, Rousseau . . .', written between 1800 and 1804, and ending with a contemptuous reference to 'the atoms of Democritus', coupling them with 'Newton's particles of light' (William Blake, *Selected Poems* [Oxford: Oxford University Press, 1996], 148).

57 A. N. Wilson, *God's Funeral* (London: John Murray, 1999).

58 Pope, 'Intended for Sir Isaac Newton', in *The Poetical Works of Alexander Pope* (London: Frederick Warne, n.d.), 371. A footnote points out that Newton was born on the very day that Galileo died. Pope's couplet produced an eventual response from J. C. Squire (1884–1958): 'It did not last: the Devil, howling "Ho!/ Let Einstein be!" restored the status quo' (sourced at https://en.wikiquote.org/wiki/J._C._Squire).

59 See Edelstein, *Enlightenment*, 22, 28: the first theories of 'Enlightenment' started out as celebratory histories of 'the scientific revolution', but they were at the same time a retrieval of 'the ancients'.

60 See Taylor, *Secular Age*, 19.

61 *The Oxford Book of English Verse*, ed. H. Gardner (Oxford: Oxford University Press, 1972), 792.

62 See *St Andrews Citizen*, April 8, 1893; *Dictionary of National Biography* (1912 supplement), 245. Online suggestions that the degree was in Divinity seem to be misplaced.

63 See e.g. W. G. Kümmel, *The New Testament: The History of the Investigation of Its Problems* (London: SCM Press, 1973). W. Baird, *History of New Testament Research*, 3 vols.

(Minneapolis: Fortress, 1992–2013) offers a little socio-cultural context but consists mostly of a relentless chronicle of exegetical proposals.

64   J. Israel, foreword to I. Berlin, *Three Critics of the Enlightenment*, vii.

65   On Jansenism, and just how vital this phase of eighteenth-century politics in France was, see D. K. Van Kley, *The Religious Origins of the French Revolution: From Calvin to the Civil Constitution, 1560–1791* (New Haven, Conn.: Yale University Press, 1996).

66   See P. McPhee, *Robespierre: A Revolutionary Life* (New Haven, Conn.: Yale University Press, 2012). See further Van Kley, *Religious Origins of the French Revolution*; F. Tallett, 'Dechristianizing France: The Year II and the Revolutionary Experience', in F. Tallett and N. Atkin, *Religion, Society and Politics in France Since 1789* (London: Bloomsbury Academic, 1991), 1–28; and M. Vovelle, *The Revolution against the Church: From Reason to the Supreme Being* (Columbus: Ohio State University Press, 1991 [1988]).

67   Jefferson, letter to William Short, Oct. 31, 1819. He explains: Jesus was a great moral teacher, but his views were corrupted by the influx of Platonism (Jefferson's real bugbear) into the church. Greenblatt, *Swerve*, 263, points out the irony: for Lucretius, happiness would consist in withdrawal from the world, not in trying to reorganise an entire society. Jefferson turned this around: 'the pursuit of happiness'—the Lucretian goal—was now written in to the Constitution. Gay (*Enlightenment*, 1.105 n. 8) suggests that Jefferson, who owned 'as many as eight copies' of Lucretius, later regarded his philosophy of nature untenable, despite his youthful attachment, learned from Machiavelli (55).

68   See Smith and Denton, *Soul Searching*.

69   See Gillespie, *Theological Origins of Modernity*, 141.

70   Virgil, *Ecl.* 4.5. The original quotation ('Magnus ab integro saeclorum nascitur ordo', 'the great order of the ages is born afresh') was adapted for the reverse of the Great Seal of America by Charles Thomson. *Ecl.* 4 had been read as quasi-Christian prophecy for many years: see below.

71   No. 29 in *The New English Hymnal* (London: Oxford University Press, 1986). The author of the hymn was E. H. Sears (1810–1876). The problem with this essentially pagan idea in a Christian context is obvious: if the years are indeed 'ever-circling', will this 'age of gold' itself then decline once more into ages of silver, bronze and so on? On the early Christian interpretation see R. J. Tarrant, 'Aspects of Virgil's Reception in Antiquity', in *The Cambridge Companion to Virgil*, ed. C. Martindale (Cambridge: Cambridge University Press, 1997), 56–72 (70).

72   For an explicit statement of this see E. P. Sanders, 'Christianity, Judaism and Humanism', in his *Comparing Judaism and Christianity: Common Judaism, Paul, and the Inner and the Outer in Ancient Religion* (Minneapolis: Fortress, 2016), 429–45. His heroes are Jesus, John Locke and Thomas Jefferson.

73   See the discussion in Taylor, *Secular Age*, 328, 332. On all this see now T. M. Lessl, *Rhetorical Darwinism: Religion, Evolution and the Scientific Identity* (Waco, Tex.: Baylor University Press, 2012).

74   See J. Uglow, *The Lunar Men: The Friends Who Made the Future, 1730–1810* (London: Faber, 2002).

75   Uglow, *Lunar Men*, 152f., citing D. King-Hele, *Erasmus Darwin: A Life of Unequalled Achievement* (London: Giles de la Mare, 1999), 89. Thomas Seward (1708–1790), like Darwin a graduate of St John's College, Cambridge, lived in the Bishop's Palace at the north-east corner of the Close (the Bishop lived in his castle near Stafford) and knew the Lunar Men well. His daughter, the poet Anna Seward, became one of the group in her own right

(Uglow, *Lunar Men*, 40f. and elsewhere). Uglow's study of Darwin's personal life shows that the accusation of Epicureanism had other dimensions beyond scientific theories.

76 On Erasmus Darwin see too Greenblatt, *Swerve*, 262: Lucretius's vision had 'directly influenced' him.

77 See J. Norman, *Adam Smith: What He Thought and Why It Matters* (London: Allen Lane, 2018).

78 Gay, *Enlightenment*, 1.172; 2.354; Gay summarizes him as 'a modern moderate Stoic' (2.361).

79 Gay, *Enlightenment*, 1.58, summarizing an important discussion.

80 Details in W. Baird, *History of New Testament Research*, vol. 1 (Minneapolis: Fortress, 1992), 77. See also the recent treatments in M. H. de Lang, 'Literary and Historical Criticism as Apologetics: Biblical Scholarship at the End of the Eighteenth Century', *Nederlands archief voor kerkgeschiedenis/ Dutch Review of Church History* 72.2 (1992), 149–65; Jonathan Israel, 'The Philosophical Context of Hermann Samuel Reimarus' Radical Bible Criticism', in *Between Philology and Radical Enlightenment: Hermann Samuel Reimarus (1694–1768)*, ed. M. Mulsow (Leiden: Brill, 2011), 183–200. Reimarus's *Fragments* is available in an edition by C. H. Talbert (Philadelphia: Fortress, 1970).

81 Gay, *Enlightenment*, 2.389, speaks of 'the expulsion of God from the historical stage'.

82 Adam Smith hailed Hume as 'by far the most illustrious philosopher and historian of the present age' (*Wealth of Nations*, 742; quoted in Gay, *Enlightenment*, 2.359). On Hume see now J. A. Harris, *Hume: An Intellectual Biography* (Cambridge: Cambridge University Press, 2018).

83 'Dare not to know': see Edelstein, *Enlightenment* 34.

84 For the many variations, see Leddy and Lifschitz, *Epicurus in the Enlightenment*.

85 See Gillespie, *Theological Origins*, 5–7.

86 On the various secular eschatologies see particularly J. Moltmann, *The Coming of God*, trans. Margaret Kohl (Minneapolis: Fortress, 1996 [1995]), Part III. Moltmann sees Hegel's myth of progress as a 'millenarianism without apocalyptic', enabling a new age simply to emerge without any rupture, and conversely Nietzsche's nihilism as 'apocalypticism without millenarianism', a meaningless world with a bleak future. Some might call this 'eschatological naturalism', a label which M. Allen, *Grounded in Heaven: Recentering Christian Hope and Life on God* (Grand Rapids: Eerdmans, 2018) curiously tries to fasten on to my work and that of some others. The present volume, particularly chs. 5 and 6, offers an implicit rebuttal.

87 Quoted in 'Progress', in *The Oxford Companion to Philosophy*, ed. T. Honderich (Oxford: Oxford University Press, 1995), 722. Condorcet's *Esquisse d'un tableau historique des progrès de l'esprit humain* was published posthumously in 1794. 'Daniel Malthus [father of Thomas] believed, with such sages as Condorcet, Jean-Jacques Rousseau and William Godwin, that society was advancing towards perfection' (A. N. Wilson, *The Victorians* [London: Hutchinson, 2002], 11).

88 Gay, *Enlightenment*, 2.364.

89 F. M. Turner, *European Intellectual History from Rousseau to Nietzsche* (New Haven, Conn.: Yale University Press, 2014), 49.

90 See e.g. M. Tournier, '"Le Grand Soir": Un Mythe de Fin de Siècle', *Mots: Les Langages du Politique* 19 (1989), 79–94.

91 'The French Revolution of 1789 introduced "new time" as a defining temporal quality for modern society and politics' . . . 'The modern vision of revolutionary upheaval shaped the French political imagination in the nineteenth century': so Julian Wright, *Socialism and the Experience of Time* (Oxford: Oxford University Press, 2017), 13, 14, with various citations.

Wright goes on to point out, however, that this in turn generated anxieties about how to care for society in the interim.

92 So e.g. R. Nisbet, *History of the Idea of Progress* (New York: Basic Books, 1980).

93 For a relatively recent study of the poem, see ch. 4 of John Barnard, *John Keats* (Cambridge: Cambridge University Press, 1987).

94 On 'progress' as itself a developing belief in recent centuries see J. R. Middleton and B. J. Walsh, *Truth Is Stranger than It Used to Be: Biblical Faith in a Postmodern Age* (Downers Grove, Ill.: IVP, 1995), 13–20. Seminal thinkers here include Francis Bacon, *The New Atlantis*; Pico della Mirandola, *Oration on the Dignity of Man*; and Kant, 'On Progress'. Older studies include J. B. Bury, *The Idea of Progress: An Enquiry into Its Origin and Growth* (London: Macmillan, 1920); Nisbet, *History of the Idea of Progress*; more recently, C. Lasch, *The True and Only Heaven: Progress and Its Critics* (New York: Norton, 1991).

95 Strictly speaking this would be more complex than it sounds, since a Deist god would be pure spirit while an Epicurean one would be made of very fine atoms; but in popular consciousness the point would be irrelevant.

96 Even Lucretius may hint at this, however paradoxically: see Wilson, *Epicureanism*, 140: 'Lucretius' confidence in the renewing and reconstructive powers of nature complemented his theory of limits and dissolution, leading him to ascribe powers and even a divine status to nature seemingly at odds with the anti-theology underlying his text'. See *Rer. nat.* 1.577ff. This may also explain the otherwise puzzling opening invocation of Venus in *Rer. nat.* 1.1–43; see e.g. Greenblatt, *Swerve*, 237f., and my comments in *PFG*, 212 n. 45.

97 Jones, *Karl Marx*, 80–82.

98 For a recent discussion see e.g. Ø. Larsen, 'Kierkegaard's Critique of Hegel: Existentialist Ethics versus Hegel's Sittlichkeit in the Institutions of Civil Society of the State', *Nordicum Mediterraneum* 11.2 (2016), accessed at https://nome.unak.is/wordpress/08-3/c69-conference-paper/kierkegaard-s-critique-of-hegel-existentialist-ethics-versus-hegel-s-sittlichkeit-in-the-institutions-of-civil-society-of-the-state/.

99 'We have seen the future . . .' is attributed to Lincoln Steffens after his visit to the Soviet Union in 1919. The British couple Beatrice and Sidney Webb visited in 1932 and produced *Soviet Communism: A New Civilisation?* (London: Longmans, Green) the following year (subsequent editions omitted the question mark). They expressed similar views in their final book, *The Truth about the Soviet Union* (London: Longmans, Green, 1944).

100 Wilson, *Victorians*, 15.

101 See e.g. S. Pinker, *The Better Angels of Our Nature* (London: Penguin, 2012) and now *Enlightenment Now: The Case for Reason, Science, Humanism, and Progress* (London: Penguin, 2018).

102 Eastern Europe of course lived for two generations on the myth that its Marxist pedigree rendered it automatically 'superior', a fiction still believed in North Korea. In that sense, the Cold War was fought between right-wing and left-wing Epicureanism.

103 See my *Evil and the Justice of God* and also *Revolution*.

104 This is routinely assumed by atheist commentators: e.g. Simon Blackburn, reviewing John Gray's *Seven Types of Atheism* and Edward Feser's *Five Proofs of the Existence of God* in the *Times Literary Supplement* for September 7, 2018, 4, speaks of 'evidence of historical unreliability' as one of the three reasons for the widespread Western abandonment of 'religions'—the others being 'philosophical scepticism' and 'a liberal distaste for authoritarian yet apparently arbitrary commands and prohibitions'.

105 I have noted in many cases the citing of Geza Vermes, whose many works, starting with *Jesus the Jew* (London: Collins, 1973), served to support his own de-conversion which he

graphically describes in his autobiography, *Providential Accidents* (London: SCM Press, 2011 [1998]).

106 B. F. Meyer, *The Aims of Jesus* (London: SCM Press, 1979), 29.

107 Lessing of course believed that, even if the Gospels were historically accurate, 'history' could still not be the basis for theological conclusions; Reimarus argued that the Gospels were in any case fictitious.

108 In this later analysis the obvious exception is Philo of Alexandria, who like Clement employed sophisticated Hellenistic philosophy to interpret his Jewish traditions.

109 Famously by E. P. Sanders, *Paul and Palestinian Judaism* (London: SCM Press, 1977), but also by many others before and since. There has also been strong reaction to Sanders. See my *Paul and His Recent Interpreters* (London: SPCK, 2015) (hereafter *PRI*), chs. 3–5.

110 See e.g. D. A. Knight, 'The Pentateuch', in *The Hebrew Bible and Its Modern Interpreters*, ed. D. A. Knight and G. M. Tucker (Chico, Calif.: Scholars Press, 1985), 263–96; J. Conrad, *Karl Heinrich Grafs Arbeit am Alten Testament* (Berlin: de Gruyter, 2011); and E. Nicholson, *The Pentateuch in the Twentieth Century: The Legacy of Julius Wellhausen* (Oxford: Oxford University Press, 2003). For a Jewish perception of the German scholarship involved see e.g. C. Potok, *The Promise* (London: Penguin, 1982).

111 See e.g. Hans Küng, *The Church* (London: Burns and Oates, 1968), 136: 'For German Idealism, notably for Hegel, Judaism figured as the manifestation of the evil principle'.

112 See *Surprised by Hope* (London: SPCK, 2007) and, behind that, *The Resurrection of the Son of God*, Christian Origins and the Question of God 3 (London: SPCK, 2003) (hereafter *RSG*).

113 That was the word on the stone, found among the ruins of the old St Paul's Cathedral after the London fire of 1666, which Christopher Wren saw as the motto for his own rebuilding: see L. Jardine, *On a Grander Scale: The Outstanding Career of Sir Christopher Wren* (London: HarperCollins, 2002), 428.

114 See e.g. 'Leader of Faithful Souls, and Guide of All That Travel to the Sky', whose second stanza declares that 'the earth, we know, is not our place', since we will swiftly 'to our heavenly country move, our everlasting home above'. Similarly, the final stanza of 'Love Divine, All Loves Excelling' offers a closing scene ('Till in heaven we take our place') which is based, not on the final vision of new heavens and new earth in Rev 21, but on the *present* 'heaven' of Rev 4 and 5 ('till we cast our crowns before thee').

115 See his treatise *On Exile* 607C–E. See E. Radner, 'Exile and Figural History', in *Exile: A Conversation with N. T. Wright*, ed. J. M. Scott (Downers Grove, Ill.: IVP Academic, 2017), 273–301, and my response in the same volume, at 328–32. Of course, much popular piety had continued to travel the same road (see *Surprised by Hope*, ch. 2, with many examples). For an explicit appeal for a Christian-Platonist synthesis in contemporary theology see e.g. H. Boersma, *Heavenly Participation: The Weaving of a Sacramental Tapestry* (Grand Rapids: Eerdmans, 2011).

116 See e.g. Bishop Berkeley, opposing materialism with an explicit Platonic dualism in which 'matter is both unreal *and* evil' (Wilson, *Epicureanism*, 177, italics original; see Berkeley, *Works*, 5.164). The philosopher climbs a ladder from the sensual to the intellectual, but one cannot infer the latter from the former (see Berkeley, *Works*, 5.137). This is ultimately the same as Lessing's ugly ditch. Plutarch, again (*On Exile* 1086C–1107C): Epicureanism cannot produce true happiness.

117 'Abide with Me' (no. 331 in *The New English Hymnal* [London: Oxford University Press, 1986]. The author of the hymn was H. F. Lyte [1793–1847]). Allen, *Grounded in Heaven*, 4, tries to suggest that this line is not Platonic, but rather seeks for heaven's light to shine on

earth in a new dawn; but the line, in context, clearly speaks of death itself in terms of leaving earth and going to heaven (just like Plutarch, in other words).

118   On the 'rapture' see my discussion in *Surprised by Hope*, over against the famous 'Left Behind' series of novels by Tim LaHaye and Jerry B. Jenkins.

119   See e.g. H. Bloom, *The American Religion: The Emergence of the Post-Christian Nation* (New York: Simon and Schuster, 1992) and, for the relevance of this to the churches, P. J. Lee, *Against the Protestant Gnostics*, 2nd edn. (New York: Oxford University Press, 1993 [1987]). See the discussion in my *Judas and the Gospel of Jesus* (London: SPCK, 2006), ch. 6.

120   See Samuel's remark about the choice of David in 1 Sam 16.7; cp. 2 Cor 4.18.

121   One notable counterblast was that of C. S. Lewis in his Cambridge inaugural lecture, '*De Descriptione Temporum*', in *Selected Essays* (Cambridge: Cambridge University Press, 1969), ch. 1.

122   On this and what follows, see *PFG*, chs. 4, 13. On the weaving of religion into every part of ancient life see e.g. O'Meara, *Cosmology and Politics in Plato's Later Works*, 122–29. On the modern meaning of 'religion' (which, prior to the seventeenth century, had referred mainly to the right ordering of worship), see e.g. W. Pannenberg, *Christianity in a Secularised World* (London: SCM Press, 1989) and esp. K. Barth, *Church Dogmatics*, vol. 1, *The Doctrine of the Word of God*, part 2, trans. G. T. Thomson and Harold Knight (Edinburgh: T&T Clark, 1956 [1938]), 284, discussing Paul de Lagarde on the way 'religion' had come to be placed over against 'revelation'.

123   On the *religionsgeschichtliche Schule* and its powerful influence on twentieth-century New Testament scholarship, see *PRI*. Much of Bultmann's developing hypotheses about early Christianity included (notoriously unsuccessful) attempts at such genealogy.

124   Lord Gifford certainly seemed to be presupposing something like this antithesis: see the preface, note 4.

125   Lessing says, 'I live in the eighteenth century, in which miracles no longer happen' ('On the Proof of the Spirit and of Power', 52). C. S. Lewis frames that kind of position in the Narnia stories, when the children examine the wardrobe and find that it is indeed only a wardrobe. It is a pity Lessing never met Wesley or Whitefield.

126   See e.g. C. Rowland, 'Natural Theology and the Christian Bible', *OHNT*, 31: in reference to Matt 25, 'the divide between natural and supernatural is not as great as one might have thought'.

127   See Wis 2 (cp. *PFG*, ch. 3, 239–43); mSanh. 10.2.

128   See Lucretius, *Rer. nat.* 4.1058–1191, with Wilson, *Epicureanism*, 255f. On Wilde see e.g. 'The Picture of Dorian Gray', in *The Works of Oscar Wilde* (Leicester: Galley Press, 1987), 137: 'A man can be happy with any woman, as long as he does not love her'.

129   J. W. Goethe, *Faust: Eine Tragödie. Erster Theil*, ed. E. Gaier (Stuttgart: Reclam, 2011), 71 (line 1700): 'Do please stay; you are so beautiful'.

130   Thomas Mann, *Doctor Faustus: The Life of the German Composer Adrian Leverkühn as Told by a Friend*, trans. H. T. Lowe-Porter (London: Vintage Books, 2015 [1947]), 361: 'Thou maist not love'; 242: 'Love is forbidden you, insofar as it warms'.

131   Wagner picks up the same point as the plot of the *Ring* gets under way: Alberich the Niebelung gives up love in order to get the Rhine-gold and, with it, the dark power that drives the story.

132   This is exactly cognate with Iain McGilchrist's remarkable thesis in *The Master and His Emissary: The Divided Brain and the Making of the Western World* (New Haven, Conn.: Yale University Press, 2009): the left brain has taken over from the right. We have become a

schizophrenic culture, in which music, faith, metaphor and love itself are marginal and minority interests.

133 On Schweitzer and Goethe see e.g. T. X. Qu, "'In the Drawing Power of Goethe's Sun": A Preliminary Investigation into Albert Schweitzer's Reception of Goethe', in *Albert Schweitzer in Thought and Action*, ed. J. C. Paget and M. J. Thate (Syracuse, N.Y.: Syracuse University Press, 2016), 216–33. Schweitzer won the Goethe Prize in 1928; he had Goethe's complete works with him at Lambarene and apparently used to read *Faust* every year during the Easter season (Qu, "'In the Drawing Power of Goethe's Sun"', 218).

134 On love as homecoming see now S. May, *Love: A New Understanding of an Ancient Emotion* (New York: Oxford University Press, 2019).

135 On Bernard Lonergan's proposal for an 'enlarged epistemology', see his *Method in Theology* (London: Darton, Longman and Todd, 1972), 28–56, 81–84, 155–265 and 311–37. Treating 'love' as central to knowledge goes back at least to Aquinas (I would argue, to St Paul) and has been powerfully expressed by von Balthasar among others. There is a sense in which this is what 'hermeneutics' has been all about at least since Gadamer, and in a line going back to G. B. Vico in his opposition (in Thiselton's phrase, in *Hermeneutics of Doctrine* [Grand Rapids: Eerdmans, 2007], xvii) to the 'timeless, individual-centred rationalism of Descartes': see H.-G. Gadamer, *Truth and Method*, 2nd rev. edn. (London: Sheed and Ward, 1989 [1960]), 17, and I. Berlin, *Three Critics of the Enlightenment*, 26–207. Berlin declares (206) that Vico's insistence upon the specificity of different cultures 'makes it difficult, if not impossible, . . . to return to the conceptions of human nature and the real world held by Descartes or Spinoza or Voltaire or Gibbon'. That, however, is what most supposed 'historical criticism' has done.

CHAPTER 2: THE QUESTIONED BOOK

1 Details and larger context in e.g. Reventlow, *Authority of the Bible and the Rise of the Modern World*, Part III.

2 On Toland's relation to and influence on philology and biblical criticism, cf. Luisa Simonutti, 'Deism, Biblical Hermeneutics, and Philology', in *Atheism and Deism Revalued: Heterodox Religious Identities in Britain, 1650–1800*, ed. Wayne Hudson, Lucci Diego and Jeffrey R. Wigelsworth (Farnham: Ashgate, 2014), 45–62.

3 On Reimarus and Lessing see ch. 1 above.

4 A. Schweitzer, *The Quest of the Historical Jesus: First Complete Edition*, ed. J. Bowden (London: SCM Press, 2000 [1906]), 14–26.

5 The *OHNT* has no index entries for either 'Jesus' or 'gospels', and under 'Christology' has only fleeting references, including the two mentioned in the next note.

6 In the latter category of course we find Karl Barth, both in his famous negative response to Emil Brunner and in his 1937 Giffords (K. Barth, *Nein! Antwort an Emil Brunner* [Zurich: Theologischer Verlag, 1934]; and *The Knowledge of God and the Service of God according to the Teaching of the Reformation*, trans. J. L. M. Haire and Ian Henderson [London: Hodder and Stoughton, 1938]). See the brief discussion in Russell Re Manning, 'Protestant Perspectives on Natural Theology', *OHNT*, 197–212 (198f.). T. F. Torrance, in some writings at least, followed Barth in this respect: see R. D. Holder, 'Natural Theology in the Twentieth Century', *OHNT*, 118–34 (127–29).

7 See e.g. L. Lessius and M. Marsenne, discussed by M. J. Buckley in *At the Origins of Modern Atheism* (New Haven, Conn.: Yale University Press, 1987), referred to by D. Edwards in 'Catholic Perspectives on Natural Theology', *OHNT*, 182–96 (183–84).

8 This in turn collapses into the caricature once portrayed in the TV series *Yes, Prime Minister*. The premier explains to his wife that they have to keep the balance in the Church of England. 'What balance?' she asks. 'Between those who believe in God and those who don't', comes the reply.

9 Grace Davie, *Religion in Britain: A Persistent Paradox*, 2nd edn. (Malden, Mass.: Wiley Blackwell, 2015 [1994]). See Jeff Astley, *Ordinary Theology: Looking, Listening and Learning in Theology* (London: Routledge, 2002), 45f., discussing Michael Langford and Maurice Wiles as representing different kinds of non-interventionist theism.

10 See above, ch. 1, in reference to the thesis of Christian Smith.

11 This seems to be ignored by Schweitzer's recent biographer, N. O. Oermann, who refers to the book uncomplicatedly by its English title. See the remarks of D. E. Nineham in his 'Foreword to the Complete Edition' in the 2000 edition of Schweitzer's *Quest*, xiv, xxii; though Nineham, here as elsewhere, seems not to grasp the full significance.

12 See ch. 3 below on von Ranke's (wrongly) supposed positivism.

13 See e.g. E. Gibbon, *The Decline and Fall of the Roman Empire*, vol. 1 (London: Frederick Warne, n.d.), 347.

14 On Wrede see *JVG*, 28f., 478; and see the discussions in e.g. C. Tuckett, ed., *The Messianic Secret* (London: SPCK, 1983). Schweitzer criticises Wrede (*Quest*, chs. 19, 20); but he employs a similar developmental scheme, placing it in the mind of Jesus rather than in the later fiction of the evangelists (*Quest*, ch. 21). On Bultmann and the reasons for his type of form criticism see *The New Testament and the People of God*, Christian Origins and the Question of God 1 (London: SPCK, 1992) (hereafter *NTPG*), ch. 14; *JVG*, 113f. For the long entail of Wrede's view see *JVG*, ch. 2, *passim*.

15 E.g. Kümmel, *New Testament*, and Baird, *History of New Testament Research*, cited in ch. 1 above.

16 On McGilchrist, *Master and His Emissary*, and the truth of his analysis in New Testament scholarship, see my inaugural lecture, 'Imagining the Kingdom: Mission and Theology in Early Christianity', *SJT* 65.4 (2012), 379–401 (and to be reprinted in a forthcoming collection of essays).

17 On Strauss and Renan see Schweitzer, *Quest*, chs. 7–9, 13.

18 For nineteenth-century salvation-history theories see R. W. Yarbrough, *The Salvation Historical Fallacy? Reassessing the History of New Testament Theology* (Leiden: Deo Publishing, 2004).

19 On Barth's early sympathy with Marxism, leading to his being called 'the red pastor of Safenwil', see e.g. E. Busch, *Karl Barth: His Life from Letters and Autobiographical Texts* (Grand Rapids: Eerdmans, 1994) and K. Barth and E. Thurneysen, *Revolutionary Theology in the Making: Barth-Thurneysen Correspondence, 1914–1925* (London: Epworth, 1964).

20 A case in point—though this would of course be controversial—might be the widely held Christological position known as the *extra Calvinisticum*, in which the Logos is said to have remained in heaven while Jesus was on earth.

21 An obvious recent example is D. W. Congdon, both in *The God Who Saves: A Dogmatic Sketch* (Eugene, Ore.: Cascade, 2016) and his shorter book *Rudolf Bultmann: A Companion to His Theology* (Eugene, Ore.: Cascade, 2015). See too e.g. his article on Jüngel's Pneumatology, 'The Spirit of Freedom: Eberhard Jüngel's Theology of the Third Article', in

Indicative of Grace—Imperative of Freedom: Essays in Honour of Eberhard Jüngel in His 80th Year, ed. D. R. Nelson (London: Bloomsbury/T&T Clark, 2014), 13–27, at section III.

22   On the different senses of 'myth' see esp. A. C. Thiselton, *The Two Horizons: New Testament Hermeneutics and Philosophical Description with Special Reference to Heidegger, Bultmann, Gadamer and Wittgenstein* (Grand Rapids: Eerdmans, 1984), 252–58.

23   I am here, and in ch. 4, redeploying much of the argument I set out in my article 'Hope Deferred? Against the Dogma of Delay', *Early Christianity* 9.1 (2018), 37–82. An obvious example of the line of thought I am opposing is Nineham's foreword to the modern edition of Schweitzer's *Quest* (see above).

24   See e.g. A. Schweitzer, *The Mysticism of the Apostle Paul*, trans. William Montgomery (London: A&C Black, 1931 [1911]), 23–25, proposing that Paul's 'mysticism', unlike Hellenistic varieties, was fused with 'the expectation of the end of the world' (24); that, for Paul, 'by the death and resurrection of Jesus Christ the end of the dominion of the angelic powers, and therewith the end of the natural world, is brought about', meaning that the second coming cannot long be delayed (25). See too W. Wrede, *Paul*, trans. Edward Lumis (London: Philip Green, 1907 [1904]), e.g. 47, 105.

25   K. Koch, *The Rediscovery of Apocalyptic: A Polemical Work on a Neglected Area of Biblical Studies and Its Damaging Effects on Theology and Philosophy* (London: SCM Press, 1972), ch. 1. See too my *PRI*, ch. 6, esp. 136f.

26   D. F. Strauss, *Die christliche Glaubenslehre in ihrer geschichtlichen Entwicklung und im Kampfe mit der modernen Wissenschaft*, 2 vols. (Tübingen: C. F. Osiander, 1840).

27   See B. Magee, *Wagner and Philosophy* (London: Penguin, 2001); and see ch. 3 below.

28   See again A. C. Thiselton, *Two Horizons*, 252–63.

29   Against e.g. D. W. Congdon, *The Mission of Demythologizing: Rudolf Bultmann's Dialectical Theology* (Minneapolis: Fortress, 2015), 407–31.

30   See recently e.g. C. Grottanelli, 'Nietzsche and Myth', *History of Religions* 37.1 (1997), 3–20, on Nietzsche's changing attitudes to 'myth', and the linking of this with his changing attitude to Wagner.

31   For the wider context of eschatological expectations in different religious traditions, see e.g. J. L. Walls, ed., *The Oxford Handbook of Eschatology* (Oxford: Oxford University Press, 2008).

32   A gentler reading of the cultural divide is offered by F. C. Burkitt in his 'Prefatory Note' to Schweitzer's *Mysticism* (v–vi).

33   See M. D. Eddy, 'Nineteenth Century Natural Theology', *OHNT*, 100–117. The idea of 'natural theology' was very much present to British culture in the nineteenth century, capable of very varied exposition, e.g. R. Browning's poem, 'Caliban upon Setebos; or, Natural Theology in the Island', in *The Poems of Robert Browning* (Oxford: Oxford University Press, 1905), 650–55.

34   See Matt 26.36–46/Mark 14.32–42; Matt 27.46/Mark 15.34.

35   See Jones, *Karl Marx*, 79–92.

36   See e.g. Schweitzer, *Quest* (2000 edn.), 478–87.

37   Schweitzer, *Quest*, 478.

38   Schweitzer, *Quest* (1954 edn.), 401. This sentence seems to have disappeared from the 2000 edn., though the same point is made in other ways.

39   A. Schweitzer, *J. S. Bach*, trans. Ernest Newman, 2 vols. (London: A&C Black, 1923 [1908]), e.g. 1.257–259; 2.21–23, 48–51. N. O. Oermann, in private correspondence (Jan. 22, 2018), suggests to me that Schweitzer's 'proprium', his main task in this respect, was 'to overcome

the hard gap between Jesus and Nietzsche on the one hand and Bach and Wagner on the other hand'.

40   See e.g. C. R. Joy, ed., *Music in the Life of Albert Schweitzer* (New York: Harper, 1951) and E. R. Jacobi, *Albert Schweitzer und Richard Wagner: Eine Dokumentation* (Tribschen: Schweizerische Richard-Wagner-Gesellschaft, 1977).

41   Harald Schützeichel, *Die Konzerttätigkeit Albert Schweitzers* (Bern: Haupt, 1991).

42   P. Berne, 'Albert Schweitzer und Richard Wagner', in *Die Geistigen Leitsterne Albert Schweitzers*, Jahrbuch 2016 für die Freunde von Albert Schweitzer (= Albert-Schweitzer-Rundbrief 108), ed. E. Weber (2016), 55–76 (available online at https://albert-schweitzer-heute.de/wp-content/uploads/2017/12/DHV-Rundbrief-2016.pdf).

43   P. Kitcher and R. Schacht, *Finding an Ending: Reflections on Wagner's* Ring (Oxford: Oxford University Press, 2004).

44   D. Cooke, *I Saw the World End: A Study of Wagner's* Ring (Oxford: Oxford University Press, 1979).

45   Joy, *Music in the Life of Albert Schweitzer*, 15. It is perhaps surprising that Schweitzer's recent biographer does not draw out this connection (N. O. Oermann, *Albert Schweitzer: A Biography* [Oxford: Oxford University Press, 2017], see e.g. 57–59).

46   R. Scruton, *The Ring of Truth: The Wisdom of Wagner's Ring of the Nibelung* (London: Penguin, 2017), 199.

47   Scruton, *Ring of Truth*, 145.

48   Scruton, *Ring of Truth*, 46f.

49   See J. Moltmann, *Theology of Hope: On the Ground and Implications of a Christian Eschatology*, trans. James W. Leitch (London: SCM Press, 1967 [1965]), ch. 1, esp. 37–42.

50   See Oermann, *Albert Schweitzer*, 74–76.

51   A. Schweitzer, *The Mystery of the Kingdom of God: The Secret of Jesus' Messiahship and Passion*, trans. Walter Lowrie (New York: Dodd, Mead, 1914 [1901]), 3, cf. 25. See Lucien Hölscher, *Weltgericht oder Revolution: Protestantische und sozialistische Zukunftsvorstellungen im deutschen Kaiserreich* (Stuttgart: Klett-Cotta, 1989); also his 'Mysteries of Historical Order: Ruptures, Simultaneity and the Relationship of the Past, the Present and the Future', in *Breaking Up Time: Negotiating the Borders between Present, Past and Future*, ed. C. Lorenz and B. Bevernage (Göttingen: Vandenhoeck & Ruprecht, 2013), 134–51.

52   See M. D. Chapman, *The Coming Crisis: The Impact of Eschatology on Theology in Edwardian England* (Sheffield: Sheffield Academic Press, 2001), 81–86. See also e.g. F. C. Burkitt, 'The Eschatological Idea in the Gospel', in *Essays on Some Biblical Questions of the Day by Members of the University of Cambridge*, ed. H. B. Swete (London: Macmillan, 1909), 193–214, insisting that the message of Jesus was relevant precisely because it was geared to 'the expectations of sudden and complete catastrophe' rather than of 'gradual and progressive evolutionary change' (208).

53   In a revealing note in the preface of *Mysticism* (ix), Schweitzer acknowledges the help of G. Kittel and K. H. Rengstorf in the worlds of *Spätjudentum* and Rabbinics. That clearly implies (among other things) that in the early period he was not himself familiar with the relevant texts. Even in *Mysticism*, he mostly cites *2 Baruch*, *4 Ezra* and *1 Enoch*, with brief references to *Jubilees* and the *Psalms of Solomon* and one reference each to the *Ascension of Moses*, the *Life of Adam and Eve* and the *Testaments of the Twelve Patriarchs*. His treatment indicates that he shared with his contemporaries a largely unhistorical (and certainly unpolitical) understanding of those texts (see again *PRI*, ch. 6). Sadly the various editions of *Quest* have no index of ancient texts.

54 Against e.g. P. Vielhauer, followed here by e.g. J. L. Martyn in his *Galatians* commentary (AB [New York: Doubleday, 1997]): see *PRI*, Part II.

55 Cf. 'in the latter days' etc. in e.g. Hos 3.5; Micah 4.1; Isa 2.2; Jer 23.20, 30.24. These look back to e.g. Gen 49.1; Num 24.14; Deut 4.30; 31.29.

56 For the different senses of 'history' see ch. 3 below.

57 On the bar-Kochba revolt see e.g. P. Schäfer, *The Bar Kokhba War Reconsidered: New Perspectives on the Second Jewish Revolt against Rome* (Tübingen: Mohr Siebeck, 2003) and W. Horbury, *Jewish War under Trajan and Hadrian* (Cambridge: Cambridge University Press, 2014).

58 Cf. Schweitzer, *Mysticism*, 54: 'Jesus Christ has made an end of the natural world and is bringing in the Messianic Kingdom'.

59 See e.g. E. P. Sanders, *Judaism: Practice and Belief, 63 BCE–66 CE* (London: SCM Press, 1992), e.g. 298, 303, 456f.; at 368 he says, as though the point were obvious, that 'like other Jews the Essenes did not think that the world would end'.

60 There are of course myriad secondary sources on Bultmann in general and not least his Giffords. D. W. Congdon's fuller study (*Mission of Demythologizing*) is complemented by his shorter *Rudolf Bultmann*. These remain useful though I have serious criticisms at certain points. An important older study is D. Fergusson, *Rudolf Bultmann*, 2nd edn. (New York: Continuum, 2000 [1992]). See too the classic study in Thiselton, *Two Horizons*, chs. 8, 9 and 10.

61 On Bultmann and 'myth' see his various related works: *The New Testament and Mythology* (1941), *Kerygma and Myth* (1953) and *Jesus Christ and Mythology* (1958). He argued in his commentary on John (1941; ET 1971) that the Fourth Gospel represented a demythologising of the earlier tradition, which for Bultmann was what it needed. See, among many discussions, Thiselton, *Two Horizons*, 252–63. I shall discuss Bultmann's Giffords more fully in ch. 3 below.

62 See e.g. A. Portier-Young, *Apocalypse against Empire: Theologies of Resistance in Early Judaism* (Grand Rapids: Eerdmans, 2011). See also *NTPG*, 280–86.

63 See A. Standhartinger, 'Bultmann's *Theology of the New Testament* in Context', in *Beyond Bultmann: Reckoning a New Testament Theology*, ed. B. W. Longenecker and M. C. Parsons (Waco, Tex.: Baylor University Press, 2014), 233–55. On the famine, see B. Winter, *After Paul Left Corinth: The Influence of Secular Ethics and Social Change* (Grand Rapids: Eerdmans, 2001), 216–25, and e.g. A. C. Thiselton, *The First Epistle to the Corinthians: A Commentary on the Greek Text* (Grand Rapids: Eerdmans, 2000), 578–86.

64 R. Bultmann, *History and Eschatology: The Presence of Eternity*, new edn. (Waco, Tex.: Baylor University Press, 2019 [1955]) (hereafter *H&E*). The pagination of the new edition follows the original, 154f.

65 Against basing faith on history see e.g. R. Bultmann, *Theology of the New Testament*, trans. Kendrick Grobel, 2 vols. (London: SCM Press, 1951–1955; repr., Waco, Tex.: Baylor University Press, 2007), 2.127.

66 See e.g. Congdon, *Rudolf Bultmann*, 10f.

67 See my earlier comments on a similar point in *PFG*, ch. 16.

68 See W. Benjamin, *Illuminations*, ed. Hannah Arendt, trans. Harry Zohn (New York: Schocken Books, 1968 [1958]), with the discussion in *PFG*, 1473–84. Klee's painting 'Angelus Novus' is now in the Israel Museum in Jerusalem. Benjamin interpreted the painting, in which the angel looks back on 'history' as a pile of rubble, as a sign that no good thing could come from 'progress'.

69 K. Barth, *Dogmatics in Outline*, trans. G. T. Thompson (London: SCM Press, 1966 [1949]), 7. See too K. Koch, *Rediscovery of Apocalyptic*, 67f. ('nearly all discerning Christians had finally lost faith in a divinely willed progress in history after the outbreak of the Second World War'), 70.

70 E. Käsemann, *Perspectives on Paul*, trans. Margaret Kohl (London: SCM Press, 1971 [1969]), 64. See the discussion in *PRI*, 50–53.

71 H. Conzelmann, *The Theology of St. Luke*, trans. Geoffrey Buswell (New York: Harper and Row, 1961 [1953]).

72 See again *PFG*, ch. 16.

73 On 2 Pet 3.10 see *RSG*, 462f. For discussion see e.g. R. J. Bauckham, *Jude, 2 Peter* (Waco, Tex.: Word, 1983), 283–322, and B. W. Witherington, *Letters and Homilies for Hellenized Christians*, vol. 2, *A Socio-rhetorical Commentary on 1–2 Peter* (Downers Grove, Ill.: IVP Academic, 2007), 363–91. 'Peter' is in any case warning against what certain 'deceivers' may say, not giving a report as to what the early church as a whole believed. The ending of John easily admits of many interpretations; insofar as it expresses uncertainty about the timing of the Lord's return, it precisely expresses uncertainty, not the certainty required for the theory.

74 J. B. Priestley, *An Inspector Calls: A Play in Three Acts* (London: Heinemann, 1947).

75 On the sketchy but hardly trouble-free history of early Christianity see *NTPG*, Part IV.

76 See A. S. Janick and S. E. Toulmin, *Wittgenstein's Vienna* (Minneapolis: Ivan R. Dee, 1996).

77 See ch. 3 below.

78 See too Longenecker and Parsons, eds., *Beyond Bultmann*, and the various works by D. W. Congdon already cited.

CHAPTER 3: THE SHIFTING SAND

1 See the discussion in *JVG*, 84–97.

2 A. C. Swinburne (1837–1909), whose 'Hymn to Proserpine', a bitter attack on a killjoy Christianity, contains the lines, 'Thou hast conquered, O pale Galilean; the world has grown grey from thy breath'. This too is an allusion, in this case to the dying words of the emperor Julian the Apostate (c. 331–363), 'Vicisti, Galilaee', 'Thou hast conquered, Galilean' (Theodoret, *Hist. eccl.* 3.20). Chadwick's insight, to line up Vermes by implication with both Swinburne and Julian, was typical of the man.

3 The present discussion stands on the shoulders of the one in *NTPG*, ch. 4. An earlier version of the chapter was given as the 2017 Analytic Theology Lecture at the Boston meeting of the American Academy of Religion (see preface, note 14).

4 See e.g. R. Koselleck, *Futures Past: On the Semantics of Historical Time* (Boston: MIT Press, 1985).

5 From *Die Götter Griechenlands*, composed in November 1819 [D677]. Schiller's original poem was published in 1788, and a shorter version in 1800.

6 'Ach von jenem leben warmen Bilde/ blieb der Schatten nur zurück'.

7 See e.g. Mark 8.31–33; 14.47 (with John 18.10f., identifying Peter as the attacker); 14.66–72.

8 See e.g. E. H. Carr, *What Is History?* (Cambridge: Cambridge University Press 1961); G. R. Elton, *The Practice of History*, 2nd edn. (Oxford: Blackwell, 2002 [1967]); and many other classic texts; recently, e.g. P. Burke, *What Is History Really About?* (Brighton: EER Publishers, 2018). A creative fresh approach is that of S. Mason, *Orientation to the History of Roman Judaea* (Eugene, Ore.: Cascade, 2016), Part I. My own earlier account is in *NTPG*, ch. 4.

9 Stephen Kotkin, 'When Stalin Faced Hitler', *Foreign Affairs* 96.6 (2017), 54.

10   Anand Menon, reviewing books on Brexit in the same issue, 122–26.

11   Alan Bennett, *Keeping On Keeping On* (London: Faber, 2016), 347.

12   Bennett, *Keeping On Keeping On*, 43. He puts K. B. McFarlane in the first category, and H. Weldon and the celebrated A. J. P. Taylor in the second. See below on von Ranke.

13   M. Bradbury, *To the Hermitage* (London: Picador, 2012 [2000]), xxi.

14   Joel Green, 'History, Historiography', in *New Interpreters Dictionary of the Bible*, vol. 2, *D–H*, ed. K. D. Sakenfeld (Nashville: Abingdon, 2007), 830.

15   Which is why Pannenberg was surprised that Collingwood thought the Greeks, not the Israelites, invented 'history'. Collingwood was thinking of *investigation*; Pannenberg was thinking of 'the larger course of events under the divine purpose'. See his *Basic Questions in Theology*, trans. G. H. Kelm, 3 vols. (London: SPCK, 1970–1973 [1967]), 1.67: 'it is obviously requisite that one should have history as a whole in view, corresponding to the universality of God'.

16   C. S. Lewis, *Christian Reflections* (London: Geoffrey Bles, 1967), 105, distinguishes (a) all events, past, present and future; (b) all past events; (c) all discoverable past events; (d) all past events actually discovered; (e) all past events now written up by historians; and (f) 'that vague, composite picture of the past which floats, rather hazily, in the mind of the ordinary educated man'.

17   The great historian Asa Briggs explained why he and other historians had been recruited to the Bletchley Park code-breaking establishment during World War II: historians, he said, were 'well read, drawn to lateral thinking, and taught to get inside the mind of people totally different from themselves' (A. Briggs, *Secret Days: Code-Breaking in Bletchley Park* [London: Frontline Books, 2011], 78).

18   See *RSG*, 12 n. 21.

19   'Thucydides, an Athenian, wrote the history of the war between the Peloponnesians and the Athenians, beginning at the moment that it broke out, and believing that it would be a great war, and more worthy of relation than any that had proceeded it' (Thucydides, *War* 1.1.1, trans. R. Crawley). Of course, writing a book is itself an event, but not (or not normally) the event to which the book itself is referring.

20   See the discussion in J. Moltmann, *God in Creation: An Ecological Doctrine of Creation*, trans. M. Kohl (London: SCM Press, 1985), 130; Pannenberg, *Basic Questions in Theology*, 1.21, 24.

21   L. von Ranke, *Sämtliche Werke*, vol. 33/34, 2nd edn. (Leipzig, 1874 [1824]), vii. People often mistakenly add 'ist' to this clause, but von Ranke did not. See e.g. J. B. Bury, 'History as a Science', in *The Varieties of History from Voltaire to the Present,* ed. F. Stern, 2nd edn. (New York: Vintage, 1973 [1956]), 209–23 (215); C. A. Beard, 'Historical Relativism', in Stern, ed., *Varieties of History*, 314–28 (327).

22   On von Ranke see Stern, *Varieties of History*, 16, and the section on von Ranke at p. 55; and see M. Bentley, *Modern Historiography: An Introduction* (London: Routledge, 1999), 39.

23   See C. S. Lewis, *The Discarded Image* (Cambridge: Cambridge University Press, 1964), 177.

24   That would be the equivalent, in historical theory, of the phenomenalist's trap, supposing that when we think we are talking about everyday material realities we are actually only talking about our own sense-data. That way lies solipsism. See the discussion in *NTPG*, 33.

25   Mason, *Orientation to the History of Roman Judaea*, 55.

26   M. MacMillan, *The War That Ended Peace* (London: Profile Books, 2014), 402f., citing Franz Ferdinand's previous restraining of earlier warmongering.

27   On this, see my *The Paul Debate* (Waco, Tex.: Baylor University Press, 2016), 100–107.

28   For the first: a fine example is in the 'painted hall' at Chatsworth House in Derbyshire. As its website explains, the first Duke of Devonshire, who built the hall between 1689 and 1694, chose to flatter the new King, William of Orange, by decorating it with scenes from the life of Julius Caesar: see https://www.chatsworth.org/media/11113/chatsworth_room -cards_english_web-allcompressed.pdf. For the second: Jefferson's retrieval of Virgil's 'Novus Ordo Seclorum', on US banknotes to this day. See above, p. 285 n. 70.

29   On 'providence' see recently G. Lloyd, *Providence Lost* (Cambridge, Mass.: Harvard University Press, 2008); M. W. Elliott, *Providence Perceived: Divine Action from a Human Point of View* (Berlin: de Gruyter, 2015); and Fergusson, *Providence of God*.

30   See Moltmann, *God in Creation*, 124f., 135.

31   I have explored this in the final chapter of *Revolution* and in *Spiritual and Religious* (London: SPCK, 2017).

32   The Septuagint translator, unable to imitate the fine literary restraint, explained that 'the Lord took away the king's sleep'.

33   See R. B. Hays, *Echoes of Scripture in the Gospels* (Waco, Tex.: Baylor University Press, 2016).

34   See my *PFG*, ch. 5.

35   For the entire context the work of Taylor, *Secular Age*, remains seminal.

36   C. K. Barrett, "J. B. Lightfoot as Biblical Commentator," appendix F, in J. B. Lightfoot, *The Epistles of 2 Corinthians and 1 Peter*, ed. B. W. Witherington and T. D. Still (Downers Grove, Ill.: IVP, 2016), 302 (originally in *Durham University Journal* 64 [1992], 193–204). Barrett (1917–2011) was Professor of New Testament at Durham; Lightfoot (1828–1889) was a Cambridge professor before becoming Bishop of Durham in 1879.

37   This is the effect of e.g. Murray Rae, *History and Hermeneutics* (London: T&T Clark, 2005), e.g. 2, 17, 55, 147, 154f. See further below.

38   On the three principles see e.g. M. Hengel, *Acts and the History of Earliest Christianity*, trans. John Bowden (London: SCM Press, 1979), 129f., and R. Deines, *Acts of God in History* (Tübingen: Mohr Siebeck, 2013), 10–13.

39   See *H&E*, 141–43. We shall discuss 'historicism' in due course.

40   See Bultmann, *H&E*, 40, 51, 73, 141–43.

41   Bultmann, *H&E*, 125f. On Croce see e.g. Stern, *Varieties of History*, 323–25. For Strauss, see above. For Collingwood see esp. *The Idea of History*, 2nd edn., ed. J. van der Dussen (New York: Oxford University Press, 1994 [1946]). I wonder if this is the only time in his work that Bultmann comes out in support of a British writer?

42   See p. 90 above on Bultmann's distinctive usage of these terms.

43   Bultmann, *H&E*, 131, 144. It therefore results in autobiography (146f., 149).

44   See *H&E*, 150–51.

45   See ch. 4 below; and *PRI*, Part II.

46   S. V. Adams, *The Reality of God and Historical Method* (Downers Grove, Ill.: IVP Academic, 2015), 185.

47   Adams, *Reality of God and Historical Method*, 185.

48   I have in mind here particularly Rae, *History and Hermeneutics*, e.g. 74, 154. See his programmatic statement (2): he aims to offer 'an account of history drawn from the Bible itself in which history is recognized as the space and time given to humankind to be truly itself as the covenant partner of God', so that 'it is within this framework of creation and divine promise that an account is given of what human history is'. This is a kind of outflanking movement, using one meaning of 'history' (everything that has ever happened or ever will, under general divine providence) to erase its other normal (and in my view necessary)

meanings, as explored in the present chapter. Rae seems to suppose that all history-writing of the normal kind is fatally infected with Troeltschian scepticism, requiring something he calls 'a new historiography' or 'a different historiography' (74, 154), in which the aims, tools and methods of ordinary historians are not required. Like Bultmann, one can settle for a *Dass*, only this time a maximal one (everything that ever happens) rather than Bultmann's minimalism.

49 Bultmann, *H&E*, 153; see above, p. 62. Bultmann's sense of this, including his idea of Christ being 'the end of history' as he is 'the end of the Law', is then a demythologisation of what he took to be the view of the early Christians, that the space-time universe would shortly cease to exist; see the discussions in chs. 2 and 4 of the present book.

50 This corresponds, *mutatis mutandis*, to the Lutheran *simul iustus et peccator*.

51 *H&E*, 153.

52 E.g. Adams, *Reality of God and Historical Method*, 232 and elsewhere.

53 Adams, *Reality of God and Historical Method*, 166. This results, for instance, in a 'resurrection' which seems to have nothing to do with the body of Jesus and hence with an empty tomb.

54 See the fuller treatment in ch. 2 above.

55 *H&E*, 110, 111, 131.

56 His book *Primitive Christianity in Its Contemporary Setting*, trans. R. H. Fuller (London: Collins, 1956) is an extraordinary example of putting the telescope to the blind eye.

57 *H&E*, 155, the last line of the book.

58 Benjamin, *Illuminations*, 264. See my discussion in *PFG*, 1473–75.

59 Wright, *NTPG*, Part II, drawing especially on Meyer, *Aims of Jesus*. See too e.g. Meyer, *Critical Realism and the New Testament* (Allison Park, Pa.: Pickwick, 1989). For a recent critique of my work in this area see S. E. Porter and A. W. Pitts, 'Critical Realism in Context: N. T. Wright's Historical Method and Analytic Epistemology', *Journal for the Study of the Historical Jesus* 13 (2015), 276–306. J. Bernier responds in the next issue (14 [2016], 186–93) and Porter and Pitts respond again (241–47). This is not the place to engage the debate further.

60 This is cognate with, though not identical to, Heisenberg's 'uncertainty principle', which noted that the more precisely a particle's position could be determined the less certain one could be about its momentum, and vice versa. See W. Heisenberg, 'Über den anschaulichen Inhalt der quantentheoretischen Kinematik und Mechanik', *Zeitschrift für Physik* 43.3–4 (1927), 172–98.

61 See G. M. Trevelyan, 'Clio Rediscovered', in Stern, ed., *Varieties of History*, 227–45 (239), calling the three stages 'the scientific, the imaginative or speculative, and the literary'. Compare the three steps set out by Martin Hengel (*Acts and the History of Early Christianity*, 131: knowing, understanding, assembling; see Deines, *Acts of God in History*, 25f.).

62 Trevelyan, 'Clio Rediscovered', in Stern, ed., *Varieties of History*, 239.

63 See *RSG*, 16–18.

64 Berlin, *Three Critics of the Enlightenment*, 52. The whole chapter is relevant to the present discussion.

65 Berlin, *Three Critics of the Enlightenment*, 19.

66 J. G. Hamann, *Sämtliche Werke*, ed. J. Nadler (Vienna: Herder, 1949–1957), 2.172.21, 171.15, cited in Berlin, *Three Critics of Enlightenment*, 19.

67 An obvious example: E. P. Sanders, asking about Jesus' motivation in going to the cross, suggests that if he really expected and even intended to die that would make him 'weird' (*Jesus and Judaism* [London: SCM Press, 1985], 333: 'the view that he plotted his own redemptive death makes him strange in any century').

68 One of my favourite examples is from MacMillan's *The War That Ended Peace*, ch. 9, entitled 'What Were They Thinking? Hopes, Fears, Ideas and Unspoken Assumptions'. The fact that many of those hopes, fears and unspoken assumptions seem completely alien to most Europeans a mere century later shows the importance of the task.

69 This was explained thoroughly in *NTPG*, Part II, and again from different angles in *PFG*, 23–36, 63–66 and elsewhere.

70 Against Adams, *Reality of God and Historical Method*, 211f., 250–258 and elsewhere. See Berlin, *Three Critics*, 111f. on Vico, stressing the need to take into account the vast amount of social complexity: 'to each stage of social change there correspond its own types of law, government, religion, art, myth, language, manners, . . . that together they form a single pattern of which each element conditions and reflects the others, and that this pattern is the life of a society'.

71 See Adams, *Reality of God and Historical Method*, 251. He mistakes 'worldview', a heuristic tool for making sure we are understanding aims and motives, for a theological category (251, 256), and wrongly imagines that using this tool means that one's historical method 'remains bound' to 'immanence' (255). This is a long-term result of the mistakes I highlighted in the first chapter.

72 On the Sabbath within Jewish worldviews see ch. 5 below.

73 See Berlin, *Three Critics of Enlightenment*, 111f. on the way in which Vico already saw the importance of multiple social differentia, long before the theme was taken up by Hegel and Marx.

74 Pannenberg, *Basic Questions in Theology*, 1.39f.; cf. 33, speaking of a 'deterioration' in which 'since the Enlightenment, since Vico and Voltaire, man has been exalted to the place of God as the one who bears history'. This skates over the fact that Vico was one of the primary *critics* of the early Enlightenment.

75 This word and this pedigree, too, is often unknown, though the process is familiar: like Molière's Monsieur Jourdain, surprised that he'd been speaking prose all his life, people do abduction without realising it. Pierce's method is lucidly summarized in A. J. P. Kenny, *A New History of Western Philosophy* (Oxford: Clarendon, 2010), 837f. See too particularly C. Ginzburg, *Clues, Myths and the Historical Method*, trans. John and Anne C. Tedeschi, new edn. (Baltimore: Johns Hopkins University Press, 2013 [1986]) and U. Eco, 'Horns, Hooves, Insteps: Some Hypotheses on Three Types of Abduction', in *Dupin, Holmes, Peirce: The Sign of Three*, ed. U. Eco and T. A. Sebeok (Bloomington: Indiana University Press, 1983), 198–220.

76 See, again, *Paul Debate*, 100–107.

77 Pierce speaks of 'guesses', as does Trevelyan, 'Clio Rediscovered', in Stern, ed., *Varieties of History*, 239. Trevelyan clearly does not imply that these guesses are random; and we should remember that when an American says 'I guess that's right' this means what in British English one might say with 'I think that's right'. 'Guess' in Britain might imply a stab in the dark; 'think' in America might imply uncertainty.

78 See my *Paul: A Biography* (San Francisco and London: HarperOne and SPCK, 2017), ch. 3.

79 R. Syme, *The Roman Revolution* (Oxford: Oxford University Press, 1939).

80 A modern successor to Gibbon: C. Nixey, *The Darkening Age: The Christian Destruction of the Classical World* (London: Macmillan, 2017). On the other side: e.g. R. Stark, *The Rise of Christianity* (Princeton: Princeton University Press, 1996).

81 Lewis, *Christian Reflections*, 1. The whole passage is relevant to the present discussion.

82 Acts 26.26.

83 'If no historical truth can be demonstrated, then nothing can be demonstrated by means of historical truths. That is: accidental truths of history can never become the proof of necessary truths of reason . . . That, then, is the ugly, broad ditch which I cannot get across, however often and however earnestly I have tried to make the leap' (G. E. Lessing, 'On the Proof of the Spirit and of Power', in *Lessing's Theological Writings*, trans. and ed. H. Chadwick [Stanford: Stanford University Press, 1956], 53, 55). Original in Lessing's *Gesammelte Werke*, ed. P. Rilla (Berlin: Aufbau-Verlag, 1956), 8.12, 14.

84 See e.g. C. Stephen Evans, 'Methodological Naturalism in Historical Biblical Scholarship', in *Jesus and the Restoration of Israel: A Critical Assessment of N. T. Wright's Jesus and the Victory of God*, ed. C. Newman, 2nd edn. (Waco, Tex.: Baylor University Press, 2018 [1999]), 180–205. I think Evans has since modified his view.

85 One might cite e.g. J. B. Davis and D. Harink, *Apocalyptic and the Future of Theology: With and beyond J. Louis Martyn* (Eugene, Ore.: Cascade, 2012) and Adams, *Reality of God and Historical Method*. See too the altogether more hopeful book from Ziegler, *Militant Grace*.

86 See e.g. *PRI*, Part II.

87 See Wright, 'Apocalyptic and the Sudden Fulfilment of Divine Promise', in *Paul and the Apocalyptic Imagination*, ed. J. K. Goodrich, B. Blackwell and J. Mastin (Philadelphia: Fortress, 2016), 111–34. See too J. P. Davies, *Paul among the Apocalypses? An Evaluation of the Apocalyptic Paul in the Context of Jewish and Christian Apocalyptic Literature* (London: T&T Clark, 2018).

88 See *Scripture and the Authority of God* (London: SPCK, 2005).

89 On 'historicism' see e.g. Mason, *Orientation to the History of Roman Judaea*, 41–43. An important survey is that of G. Scholtz, 'The Notion of Historicism and 19th Century Theology', in *Biblical Studies and the Shifting of Paradigms, 1850–1914*, ed. H. Graf Reventlow and W. R. Farmer (London: Bloomsbury, 1995), 149–67.

90 A fascinating popular-level illustration of this is found in J. Hawes, *The Shortest History of Germany* (Yowlestone House, Devon: Old Street Publishing, 2017), expounding the ways in which modern Germany has continued to retrieve, consciously and unconsciously, elements of its Roman origins.

91 The best short summary I have found is that of P. L. Gardiner in *The Oxford Companion to Philosophy*, ed. T. Honderich (Oxford: Oxford University Press, 1995), 357. Admitting that the word is confusing, he indicates three senses: (a) the need to recognise the individuality of human phenomena within their specific contexts; (b) the need to see all phenomena within a process of historical development; (c) the social-scientific prediction of development on the basis of discoverable laws of historical change.

92 See *PRI*, Part III on sociological studies of Paul's communities, and the two main branches of that study.

93 London: Routledge, 2002 (1957).

94 K. Popper, *The Open Society and Its Enemies* (London: Routledge and Kegan Paul, 1952; many reprints).

95 A famous attempt to translate this into a Christian register was that of P. Teilhard de Chardin, *The Phenomenon of Man*, trans. Bernard Wall (London: Collins Fontana, 1965; frequently reprinted).

96 Of course, we can use 'must' in proper historical investigation. If we find an undated letter from Churchill describing flying in an aeroplane, it *must* be dated to the twentieth century. When he fought in the Boer War nobody except one or two wild-eyed inventors was taking to the air. But the historicist uses 'must' to enforce the *a priori*.

97 See ch. 2.

98 There is a very interesting early critique by (the then quite young) Charles Taylor available online at https://www.scribd.com/document/357693818/Taylor-Poverty-of-the-Poverty-of-Historicism. Mason, *Orientation to the History of Roman Judaea*, 42 n. 73, criticizes Popper for using the word, suggesting that what he was attacking was really 'positivist-systemic' history.

99 Lewis, *Christian Reflections*, 100–113; *Discarded Image*, 174–77.

100 Lewis, *Christian Reflections*, 101. We should distinguish where Lewis does not. When Carlyle spoke of history as 'a book of revelations', he was referring to what we can see in the lives of 'great men', which is not the same as a Hegelian scheme or as Keats's invocation of a pagan developmentalism. See T. Carlyle, 'History as Biography', in Stern, ed., *Varieties of History*, 90-107, at p. 95f.: if History is 'Philosophy teaching by Experience', the historian would have to be all-knowing and all-wise. What's more, Carlyle's 'book of revelations' is precisely the lives of 'great men', making him in a sense a Rankian historicist (see below); but he insists that there are times when the 'great men' fail to arrive on cue, which shows that he is precisely not a Hegelian one.

101 Turner, *European Intellectual History*, 126.

102 E.g. E. Radner, *Time and the Word: Figural Reading of the Christian Scriptures* (Grand Rapids: Eerdmans, 2016), 81: 'however much one might wish to rail against the coercive historical-critical reduction of scriptural meaning, historicism remains the working metaphysical assumption of most modern readers'. On 'historical-critical' see below.

103 Mason, *Orientation to the History of Roman Judaea*, 28–56.

104 Mason, *Orientation to the History of Roman Judaea*, 51.

105 Mason, *Orientation to the History of Roman Judaea*, 42–43.

106 Turner, *European Intellectual History*, 234–35, italics added.

107 Bentley, *Modern Historiography*, 23.

108 Bentley, *Modern Historiography*, 23.

109 Bentley, *Modern Historiography*, 23.

110 Bentley, *Modern Historiography*, 19.

111 J. Burrow, *A History of Histories* (London: Penguin, 2007), 460f. See the discussions of e.g. C. A. Beard, 'Historical Relativism', in Stern, ed., *Varieties of History*, 317–20.

112 Bentley, *Modern Historiography*, 22 n. 27.

113 Bentley, *Modern Historiography*, 22.

114 Beard, 'Historical Relativism', in Stern, ed., *Varieties of History*, 320, 323, 325, 327.

115 Bury, 'History as a Science', in Stern, ed., *Varieties of History*, 214, going on to cite Leibniz.

116 Bury, 'History as a Science', in Stern, ed., *Varieties of History*, 25.

117 Bury, 'History as a Science', in Stern, ed., *Varieties of History*, 223.

118 Bury, 'History as a Science', in Stern, ed., *Varieties of History*, 210, 223.

119 So Stern, *Varieties of History*, 209, introducing Bury: he 'grew sceptical about the possibility of establishing historical causality and in his last writings stressed the role of contingency, of mere chance, in history'. See too Bury's later work, *Idea of Progress*.

120 Trevelyan, 'Clio Rediscovered', in Stern, ed., *Varieties of History*, 227–45.

121 Trevelyan, 'Clio Rediscovered', in Stern, ed., *Varieties of History*, 233.

122 Trevelyan, 'Clio Rediscovered', in Stern, ed., *Varieties of History*, 238.

123 Trevelyan, 'Clio Rediscovered', in Stern, ed., *Varieties of History*, 239.

124 Trevelyan, 'Clio Rediscovered', in Stern, ed., *Varieties of History*, 243. See Lewis, *Christian Reflections*, 102: a phrase like 'the judgement of history' 'might lure us into the vulgarest of

all vulgar errors, that of idolizing as the goddess History what manlier ages belaboured as the strumpet Fortune'.

125 Berlin, *Three Critics of Enlightenment*, 70.

126 Collingwood, *Idea of History*, xxii (editor's intro., quoting a letter of Collingwood).

127 On the objection see Lewis, *Christian Reflections*, 106–12.

128 See Stern, *Varieties of History*, 54f., indicating that Stern at least uses the term to mean that 'the particular had to be grasped as part of universal history'.

129 In between the sixteenth century and the twenty-first there have been many similar movements. The early Hanoverians were hailed as the leading edge of 'history', not least in the architecture and iconography of Edinburgh's 'New Town'. Thomas Jefferson made the same claim, as we saw, on the dollar bill; the Prussians, including von Ranke, in their celebration of 1813.

130 Lewis, 'Virgil and the Subject of Secondary Epic', in *A Preface to Paradise Lost* (Oxford: Oxford University Press, 1942), 32ff., suggests that Virgil was following earlier models.

131 Rom 8.18–30; 1 Cor 15.20–28; Rev 21.1–2; 2 Pet 3.13; cf. Isa 65.17; 66.22.

132 E.g. Mark 13.14–23 and parallels; Mark 13.32–37 and parallels; Luke 12.39f.; 1 Thess 5.6.

133 Lewis, *Discarded Image*, 175–77, also mentions in this connection Orosius's *History against the Pagans* and Dante's *De Monarchia*.

134 The book of Revelation, offering comfort and guidance for the persecuted church, envisages the victory of the Lamb and the arrival of the New Jerusalem through faith and hope, not an immanent historical progress.

135 See e.g. Rae, *History and Hermeneutics*. On the subject see Hengel, *Acts and the History of Earliest Christianity*, 129–36: an important discussion, but it seems that in the final analysis (132f.) Lessing is still ruling the roost.

136 See *JVG*, ch. 1.

137 See G. Vermes, *Providential Accidents*, and Sanders, *Comparing Judaism and Christianity*, ch. 1 n. 72. See too Vermes, *The Religion of Jesus the Jew*, 4, and Sanders, *Jesus and Judaism*, 333f. See further Rae, *History and Hermeneutics*, 91.

138 Martin Kähler, *Der sogenannte historische Jesus und der geschichtliche, biblische Christus* (Leipzig: Deichert, 1892); Lewis, *Screwtape Letters*, Letter 23; L. T. Johnson, *The Real Jesus: The Misguided Quest for the Historical Jesus and the Truth of the Traditional Gospels* (New York: HarperCollins, 1997); several of the essays in R. B. Hays and B. Gaventa, eds., *Seeking the Identity of Jesus: A Pilgrimage* (Grand Rapids: Eerdmans, 2008). Lewis's protest comes uncomfortably close to the Bultmann he rejects in his 'Modern Theology and Biblical Criticism', in *Christian Reflections*, 152–66.

139 See again e.g. C. Stephen Evans, 'Methodological Naturalism in Historical Biblical Scholarship'.

140 See *NTPG*, 199, citing mAbot 3.5, a saying of Rabbi Nehunya ben ha-Kanah.

141 See *PFG*, 80–90, and indeed the whole of ch. 2 of that work.

142 At the time of first drafting of this chapter, *First Things* (Nov. 2, 2017) carried an article by Francesca Aran Murphy whose title claims the opposite: 'Everything Is Outside the Text' (https://www.firstthings.com/web-exclusives/2017/11/everything-is-outside-the-text). Judaism and Christianity, she argues, have scriptures which constantly witness to something other than themselves, something 'infinitely greater', namely God's presence with his people. While the point is well taken, there might be a danger in then forgetting that for both Jews and Christians that divine presence has regularly been experienced precisely in and through the reading and study of scripture. It isn't an either/or, though I would certainly affirm the *primacy* of the extra-textual reality. The idea of there being no 'extra-textual' world is often attributed

to Jacques Derrida; but his famous saying, 'Il n'y a pas de hors-texte', literally means, not that there is no extra-textual reality, but that there is no 'outside-text', which as M. Wood explains in the *London Review of Books* 38.3 (Feb. 4, 2016), 7–9, is a reference to an unnumbered page in a printed book, which, though it lacks a number, is nevertheless what it is in relation to the rest. Context, in other words, always matters, even when it is unstable. Discussing what Derrida 'meant' by a saying, however, seems inherently peculiar.

143   Luke 1.1–4; 3.1–2.

144   Of course, some within the post-Bultmann world wanted to reject Luke for exactly this reason: he, unlike Mark at least, thought that these stories had to do with actual events . . .

145   The work of Richard Burridge and others on the Gospels as biography, and the remarkable proposal of Richard Bauckham about eyewitness traditions, have created a new context: see R. Burridge, *What Are the Gospels? A Companion with Graeco-Roman Biography*, SNTSMS 70 (Cambridge: Cambridge University Press 1992; 2nd edn., Grand Rapids: Eerdmans 2004; 25th anniv. edn., Waco, Tex.: Baylor University Press, 2018); R. J. Bauckham, *Jesus and the Eyewitnesses: The Gospels as Eyewitness Testimony*, 2nd edn. (Grand Rapids: Eerdmans, 2017). There is much to be said about both, but both offer well-grounded ways forward. Of course, both generate further discussion: see e.g. J.-N. Aletti, *The Birth of the Gospels as Biographies* (Rome: G & BP, 2017).

146   See e.g. Sanders, *Jesus and Judaism*; and my own *JVG*.

147   R. J. Bauckham, *Jesus and the God of Israel* (Grand Rapids: Eerdmans, 2009); L. W. Hurtado, *Lord Jesus Christ: Devotion to Jesus in Earliest Christianity* (Grand Rapids: Eerdmans, 2003) and e.g. *How on Earth Did Jesus Become a God?* (Grand Rapids: Eerdmans, 2005). In my own work, see e.g. *PFG*, chs. 2, 9, citing earlier work as well.

148   On all this see my *RSG*.

149   H. Chadwick, 'The Chalcedonian Definition', in *Selected Writings*, ed. William G. Rusch (Grand Rapids: Eerdmans, 2017), 101–14. Originally in *Actes du Concile de Chalcedoine: Sessions III–VI*, trans. A.-J. Festugière, Cahiers d'Orientalism IV (Geneva: Patrick Cramer, 1983). See esp. 113: 'The technical philosophical terms and the negative adverbs . . . convey a sense of abstraction inadequate to express the richness of a biblical Christology . . . Abstract terms do not do justice to the vivid figure of the four Gospels, and by their abstraction may seem to take him out of the particularity of the historical process'. This casts doubt, in my mind, on Chadwick's final claim (114) that the Definition is helping the church to hold on to 'the two main patterns of Christology inherited from the New Testament itself'. We might compare the striking sentences of Karl Barth in *Church Dogmatics*, vol. 4, *The Doctrine of Reconciliation*, part 2, trans. G. W. Bromiley (Edinburgh: T&T Clark, 1956 [1953]), 127: 'In Himself and as such the Christ of Nicaea and Chalcedon naturally was and is a being which even if we could consistently and helpfully explain His unique structure conceptually could not possibly be proclaimed and believed as One who acts historically because of the timelessness and historical remoteness of the concepts . . . He could not possibly be proclaimed and believed as the One whom in actual fact the Christian Church has always and everywhere proclaimed and believed under the name Jesus Christ'.

150   See *JVG*, ch. 2, and the other literature cited there.

151   The idea of a 'kenotic' Christology emerged from some readings of Phil 2.7, where Jesus 'emptied himself' (*ekenōsen heauton*). Different meanings have been attached to this. See *PFG*, 680–89.

152   See too 1.68; 19.44.

153   Luke 24.21: 'we were hoping that he was going to redeem Israel!'

CHAPTER 4: THE END OF THE WORLD?

1   On 'apocalyptic' in the modern period, and particularly with reference to contemporary Pauline studies, see *PRI*, Part II.

2   Among my earlier discussions of the whole theme, see esp. *NTPG*, 280–338 and 459–64.

3   See G. B. Caird, *The Language and Imagery of the Bible* (London: Duckworth, 1980), ch. 14. See too my summary of different current meanings in *JVG*, 208.

4   Some still use the word as though this was its univocal meaning: e.g. R. Morgan, 'Albert Schweitzer's Challenge and the Response from New Testament Theology', in *Albert Schweitzer in Thought and Action*, ed. J. C. Paget and M. J. Thate (Syracuse: Syracuse University Press, 2016), 71–104 (72).

5   Cf. C. H. Dodd, *Parables of the Kingdom*, rev. edn. (London: Nisbet, 1961 [1935]) and elsewhere.

6   See the critique in Moltmann, *Coming of God*, 13–22, also criticizing Barth and Bultmann for losing the 'futurity' of the eschaton as they look instead for the 'eternal moment'.

7   Caird then lists two interpretations of Old Testament prophecy well known in the last generation, those of Lindblom and Clements. These are the prophetic hope that God will 'do a new thing', and the providential belief in God's purposes being worked out steadily and gradually.

8   See ch. 3 above and *NTPG*, 199f., on the Rabbis giving up 'apocalyptic' and 'kingdom of God'—i.e. scripturally driven visions of revolution—in the mid-second century.

9   On the question of 'dualism' here and elsewhere see the discussion by R. Bauckham, 'Dualism and Soteriology in Johannine Theology', in Longenecker and Parsons, eds., *Beyond Bultmann*, 133–53, citing esp. J. G. Gammie, 'Spatial and Ethical Dualism in Jewish Wisdom and Apocalyptic Literature', *JBL* 93 (1974), 356–85; *NTPG*, 280–99; and *PFG*, 370f. See too Bauckham's older article, 'The Delay of the Parousia', *TynBul* 31 (1980), 3–36.

10   On Jewish views of life after death in this period see *RSG*, chs. 3, 4.

11   See the sharp critique of this kind of view in J. Moltmann, 'The Liberation of the Future from the Power of History', in *God Will Be All in All: The Eschatology of Jürgen Moltmann*, ed. R. Bauckham (London: T&T Clark, 1999), 265–89.

12   Luke 11.20. The parallel in Matt 12.28 has 'spirit' for 'finger', but the point is the same.

13   See here particularly my response to Jörg Frey in *God and the Faithfulness of Paul*, ed. C. Heilig, J. T. Hewitt and M. F. Bird (Grand Rapids: Eerdmans, 2017), 743–54.

14   See *PRI*, Part II.

15   By this I mean the Barth of the later volumes of the *Church Dogmatics*, and also of *The Humanity of God*, trans. Thomas Wieser and John Newton Thomas (Philadelphia: Westminster John Knox, 1998 [1960], from three German monographs) as opposed to the Barth of the first Romans commentary. Reflecting upon his monumental second edition commentary on Romans, Barth suggests to the reader in *Church Dogmatics* I/2 that he has undergone a change of mind. Whereas in his commentary he famously suggested that revelation touches time 'as a tangent touches a circle, that is, without touching it' (*The Epistle to the Romans*, 2nd edn., trans. Edwyn C. Hoskins [Oxford: Oxford University Press, 1933 (1922)], 29), he now believes that revelation 'does not remain transcendent over time, [and] it does not merely meet it at a point, but it enters time; nay it assumes time' (*CD* I/2, 50).

16   See again *PRI*, Part II. This raises a host of other questions not relevant to our present discussion.

17 See, among many possible scholarly sources, C. C. Rowland, *The Open Heaven: A Study of Apocalyptic in Judaism and Early Christianity* (New York: Crossroad, 1982); J. J. Collins, *The Apocalyptic Imagination* (New York: Crossroad, 1987); and recently, B. E. Reynolds and L. T. Stuckenbruck, eds., *The Jewish Apocalyptic Tradition and the Shaping of New Testament Thought* (Minneapolis: Fortress, 2017).

18 See e.g. J. P. Davies, *Paul among the Apocalypses?*

19 See M. Eliade, 'Sacred Space and Making the World Sacred', in *Cult and Cosmos: Tilting towards a Temple-Centered Theology*, ed. L. M. Morales (Leuven: Peeters, 2014), 195–316, on the way in which heaven-and-earth symbols function cross-culturally.

20 On 'dualism' in this connection see *NTPG*, 252–56, and above, p. 304 n. 9.

21 See e.g. D. C. Allison, *The Historical Christ and the Theological Jesus* (Grand Rapids: Eerdmans, 2009), 90–101, a brief summary of a position Allison has argued at more length elsewhere: e.g. *Constructing Jesus: Memory, Imagination, and History* (Grand Rapids: Baker, 2010), esp. ch. 2.

22 See Isa 13.10; 24.23; cf. Ezek 32.7f.; Joel 2.10, 30f.; 3.15; Amos 8.9.

23 Cf. Caird, *Language and Imagery*, 259 (discussed in *PFG*, 168–70).

24 In what follows I draw freely on my article 'Hope Deferred? Against the Dogma of Delay', *Early Christianity* 9.1 (2018), 37–82.

25 Note also Paul's references to 'the day of the Lord' (1 Cor 1.8; 2 Cor 1.14; Phil 1.6, 10; 1 Thess 5.2), which seems to be an adaptation of the biblical 'day of YHWH'. On all this see *PFG*, 1078–95.

26 See *NTPG*, 421f.

27 See e.g. Winter, *After Paul Left Corinth*, 216–25. Similar things could be said about Rom 13.11 ('our salvation is nearer now than it was when we first came to faith').

28 See above, p. 65.

29 A recent publication that takes the received dogma for granted and tries to work around it is C. M. Hays, ed., *When the Son of Man Didn't Come: A Constructive Proposal on the Delay of the Parousia* (Minneapolis: Fortress, 2016). Several scholars have pushed back hard at the still standard 'dogma of delay', e.g. C. F. D. Moule, *The Birth of the New Testament*, 3rd edn. (London: A&C Black, 1982 [1962]), 139f., 143f.; M. Hengel, *Between Jesus and Paul: Studies in the Earliest History of Christianity*, trans. John Bowden (London: SCM Press, 1983; repr., Waco, Tex.: Baylor University Press, 2013), 184 n. 55, describing the 'delay of the parousia' as 'a tired cliché'; Sanders, *Judaism*, e.g. 298, 303, 456f., and especially the passage at 368 which I quoted above at p. 294 n. 59; J. J. Collins, as summarized in *NTPG*, 333f.; and see the fuller discussions in that volume, 280–99, 459–64; *JVG*, 339–67; and *PFG*, 163–75.

30 See the discussion in *PFG*, 1402f.

31 See again Congdon, *Rudolf Bultmann*, 10: the combination of present and future eschatology into an 'already but not yet' scheme is a 'simplistic dismissal of the problem', invented in the mid-twentieth century, offering 'an easy way out' which has become 'immensely attractive for obvious reasons' so that 'all problems immediately disappear'.

32 See *PFG*, 1076–85.

33 Bultmann might have agreed at this point, since for him the Transfiguration narrative which follows (Mark 9.2–8) was a misplaced 'resurrection' story designed to 'fulfil' this prediction.

34 On the 'royal' interpretation of the 'son of man' in Ps 8 see my article 'Son of Man—Lord of the Temple? Gospel Echoes of Ps 8 and the Ongoing Christological Challenge', in *The Earliest Perceptions of Jesus in Context: Essays in Honour of John Nolland on His 70th Birthday*, ed. A. W. White, D. Wenham and C. A. Evans (London: Bloomsbury/T&T Clark), 77–96.

In Heb 2.5–9 the psalm is seen as *partially* fulfilled in Jesus. In discussing Ps 8 I am using the verse-numbering from the LXX.

35 See J. T. Hewitt, *In Messiah: Messiah Discourse in Ancient Judaism and 'In Christ' Language in Paul* (Tübingen: Mohr Siebeck, 2019).

36 There are slight variations here between LXX and Theodotion but the sense is the same.

37 One could focus the debate between Pannenberg and Moltmann on the meaning of 'within' here. For both, the resurrection is 'historical' in the sense of an actual happening in space and time; the question tends to polarize between those who might suggest that the event arises from latent capacities within the created order (and thus may be subjected to historical study as any other event) and those who see it as the result of quite fresh divine action (and thus is in principle not able to be demonstrated on historical grounds alone).

38 I am assuming that Paul at least is taking Ps 8.6 (8.5 EVV) as a sequence (from an earlier humiliation to a subsequent exaltation) rather than a static paradox (simultaneous humiliation and exaltation), though as it stands—and perhaps in Johannine interpretation—the latter is a possible reading. I am grateful to Prof. W. Moberly for pointing this out to me.

39 That same future is re-emphasised in 2.15, alluding to Dan. 12.3; cf. too the echoes both of the poem and of Ps 8 in Phil 3.20–21.

40 Against the elegant exposition of S. Motyer, *Come, Lord Jesus! A Biblical Theology of the Second Coming of Christ* (London: Apollos, 2016), 100–105. The point deserves fuller discussion.

41 This discussion could be made more complex by reflecting on the meaning which Matthew and Luke intended for the relevant sayings if, as most still think, those Gospels were written after AD 70.

42 I have argued in *PFG*, ch. 9, that this theme—Yhwh's return—was central to early Christology. On the Isaianic and similar traditions behind this belief see recently C. Ehring, *Die Rückkehr JHWHs: Traditions- und religionsgeschichtliche Untersuchungen zu Jesaja 40,1–11, Jesaja 52,7–10 und verwandten Texten* (Neukirchen: Neukirchener Verlag, 2007).

43 See the discussion in Hays, *Echoes of Scripture in the Gospels*, 22, 374f. nn. 17, 22.

44 On all this, see *JVG*, 348–60.

45 See N. T. Wright, 'Son of God and Christian Origins', forthcoming in *Son of God: Divine Sonship in Jewish and Christian Antiquity*, ed. G. V. Allen et al. (University Park, Pa: Eisenbrauns, 2019), 120–36.

46 See again Bauckham, 'Delay of the Parousia'. The theme goes back through Habakkuk to the Psalms at least.

47 See the full discussions in Schäfer, *Bar Kokhba War*, and Horbury, *Jewish War*.

48 This is the thesis, particularly, of the commentary of A. C. Thiselton (*First Epistle to the Corinthians*). However much his argument about 1 Corinthians may need modification (see, for instance, R. B. Hays, *The Conversion of the Imagination: Paul as Interpreter of Israel's Scriptures* [Grand Rapids: Eerdmans, 2005]), the larger theological point remains valid.

49 On the transition from 'hope' (the dominant note among Second Temple Jews) to 'joy' see *NTPG*, Part IV.

50 D. E. Nineham, foreword to the 2000 edn. of Schweitzer's *Quest*, xxiii–xxv. Nineham, of course, wanted to be able to say that ancient Jewish kingdom-language was end-of-the-world talk, and that Jesus made no attempt to change it. This is wrong on both counts.

51 As in Matt 10.28 and Luke 12.4–5.

52 Specifically, vv. 13–14, 18, 22, 27.

53 Matthew: 'All authority has been given to me in heaven and upon earth'; Daniel: 'Authority was given to him so that all the nations of the earth would serve him'.

54 Cf. Dan 7.27.
55 See Wright, 'Son of Man—Lord of the Temple?', in White, Wenham and Evans, eds., *Earliest Perceptions of Jesus in Context*, 77–96.
56 Cp. Acts 5.31.
57 On the passage, see recently M. Botner, *Jesus Christ as the Son of David in the Gospel of Mark* (Cambridge: Cambridge University Press, 2019). On the Temple in Mark, see esp. T. C. Gray, *The Temple in the Gospel of Mark: A Study in Its Narrative Role* (Tübingen: Mohr, 2008).
58 I have discussed this in detail elsewhere: see *JVG*, 320–67.
59 John 2.18–22; see esp. vv. 21 ('He was speaking about the 'temple' of his body') and 22 ('So when he was raised from the dead, his disciples remembered that he had said this, and they believed the Bible and the word which Jesus had spoken').
60 As Jeremiah had said: Jer 7.11, quoted at Mark 11.17.
61 The attempt by E. Adams, in *The Stars Will Fall from Heaven: Cosmic Catastrophe in the New Testament and Its World* (London: T&T Clark, 2007), 165, to suggest that the events before which the generation will not have passed away (Mark 13.30) does not include the events of vv. 24–27, but only those of vv. 5–23, strikes me as desperate, especially in view of 'all these things' in v. 30. For my response to Adams see *PFG*, 167–75.
62 For the fascinating suggestion that the chapter is replete with hints towards the coming passion narrative, see P. G. Bolt, 'Mark 13: An Apocalyptic Precursor to the Passion Narrative', *RTR* 54 (1995), 10–30 (http://mydigitalseminary.com/wp-content/uploads/2015/11/Bolt-PG-Mark-13-An-Apocalyptic-Precursor-to-the-Passion-Narrative.pdf).
63 See the full discussion in *JVG*, ch. 8.
64 On the interpretation of Dan 7 see e.g. J. E. Goldingay, *Daniel* (Dallas: Word Books, 1989), 137–93; J. J. Collins, *Daniel* (Minneapolis: Fortress, 1993), 274–324.
65 On the ways in which the Gospel traditions reflect Jesus' own situation rather than that of the early church, see *NTPG*, 421f.
66 See *NTPG*, 462–64; and, for the larger picture, B. E. Daley, *The Hope of the Early Church: A Handbook of Patristic Eschatology* (Grand Rapids: Baker Academic, 2010 [1991]). It is noticeable that in *Barn.* 15.4f. the writer takes it for granted that the 'end' will come after six thousand years of world history, presumably understanding that as stretching a long way into the future. See too T. F. Torrance, *Space, Time and Resurrection* (Edinburgh: Handsel Press, 1976), 153f.
67 See again *PRI*, Part II.
68 See e.g. John Hick, ed., *The Myth of God Incarnate* (London: SCM Press, 1977). Keith Ward, in *Christ and the Cosmos: A Reformulation of Trinitarian Doctrine* (Cambridge: Cambridge University Press, 2015), xii, 10, simply repeats the twentieth-century tradition: for the early Christians 'the world was due to end at any moment', so that we, who know they were wrong, may need to think differently.

CHAPTER 5: THE STONE THE BUILDERS REJECTED

1 An important survey of relevant Second Temple material is provided by R. Hayward, *The Jewish Temple: A Non-biblical Sourcebook* (London: Routledge, 1996); and cf. e.g. J. M. Lundquist, *The Temple of Jerusalem: Past, Present, and Future* (Santa Barbara: Praeger, 2008), 94–96.
2 Though Margaret Barker has done remarkable work in alerting scholarly and popular circles to 'Temple'-based theological understanding (see e.g. M. Barker, *The Gate of Heaven: The History and Symbolism of the Temple in Jerusalem* [London: SPCK, 1991)] and *Temple Theology: An Introduction* [London: SPCK, 2014]), most would be cautious at least about

her larger hypotheses e.g. about early Israelite non-monotheism. Some have expressed similar caution about the maximalist exegesis of G. K. Beale, *The Temple and the Church's Mission* (Downers Grove, Ill.: IVP, 2004), though it remains extremely suggestive. Equally, the themes I am exploring are more or less absent from J. Day, ed., *Temple and Worship in Biblical Israel* (London: T&T Clark, 2007); and C. Koester's study *The Dwelling of God: The Tabernacle in the Old Testament, Intertestamental Jewish Literature and the New Testament* (Washington, D.C.: Catholic Bible Association, 1989) only raises them in connection with Philo and Josephus.

3 See too 2 Macc 2.8, in connection with the promised rebuilding of the Temple, indicating how this promise of returning divine glory would be seen in the Second Temple period.

4 Focused here on v. 21.

5 J. D. Levenson, *Creation and the Persistence of Evil: The Jewish Drama of Divine Omnipotence* (Princeton: Princeton University Press, 1994 [1988]), 86.

6 A brief statement, with an indicative bibliography at the time, is given by R. Middleton, *The Liberating Image: The Imago Dei in Genesis 1* (Grand Rapids: Brazos, 2005), 84f. Many of the articles he cites are now conveniently reprinted in Morales, *Cult and Cosmos*. See too e.g. J. H. Walton, *The Lost World of Genesis One: Ancient Cosmology and the Origins Debate* (Downers Grove, Ill.: IVP, 2009) and *Genesis 1 as Ancient Cosmology* (Winona Lake, Ind.: Eisenbrauns, 2011); Beale, *Temple and the Church's Mission*. P. Renwick, *Paul, the Temple, and the Presence of God* (Atlanta: Scholars Press, 1991), suggestively explores the connections in relation to 2 Cor 3 and Jewish ideas about the Temple. The parallel of Genesis 1 with the instructions for the Tabernacle in Exodus have long been noted by Jewish interpreters; cf. e.g. J. Klawans, *Purity, Sacrifice and the Temple: Symbolism and Supersessionism in the Study of Ancient Judaism* (Oxford: Oxford University Press, 2006), 111–44; M. Fishbane, *Biblical Text and Texture: A Literary Reading of Selected Biblical Texts* (Oxford: Oneworld, 1998 [1979]), 12, citing Martin Buber, *Die Schrift und ihre Verdeutschung* (Berlin: Schocken, 1936), 39ff.; A. Green, 'Sabbath as Temple: Some Thoughts on Space and Time in Judaism', in *Go and Study: Essays and Studies in Honor of Alfred Jospe*, ed. R. Jospe and S. Z. Fishman (Washington, D.C.: B'nai B'rith Hillel Foundation, 1982), 287–305 (294–96). The meaning Fishbane (following Buber) assigns to this parallel, however, seems lame and restricted: that humans 'have to extend and complete on earth the divine work of creation' (10), or that the parallels serve to 'valorize' the Tabernacle (11). More profound is Fishbane's comment at p. 136: 'the historical representation of past and future in terms of cosmogonic paradigms discloses the deep biblical presentiment that all historical renewal is fundamentally a species of world renewal'. On wider issues see B. M. Bokser, 'Approaching Sacred Space', *HTR* 78 (1985), 279–99.

7 See the texts in the previous and following notes.

8 Levenson, *Creation and the Persistence of Evil*, 74–75, 85–86. See too e.g. Eliade, 'Sacred Space and Making the World Sacred', in Morales, ed., *Cult and Cosmos*, 295–316; E. Burrows, 'Some Cosmological Patterns in Babylonian Religion', in Morales, ed., *Cult and Cosmos*, 27–48; M. Hundley, *Gods in Dwellings* (Atlanta: SBL, 2013), 135f.; J. M. Lundquist, 'The Common Temple Ideology of the Ancient Near East', in Morales, ed., *Cult and Cosmos*, 49–68 (49): 'in the ancient Near East up to approximately late Hellenistic times, there was a common ritual language and praxis centered around great temples', citing other relevant studies and work by Peter Brown, J. Z. Smith and Jacob Milgrom. See also G. J. Wenham, 'Sanctuary Symbolism in the Garden of Eden Story', in Morales, ed., *Cult and Cosmos* 161–66.

9   E.g. Isa 2.2–5; Micah 4.1–5; Ps 48.1f.

10   Gen 7.1–8.22; 11.1–9; 28.10–22. For discussion, see e.g. on Noah, S. W. Holloway, 'What Ship
     Goes There? The Flood Narrative in the Gilgamesh Epic and Genesis Considered in the
     Light of Ancient Near Eastern Temple Ideology', in Morales, ed., *Cult and Cosmos*, 183–208
     (202–7), likening Noah's Ark to Solomon's Temple with Noah as a priestly figure; Fishbane,
     Biblical Interpretation, 113; see too M. Fishbane, 'The Sacred Center: The Symbolic Struc-
     ture of the Bible', in Morales, ed., *Cult and Cosmos* 289–408 (394f.), suggesting that Noah
     recapitulates Adam and (402) anticipates David.

11   For this theme see esp. R. Luyster, 'Wind and Water: Cosmogonic Symbolism in the Old
     Testament', in Morales, ed., *Cult and Cosmos*, 249–58, citing inter alia Pss 89, 93, 18, 29, 104;
     Nahum 1.4; Isa 44.27; 11.15; 51.10. See too H. G. May, 'Some Cultic Connotations of *Mayyim
     Rabbîm*, "Many Waters"', in Morales, ed., *Cult and Cosmos*, 259–72, stressing that the 'waters'
     are regularly a mythical representation of actual human enemies, and pointing out the obvi-
     ous link of this theme with Dan 7 (on which see below).

12   Exod 15.17.

13   2 Sam 7.1; cf. 1 Chr 23.25, where God has given 'rest' to his people and now will himself
     reside in Jerusalem.

14   1 Kgs 5.4. This also includes, we may assume, his dealing with threats to his own rule.

15   Cf. 132.8, 14; other elements in the narrative are visible with the mention of David's hard-
     ships (v. 1) and his enemies (v. 18).

16   See e.g. Acts 4.25–26; Wis 1–6, with the whole narrative of the wicked nations raging
     against the true God and his people and God then startling them by installing his king and
     summoning the peoples to learn wisdom.

17   Ezek 40–47; see esp. 47.9f.

18   1 Kgs 8.27; 2 Chr 2.6; 6.18.

19   In his classic work *The Sabbath: Its Meaning for Modern Man* (New York: Farrar, Straus and
     Giroux, 2005 [1951]), Abraham J. Heschel argues from Gen 1 that the Sabbath is primary
     and the Temple secondary, since time is more important than space. The Ten Command-
     ments ignore the Temple but make Sabbath-keeping central. Even granted Heschel's desire
     to be relevant to the modern world many centuries after the Temple's destruction (see
     too Green, 'Sabbath as Temple', 292f.), these are significant points for a careful reading of
     Genesis and Exodus. See now e.g. H. Weiss, *A Day of Gladness: The Sabbath among Jews and
     Christians in Antiquity* (Columbia: University of South Carolina Press, 2003), esp. 25–31: for
     Jubilees and the *Songs of the Sabbath Sacrifice*, 'the Sabbath becomes a foretaste of that escha-
     tological social order' (26). The full study by L. Doering, *Schabbat: Sabbathalacha und –praxis
     im antiken Judentum und Urchristentum* (Tübingen: Mohr Siebeck, 1999) concentrates on
     other aspects of the Sabbath, but does note at one point the possibility of Jesus invoking
     an *Urzeit–Endzeit* scheme in which the Sabbath would be a foretaste of the age to come:
     see pp. 455f., with full refs. at p. 456 n. 327. Weiss and Doering, like most Christian scholars,
     focus mainly on the questions of Jewish rules for observance and on early Christian retriev-
     als or readjustments of these. On the historical and textual problems related to the biblical
     notion of 'rest' see G. von Rad, 'There Remains Still a Rest for the People of God', in *The
     Problem of the Hexateuch and Other Essays*, trans. Rev. E. W. Trueman Dicken (London:
     SCM Press, 2012 [1965]), 94–102.

20   W. P. Brown, *The Ethos of the Cosmos: The Genesis of Moral Imagination in the Bible* (Grand
     Rapids: Eerdmans, 1999), 131. See again Green, 'Sabbath as Temple'.

21 I here follow Levenson, *Creation and the Persistence of Evil*, 108. See Doering, *Schabbat*, 67 (though he disclaims any eschatological reference here), and e.g. A.-M. Schwemer, 'Gott als König und seine Königsherrschaft in den Sabbatliedern aus Qumran', in *Königsherrschaft und himmlischer Kult im Judentum, Urchristentum und in der hellenistischen Welt*, ed. M. Hengel and A.-M. Schwemer, WUNT 55 (Tübingen: Mohr Siebeck 1991), 45–118 (53f.).

22 Ps 132.8, 14.

23 mTamid 7.4.

24 bRosh Has. 31a; see too ARN 3; Mek. Exod 31.13; other refs in A. T. Lincoln, 'Sabbath, Rest and Eschatology in the New Testament', in *From Sabbath to Lord's Day: A Biblical, Historical and Theological Investigation*, ed. D. A. Carson (Eugene, Ore.: Wipf & Stock, 1982), 198–220. In another tradition (Zohar Hadash Gen 2.4.22a) all creation, busy during the rest of the week, finally breaks into celebratory song on the Sabbath 'when God ascended upon his throne' (see L. Ginzberg, *The Legends of the Jews*, 14th edn. [Philadelphia: Jewish Publication Society of America, 1937 (1909)], 1.83).

25 See T. Friedman, 'The Sabbath: Anticipation of Redemption', *Judaism* 16 (1967), 445–52; and the quite full discussion of Lincoln, 'Sabbath, Rest and Eschatology in the New Testament', in Carson, ed., *From Sabbath to Lord's Day*.

26 So too e.g. 2 *Bar.* 72.2; 73.1; *Test. Dan* 5.11–12.

27 *LAE* 51.2. In the parallel text *Apoc. Mos.* 43.3 the 'resurrection' has been replaced by 'the migration from the earth of a righteous soul'. Related to all this (though perhaps a Christian interpolation?) is 2 *En.* 33.1–2 which speaks of the coming 'eighth day' of new creation.

28 Friedman, 'Sabbath', 445.

29 PRE 18; ARN 1; so Friedman, 'Sabbath', 447f.

30 So Friedman, 'Sabbath', 443. He suggests that the Rabbis developed this notion through meditation on the biblical promises of creation restored.

31 Cf. e.g. *Jub.* 50.8 (no intercourse allowed on the Sabbath); similarly CD 11.4b–5a; and see Doering, *Schabbat*, 174, citing too Bokser, 'Approaching Sacred Space', 285.

32 See CD 10–12 on Sabbath observance and ShirShabb (4Q400–407: G. Vermes, ed. and trans., *The Complete Dead Sea Scrolls in English* [Harmondsworth: Penguin, 1997], 139–41; 322–30) where the point is that the earthly liturgy is sharing exactly in the heavenly one, so that (4Q405.14–15) the worship constitutes an entry into the true Temple. See however Weiss, 'A Day of Gladness', who sees the eschatological meaning in Qumran as well.

33 Levenson, *Creation and the Persistence of Evil*, 77, 82: history and cosmology work together.

34 Levenson, *Creation and the Persistence of Evil*, 120, italics original.

35 Levenson, *Creation and the Persistence of Evil*, 82; see too S. Bacchiocchi, 'Sabbatical Typologies of Messianic Redemption', *JSJ* 17.2 (1986), 153–76 (166f.). Doering, *Schabbat*, 111, notes that the 364-day calendar of *Jubilees* gave an advantage: major festivals would never occur on ordinary Sabbaths.

36 See Bacchiocchi, 'Sabbatical Typologies of Messianic Redemption', 170f., linking these institutions back to the Sabbath and forward to the messianic redemption.

37 *Jub.* 1.26, 29.

38 *Jub.* 50.5; the book then closes with a stern, detailed warning about the importance of Sabbath-keeping. This idea of the purified land is 'translated' by Paul in Rom 8 into the idea of the 'inheritance' which is the entire redeemed creation. See *PFG*, 366f., 635, 659, 730.

39 Variations on this: *Jub.* 50.5–11; 2 *En.* 33.2 (though this may be a Christian addition); and bSanh. 97a. See further Lincoln 'Sabbath, Rest and Eschatology in the New Testament', in Carson, ed., *From Sabbath to Lord's Day*, 200.

40 See e.g. 2 Pet 3.8. The *Letter of Barnabas* carefully explains (15.4–8) that the Jewish Sabbath is now irrelevant, because Genesis 2.2 is a prophecy of a six-thousand-year creation followed by the judgment, after which God will 'rest' indeed, as will those whom the gospel has made holy and who now celebrate the 'eighth day' because of Jesus' resurrection and ascension (15.9). The letter goes on at once to explain that the Jerusalem Temple, now destroyed, was never the ultimate dwelling-place of God, and that the church, renewed through repentance and faith, is indwelt by God and is thus a 'spiritual temple' (16.1–10).

41 Dan 9.24. Alternative translations of the final phrase include 'a most holy one'. Other obvious occurrences of multiplying 'sevens' to emphasise completeness include Gen 4.24; Matt 18.21f.

42 See esp. *NTPG*, 312–17; *PFG*, 116f., 130, 142f., 293, 1065, and the other literature referred to there.

43 See the use of Lev 25.13; Deut 15.2; Isa 52.7; 61.1 in 11QMelch: see Bacchiocchi, 'Sabbatical Typologies of Messianic Redemption', 175f., referring to other discussions.

44 Here I follow quite closely Middleton, *Liberating Image*.

45 See my article 'Son of Man—Lord of the Temple?' in White, Wenham and Evans, eds., *Earliest Perceptions of Jesus in Context*.

46 This is directly related to the stance of Jürgen Moltmann over against, for instance, H. U. von Balthasar: see Moltmann, 'The World in God or God in the World?' in Bauckham, ed., *God Will Be All in All*, 35–42.

47 Details in *PFG*, 328f.

48 Ps 48.2. The whole psalm displays many aspects of the 'cosmic Temple' narrative, including God's dismaying the surrounding nations, as in Ps 2 (and as, in a different but related connection, Isa 52.13–15).

49 This highlights of course the extraordinary nature of the portrait of Jesus in the four Gospels, where he regularly comes into physical contact with various kinds of impurity.

50 This is paralleled by the repeated promises in the Scrolls that the members of the sect will receive 'all the glory of Adam': e.g. 1QS 4.22f.; 4QpPs37 3.1f.; see *NTPG*, 265f.; *PFG*, 783–95.

51 Sir 24.1–34.

52 See e.g. Lundquist, 'Common Temple Ideology of the Ancient Near East', in Morales, ed., *Cult and Cosmos*, 54–61.

53 See e.g. Fishbane, *Biblical Interpretation*, 370, citing Pss 46.5; 48.2–4, 12–14; Isa 51.3; Ezek 36.35; 47.1–12; also Joel 2.3; 4.18–21; Zech 14.8–11; and cp. L. E. Stager, 'Jerusalem and the Garden of Eden', in Morales, ed., *Cult and Cosmos*, 99–116 (112): the original Temple of Solomon was 'a mythopoeic realization of heaven on earth, of Paradise, the Garden of Eden'.

54 On the 'abduction' by which such narratives are detected, and its important difference from the 'deduction' with which it is often confused, see above, ch. 3.

55 Plato himself, in the *Timaeus*, regarded the present world as beautiful: see recently O'Meara, *Cosmology and Politics in Plato's Later Works*, esp. Part II and ch. 4.

56 Exod 19.5f.; 1 Pet 2.9; Rev 1.6; 5.10; 20.6.

57 A. Green, 'Sabbath as Temple', 291, sees more sharply than most Christian commentators the way in which Jesus becomes the Temple in person: 'as Jesus the Christ is Torah enfleshed, so is he God's house re-established'. See now N. Perrin, *Jesus the Temple* (London: SPCK, 2010).

58 For this theme in the Gospels, see *Revolution*.

59 H. G. May, 'Some Cosmic Connotations', *JBL* 74.1 (1955), 9–21, sees the link but, despite acknowledging that it makes sense within the strong monotheism of the 'P' tradition, insists that in 'apocalyptic' this produces 'cosmic dualism' (262). I regard this as very misleading;

see *NTPG*, 252–56, and *PFG*, 370f. See also R. R. Wilson, 'Creation and New Creation: The Role of Creation Imagery in the Book of Daniel', in *God Who Creates: Essays in Honor of W. Sibley Towner*, ed. W. P. Brown and S. D. McBride (Grand Rapids: Eerdmans, 2000), 190–203, stressing (202) that the vision of Daniel is about the restoration of creation, not the establishment of an alternative 'heavenly realm'.

60 T. Friedman, 'The Sabbath', 446f., suggests that the prophecies of messianic healing in Isa 35 relate to a supposed restoration of the pre-fall state of humans. Some Rabbis and others may have thought like that, though the idea of a return to a pre-fall state, as though the point of salvation were to return to the beginning, is absent from the New Testament.

61 See e.g. W. D. Davies and D. C. Allison, *A Critical and Exegetical Commentary on the Gospel according to Saint Matthew*, vol. 2 (Edinburgh: T&T Clark, 1991), 288f., citing various other primary and secondary sources; Lincoln, 'Sabbath, Rest and Eschatology in the New Testament', in Carson, ed., *From Sabbath to Lord's Day,* 202; and e.g. S. Bacchiocchi, 'Matthew 11:28–30: Jesus' Rest and the Sabbath', *Andrews University Seminary Studies* 22.3 (Autumn 1984), 289–316, esp. at 299f.

62 Lincoln, 'Sabbath, Rest and Eschatology in the New Testament', in Carson, ed., *From Sabbath to Lord's Day*, 202–5.

63 For the Christology of Colossians see *PFG*, 670–77.

64 See D. M. Moffitt, *Atonement and the Logic of Resurrection in the Epistle to the Hebrews* (Leiden: Brill, 2013).

65 Examples of real innovation might include the use of Isa 7.14 in Matt 1.23, and of 2 Sam 7.12 in Rom 1.3f. So far as we know, nobody prior to the early Christians had seen the former as a prediction of a virginal conception, or the latter as a prediction of a resurrected 'son of David'.

CHAPTER 6: THE NEW CREATION

1 L. Wittgenstein, *Culture and Value: A Selection from the Posthumous Remains*, ed. G. H. von Wright et al., trans. P. Winch (Oxford: Blackwell, 1998 [1970]), 39.

2 McGilchrist, *Master and His Emissary*. Brain scientists themselves are still working on the left brain/right brain problem but McGilchrist's analysis makes a great deal of sense in the academic fields I know.

3 See particularly 2 Cor 4.1–6; 5.1–10; 6.2 (quoting Isa 49.8).

4 T. Kuhn, *The Structure of Scientific Revolutions*, 2nd edn. (Chicago: University of Chicago Press, 1970 [1962]).

5 On the 'new perspective', see *PRI*, chs. 3, 4 and 5; on the 'third quest', see *JVG*, ch. 3. I have outlined a more autobiographical approach in my essays in *Jesus, Paul and the People of God: A Theological Dialogue with N. T. Wright*, ed. N. Perrin and R. B. Hays (Downers Grove, Ill.: IVP Academic, 2011).

6 On emperors in this connection, see *RSG*, 684, quoting Oscar Wilde's play *Salome*. Death is the last weapon of the tyrant; resurrection indicates (as the Maccabean martyrs already knew) that this weapon is no longer ultimate.

7 For the routine denial in ancient paganism, see *RSG*, ch. 2.

8 See *RSG*, ch. 18.

9 See *RSG*, 599–602.

10 *RSG*, 602–8.

11 See *RSG* 347–56; *PFG* 1398–403.

12 Torrance, *Space, Time and Resurrection*, xi.

13 The original docetic heresy had to do with Jesus prior to his death, that he only 'seemed' to be human. Barth and Torrance here seem to have used it in an extended sense: that the risen Jesus only 'seemed' to be bodily raised.

14 See *RSG* 534–51. Contrast the other second-century writers surveyed in *RSG*, 480–534.

15 This is a problem in the work of e.g. R. Jenson, *Systematic Theology*, vol. 1, *The Triune God* (New York: Oxford University Press, 1997), 194. Jenson suggests that the early Christian belief that Jesus was now in 'heaven' makes some sense within a Ptolemaic universe but not in a Copernican one (201f.). But things are more complicated. Ptolemy (second century AD) knew that the earth was tiny in comparison to the larger universe: see *The Almagest: Introduction to the Mathematics of the Heavens*, trans. B. M. Perry, ed. W. H. Donahue (Santa Fe, N.Mex.: Green Lion, 2014), 32.

16 See recently e.g. A. Lindemann, 'The Resurrection of Jesus: Reflections on Historical and Theological Questions', *Ephemerides Theologicae Lovanienses* 93.4 (2017), 557–79.

17 Jenson, *Systematic Theology*, 1.205.

18 See, in considerable detail, *RSG*, ch. 2.

19 Luke perhaps intends a reference back to Acts 4.25–26, where the Jerusalem church prays Ps 2, with 'the nations' raging against God's Messiah, and applies this directly to Pontius Pilate and Herod Antipas.

20 *Surprised by Hope*, 52–59.

21 Individual items from this list are paralleled here and there, so that (for instance) the Qumran scrolls speak of the community in terms of a new Temple. The uniqueness lies in some of the features but particularly in their combination.

22 On the ways in which the early Christians were, and were not, a 'religious' movement, see *PFG*, ch. 13.

23 See particularly Hays, *Echoes of Scripture in the Gospels*, and my initial reflections in 'Pictures, Stories, and the Cross: Where Do the Echoes Lead?' *JTI* 11.1 (2017), 53–73.

24 This is the argument of *RSG*, ch. 18.

25 That was the conclusion of my former philosophy tutor, Christopher Kirwan of Exeter College, Oxford, on reading *RSG*.

26 Or not, at least, in the usual sense; one can imagine a Gnostic deducing from present experience (a) that the dark and wicked world is the creation of a Demiurge and (b) that the inner human spark possessed by a favoured few is a distant signal of a different god . . .

27 See my article, 'Apocalyptic and the Sudden Fulfilment of Divine Promise', in Goodrich, Blackwell and Mastin, eds., *Paul and the Apocalyptic Imagination*, 111–34.

28 See Hays, *Echoes of Scripture in the Gospels*.

29 See *PRI*, Part II.

30 *Resurrection and Moral Order*, 2nd edn. (Leicester: IVP, 1994 [1986]).

31 As I have argued in *Virtue Reborn* (London: SPCK, 2010; US title *After You Believe* [San Francisco: HarperOne, 2010]), these were never seen as virtues in the ancient non-Jewish world, but quickly became central among Jesus' followers.

32 *RSG*, and *Surprised by Hope*.

33 See *PFG*, 733–37 and frequently.

34 The theme of the 'first day' of the new week is prominent in John's presentation of the resurrection: see 21.1, 19. On the question of whether the early Christians saw Sunday as a 'new Sabbath' see S. Bacchiocchi, *From Sabbath to Sunday: A Historical Investigation of the Rise of Sunday Observance in Early Christianity* (Rome: Pontifical Gregorian University Press,

1979) and D. A. Carson, ed., *From Sabbath to Lord's Day* (Eugene, Ore.: Wipf & Stock, 1982). Key texts include *Barn.* 15.8–9; Justin Martyr, *Dial.* 41.

35 It should not be necessary to point out the difference between this and the 'promise-fulfilment' theme of an older style of Christian apologetics. That was about the apparently random 'supernatural' promises of scripture which were now 'fulfilled' in Jesus-events to which they had only a tangential connection. We are here dealing with something far more organic.

36 This received classic expression in A. J. Ayer, *Language, Truth and Logic* (London: Penguin Modern Classics, 2001 [1936]).

37 See *NTPG*, 33.

38 On 'power' see further ch. 7 below.

CHAPTER 7: BROKEN SIGNPOSTS?

1   On the hermeneutical implications of the passage see Hays, *Echoes of Scripture in the Gospels*.

2   See *NTPG*, Part IV.

3   For this reading of Luke, see e.g. Conzelmann, *Theology of St. Luke*; for this (so-called 'apocalyptic') reading of Paul, see my discussion in *PRI*, Part II.

4   For a summary of the many answers to this question, see the preface, pp. x–xi.

5   See M. D. Eddy, 'Nineteenth-Century Natural Theology', *OHNT*, 100–117 (101f.).

6   Kant, as quoted in Eddy, 'Nineteenth-Century Natural Theology', 104.

7   Kant, as quoted in Eddy, 'Nineteenth-Century Natural Theology', 104.

8   See *Revolution*.

9   There might be more mileage in looking at the human capacity for words. Rowan Williams examined that in his Gifford Lectures: *The Edge of Words: God and the Habit of Language* (London: Bloomsbury Continuum, 2014).

10 See *PRI*, Part II.

11 For a historical survey of the development and outcome of the Barth/Brunner debate cf. Hart, *Karl Barth vs. Emil Brunner*.

12 See, for a not uncontroversial perspective, McGrath, *Emil Brunner*.

13 The debate is easily accessible in Fraenkel, trans., *Natural Theology*.

14 See esp. *Revolution*, and the other works listed in the preface, n. 1.

15 I have explored these in somewhat more depth in a forthcoming book centred on the Gospel of John.

16 See *Simply Christian* (London and San Francisco: SPCK and HarperOne, 2005), Part I.

17 Despite the haunting imagery associated with it in 'The Dry Salvages', the third of T. S. Eliot's *Four Quartets* (Orlando: Harcourt, 1971 [1943]), lines 200–205, speaking of 'the point of intersection of the timeless with time', which proves (215) to be a 'hint half guessed' and a 'gift half understood', namely Incarnation.

18 Ezra 9.8f. and Neh. 9.36 complain of being 'slaves in our own land'. See the full treatment in *PFG*, 139–63, and J. M. Scott, ed., *Exile: A Conversation with N. T. Wright* (Downers Grove, Ill.: IVP Academic, 2017).

19 This is the thesis of Bernard Williams's last book, *Truth and Truthfulness: An Essay in Genealogy* (Princeton: Princeton University Press, 2002).

20 On different theories of 'truth' see the helpful summary articles of P. Horwich, 'Truth', in *The Cambridge Dictionary of Philosophy*, 2nd edn. (Cambridge: Cambridge University Press, 1999), 929–31, and his larger study *Truth* (Oxford: Oxford University Press, 1990); R. L.

Kirkham, *Theories of Truth: A Critical Introduction* (Cambridge, Mass.: MIT Press, 1992); Walsh and Middleton, *Truth Is Stranger than It Used to Be*; and S. Blackburn, *Truth: A Guide for the Perplexed* (London: Penguin, 2006 [2005]).

21 See above, ch. 3 n. 58 (p. 298).

22 W. Pannenberg, *Anthropology in Theological Perspective*, trans. M. J. O'Connell (Edinburgh: T&T Clark, 1999), esp. 43–79.

23 See Jonathan Sacks, *Not in God's Name: Confronting Religious Violence* (London: Hodder & Stoughton, 2015).

24 The desire for God will out: as the novelist Julian Barnes says at the start of his book *Nothing to Be Frightened Of* (London: Random House, 2008): 'I don't believe in God, but I miss him'.

25 R. B. Hays, *Reading Backwards* (Waco, Tex.: Baylor University Press, 2015) and, more fully, *Echoes of Scripture in the Gospels*.

26 This emerges particularly in Rom 9–11: see *PFG*, ch. 11.

27 See e.g. M. Hengel, *Crucifixion in the Ancient World and the Folly of the Message of the Cross*, trans. J. Bowden (London: SCM Press, 1976).

28 For the details, see *NTPG*, 170–81.

29 On the 'cry of dereliction' from Ps 22.1 see also *JVG*, 600–601.

30 Cf. Luke 23.35.

31 E. Shillito, *Jesus of the Scars and Other Poems* (London: Hodder and Stoughton, 1919).

32 See Rom 8.29; Col 3.10.

33 R. Bultmann, 'Die Bedeutung des geschichtlichen Jesus für die Theologie des Paulus', in *Glauben und Verstehen*, vol. 1 (Tübingen: Mohr, 1933), 188–213 (205).

34 The danger of this is exemplified in the attempts to fuse a biblical understanding of God with empirical observation, as in the use made by Thomas Chalmers of the work of Newton: see Eddy, 'Nineteenth Century Natural Theology', 102.

35 See J. Moltmann, *God in Creation*, 277–79: the promise of the eschatological Sabbath is built in to creation's original fabric, though only discernible as such in the light of Easter.

36 Sellars explained this in a broadcast talk on BBC Radio 3 on September 6, 2014. I have discussed it further in *Revolution*, 9. A similar point could be made from Chaim Potok's novel *My Name Is Asher Lev* (London: Heinemann, 1972), where the young Jewish artist discovers that only the crucifixion—in shocking new expressions—can do justice to the pain of being a Jew in the modern world.

37 *Revolution*, 8, 37.

38 See *Revolution*, 11f. When writing that book I did not know the archbishop's name; I have since discovered it.

39 See *Evil and the Justice of God* and *Revolution*.

CHAPTER 8: THE WAITING CHALICE

1 Hopkins, 'God's Grandeur', in *The New Oxford Book of English Verse*, ed. H. Gardner (Oxford: Oxford University Press, 1972), 786.

2 John 18.36 has regularly been misread ('not of this world') as though it were advocating an other-worldly 'kingdom'. The Greek is clear: the kingdom is not *ek tou kosmou toutou*. It does not arise from within the world, but it is designed to replace the usurping rule of the dark force referred to in 12.31.

3   For a helpful discussion of a new kind of 'natural theology', cast within an eschatological frame-work, see J. Moltmann, *Experiences in Theology: Ways and Forms of Christian Theology*, trans. M. Kohl (London: SCM Press, 2000), 64–86. My proposal, though different from his, aligns to this extent: that the true 'nature' of anything is revealed in its eschatological mode of existence, and it is on that new-creational basis that a Christian 'natural theology' can be constructed.

4   As I stressed before, I am not suggesting that 'all Jews', at any particular period, thought in exactly the way I have described. I am proposing, on good historical grounds, that many did, and that Jesus and his first followers picked up these strands of thought and developed them in new ways.

5   Cf. Isa 66.1; Wis 1.7; 12.1.

6   On 'image' and monarchy see ch. 5.

7   See Moltmann, *Coming of God*, 283.

8   Moltmann, *God in Creation*, 152–57.

9   For Paul's idea of the *arrabōn*, see Rom 8.23; 2 Cor 1.22; 5.5; Eph 1.14.

10   See *PFG*, 879–85.

11   See 2 Cor 12.12.

12   See particularly 2 Cor 4.7–18; 6.3–10; 11.21–33; 12.7–10.

13   As in the combination of e.g. Exod 15.8 and Pss 75.13–15; 89.9–10.

14   The idea of seeing this 'glory' in relation to Ps 8 was pointed out to me by Dr H. G. Jacob: see her study, *Conformed to the Image of His Son: Reconsidering Paul's Theology of Glory in Romans* (Downers Grove, Ill.: IVP Academic, 2018). She has not yet, in my view, integrated this with the Temple-related and 'divine' meanings of *doxa* in this passage (this is cognate with her somewhat strange criticisms of C. C. Newman, *Paul's Glory-Christology: Tradition and Rhetoric* [Leiden: Brill, 1992; repr., Waco, Tex.: Baylor University Press, 2017]).

15   I first noticed this in G. K. Beale, *The Book of Revelation: A Commentary on the Greek Text* (Grand Rapids: Eerdmans, 1999); he develops it further in *Temple and the Church's Mission*, which raised many points that are important both for ch. 5 and for my present argument.

16   See too 1.6; 5.10; 1 Pet 2.5, 9; and for the background Exod 19.6; Isa 61.6.

17   See not only the obvious link from John 1.1 to Gen 1.1 but the *eskēnōsen* of John 1.14, reso-nating with the *skēnē*, the tent or Tabernacle, of Exod 25–40.

18   The alternative punctuation (literally, 'If any thirst, let them come to me, and let the one drink who believes in me; as the scripture says, out of his heart will flow rivers of living water') would see the living water flowing from Jesus himself, not from his believing fol-lowers. See e.g. C. Keener, *The Gospel of John: A Commentary*, 2 vols. (Peabody, Mass.: Hen-drickson, 2003), 1.728f., with detailed reference to other discussions. But Rev 21.19–24 may suggest that the more traditional reading is correct, echoing Ezek 47 and e.g. Zech 14.8: so e.g. B. F. Westcott, *The Gospel according to St John* (London: John Murray, 1903 [1881]), 123). This would then see the church as the new Temple, refreshing the whole creation. Of course, Jesus remains the ultimate source of the 'living water', as in John 4.10–15. See too my article 'The Powerful Breath of New Creation', in *Veni, Sancte Spiritus! Festschrift für Barbara Hallensleben zum 60. Geburtstag*, ed. W. Dürr, J. Negel, G. Vergauwen and A. Ste-ingruber (Münster: Aschendorff Verlag, 2018), 1–15.

19   See my article with J. P. Davies, 'John, Jesus, and "The Ruler of This World": Demonic Politics in the Fourth Gospel?' in *Conception, Reception and the Spirit: Essays in Honor of Andrew T. Lincoln*, ed. J. G. McConville and L. K. Pietersen (Eugene, Ore.: Wipf & Stock, 2015), 71–89.

20   For the detail, see ch. 4 above.

21 I am reminded of Karl Barth's legendary response to someone asking whether the serpent in Genesis actually spoke; what matters, he replied, is not whether the serpent spoke, but *what the serpent said* (see R. E. Burnett, *Karl Barth's Theological Exegesis: The Hermeneutical Principles of the Römerbrief Period* [Tübingen: Mohr Siebeck, 2001], 262).

22 One might indeed discuss the extent to which a philosopher like Epictetus was an exception to this: see e.g. *Discourses* 2.22, and the discussion in *PFG*, 223–27.

23 At this point one should note the extraordinary slip in the NRSV translation of Rev 21.3, 'the home of God is among mortals'. This is of course a way of avoiding gender-specific terms, but 'mortals' is precisely wrong: the humans in question have been raised to new and undying life (cp. Luke 20.36).

24 On holding the rulers to account see e.g. my *Creation, Power and Truth* (London: SPCK, 2013).

25 One thinks, of course, of the ongoing feud between fundamentalist 'creationists' and the 'new atheists', on which see John Gray's remarks quoted at 281 n. 10 above.

26 On the 'back story' of science see now the remarkable work by R. Wagner and A. Briggs, *The Penultimate Curiosity: How Science Swims in the Slipstream of Ultimate Questions* (Oxford: Oxford University Press, 2016).

27 See my article on 'Christ and the Cosmos: Kingdom and Creation in Gospel Perspective', in *Christ and the Created Order: Perspectives from Theology, Philosophy and Science*, ed. A. B. Torrance and T. H. McCall (Grand Rapids: Zondervan, 2018), 97–109.

28 It is perhaps significant that Bultmann thought the original meaning of the parable of the 'sower' was irrecoverable: see *The History of the Synoptic Tradition*, trans. J. Marsh (Oxford: Blackwell, 1968 [1921]), 199f.

29 This goes back at least to Augustine's notion of the 'book of nature', and was variously developed in the Middle Ages before being adopted again after the Napoleonic Wars. See e.g. A. W. Hall, 'Natural Theology in the Middle Ages', *OHNT*, 57–74 (69f.), with reference to Raymonde of Sabunde (d. 1436), and M. D. Eddy, 'Nineteenth-Century Natural Theology', 105.

30 L. Wittgenstein, *Tractatus Logico-Philosophicus* (London: Routledge, 1974 [1921]), 7.1.

31 All the images in this last paragraph are of course just that: images, designed to point beyond themselves. I am well aware that none of them can fully embody or exemplify the argument of this book as a whole.

32 A British radio station which normally plays short extracts rather than full works.

33 Not least in my *God in Public* (London: SPCK, 2016).

34 Any who might be tempted to question the 'God-given' nature of human authority should study John 19.10–11. This too is a 'broken signpost' in that, as in that same passage, the authority can be and often is horribly abused. When I speak in general terms of the 'structures of the world', I do not intend to affirm all the theories that have used that kind of language.

35 A. Schmemann, *World as Sacrament* (London: Darton, Longman and Todd, 1974).

36 R. Jenson, *Visible Words: The Interpretation and Practice of Christian Sacraments* (Minneapolis: Fortress, 2010). For Jenson's view of the resurrection see, briefly, ch. 6 above.

37 I am grateful for many conversations on this topic with Professor Alan Torrance.

Bibliography

Adams, E. *The Stars Will Fall from Heaven: Cosmic Catastrophe in the New Testament and Its World.* London: T&T Clark, 2007.

Adams, S. V. *The Reality of God and Historical Method.* Downers Grove, Ill.: IVP Academic, 2015.

Albury, W. R. 'Halley's Ode on the *Principia* of Newton and the Epicurean Revival in England'. *Journal of the History of Ideas* 39 (1978), 24–43.

Aletti, J.-N. *The Birth of the Gospels as Biographies.* Rome: G & BP, 2017.

Allen, M. *Grounded in Heaven: Recentering Christian Hope and Life on God.* Grand Rapids: Eerdmans, 2018.

Allison, D. C. *Constructing Jesus: Memory, Imagination, and History.* Grand Rapids: Baker, 2010.

———. *The Historical Christ and the Theological Jesus.* Grand Rapids: Eerdmans, 2009.

Annas, Jula and Jonathan Barnes. *Sextus Empiricus: Outlines of Scepticism.* Cambridge: Cambridge University Press, 2000.

Ayer, A. J. *Language, Truth and Logic.* London: Penguin Modern Classics, 2001 (1936).

Bacchiocchi, S. 'Matthew 11:28–30: Jesus' Rest and the Sabbath'. *Andrews University Seminary Studies* 22.3 (Autumn 1984), 289–316.

———. *From Sabbath to Sunday: A Historical Investigation of the Rise of Sunday Observance in Early Christianity.* Rome: Pontifical Gregorian University Press, 1979.

———. 'Sabbatical Typologies of Messianic Redemption'. *JSJ* 17.2 (1986), 153–76.

Baird, W. *History of New Testament Research.* 3 vols. Minneapolis: Fortress, 1992–2013.

Barker, M. *The Gate of Heaven: The History and Symbolism of the Temple in Jerusalem.* London: SPCK, 1991.

———. *Temple Theology: An Introduction.* London: SPCK, 2014.

Barnes, Julian. *Nothing to Be Frightened Of.* London: Random House, 2008.

Barrett, C. K. 'J. B. Lightfoot as Biblical Commentator'. Appendix F in J. B. Lightfoot, *The Epistles of 2 Corinthians and 1 Peter*, edited by B. W. Witherington and T. D. Still. Downers Grove, Ill.: IVP, 2016.

Barth, K. *Church Dogmatics*. Vol. 1, *The Doctrine of the Word of God*. Part 2. Translated by G. T. Thomson and Harold Knight. Edinburgh: T&T Clark, 1956 (1938).

―――. *Church Dogmatics*. Vol. 4, *The Doctrine of Reconciliation*. Part 2. Translated by G. W. Bromiley. Edinburgh: T&T Clark, 1956 (1953).

―――. *Dogmatics in Outline*. Translated by G. T. Thompson. London: SCM Press, 1966 (1949).

―――. *The Epistle to the Romans*. 2nd edn. Translated by Edwyn C. Hoskins. Oxford: Oxford University Press, 1933 (1922).

―――. *The Humanity of God*. Translated by Thomas Wieser and John Newton Thomas. Philadelphia: Westminster John Knox, 1998 (1960).

―――. *The Knowledge of God and the Service of God according to the Teaching of the Reformation*. Translated by J. L. M. Haire and Ian Henderson. London: Hodder and Stoughton, 1938.

―――. *Nein! Antwort an Emil Brunner*. Zurich: Theologischer Verlag, 1934.

Barth, K. and E. Thurneysen. *Revolutionary Theology in the Making: Barth-Thurneysen Correspondence, 1914–1925*. London: Epworth, 1964.

Bauckham, R. J. 'The Delay of the Parousia'. *TynBul* 31 (1980), 3–36.

―――. 'Dualism and Soteriology in Johannine Theology'. In *Beyond Bultmann: Reckoning a New Testament Theology*, edited by B. W. Longenecker and M. C. Parsons, 133–53. Waco, Tex.: Baylor University Press, 2014.

―――. *Jesus and the Eyewitnesses: The Gospels as Eyewitness Testimony*. 2nd edn. Grand Rapids: Eerdmans, 2017 (2008).

―――. *Jesus and the God of Israel*. Grand Rapids: Eerdmans, 2009.

―――. *Jude, 2 Peter*. Waco, Tex.: Word, 1983.

Beale, G. K. *The Book of Revelation: A Commentary on the Greek Text*. Grand Rapids: Eerdmans, 1999.

―――. *The Temple and the Church's Mission*. Downers Grove, Ill.: IVP, 2004.

Behler, E. 'Nietzsche in the Twentieth Century'. In *The Cambridge Companion to Nietzsche*, edited by B. Magnus and K. M. Higgins. Cambridge: Cambridge University Press, 1996.

Benjamin, W. *Illuminations*. Edited by Hannah Arendt. Translated by Harry Zohn. New York: Schocken Books, 1968 (1958).

Bennett, Alan. *Keeping On Keeping On*. London: Faber, 2016.

Bentley, M. *Modern Historiography: An Introduction*. London: Routledge, 1999.

Berlin, I. *Three Critics of the Enlightenment: Vico, Hamann, Herder*. 2nd edn. London: Pimlico, 2013 (2000).

Berne, P. 'Albert Schweitzer und Richard Wagner'. In *Die Geistigen Leitsterne Albert Schweitzers*, Jahrbuch 2016 für die Freunde von Albert Schweitzer (= Albert-Schweitzer-Rundbrief 108). Edited by E. Weber (2016), 55–76. Available online at https://albert-schweitzer-heute.de/wp-content/uploads/2017/12/DHV-Rundbrief-2016.pdf.

Blackburn, S. *Truth: A Guide for the Perplexed*. London: Penguin, 2006 (2005).

Blake, William. *Selected Poems*. Oxford: Oxford University Press, 1996.

Bloom, H. *The American Religion: The Emergence of the Post-Christian Nation*. New York: Simon and Schuster, 1992.

Boersma, H. *Heavenly Participation: The Weaving of a Sacramental Tapestry*. Grand Rapids: Eerdmans, 2011.

Bokser, B. M. 'Approaching Sacred Space'. *HTR* 78 (1985), 279–99.

Bolt, P. G. 'Mark 13: An Apocalyptic Precursor to the Passion Narrative'. *RTR* 54 (1995), 10–30.

Botner, M. *Jesus Christ as the Son of David in the Gospel of Mark*. Cambridge: Cambridge University Press, 2019.

Bradbury, M. *To the Hermitage*. London: Picador, 2012 (2000).

Brewer, Christopher R. 'Beginning All Over Again: A Metaxological Natural Theology of the Arts'. PhD thesis, University of St Andrews, 2015.

———. *Understanding Natural Theology*. Grand Rapids: Zondervan Academic, forthcoming.

Briggs, A. *Secret Days: Code-Breaking in Bletchley Park*. London: Frontline Books, 2011.

Brown, W. P. *The Ethos of the Cosmos: The Genesis of Moral Imagination in the Bible*. Grand Rapids: Eerdmans, 1999.

Browning, R. 'Caliban upon Setebos; or, Natural Theology in the Island'. In *The Poems of Robert Browning*, 650–55. Oxford: Oxford University Press, 1905.

Buber, Martin. *Die Schrift und ihre Verdeutschung*. Berlin: Schocken, 1936.

Buckley, M. J. *At the Origins of Modern Atheism*. New Haven, Conn.: Yale University Press, 1987.

Bultmann, R. 'Die Bedeutung des geschichtlichen Jesus für die Theologie des Paulus'. In *Glauben und Verstehen*, vol. 1, 188–213. Tübingen: Mohr, 1933.

———. *The Gospel of John: A Commentary*. Translated by G. R. Beasley-Murray, R. W. N. Hoare, and J. K. Riches. Philadelphia: Westminster, 1971 (1941).

———. *History and Eschatology: The Presence of Eternity*. New edn. Waco, Tex.: Baylor University Press, 2019 (1955).

———. *The History of the Synoptic Tradition*. Translated by J. Marsh. Oxford: Blackwell, 1968 (1921).

———. *Jesus Christ and Mythology*. New York: Scribner, 1958.

———. *The New Testament and Mythology and Other Basic Writings*. Edited and translated by Schubert M. Ogden. Philadelphia: Fortress, 1984 (1941).

———. *Primitive Christianity in Its Contemporary Setting*. Translated by R. H. Fuller. London: Collins, 1956.

———. *Theology of the New Testament*. Translated by Kendrick Grobel. 2 vols. London: SCM Press, 1951–1955. Repr., Waco, Tex.: Baylor University Press, 2007.

Bultmann, R. et al. *Kerygma and Myth: A Theological Debate*. Translated by Reginald H. Fuller. London: SPCK, 1953 (1941).

Burke, P. *What Is History Really About?* Brighton: EER Publishers, 2018.

Burkitt, F. C. 'The Eschatological Idea in the Gospel'. In *Essays on Some Biblical Questions of the Day by Members of the University of Cambridge*, edited by H. B. Swete, 193–214. London: Macmillan, 1909.

Burnett, R. E. *Karl Barth's Theological Exegesis: The Hermeneutical Principles of the Römerbrief Period*. Tübingen: Mohr Siebeck, 2001.

Burridge, R. *What Are the Gospels? A Companion with Graeco-Roman Biography*. SNTSMS 70. Cambridge: Cambridge University Press, 1992. 2nd edn., Grand Rapids: Eerdmans, 2004. 25th anniv. edn., Waco, Tex.: Baylor University Press, 2018.

Burrow, J. *A History of Histories*. London: Penguin, 2007.

Bury, J. B. *The Idea of Progress: An Enquiry into Its Origin and Growth*. London: Macmillan, 1920.

Caird, G. B. *The Language and Imagery of the Bible*. London: Duckworth, 1980.

Carr, E. H. *What Is History?* Cambridge: Cambridge University Press, 1961.

Carson, D. A., ed. *From Sabbath to Lord's Day*. Eugene, Ore.: Wipf & Stock, 1982.

Chadwick, H. 'The Chalcedonian Definition'. In *Selected Writings*, edited by William G. Rusch, 101–14. Grand Rapids: Eerdmans, 2017 (1983).

Chambers, E. *Cyclopedia, or a Universal Dictionary of Arts and Sciences.* London: Knapton, Darby and Midwinter, 1728.

Chapman, M. D. *The Coming Crisis: The Impact of Eschatology on Theology in Edwardian England.* Sheffield: Sheffield Academic Press, 2001.

Collingwood, R. G. *The Idea of History.* 2nd edn. Edited by J. van der Dussen. New York: Oxford University Press, 1994 (1946).

Collins, J. J. *The Apocalyptic Imagination.* New York: Crossroad, 1987.

———. *Daniel.* Minneapolis: Fortress, 1993.

Collins, R. *The Sociology of Philosophies: A Global Theory of Intellectual Change.* Cambridge, Mass.: Belknap Press of Harvard University Press, 1998.

Congdon, D. 'The Spirit of Freedom: Eberhard Jüngel's Theology of the Third Article', in Congdon, D. *Indicative of Grace—Imperative of Freedom: Essays in Honour of Eberhard Jüngel in His 80th Year,* edited by D. R. Nelson, 13–27. London: Bloomsbury/T&T Clark, 2014.

Congdon, D. W. *The God Who Saves: A Dogmatic Sketch.* Eugene, Ore.: Cascade, 2016.

———. *The Mission of Demythologizing: Rudolf Bultmann's Dialectical Theology.* Minneapolis: Fortress, 2015.

———. *Rudolf Bultmann: A Companion to His Theology.* Eugene, Ore.: Cascade, 2015.

Conzelmann, H. *The Theology of St. Luke.* Translated by Geoffrey Buswell. New York: Harper and Row, 1961 (1953).

Cook, H. *The Young Descartes: Nobility, Rumor and War.* Chicago: University of Chicago Press, 2018.

Cooke, D. *I Saw the World End: A Study of Wagner's* Ring. Oxford: Oxford University Press, 1979.

Craig, William Lane and J. P. Moreland. *The Blackwell Companion to Natural Theology.* Malden, Mass.: Wiley-Blackwell, 2012.

Daley, B. E. *The Hope of the Early Church: A Handbook of Patristic Eschatology.* Grand Rapids: Baker Academic, 2010 (1991).

Davies, J. P. *Paul among the Apocalypses? An Evaluation of the Apocalyptic Paul in the Context of Jewish and Christian Apocalyptic Literature.* London: T&T Clark, 2018.

Davies, W. D. and D. C. Allison. *A Critical and Exegetical Commentary on the Gospel according to Saint Matthew.* Vol. 2. Edinburgh: T&T Clark, 1991.

Davis, J. B. and D. Harink. *Apocalyptic and the Future of Theology: With and beyond J. Louis Martyn.* Eugene, Ore.: Cascade, 2012.

Day, J., ed. *Temple and Worship in Biblical Israel.* London: T&T Clark, 2007.

de Chardin, P. Teilhard. *The Phenomenon of Man.* Translated by Bernard Wall. London: Collins Fontana, 1965 (1955).

de Lang, M. H. 'Literary and Historical Criticism as Apologetics: Biblical Scholarship at the End of the Eighteenth Century'. *Nederlands archief voor kerkgeschiedenis/ Dutch Review of Church History* 72.2 (1992), 149–65.

Deines, R. *Acts of God in History.* Tübingen: Mohr Siebeck, 2013.

Dodd, C. H. *Parables of the Kingdom.* Rev. edn. London: Nisbet, 1961 (1935).

Doering, L. *Schabbat: Sabbathalacha und –praxis im antiken Judentum und Urchristentum.* Tübingen: Mohr Siebeck, 1999.

Eco, U. 'Horns, Hooves, Insteps: Some Hypotheses on Three Types of Abduction'. In *Dupin, Holmes, Peirce: The Sign of Three,* edited by U. Eco and T. A. Sebeok, 198–220. Bloomington: Indiana University Press, 1983.

Edelstein, D. *The Enlightenment: A Genealogy.* Chicago: University of Chicago Press, 2010.

Ehring, C. *Die Rückkehr JHWHs: Traditions- und religionsgeschichtliche Untersuchungen zu Jesaja 40,1–11, Jesaja 52,7–10 und verdandten Texten.* Neukirchen: Neukirchener Verlag, 2007.

Eliot, T. S. *Four Quartets.* Orlando: Harcourt, 1971 (1943).

Elliott, M. W. *Providence Perceived: Divine Action from a Human Point of View.* Berlin: de Gruyter, 2015.

Elton, G. R. *The Practice of History.* 2nd edn. Oxford: Blackwell, 2002 (1967).

Evans, C. Stephens. 'Methodological Naturalism in Historical Biblical Scholarship'. In *Jesus and the Restoration of Israel: A Critical Assessment of N. T. Wright's* Jesus and the Victory of God, edited by C. Newman, 2nd edn., 180–205. Waco, Tex.: Baylor University Press, 2018 (1999).

Fergusson, D. *The Providence of God: A Polyphonic Approach.* Cambridge: Cambridge University Press, 2018.

———. *Rudolf Bultmann.* 2nd edn. New York: Continuum, 2000 (1992).

Fishbane, M. *Biblical Text and Texture: A Literary Reading of Selected Biblical Texts.* Oxford: Oneworld, 1998 (1979).

Fraenkel, Peter, trans. *Natural Theology: Comprising 'Nature and Grace' by Professor Dr. Emil Brunner and the Reply 'No!' by Dr. Karl Barth.* Eugene, Ore.: Wipf & Stock, 2002 (1946).

Friedman, T. 'The Sabbath: Anticipation of Redemption'. *Judaism* 16 (1967), 445–52.

Gadamer, H.-G. *Truth and Method.* 2nd rev. edn. London: Sheed and Ward, 1989 (1960).

Gale, M. R. *Oxford Readings in Classical Studies: Lucretius.* Oxford: Oxford University Press, 2007.

Gammie, J. G. 'Spatial and Ethical Dualism in Jewish Wisdom and Apocalyptic Literature'. *JBL* 93 (1974), 356–85.

Gardiner, P. L. 'Historicism'. In *The Oxford Companion to Philosophy*, edited by T. Honderich, 357. Oxford: Oxford University Press, 1995.

Gardner, H., ed. *The Oxford Book of English Verse.* Oxford: Oxford University Press, 1972.

Gay, Peter. *The Enlightenment: The Rise of Modern Paganism.* 2 vols. New York: Knopf, 1966.

Gibbon, E. *The Decline and Fall of the Roman Empire.* Vol. 1. London: Frederick Warne, n.d.

Ginzberg, L. *The Legends of the Jews.* 14th edn. Philadelphia: Jewish Publication Society of America, 1937 (1909).

Ginzburg, C. *Clues, Myths and the Historical Method.* Translated by John and Anne C. Tedeschi. New edn. Baltimore: Johns Hopkins University Press, 2013 (1986).

Goethe, J. W. *Faust: Eine Tragödie. Erster Theil.* Edited by E. Gaier. Stuttgart: Reclam, 2011.

Goldingay, J. E. *Daniel.* Dallas: Word Books, 1989.

Gordon, D. R. and D. B. Suits. *Epicurus: His Continuing Influence and Contemporary Relevance.* Rochester, N.Y.: RIT Cary Graphic Arts Press, 2003.

Gray, John. *Seven Types of Atheism.* London: Allen Lane, 2018.

Green, A. 'Sabbath as Temple: Some Thoughts on Space and Time in Judaism'. In *Go and Study: Essays and Studies in Honor of Alfred Jospe*, edited by R. Jospe and S. Z. Fishman, 287–305. Washington, D.C.: B'nai B'rith Hillel Foundation, 1982.

Green, Joel. 'History, Historiography'. In *New Interpreters Dictionary of the Bible*, vol. 2, *D–H*, edited by K. D. Sakenfeld, 830. Nashville: Abingdon, 2007.

Greenblatt, S. *The Swerve: How the Renaissance Began.* London: Bodley Head, 2011.

Grottanelli, C. 'Nietzsche and Myth'. *History of Religions* 37.1 (1997), 3–20.

Harris, J. A. *Hume: An Intellectual Biography.* Cambridge: Cambridge University Press, 2018.

Hart, J. W. *Karl Barth vs. Emil Brunner: The Formation and Dissolution of a Theological Alliance, 1916–1936.* New York: Peter Lang, 2001.

Hatton, B. *Queen of the Sea: A History of Lisbon.* London: C. Hurst, 2018.

Hawes, J. *The Shortest History of Germany.* Yowlestone House, Devon: Old Street Publishing, 2017.

Hays, C. M., ed. *When the Son of Man Didn't Come: A Constructive Proposal on the Delay of the Parousia*. Minneapolis: Fortress, 2016.

Hays, R. B. *The Conversion of the Imagination: Paul as Interpreter of Israel's Scriptures*. Grand Rapids: Eerdmans, 2005.

———. *Echoes of Scripture in the Gospels*. Waco, Tex.: Baylor University Press, 2016.

———. *Reading Backwards*. Waco, Tex.: Baylor University Press, 2015.

Hays, R. B. and B. Gaventa, eds. *Seeking the Identity of Jesus: A Pilgrimage*. Grand Rapids: Eerdmans, 2008.

Hayward, R. *The Jewish Temple: A Non-biblical Sourcebook*. London: Routledge, 1996.

Heilig, C., J. T. Hewitt and M. F. Bird, eds. *God and the Faithfulness of Paul*. Grand Rapids: Eerdmans, 2017.

Heisenberg, W. 'Über den anschaulichen Inhalt der quantentheoretischen Kinematik und Mechanik'. *Zeitschrift für Physik* 43.3–4 (1927), 172–98.

Hengel, M. *Acts and the History of Earliest Christianity*. Translated by John Bowden. London: SCM Press, 1979.

———. *Between Jesus and Paul: Studies in the Earliest History of Christianity*. Translated by John Bowden. London: SCM Press, 1983. Repr., Waco, Tex.: Baylor University Press, 2013.

———. *Crucifixion in the Ancient World and the Folly of the Message of the Cross*. Translated by John Bowden. London: SCM Press, 1976.

Heschel, Abraham J. *The Sabbath: Its Meaning for Modern Man*. New York: Farrar, Straus and Giroux, 2005 (1951).

Hewitt, J. T. *In Messiah: Messiah Discourse in Ancient Judaism and 'In Christ' Language in Paul*. Tübingen: Mohr, 2019.

Hick, John, ed. *The Myth of God Incarnate*. London: SCM Press, 1977.

Hölscher, Lucien. 'Mysteries of Historical Order: Ruptures, Simultaneity and the Relationship of the Past, the Present and the Future'. In *Breaking Up Time: Negotiating the Borders between Present, Past and Future*, edited by C. Lorenz and B. Bevernage, 134–51. Göttingen: Vandenhoeck & Ruprecht, 2013.

———. *Weltgericht oder Revolution: Protestantische und sozialistische Zukunftsvorstellungen im deutschen Kaiserreich*. Stuttgart: Klett-Cotta, 1989.

Honderich, T., ed. *The Oxford Companion to Philosophy*. Oxford: Oxford University Press, 1995.

Horbury, W. *Jewish War under Trajan and Hadrian*. Cambridge: Cambridge University Press, 2014.

Horwich, P. *Truth*. Oxford: Oxford University Press, 1990.

———. 'Truth'. In *The Cambridge Dictionary of Philosophy*, 2nd edn., 929–31. Cambridge: Cambridge University Press, 1999.

Hundley, M. *Gods in Dwellings*. Atlanta: SBL, 2013.

Hurtado, L. W. *How on Earth Did Jesus Become a God?* Grand Rapids: Eerdmans, 2005.

———. *Lord Jesus Christ: Devotion to Jesus in Earliest Christianity*. Grand Rapids: Eerdmans, 2003.

Israel, Jonathan. 'The Philosophical Context of Hermann Samuel Reimarus' Radical Bible Criticism'. In *Between Philology and Radical Enlightenment: Hermann Samuel Reimarus (1694–1768)*, edited by M. Mulsow, 183–200. Leiden: Brill, 2011.

Jacob, H. G. *Conformed to the Image of His Son: Reconsidering Paul's Theology of Glory in Romans*. Downers Grove, Ill.: IVP Academic, 2018.

Jacobi, E. R. *Albert Schweitzer und Richard Wagner: Eine Dokumentation*. Tribschen: Schweizerische Richard-Wagner-Gesellschaft, 1977.

Janick, A. S. and S. E. Toulmin. *Wittgenstein's Vienna*. Minneapolis: Ivan R. Dee, 1996.

Jardine, L. *On a Grander Scale: The Outstanding Career of Sir Christopher Wren.* London: Harper-Collins, 2002.

Jenson, R. *Systematic Theology.* Vol. 1, *The Triune God.* New York: Oxford University Press, 1997.

———. *Visible Words: The Interpretation and Practice of Christian Sacraments.* Minneapolis: Fortress, 2010.

Johnson, L. T. *The Real Jesus: The Misguided Quest for the Historical Jesus and the Truth of the Traditional Gospels.* New York: HarperCollins, 1997.

Johnson, W. R. *Lucretius and the Modern World.* London: Duckworth, 2000.

Jones, G. S. *Karl Marx: Greatness and Illusion.* London: Penguin, 2017.

Jones, H. *The Epicurean Tradition.* London: Routledge, 1989.

Joy, C. R., ed. *Music in the Life of Albert Schweitzer.* New York: Harper, 1951.

Kähler, Martin. *Der sogenannte historische Jesus und der geschichtliche, biblische Christus.* Leipzig: Deichert, 1892.

Kant, Immanuel. 'Beantwortung der Frage: Was ist Aufklärung?' *Berlinische Monatsschrift* 12 (1784), 481–94.

Käsemann, E. *Perspectives on Paul.* Translated by M. Kohl. London: SCM Press, 1971 (1969).

Keener, C. *The Gospel of John: A Commentary.* 2 vols. Peabody, Mass.: Hendrickson, 2003.

Kenny, A. J. P. *A New History of Western Philosophy.* Oxford: Clarendon, 2010.

King-Hele, D. *Erasmus Darwin: A Life of Unequalled Achievement.* London: Giles de la Mare, 1999.

Kirkham, R. L. *Theories of Truth: A Critical Introduction.* Cambridge, Mass.: MIT Press, 1992.

Kitcher, P. and R. Schacht, *Finding an Ending: Reflections on Wagner's* Ring. Oxford: Oxford University Press, 2004.

Klawans, J. *Purity, Sacrifice and the Temple: Symbolism and Supersessionism in the Study of Ancient Judaism.* Oxford: Oxford University Press, 2006.

Knight, D. A. 'The Pentateuch'. In *The Hebrew Bible and Its Modern Interpreters,* edited by D. A. Knight and G. M. Tucker, 263–96. Chico, Calif.: Scholars Press, 1985.

Koch, K. *The Rediscovery of Apocalyptic: A Polemical Work on a Neglected Area of Biblical Studies and Its Damaging Effects on Theology and Philosophy.* London: SCM Press, 1972.

Koester, C. *The Dwelling of God: The Tabernacle in the Old Testament, Intertestamental Jewish Literature and the New Testament.* Washington, D.C.: Catholic Bible Association, 1989.

Koselleck, R. *Futures Past: On the Semantics of Historical Time.* Boston: MIT Press, 1985.

Kotkin, Stephen. 'When Stalin Faced Hitler'. *Foreign Affairs* 96.6 (2017), 54.

Kuhn, T. *The Structure of Scientific Revolutions.* 2nd edn. Chicago: University of Chicago Press, 1970 (1962).

Küng, Hans. *The Church.* London: Burns and Oates, 1968.

Larsen, Ø. 'Kierkegaard's Critique of Hegel: Existentialist Ethics versus Hegel's Sittlichkeit in the Institutions of Civil Society of the State'. *Nordicum Mediterraneum* 11.2 (2016). https://nome.unak.is/wordpress/08-3/c69-conference-paper/kierkegaard-s-critique-of-hegel-existentialist-ethics-versus-hegel-s-sittlichkeit-in-the-institutions-of-civil-society-of-the-state/.

Lasch, C. *The True and Only Heaven: Progress and Its Critics.* New York: Norton, 1991.

Leddy, N. and A. S. Lifschitz, eds. *Epicurus in the Enlightenment.* Oxford: Voltaire Foundation, 2009.

Lee, P. J. *Against the Protestant Gnostics.* 2nd edn. New York: Oxford University Press, 1993 (1987).

Leibniz, Gottfried Wilhelm. *Die Philosophischen Schriften von Gottfried Wilhelm Leibniz.* Edited by C. I. Gerhardt. 7 vols. Berlin: 1875–1890. Repr., Hildesheim: Olms, 1965.

Lessing, G. E. 'On the Proof of the Spirit and of Power'. In *Lessing's Theological Writings*, translated and edited by H. Chadwick. Stanford: Stanford University Press, 1956.

Lessl, T. M. *Rhetorical Darwinism: Religion, Evolution and the Scientific Identity*. Waco, Tex.: Baylor University Press, 2012.

Levenson, J. D. *Creation and the Persistence of Evil: The Jewish Drama of Divine Omnipotence*. Princeton: Princeton University Press, 1994 (1988).

Lewis, C. S. *Christian Reflections*. London: Geoffrey Bles, 1967.

———. *The Discarded Image*. Cambridge: Cambridge University Press, 1964.

———. *A Preface to Paradise Lost*. Oxford: Oxford University Press, 1942.

———. *The Screwtape Letters*. London: Geoffrey Bles, 1942.

Lincoln, A. T. 'Sabbath, Rest and Eschatology in the New Testament'. In *From Sabbath to Lord's Day: A Biblical, Historical and Theological Investigation*, ed. D. A. Carson, 198–220. Eugene, Ore.: Wipf & Stock, 1982.

Lindemann, A. 'The Resurrection of Jesus: Reflections on Historical and Theological Questions'. *Ephemerides Theologicae Lovanienses* 93.4 (2017), 557–79.

Lloyd, G. *Providence Lost*. Cambridge, Mass.: Harvard University Press, 2008.

Lonergan, Bernard. *Method in Theology*. London: Darton, Longman and Todd, 1972.

Long, A. A. and D. N. Sedley. *The Hellenistic Philosophers*. Vol. 1, *Translations of the Principal Sources with Philosophical Commentary*. Cambridge: Cambridge University Press, 1987.

Longenecker, B. W. and M. C. Parsons, eds. *Beyond Bultmann: Reckoning a New Testament Theology*. Waco, Tex.: Baylor University Press, 2014.

Lundquist, J. M. *The Temple of Jerusalem: Past, Present, and Future*. Santa Barbara: Praeger, 2008.

MacMillan, M. *The War That Ended Peace*. London: Profile Books, 2014.

Magee, B. *Wagner and Philosophy*. London: Penguin, 2001.

Mann, Thomas. *Doctor Faustus: The Life of the German Composer Adrian Leverkühn as Told by a Friend*. Translated by H. T. Lowe-Porter. London: Vintage Books, 2015 (1947).

Martyn, J. L. *Galatians*. AB. New York: Doubleday, 1997.

Mason, S. *Orientation to the History of Roman Judaea*. Eugene, Ore.: Cascade, 2016.

May, H. G. 'Some Cosmic Connotations'. *JBL* 74.1 (1955), 9–21.

May, S. *Love: A New Understanding of an Ancient Emotion*. New York: Oxford University Press, 2019.

Mayo, T. *Epicurus in England (1650–1725)*. Dallas: Southwest Press, 1934.

McGilchrist, I. *The Master and His Emissary: The Divided Brain and the Making of the Western World*. New Haven, Conn.: Yale University Press, 2009.

McGrath, A. E. *Emil Brunner: A Reappraisal*. Chichester: Wiley Blackwell, 2014.

———. *Re-imagining Nature: The Promise of a Christian Natural Theology*. Chichester: Wiley-Blackwell, 2017.

McPhee, P. *Robespierre: A Revolutionary Life*. New Haven, Conn.: Yale University Press, 2012.

Meeks, E. L. *Loving to Know: Covenant Epistemology*. Eugene, Ore.: Cascade, 2011.

Meyer, B. F. *The Aims of Jesus*. London: SCM Press, 1979.

———. *Critical Realism and the New Testament*. Allison Park, Pa.: Pickwick, 1989.

Middleton, J. R. *The Liberating Image: The Imago Dei in Genesis 1*. Grand Rapids: Brazos, 2005.

Middleton, J. R. and B. J. Walsh. *Truth Is Stranger than It Used to Be: Biblical Faith in a Postmodern Age*. Downers Grove, Ill.: IVP, 1995.

Moffitt, D. M. *Atonement and the Logic of Resurrection in the Epistle to the Hebrews*. Leiden: Brill, 2013.

Moltmann, J. *The Coming of God*. Translated by Margaret Kohl. Minneapolis: Fortress, 1996 (1995).

———. *Experiences in Theology: Ways and Forms of Christian Theology*. Translated by M. Kohl. London: SCM Press, 2000.

———. *God in Creation: An Ecological Doctrine of Creation*. Translated by M. Kohl. London: SCM Press, 1985.

———. 'The Liberation of the Future from the Power of History'. In *God Will Be All in All: The Eschatology of Jürgen Moltmann*, edited by R. Bauckham, 265–89. London: T&T Clark, 1999.

———. *Theology of Hope: On the Ground and the Implications of a Christian Eschatology*. Translated by James W. Leitch. London: SCM Press, 1967 (1965).

———. 'The World in God or God in the World?' In *God Will Be All in All: The Eschatology of Jürgen Moltmann*, edited by R. Bauckham, 35–42. London: T&T Clark, 1999.

Morales, L. M., ed. *Cult and Cosmos: Tilting Towards a Temple-Centered Theology*. Leuven: Peeters, 2014.

Morgan, R. 'Albert Schweitzer's Challenge and the Response from New Testament Theology'. In *Albert Schweitzer in Thought and Action*, edited by J. C. Paget and M. J. Thate, 71–104. Syracuse: Syracuse University Press, 2016.

Motyer, S. *Come, Lord Jesus! A Biblical Theology of the Second Coming of Christ*. London: Apollos, 2016.

Moule, C. F. D. *The Birth of the New Testament*. 3rd edn. London: A&C Black, 1982 (1962).

Murphy, F. A. 'Everything Is Outside the Text'. *First Things*. November 2, 2017.

Murray, Iain. *The Puritan Hope: Revival and the Interpretation of Prophecy*. Edinburgh: Banner of Truth, 1971.

Naiman, S. *Evil in Modern Thought: An Alternative History of Philosophy*. Princeton: Princeton University Press, 2002. Repr. with new preface and afterword, 2015.

The New English Hymnal. London: Oxford University Press, 1986.

Newman, C. C. *Paul's Glory-Christology: Tradition and Rhetoric*. Leiden: Brill, 1992. Repr., Waco, Tex.: Baylor University Press, 2017.

Nisbet, R. *History of the Idea of Progress*. New York: Basic Books, 1980.

Nixey, C. *The Darkening Age: The Christian Destruction of the Classical World*. London: Macmillan, 2017.

Norman, J. *Adam Smith: What He Thought and Why It Matters*. London: Allen Lane, 2018.

O'Meara, D. J. *Cosmology and Politics in Plato's Later Works*. Cambridge: Cambridge University Press, 2017.

Oermann, N. O. *Albert Schweitzer: A Biography*. Oxford: Oxford University Press, 2017.

Paice, E. *Wrath of God: The Great Lisbon Earthquake of 1755*. London: Quercus, 2009.

Pannenberg, W. *Anthropology in Theological Perspective*. Translated by M. J. O'Connell. Edinburgh: T&T Clark, 1999 (1985).

———. *Basic Questions in Theology*. Translated by G. H. Kelm. 3 vols. London: SPCK, 1970–1973 (1967).

———. *Christianity in a Secularised World*. London: SCM, 1989.

Perrin, N. *Jesus the Temple*. London: SPCK, 2010.

Perrin, N. and R. B. Hays, eds. *Jesus, Paul and the People of God: A Theological Dialogue with N. T. Wright*. Downers Grove, Ill.: IVP Academic, 2011.

Pinker, S. *The Better Angels of Our Nature*. London: Penguin, 2012.

———. *Enlightenment Now: The Case for Reason, Science, Humanism, and Progress*. London: Penguin, 2018.

Pope, Alexander. 'Intended for Sir Isaac Newton'. In *The Poetical Works of Alexander Pope*, 371. London: Frederick Warne, n.d.

Popper, K. *The Open Society and Its Enemies*. London: Routledge and Kegan Paul, 1952.

———. *The Poverty of Historicism*. London: Routledge, 2002 (1957).

Porter, S. E. and A. W. Pitts. 'Critical Realism in Context: N. T. Wright's Historical Method and Analytic Epistemology'. *Journal for the Study of the Historical Jesus* 13 (2015), 276–306.

Portier-Young, A. *Apocalypse against Empire: Theologies of Resistance in Early Judaism*. Grand Rapids: Eerdmans, 2011.

Potok, Chaim. *My Name Is Asher Lev*. London: Heinemann, 1972.

Priestley, J. B. *An Inspector Calls: A Play in Three Acts*. London: Heinemann, 1947.

Ptolemy. *The Almagest: Introduction to the Mathematics of the Heavens*. Translated by B. M. Perry. Edited by W. H. Donahue. Santa Fe, N.Mex.: Green Lion, 2014.

Qu, T. X. '"In the Drawing Power of Goethe's Sun": A Preliminary Investigation into Albert Schweitzer's Reception of Goethe'. In *Albert Schweitzer in Thought and Action*, edited by J. C. Paget and M. J. Thate, 216–233. Syracuse, N.Y.: Syracuse University Press, 2016.

Radner, E. 'Exile and Figural History'. In *Exile: A Conversation with N. T. Wright*, edited by J. M. Scott, 273–301. Downers Grove, Ill.: IVP Academic, 2017.

———. *Time and the Word: Figural Reading of the Christian Scriptures*. Grand Rapids: Eerdmans, 2016.

Rae, Murray. *History and Hermeneutics*. London: T&T Clark, 2005.

Re Manning, Russell, ed. *The Oxford Handbook of Natural Theology*. Oxford: Oxford University Press, 2013.

Renwick, P. *Paul, the Temple, and the Presence of God*. Atlanta: Scholars Press, 1991.

Reventlow, H. G. *The Authority of the Bible and the Rise of the Modern World*. London: SCM, 1984 (1980).

Reynolds, B. E. and L. T. Stuckenbruck, eds. *The Jewish Apocalyptic Tradition and the Shaping of New Testament Thought*. Minneapolis: Fortress, 2017.

Robertson, J. *The Enlightenment: A Very Short Introduction*. Oxford: Oxford University Press, 2015.

Rowland, C. C. *The Open Heaven: A Study of Apocalyptic in Judaism and Early Christianity*. New York: Crossroad, 1982.

Sanders, E. P. *Comparing Judaism and Christianity: Common Judaism, Paul, and the Inner and the Outer in Ancient Religion*. Minneapolis: Fortress, 2016.

———. *Jesus and Judaism*. London: SCM Press, 1985.

———. *Judaism: Practice and Belief, 63 BCE–66 CE*. London: SCM Press, 1992.

———. *Paul and Palestinian Judaism*. London: SCM Press, 1977.

Schäfer, P. *The Bar Kokhba War Reconsidered: New Perspectives on the Second Jewish Revolt against Rome*. Tübingen: Mohr Siebeck, 2003.

Schmemann, A. *World as Sacrament*. London: Darton, Longman and Todd, 1974.

Scholtz, G. 'The Notion of Historicism and 19th Century Theology'. In *Biblical Studies and the Shifting of Paradigms, 1850–1914*, edited by H. Graf Reventlow and W. R. Farmer, 149–67. London: Bloomsbury, 1995.

Schützeichel, Harald. *Die Konzerttätigkeit Albert Schweitzers*. Bern: Haupt, 1991.

Schweitzer, A. *J. S. Bach*. Translated by Ernest Newman. 2 vols. London: A&C Black, 1923 (1908).

———. *The Mystery of the Kingdom of God: The Secret of Jesus' Messiahship and Passion*. Translated by Walter Lowrie. New York: Dodd, Mead and Company, 1914 (1901).

———. *The Mysticism of the Apostle Paul*. Translated by William Montgomery. London: A&C Black, 1931 (1911).

———. *The Quest of the Historical Jesus: First Complete Edition*. Edited by J. Bowden. London: SCM Press, 2000 (1906).

Schwemer, A.-M. 'Gott als König und seine Königsherrschaft in den Sabbatliedern aus Qumran'. In *Königsherrschaft und himmlischer Kult im Judentum, Urchristentum und in der hellenistischen Welt*, edited by M. Hengel and A.-M. Schwemer, 45–118. WUNT 55. Tübingen: Mohr Siebeck, 1991.

Scott, J. M., ed. *Exile: A Conversation with N. T. Wright*. Downers Grove, Ill.: IVP Academic, 2017.

Scruton, R. *The Ring of Truth: The Wisdom of Wagner's Ring of the Nibelung*. London: Penguin, 2017.

Simonutti, Luisa. 'Deism, Biblical Hermeneutics, and Philology'. In *Atheism and Deism Revalued: Heterodox Religious Identities in Britain, 1650–1800*, edited by Wayne Hudson, Lucci Diego and Jeffrey R. Wigelsworth, 45–62. Farnham: Ashgate, 2014.

Smith, C. and M. L. Denton. *Soul Searching: The Religious and Spiritual Lives of American Teenagers*. New York: Oxford University Press, 2005.

Standhartinger, A. 'Bultmann's *Theology of the New Testament* in Context'. In *Beyond Bultmann: Reckoning a New Testament Theology*, edited by B. W. Longenecker and M. C. Parsons, 233–55. Waco, Tex.: Baylor University Press, 2014.

Stark, R. *The Rise of Christianity*. Princeton: Princeton University Press, 1996.

Stern, F., ed. *The Varieties of History from Voltaire to the Present*. 2nd edn. New York: Vintage, 1973 (1956).

Strauss, D. F. *Die christliche Glaubenslehre in ihrer geschichtlichen Entwicklung und im Kampfe mit der modernen Wissenschaft*. 2 vols. Tübingen: C. F. Osiander, 1840.

Syfret, R. H. 'Some Early Reactions to the Royal Society'. *Notes and Records of the Royal Society* 7 (1950).

Tallett, F. 'Dechristianizing France: The Year II and the Revolutionary Experience'. In F. Tallett and N. Atkin, *Religion, Society and Politics in France Since 1789*, 1–28. London: Bloomsbury Academic, 1991.

Tarrant, J. 'Aspects of Virgil's Reception in Antiquity'. In *The Cambridge Companion to Virgil*, edited by C. Martindale, 56–72. Cambridge: Cambridge University Press, 1997.

Taylor, C. *A Secular Age*. Cambridge, Mass.: Belknap Press of Harvard University Press, 2007.

———. 'The Poverty of the Poverty of Historicism'. *Universities and Left Review* 4 (Summer 1958), 77–78.

Tennyson, Alfred Lord. *The Complete Works of Alfred Lord Tennyson*. London: Macmillan, 1898.

Thiselton, A. C. *The First Epistle to the Corinthians: A Commentary on the Greek Text*. Grand Rapids: Eerdmans, 2000.

———. *Hermeneutics of Doctrine*. Grand Rapids: Eerdmans, 2007.

———. *The Two Horizons: New Testament Hermeneutics and Philosophical Description with Special Reference to Heidegger, Bultmann, Gadamer and Wittgenstein*. Grand Rapids: Eerdmans, 1984.

Torrance, T. F. *Space, Time and Resurrection*. Edinburgh: Handsel Press, 1976.

Tournier, M. '"Le Grand Soir": Un Mythe de Fin de Siècle'. *Mots: Les Langages du Politique* 19 (1989), 79–94.

Turner, F. M. *European Intellectual History from Rousseau to Nietzsche*. New Haven, Conn.: Yale University Press, 2014.

Uglow, J. *The Lunar Men: The Friends Who Made the Future, 1730–1810*. London: Faber, 2002.

———. *Nature's Engraver: A Life of Thomas Bewick*. London: Faber, 2006.

Van Kley, D. K. *The Religious Origins of the French Revolution: From Calvin to the Civil Constitution, 1560–1791*. New Haven, Conn.: Yale University Press, 1996.

Vermes, Geza. *Jesus the Jew*. London: Collins, 1973.

———. *Providential Accidents*. London: SCM, 2011 (1998).

Voltaire. *Toleration and Other Essays by Voltaire*. Edited with an introduction by J. McCabe. New York: Putnam's, 1912.

von Goethe, Johann Wolfgang. *Doctor Faustus*. Translated by T. Mann. London: Penguin, 1968 (1947).

von Rad, G. *The Problem of the Hexateuch and Other Essays*. Translated by Rev. E. W. Trueman Dicken. London: SCM Press, 2012 (1965).

von Ranke, L. *Sämtliche Werke*. Vol. 33/34. 2nd edn. Leipzig, 1874 (1824).

Vovelle, M. *The Revolution against the Church: From Reason to the Supreme Being*. Columbus: Ohio State University Press, 1991 (1988).

Wagner, R. and A. Briggs. *The Penultimate Curiosity: How Science Swims in the Slipstream of Ultimate Questions*. Oxford: Oxford University Press, 2016.

Walls, J. L., ed. *The Oxford Handbook of Eschatology*. Oxford: Oxford University Press, 2008.

Walsh, B. and R. Middleton. *Truth Is Stranger than It Used to Be: Biblical Faith in a Postmodern Age*. Downers Grove, Ill.: IVP, 1995.

Walton, J. H. *Genesis 1 as Ancient Cosmology*. Winona Lake, Ind.: Eisenbrauns, 2011.

———. *The Lost World of Genesis One: Ancient Cosmology and the Origins Debate*. Downers Grove, Ill.: IVP, 2009.

Ward, Keith. *Christ and the Cosmos: A Reformulation of Trinitarian Doctrine*. Cambridge: Cambridge University Press, 2015.

Webb, Beatrice and Sidney. *Soviet Communism: A New Civilisation?* London: Longmans, Green, 1933.

———. *The Truth about the Soviet Union*. London: Longmans, Green, 1944.

Weiss, H. *A Day of Gladness: The Sabbath among Jews and Christians in Antiquity*. Columbia: University of South Carolina Press, 2003.

Westcott, B. F. *The Gospel according to St John*. London: John Murray, 1903 (1881).

Wigelsworth, J. R. *Deism in Enlightenment England: Theology, Politics and Newtonian Public Science*. Manchester: Manchester University Press, 2013.

Wilde, O. *The Works of Oscar Wilde*. Leicester: Galley Press, 1987.

Williams, R. *The Edge of Words: God and the Habit of Language*. London: Bloomsbury Continuum, 2014.

Wilson, A. N. *God's Funeral*. London: John Murray, 1999.

Wilson, C. *Epicureanism at the Origins of Modernity*. Oxford: Clarendon, 2008.

Wilson, R. R. 'Creation and New Creation: The Role of Creation Imagery in the Book of Daniel'. In *God Who Creates: Essays in Honor of W. Sibley Towner*, edited by W. P. Brown and S. D. McBride, 190–203. Grand Rapids: Eerdmans, 2000.

Winter, B. *After Paul Left Corinth: The Influence of Secular Ethics and Social Change*. Grand Rapids: Eerdmans, 2001.

Witherington, B. W. *Letters and Homilies for Hellenized Christians*. Vol. 2, *A Socio-rhetorical Commentary on 1–2 Peter*. Downers Grove, Ill.: IVP Academic, 2007.

Wittgenstein, L. *Culture and Value: A Selection from the Posthumous Remains*. Edited by G. H. von Wright et al. Translated by P. Winch. Oxford: Blackwell, 1998 (1970).

———. *Tractatus Logico-Philosophicus*. London: Routledge, 1974 (1921).

Wrede, W. *Paul*. Translated by Edward Lumis. London: Philip Green, 1907 (1904).

Wright, Julian. *Socialism and the Experience of Time*. Oxford: Oxford University Press, 2017.

Wright, N. T. 'Apocalyptic and the Sudden Fulfilment of Divine Promise'. In *Paul and the Apocalyptic Imagination*, edited by J. K. Goodrich, B. Blackwell and J. Mastin, 111–34. Philadelphia: Fortress, 2016.

———. 'Christ and the Cosmos: Kingdom and Creation in Gospel Perspective'. In *Christ and the Created Order: Perspectives from Theology, Philosophy and Science*, edited by A. B. Torrance and T. H. McCall, 97–109. Grand Rapids: Zondervan, 2018.

———. *Creation, Power and Truth*. London: SPCK, 2013.

———. *The Day the Revolution Began*. London: SPCK, 2017.

———. *Evil and the Justice of God*. London: SPCK, 2006.

———. 'Get the Story Right and the Models Will Fit: Victory through Substitution in "Atonement Theology"'. In *Atonement: Sin, Salvation and Sacrifice in Jewish and Christian Antiquity* (papers from the St Andrews Symposium for Biblical Studies, 2018), edited by M. Botner, J. Duff and S. Dürr. Grand Rapids: Eerdmans, 2019.

———. *God in Public*. London: SPCK, 2016.

———. 'Hope Deferred? Against the Dogma of Delay'. *Early Christianity* 9.1 (2018), 37–82.

———. 'Imagining the Kingdom: Mission and Theology in Early Christianity'. *SJT* 65.4 (2012), 379–401.

———. *Jesus and the Victory of God*. Christian Origins and the Question of God 2. London: SPCK, 1996.

———. *Judas and the Gospel of Jesus*. London: SPCK, 2006.

———. 'The Meanings of History: Event and Interpretation in the Bible and Theology'. *Journal of Analytic Theology* 6 (2018), 1–28.

———. *The New Testament and the People of God*. Christian Origins and the Question of God 1. London: SPCK, 1992.

———. *Paul: A Biography*. San Francisco and London: HarperOne and SPCK, 2017.

———. *The Paul Debate*. Waco, Tex.: Baylor University Press, 2016.

———. *Paul and the Faithfulness of God*. Christian Origins and the Question of God 4. London: SPCK, 2013.

———. *Paul and His Recent Interpreters*. London: SPCK, 2015.

———. *Pauline Perspectives*. London: SPCK, 2013.

———. 'Pictures, Stories, and the Cross: Where Do the Echoes Lead?' *JTI* 11.1 (2017), 53–73.

———. 'The Powerful Breath of New Creation'. In *Veni, Sancte Spiritus! Festschrift für Barbara Hallensleben zum 60. Geburtstag*, edited by W. Dürr, J. Negel, G. Vergauwen and A. Steingruber, 1–15. Münster: Aschendorff Verlag, 2018.

———. 'Responding to Exile'. In *Exile: A Conversation with N. T. Wright*, edited by J. M. Scott, 328–32. Downers Grove, Ill.: IVP Academic, 2017.

———. *Resurrection and Moral Order*. Leicester: IVP, 1994 (1986).

———. *The Resurrection of the Son of God*. Christian Origins and the Question of God 3. London: SPCK, 2003.

———. *Scripture and the Authority of God*. London: SPCK, 2005.

———. *Simply Christian*. London and San Francisco: SPCK and HarperOne, 2005.

———. 'Son of God and Christian Origins'. In *Son of God: Divine Sonship in Jewish and Christian Antiquity*, edited by G. V. Allen et al., 120–36. University Park, Pa.: Eisenbrauns, 2019.

———. 'Son of Man—Lord of the Temple? Gospel Echoes of Ps 8 and the Ongoing Christological Challenge'. In *The Earliest Perceptions of Jesus in Context: Essays in Honour of John Nolland on His 70th Birthday*, edited by A. W. White, D. Wenham and C. A. Evans, 77–96. London: Bloomsbury/T&T Clark, 2016.

———. *Spiritual and Religious*. London: SPCK, 2017.

———. *Surprised by Hope*. London: SPCK, 2007.

Wright, N. T. and J. P. Davies. 'John, Jesus, and "The Ruler of This World": Demonic Politics in the Fourth Gospel?' In *Conception, Reception and the Spirit: Essays in Honor of Andrew T. Lincoln*, edited by J. G. McConville and L. K. Pietersen, 71–89. Eugene, Ore.: Wipf & Stock, 2015.

Yarbrough, R. W. *The Salvation Historical Fallacy? Reassessing the History of New Testament Theology.* Leiden: Deo Publishing, 2004.

Ziegler, P. G. *Militant Grace: The Apocalyptic Turn and the Future of Christian Theology.* Grand Rapids: Baker Academic, 2018.

Index of Modern Authors

Ritschl, Albrecht, 52, 115
Robespierre, Maximilien, 17
Robinson, John, 67
Rousseau, Jean-Jacques, 26

Sanders, E. P., 63, 117, 196, 294n59, 298n67
Schlegel, Friedrich von, 8
Schmemann, Alexander, 273
Scholem, Gershom, 94
Schweitzer, Albert, 20, 42, 44–45, 47, 48, 51–60, 65, 68, 122, 131, 291n14, 292n24, 293n53, 294n58
Sellars, Peter, 245
Seward, Thomas, 18, 385–86n72
Shillito, Edward, 241–42
Smith, Adam, 19, 23, 286n82
Smith, Theodore Clark, 112
South, Robert, 7
Stager, L. E., 311n53
Strauss, David Friedrich, 47, 49–51, 76, 90
Syme, Ronald, 103

Taylor, Charles, 36
Tindal, Matthew, 41
Toland, John, 41

Torrance, T. F., 193
Trevelyan, G. M., 113–14, 298n61, 299n77
Troeltsch, Ernst, 88, 89, 110–11
Turner, F. M., 110

Vermes, Geza, 73, 117, 287–88n105
Vico, Giambattista, 97, 114, 290n135, 299n70, 299n73
Voltaire, 7, 281n16
von Ranke, Leopold, 66–67, 82, 84, 111–13, 115

Weiss, H., 309n19
Weiss, Johannes, 48, 55–56, 136
Wells, H. G., 56
Werner, Martin, 63
Wesley, John, 6
Wilde, Oscar, 56
William of Occam, 8
Wilson, A. N., 26
Wilson, Catherine, 8–9, 11, 282–83n31
Wilson, R. R., 311–12n59
Wittgenstein, Ludwig, 66, 83, 187, 271
Wrede, William, 45, 291n14

Index of Passages